IMAGES OF WOMEN IN FICTION

IMAGES
OF
WOMEN
IN
FICTION
FEMINIST
PERSPECTIVES

Edited

By

Susan Koppelman Cornillon

Bowling Green University Popular Press
Bowling Green, Ohio 43403

Cover design by Margaret Cornillon Mattheson.
Sunflower design by Wanda Walker.

THIS BOOK IS LOVINGLY DEDICATED TO:

Frances Bollotin Koppelman Horwitz, whose love, courage, self-knowledge, and honesty have provided me with a model I am proud to emulate.

Edward Nathan Koppelman, who would be very proud of me and whom I miss.

Morris Horwitz, the kindest second father I could have imagined.

Ray Browne, who says about tentative dreams, "Why not?"

Jacques and Elizabeth Cornillon, with whom dialogue is always possible.

John Cornillon who has gone through heaven and hell with me, who has loved me and known me.

Edward Nathan Koppelman Cornillon, who likes his dolly house as much as he likes his trucks, and for whom I wish, and am working to build, a better world.

The Contributors to this book, whose dedication is evident in their work.

MY SISTERS IN STRUGGLE EVERYWHERE.

PREFACE

Female Studies I–IV lists over eight hundred new courses in women's studies in the past few years, and more than half of these are being taught with their focus on literature. Those of us who have looked to literature, and especially fiction, for answers, for models, for clues to the universal questions of who we are or might become are beginning to understand why the things we have sought have not been there. We are now beginning to understand how we have been alienated from ourselves and from the literature we loved, or hoped to love, and still do half love, by the bias of what we have been taught and the biases incorporated in the works.

People—both women and men—are beginning to see literature in new perspectives which have been opened up by the Women's Liberation Movement. The writings these people offer enlighten our understanding by helping us distance ourselves from the literature; prevent us from falling into the traps of the implications and prescriptions for behavior, for the limiting self-images and aspirations for women embodied in much of the literature that we have been taught is important. People have begun to question the value structures that insist that certain kinds of writing, certain kinds of experiences and characters, are worthy of serious consideration while others—often those that we have been taught to disdain—are beneath contempt. Obviously there is desperate need for re-evaluation of most or all of our shibboleths.

I have felt for years the need for a book like this one. I began teaching Women's Studies in 1967 and have taught various courses about and for women since. In all courses I felt the desperate need for books that would study literature as being writings about *people*. This volume is an effort to supply that need.

This collection of essays deals with the new forms of analysis growing out of the new consciousness. I have limited the panorama to fiction because to have attempted to cover other forms of literature would have made a huge task unmanageably large. These essays illustrate the beginnings of new directions for women in reading and understanding fiction, and therefore new directions and depths for women in their personal paths. These essays lead us into fiction and then back out again into reality, into ourselves and our own lives.

This book will be useful in several ways. It will help in classrooms where investigations about the real meaning of fiction and the role of women in and out of it are being undertaken. In choosing these essays I have brought together some of the important conclusions reached so far. One of the best ways we grow is by listening to one another and building on the ideas others share with us. This book will be a useful tool for raising consciousness not only in classrooms, but for those not involved in the academic world who are committed to personal growth. Hopefully it will be valuable in other ways, too.

This book is divided into four sections depicting the roles women have been forced to assume in society and are now beginning to occupy, beginning with the most desiccated and lifeless traditional stereotypes of woman as heroine, and as invisible person, progressing through an awakening to reality, wherein the woman is treated as person, and ending with the newest insistence by women that we are equal in all respects to men.

Woman as Heroine. This section consists of analyses of traditional views of women, of the "sugar 'n' spice and everything nice" stereotype that insults most fiction. There are discussions of traditional women, of myths about women, stereotypes of women's roles, needs, attributes, and potentials.

The Invisible Woman. This investigation covers the roles women are forced to play in much fiction: as the Other, the thing, as non-cognating phenomenon for the hero to test himself against as he would against hurricane or high mountain or disease, as symbol. In these essays we search for the women we cannot find in literature, either as authors or characters for the experiences not recorded in belles lettres, and we recognize the weird distortions of the meanings of women's experience.

The Woman as Hero. These essays investigate the fiction in which women are portrayed as whole people or as people in the process of creating or discovering their wholeness, of women seeking and finding other metaphors for existence than men, or martyrdom, or selflessness, or intrinsic worthlessness. Women are revealed as working, being political, creating, of living in relationships with other women, of being alive, adventuresome, self-determining, growing, making significant choices, questioning and finding viable answers and solutions—of being, in other words, human beings.

Feminist Aesthetics. In these determined and courageous statements are revealed portions of the credo and manifesto of women, in which is made patently clear women's desires and determinations and their abilities to achieve, at least as much as men do, their goals.

The people who have written this book range in age from twenty one to the late sixties. Some of us haven't gone in formal education beyond high school and some of us have Ph.D.'s. Some have been published before and some of us have never written before. Some are married, some single, some divorced. All of us are trying to belong to ourselves. About half of us are parents with children ranging from infancy through adulthood. Many of us are teachers, some are students, some are writers, some librar-

ians, some waitresses, some full-time mothers at home.
We are from all over the country and are all excited and
happy to have found one another. We are all grateful for
the opportunity to share our ideas with you.

With part of the proceeds from this book there will be
established a **new scholarship fund** at Bowling Green State
University. The scholarship will provide tuition money
for one course each quarter plus book money and child
care money. It will be awarded to a woman who has begun work towards a degree—any degree— and for financial
and/or family responsibility reasons been unable to continue. More and more scholarship funds are being established for women to return to school on a full-time basis,
but none that we know of are part-time. Too many
women are typing and babysitting their husbands' ways
through college and graduate school. We hope this scholarship will provide an opportunity for some of these
women to find their own ways. If any of you wish to
contribute to this fund, please send your checks to: The
Women's Liberation-Popular Press Scholarship Fund, c/o
The Center for the Study of Popular Culture, University
Hall, Bowling Green State University, Bowling Green,
Ohio 43403. Contributions are tax deductible. Ralph
Cohen, editor of the *New Literary History* at the University of Virginia has agreed to contribute the reprint fee
for the article "Modernism and History" to the scholarship fund.

A book of this nature is in many ways a joint ven-
ture. Without the encouragement, support, and kindness
of Ray Browne this book would still be a dream. I also
wish to thank Lois Howe, Lee Levine, and Dorothy Betts
for their endless good humor and technical assistance, and
Pat Browne, Dick Fillion, and Nora Erb for their help. My
thanks to Larry Anderson and Nancy Stepp for their help
with proofreading, and to Linda Harden, Dawn Anderson,
and Wayne and Toni Trainor for many hours of child care.
I am, of course, eternally grateful to the contributors to

this volume for their cooperation, enthusiasm, and good work. Thanks to Margaret Cornillon Mattheson for a cover I am proud of, and to Wanda Walker for the logo. And most of all, I am grateful to one of the people I live with, John Cornillon, for relieving me of hours of my share of housework and child care called for in our contract, for endless hours of help with editing and proofreading and listening to me think out loud. Thank you for your faith in me, your tenderness towards my needs, your never-ending gentle love. And finally, thank you Edward Nathan Koppelman Cornillon for helping with Mommy's book and making a picture for it and for patting my head when I got too tired. You and Daddy are my good, good friends.

SKC
Bowling Green, Ohio
September 10, 1972

CONTENTS

THE WOMAN AS HEROINE

WHAT CAN A HEROINE DO?
OR
WHY WOMEN CAN'T WRITE

1. Two strong women battle for supremacy in the early West.

2. A young girl in Minnesota finds her womanhood by killing a bear.

3. An English noblewoman, vacationing in Arcadia, falls in love with a beautiful, modest young shepherd. But duty calls; she must return to the court of Elizabeth I to wage war on Spain. Just in time the shepherd lad is revealed as the long-lost son of the Queen of a neighboring country; the lovers are united and our heroine carries off her husband and lad-in-waiting to the King of England.

4. A phosphorescently doomed poetess sponges off her husband and drinks herself to death, thus alienating the community of Philistines and businesswomen who would have continued to give her lecture dates.

5. A handsome young man, quite virginal, is seduced by an older woman who has made a pact with the Devil to give her back her youth. When the woman becomes pregnant, she proudly announces the paternity of her child; this revelation so shames the young man that he goes quite insane, steals into the house where the baby is kept, murders it, and is taken to prison where—repentant and surrounded by angel voices—he dies.

6. Alexandra the Great.

7. A young man who unwisely puts success in business before his personal fulfillment loses his masculinity and ends up as a neurotic, lonely eunuch.

8. A beautiful, seductive boy whose narcissism and instinctive cunning hide the fact that he has no mind (and in fact, hardly any sentient consciousness) drives a succes-

sion of successful actresses, movie produceresses, cow-girls, and film directresses wild with desire. They rape him.

Authors do not make their plots up out of thin air, nor are the above pure inventions; every one of them is a story familiar to all of us.[1] What makes them look so odd —and so funny—is that in each case the sex of the protagonist has been changed (and correspondingly the sex of the other characters). The result is that these very familiar plots simply will not work. They are tales for heroes, not heroines, and one of the things that handicaps women writers in our—and every other—culture is that there are so very few stories in which women can figure as protagonists.

Culture is male.[2] This does not mean that every man in Western (or Eastern) society can do exactly as he pleases, or that every man creates the culture *solus*, or that every man is luckier or more privileged than every woman. What it does mean (among other things) is that the society we live in, like all other historical societies, is a patriarchy. And patriarchies imagine or picture themselves from the male point of view. There is a female culture, but it is an underground, unofficial, minor culture, occupying a small corner of what we think of officially as possible human experience. Both men *and women* in our culture conceive the culture from a single point of view—the male.

Now writers, as I have said, do not make up their stories out of whole cloth; they are pretty much restricted to the attitudes, the beliefs, the expectations, and above all the plots, that are "in the air"—"plot" being what Aristotle called *mythos*; and in fact it is probably most accurate to call these plot-patterns *myths*. They are dramatic embodiments of what a culture believes to be true—or what it would like to be true—or what it is mortally afraid may be true. Novels, especially, depend upon what central action can be imagined as being performed by the protagonist (or protagonists)—i.e. what can a central character *do* in a book? An examination of English literature, or Western literature (or Eastern literature, for that matter) reveals that of all the possible actions people can do in fiction, very few can be done by women.

Our literature is not about women. It is not about women and men equally. It is by and about men.

But (you might object) aren't our books and our movies full of women? Isn't there a "love interest" or at least a sexual interest in every movie? What about Cleopatra? What about Juliet? What about Sophia Western, Clarissa Harlowe, Faye Greener, Greta Garbo, Pip's Estella, and the succession of love goddesses without whom film history would hardly exist? Our literature is full of women: bad women, good women, motherly women, bitchy women, faithful women, promiscuous women, beautiful women—

Plain women?

Women who have no relations with men (as so many male characters in American literature have no relations with women)?

Oddly enough, no. If you look at the plots summarized at the beginning of this article, and turn them back to their original forms, you will find not women but images of women: modest maidens, wicked temptresses, pretty schoolmarms, beautiful bitches, faithful wives, and so on. They exist only in relation to the protagonist (who is male). Moreover, look at them carefully and you will see that they do not really exist at all—at their best they are depictions of the social roles women are supposed to play and often do play, but they are the public roles and not the private women;[3] at their worst they are gorgeous, Cloudcuckooland fantasies about what men want, or hate, or fear.

How can women writers possibly use such myths?

In twentieth century American literature there is a particularly fine example of these impossible "women," a figure who is beautiful, irresistible, ruthless but fascinating, fascinating because she is somehow cheap or contemptible, who (in her more passive form) destroys men by her indifference and who (when the male author is more afraid of her) destroys men actively, sometimes by shooting them. She is Jean Harlow, Daisy Faye, Faye Greener, Mrs. Macomber, and Deborah Rojack. She is the Bitch Goddess.

Now it is just as useless to ask why the Bitch Goddess is so bitchy as it is to ask why the Noble Savage is so noble. Neither "person" really exists. In existential terms they are both The Other and The Other does not have the kind of inner life or consciousness that you and I have. In fact, The Other has no mind at all. No man in his senses ever says of himself *to himself*: I acted nobly because I am a Noble Savage. His reasons are far more prosaic: I did what I did because I was afraid, or because I was ambitious, or because I wanted to provoke my father, or because I felt lonely, or because I needed money, and so on. Look for reasons like that to explain the conduct of the Bitch Goddess and you will not find them; there is no explanation in terms of human motivation or the woman's own inner life; she simply behaves the way she does because she is a bitch. Q.E.D. No Other ever has the motives that you and I have; the Other contains a mysterious *essence* which causes it to behave as it does; in fact "it" is not a person at all, but a projected wish or fear.

The Bitch Goddess is not a person.

Virgin-victim Gretchen (see number five, above) is not a person. The faithful wife, the beautiful temptress, the seductive destroyer, the devouring momma, the healing Madonna—none of these are persons in the sense that a novel's protagonist must be a person and none is of the slightest use as myth to the woman writer who wishes to write about a female protagonist.

Try, for example, to change the Bitch Goddess/Male Victim story into a woman's story—are we to simply change the sex of the characters and write about a male "bitch" and a female victim? The myth still works in male homosexual terms—Man and Cruel Youth—but the female equivalent is something quite different. Changing the sex of the protagonist completely alters the meaning of the tale. The story of Woman/Cruel Lover is the story of so many English ballads—you have the "false true lover" and the pregnant girl left either to mourn or to die, but you do not have—to indicate only some elements of the story—the Cruel Lover as the materially sumptuous but spiritually bankrupt spirit of our civilization, the essence of sex, the "soul" of our corrupt culture, a dramatization of the split between the degrading necessities of the flesh and the transcendence of world-cleaving Will. What you have instead, if the story is told about or by the woman, is a cautionary tale warning you not to break social rules—in short, a much more realistic story of social error or transgression leading to ostracism, poverty, or death. Moral: Get Married First.

No career woman, at least in literature, keeps in the back of her mind the glamorous figure of Daisy Faye, the beautiful, rich, indifferent boy she loved back in Cleveland when she was fighting for a career as a bootlegger. Reversing sexual roles in fiction may make good burlesque or good fantasy, but it is ludicrous in terms of serious literature. Culture is male. Our literary myths are for heroes, not heroines.

What can a heroine do?

What myths, what plots, what actions are available to a female protagonist?

Very few.

For example, it is impossible to write a conventional success story with a heroine, for success in male terms is failure for a woman, a "fact" movies, books, and television plays have been earnestly proving to us for decades. Nor is the hard-drinking, hard-fighting hero imagined as female, except as an amusing fluke—e.g. Bob Hope and Jane Russell in "Paleface." Nor can our heroine be the Romantic Poet Glamorously Doomed, nor the Oversensitive Artist Who Cannot Fulfill His Worldly Responsibilities (Emily Dickinson seems to fit the latter pattern pretty well, but she is always treated as The Spinster, an exclusively female—*and sexual*—role). Nor can a heroine be the Intellectual Born Into a Philistine Small Town Who Escapes to the Big City—

a female intellectual cannot escape her problems by fleeing to the big city; she is still a woman and Woman as Intellectual is not one of our success myths.

With one or two exceptions (which I will deal with later) all sub-literary genres are closed to the heroine; she cannot be a Mickey Spillane private eye, for example, nor one of H. Rider Haggard's adventure-story Englishmen who discover a Lost Princess in some imaginary corner of Africa. (She can be the Lost Princess, but a story written with the Princess herself as protagonist would resemble the chronicle of any other monarch and would hardly fit the female figure of Haggard's romances, who is—again—the Other.) The hero whose success in business alienates him from his family is not at all in the position of the heroine who "loses her femininity" by competing with men—*he* is not desexed, but *she* is. The Crass Businessman genre (minor anyway) is predicated on the assumption that success is masculine and a good thing as long as you don't spend all your time at it; one needs to spend the smaller part of one's life recognizing the claims of personal relations and relaxation. For the heroine the conflict between success and sexuality is itself the issue, and the duality is absolute. The woman who becomes hard and unfeminine, who competes with men, finally becomes—have we seen this figure before?—a bitch. Again.

Women in twentieth-century American literature seem pretty much limited to either Devourer/Bitches or Maiden/Victims. Perhaps male authors have bad consciences.

So we come at last to the question of utmost importance to novelists—What will my protagonist(s) do? What central action can be the core of the novel? I know of only one plot or myth that is genderless, and in which heroines can figure equally with heroes; this is the Abused Child story (I mean of the Dickensian variety) and indeed many heroines do begin life as Sensitive, Mistreated Waifs. But such a pattern can be used only while the heroine is still a child (as in the first part of *Jane Eyre*). Patient Griselda, who also suffered and endured, was not a Mistreated Child but the adult heroine of a peculiar kind of love story. And here, of course, we come to the one occupation of a female protagonist in literature, the one thing she can do, and by God she does it and does it and does it, over and over and over again.

She is the protagonist of a Love Story.

The tone may range from grave to gay, from the tragedy of *Anna Karenina* to the comedy of *Emma*, but the myth is always the same: innumerable variants on Falling In Love, on courtship, on marriage, on the failure of courtship and marriage, How She Got Married. How She Did Not Get Married (always tragic). How She Fell In Love And Committed Adultery. How She Saved Her Marriage But Just Barely. How She Loved a Vile Seducer And Eloped. How She Loved a Vile Seducer, Eloped, And Died In Childbirth. As far as literature is concerned, heroines are still restricted to one vice, one virtue, and one occupation. In the novels of Doris Lessing, an authoress concerned with a great many other things besides love, the heroines still spend most of their energy and time maintaining relations with their lovers (or marrying, or divorcing, or failing to achieve orgasm, or achieving it, or worrying about their sexuality, their men, their loves, and their love lives).

For female protagonists the Love Story includes not only personal relations as such, but *bildungsroman*, worldly success or worldly failure, career, the exposition of character, crucial learning experiences, the transition to adulthood, rebellion (usually adultery) and everything else. Only in a few iconoclasts like George Bernard Shaw do you find protagonists like Vivie Warren, whose work means more to her than marriage, or Saint Joan, who has no "love life" at all. It is interesting that Martha Graham's dance version of Saint Joan's life turns the tale back into a Love Story, with Saint Michael (at one point, in the version I saw) inspiring Joan by walking astride her from head to foot, dragging his robe over her several times as she lies on her back on the stage floor.

How she lost him, how she got him, how she kept him, how she died for/with him. What else is there? A new pattern seems to have been developing in the last few years: female authors who do not wish to write Love Stories may instead write about heroines whose main action is to go mad—but How She Went Crazy will also lose its charm in time. One cannot write *The Bell Jar* or *Jane Eyre*, good as it is, forever.

A woman writer may, if she wishes, abandon female protagonists altogether and stick to male myths with male protagonists, but in so doing she falsifies herself and much of her own experience. Part of life is obviously common to both sexes—we all eat, we all get stomach-aches, and we all grow old and die—but a great deal of life is not shared by men and women. A woman who refuses to write about women ignores the whole experience of the female culture (a very different one from the official, male culture), all her specifically erotic experiences, and a good deal of her own history. She falsifies her position both artistically and humanly: she is an artist creating a world in which persons of her kind cannot be artists, a consciousness central to itself creating a world in which women have no consciousness, a successful person creating a world in which persons like herself cannot be successes. She is a Self trying to pretend that she is a different Self, one for whom her own self is Other.

If a female writer does not use the two, possibly three, myths available to a she-writer, she must drop the culture's myths altogether. Is this in itself a bad thing? Perhaps what we need here is a digression on the artistic advantages of working with myths, i.e. material that has passed through other hands, that is not raw-brand-new.

The insistence that authors make up their own plots is a recent development in literature; Milton certainly did not do it. Even today, with novelty at such a premium in all the arts, very little is written that is not—at bottom—common property. It's a commonplace that bad writers imitate and great writers steal. Even an iconoclast like

Shaw "stole" his plots wholesale, sometimes from melodrama, sometimes from history, sometimes from his friends.[4] Ibsen owes a debt to Scribe, Dickens to theatre melodrama, James to the ladies' magazine fiction of his own time—nothing flowers without a history. Something that has been worked on by others in the same culture, something that is "in the air" provides a writer with material that has been distilled, dramatized, stylized, and above all, clarified. A developed myth has its own form, its own structure, its own expectations and values, its own cues-to-nudge-the-reader. When so much of the basic work has already been done, the artist may either give the myth its final realization or stand it on its head, but in any case what he does will be neither tentative nor crude and it will not take forever; it can simply be done well. For example, the very pattern of dramatic construction which we take as natural, the idea that a story ought to have a beginning, a middle, and an end, that one ought to be led to something called a "climax" by something called "suspense" or "dramatic tension" is in itself an Occidental myth—Western artists, therefore, do not have to invent this pattern for themselves.

Hemingway, whom we call a realist, spent his whole working life capitalizing on the dramatic lucidity possible to an artist who works with developed myths. The Bitch Goddess did not appear full-blown in "The Short and Happy Life of Francis Macomber"—one can find her in Fitzgerald—or Hawthorne, to name an earlier writer—or Max Beerbohm, whose *Zuleika Dobson* is certainly a Bitch Goddess, though a less serious one than her American cousins. "Macomber" is the ultimate fictional refinement out of the mess and bother of real life. Beyond it lies only nightmare (Faye Greener in West's *Day of the Locust*) or the half-mad, satiric fantastications Mailer uses to get a little more mileage out of an almost-exhausted pattern.

"Macomber" is perfectly clear, as is most of Hemingway's work. Nobody can fail to understand that Mrs. Macomber is a Bitch, that the White Hunter is a Real Man,

and that Macomber is a Failed Man. The dramatic conflict is extremely clear, very vehement, and completely
expectable. The characters are simple, emotionally
charged, and larger-than-life. *Therefore* the fine details of
the story can be polished to that point of high gloss where
everything—weather, gestures, laconic conversation, terrain, equipment, clothing—is all of meaning. (Compare
"Macomber" with *Robinson Crusoe*, for example; Defoe
is much less sure from moment to moment of what he
wants to say or what it means.) One cannot stop to ask
why Mrs. Macomber is so bitchy—she's just a Bitch, that's
all—or why killing a large animal will restore Macomber's
manhood—everybody knows it will—or why the Bitch cannot tolerate a Real Man—these things are already explained
by the myth.

But this kind of larger-than-life simplicity and clarity
are not accessible to the woman writer unless she remains
within the limits of the Love Story. Again: what can a
heroine do?

There seem to me to be two alternatives open to the
woman author who no longer cares about How She Fell in
Love or How She Went Mad. These are (1) lyricism, and
(2) life.

By "lyricism" I do not mean purple passages or baroque raptures; I mean a particular principle of structure.

If *the narrative mode* (what Aristotle called "epic")
concerns itself with *events* connected by the *chronological
order* in which they occur, and *the dramatic mode* with
voluntary human actions which are connected both by
chronology and causation, then the principle of construction I wish to call *lyric* consists of *the organization of discrete elements* (images, events, scenes, passages, words,
what-have-you) *around an unspoken thematic or emotional center.* The lyric mode exists without chronology
or causation; its principle of connection is *associative.* Of
course no piece of writing can exist purely in any one
mode, but we can certainly talk of the predominance of
one element, perhaps two.) In this sense of "lyric" Vir-

ginia Woolf is a lyric novelist—in fact she has been criticized in just those terms, i.e., "nothing happens" in her books. A writer who employs the lyric structure is setting various images, events, scenes, or memories to circling round an unspoken, invisible center. The invisible center is what the novel or poem is about; it is also unsayable in available dramatic or narrative terms. That is, there is no action possible to the central character and no series of events which will embody in clear, unequivocal, immediately graspable terms what the artist means. Or perhaps there is no action or series of events that will embody this "center" at all. Unable to use the myths of male culture (and apparently unwilling to spend her life writing love stories) Woolf uses a structure that is basically non-narrative. Hence the lack of "plot," the repetitiousness, the gathering-up of the novels into moments of epiphany, the denseness of the writing, the indirection. There is nothing the female characters can *do*—except exist, except think, except feel. And critics (mostly male) employ the usual vocabulary of denigration: these novels lack important events; they are hermetically sealed; they are too full of sensibility; they are trivial; they lack action; they are feminine.[5]

Not every female author is equipped with the kind of command of language that allows (or insists upon) lyric construction; nor does every woman writer want to employ this mode. The alternative is to take as one's model (and structural principle) not male myth but the structure of one's own experience. So we have George Eliot's (or Doris Lessing's) "lack of structure," the obviously tacked-on ending of *Mill on the Floss*; we have Brontë's spasmodic, jerky world of *Villette*, with a structure modelled on the heroine's (and probably author's) real situation. How to write a novel about a person to whom nothing happens? A person to whom nothing but a love story is *supposed* to happen? A person inhabiting a world in which the only reality is frustration or endurance—or these plus an unbearably mystifying confusion? The movement of

Villette is not the perfect curve of *Jane Eyre* (a classic version of the female Love Story)—it is a blocked jabbing, a constant thwarting; it is the protagonist's constantly frustrated will to action, and her alternately losing and regaining her perception of her own situation.[6] There are vestiges of Gothic mystery and there is a Love Story, but the Gothic mysteries turn out to be fakery and the Love Story (which occupies only the last quarter of the book) vanishes strangely and abruptly on the last page but one. In cases like these the usual epithet is "formless," sometimes qualified by "inexperienced"—obviously life is not like *that*; life is not messy and indecisive; we know what life (and novels) are from Aristotle—who wrote about plays—and male novelists who employ male myths created by a culture that imagines itself from the male point of view. The task of art—we know—is to give form to life, i.e., the very forms that women writers cannot use. So it's clear that women can't write, that they swing wildly from lyricism to messiness once they abandon the cozy realms of the Love Story. And successes within the Love Story (which is itself imagined out of genuine female experience) are not important because the Love Story is not important. It is a commonplace of criticism that only the male myths are valid or interesting; a book as fine (and well-structured) as *Jane Eyre* fails *even to be seen* by many critics because it grows out of experiences—events, fantasies, wishes, fears, daydreams, images of self—entirely foreign to their own. As critics are usually unwilling to believe their lack of understanding to be their own fault, it becomes the fault of the book. Of the author. Of all women writers.

Western European (and North American) culture is not only male in its point of view; it is also Western European. For example, it is not Russian. Nineteenth-century Russian fiction can be criticized in much the same terms as women's fiction: "pointless" or "plotless" narratives stuffed with strange minutiae, and not obeying the accepted laws of dramatic development, lyrical in the wrong places, condensed in the wrong places, overly emotional, obsessed with things we do not understand, perhaps even grotesque. Here we have other outsiders who are trying, in less than a century, to assimilate European myths, producing strange Russian hybrids (*A King Lear of the Steppe, Lady Macbeth of Mtensk*), trying to work with literary patterns that do not suit their experiences and were not developed with them in mind. What do we get? Oddly digressive Pushkin. "Formless" Dostoevsky. (Colin Wilson has called Dostoevsky's novels "sofa pillows stuffed with lumps of concrete.") Sprawling, glacial, all-inclusive Tolstoy. And of course "lyrical" Chekhov, whose magnificent plays are called plotless to this very day.

There is an even more vivid—and tragic—example: what is an American Black writer to make of our accepted myths? For example, what is she or he to make of the still-current myth (so prominent in *King Lear*) that Suffering Brings Wisdom? This is an old, still-used plot. Does suffering bring wisdom to *The Invisible Man*? When critics do not find what they expect, they cannot imagine that the fault may lie in their expectations. I know of a case in which the critics (white and female) decided after long, nervous discussion that Baldwin was "not really a novelist" but that Orwell was.

Critical bias aside, all artists are going to be in the soup pretty soon, if they aren't already. As a culture, we are coasting on the tag-ends of our assumptions about a lot of things (including the difference between fiction and "propaganda"). As novelists we are working with myths that have been so repeated, so triply-distilled, that they are almost exhausted. Outside of commercial genres—which can remain petrified and profitable indefinitely—how many more incarnations of the Bitch Goddess can anybody stand? How many more shoot-'em-ups on Main Street? How many more young men with identity problems?

The lack of workable myths in literature, of acceptable dramatizations of what our experience means, harms

much more than art itself. We do not only choose or reject works of art on the basis of these myths; we interpret
our own experience in terms of them. Worse still, we
actually perceive what happens to us in the mythic terms
our culture provides.

The problem of "outsider" artists is the whole problem of what to do with unlabeled, disallowed, disavowed,
not-even-consciously-perceived experience, experience
which cannot be spoken about because it has no embodiment in existing art. Is one to create new forms wholesale
—which is practically impossible? Or turn to old ones, like
Blake's Elizabethan lyrics and Yeats's Noh plays? Or
"trivial," trashy genres, like Austen's ladies' fiction?

Make something unspeakable and you make it unthinkable.

Hence the lyric structure, which can deal with the unspeakable and unembodyable as its thematic center, or the
realistic piling up of detail which may (if you are lucky)
eventually *add up to* the unspeakable, undramatizable, unembodyable, action-one-cannot-name.

Outsiders' writing is always in critical jeopardy. Insiders know perfectly well that art ought to match their
ideas of it. Thus insiders notice instantly that the material
of *Jane Eyre* is trivial and the emotionality untenable, even
though the structure is perfect. George Eliot, whose point
of view is neither peccable nor ridiculously romantic, does
not know what fate to award her heroines and thus falsifies
her endings.[7] Genet, whose lyrical mode of construction
goes unnoticed, is meaningless and disgusting. Kafka, who
can "translate" (in his short stories only) certain common
myths into fantastic or extreme versions of themselves,
does not have Tolstoy's wide grasp of life. (That Tolstoy
lacks Kafka's understanding of alienation and schizophrenia is sometimes commented upon, but that does not
count, of course.) Ellison is passionate but shapeless and
crude. Austen, whose sense of form cannot be impugned,
is not passionate enough. Blake is inexplicable. Baldwin

lacks Shakespeare's gift of reconciliation. And so on and so on.

But outsiders' problems are real enough, and we will all be facing them quite soon, as the nature of human experience on this planet changes radically—unless, of course, we all end up in the Second Paleolithic, in which case we will have to set about re-creating the myths of the First Paleolithic.

Perhaps one place to look for myths which escape from the equation Culture = Male is in those genres which already employ plots not limited to one sex—i.e., myths which have nothing to do with our accepted gender roles. There seem to me to be three places one can look:

1) Detective stories, as long as these are limited to genuine intellectual puzzles ("crime fiction" is a different genre). Women write these; women read them; women even figure in them as protagonists. The slang name, "whodunit," neatly describes the myth: Finding Out Who Did It (whatever "It" is).

2) Supernatural fiction, often written by women (Englishwomen, at least) during the nineteenth and the first part of the twentieth century. These are about the intrusion of something strange, dangerous, *and not natural* into one's familiar world. What to do? In the face of the supernatural, knowledge and character become crucial; the accepted gender roles are often irrelevant. After all, potting a twelve-foot-tall batrachian with a kerosene lamp is an act that can be accomplished by either sex, and both heroes and heroines can be expected to feel sufficient horror to make the story interesting. (My example is from a short story by H. P. Lovecraft and August Derleth.) However, much of this genre is as severely limited as the detective story—they both seem to have reached the point of decadence where writers are restricted to the re-enactment of ritual gestures. Moreover, supernatural fiction often relies on very threadbare social/sexual roles, e.g., aristocratic Hungarian counts drinking the blood of beautiful,

innocent Englishwomen. (Vampire stories use the myths of an old-fashioned eroticism; other tales trade on the fear of certain animals like snakes or spiders, disgust at "mold" or "slime," human aggression taking the form of literal bestiality (lycanthropy), guilt without intention, the lex talionis, severe retribution for venial faults, supernatural "contamination"—in short, what a psychoanalyst would call the "archaic" contents of the mind.)

3) Science fiction, which seems to me to provide a broad pattern for human myths, even if the specifically futuristic or fantastic elements are subtracted. (I except the kind of male adventure story called Space Opera, which may be part of science fiction as a genre, but is not innate in science fiction as a mode.) The myths of science fiction run along the lines of exploring a new world conceptually (not necessarily physically), creating needed physical or social machinery, assessing the consequences of techno-logical or other changes, and so on. These are not stories about men *qua* Man and women *qua* Woman; they are myths of human intelligence and human adaptability. They not only ignore gender roles but—at least theoreti-cally—are not culture-bound. Some of the most fascinating characters in science fiction are not human. True, the at-tempt to break through culture-binding may mean only that we transform old myths like Black Is Bad/ White Is Good (or the Heart of Darkness myth) into new asininities like Giant Ants Are Bad/ People Are Good. At least the latter can be subscribed to by all human races and sexes. (Giant ants might feel differently.)

Darko Suvin of the University of Montreal has sug-gested that science fiction patterns often resemble those of medieval literature.[8] I think the resemblance lies in that medieval literature so often dramatizes not people's social roles but the life of the soul; hence we find the fol-lowing patterns in both science fiction and medieval tales:

I find myself in a new world, not knowing who I am or where I came from. I must find these out, and also find out the rules of the world I inhabit. (the journey of the soul from birth to death)

Society needs something. I/we must find it. (the quest)

We are miserable because our way of life is out of whack. We must find out what is wrong and change it. (the drama of sin and salvation)

Science fiction, political fiction, parable, allegory, exemplum—all carry a heavier intellectual freight (and self-consciously so) than we are used to. All are didactic. All imply that human problems are collective, as well as in-dividual, and take these problems to be spiritual, social, perceptive, or cognitive—not the fictionally sex-linked problems of success, competition, castration, education, love, or even personal identity with which we are all so very familiar. I would go even farther and say that science fiction, political fiction (when successful), and the modes (if not the content) of much medieval fiction all provide myths for dealing with the kinds of experiences we are actually having now, instead of the literary myths we have inherited, which only tell us about the kinds of experiences we think we ought to be having.

This may sound like the old cliche about the Soviet plot of Girl Meets Boy Meets Tractor. And why not? Our current fictional myths leave vast areas of human experi-ence unexplored: work for one, genuine religious experi-ence for another, and above all the lives of the traditionally voiceless, the vast majority of whom are women. (When I speak of the "traditionally voiceless" I am not pleading for descriptions of their lives—we have had plenty of that by very vocal writers—what I am talking about are fictional myths *growing out of their lives* and told by themselves for themselves.)

Forty years ago those Americans who read books at all read a good deal of fiction. Nowadays such persons read popularized anthropology, psychology, history, and philosophy. Perhaps current fictional myths no longer tell the truth about any of us.

When things are changing, those who know least about them—in the usual terms—may make the best job of them. There is so much to be written about, and here we are with nothing but the rags and tatters of what used to mean something. One thing I think we must know—that our traditional gender roles will not be part of the future, as long as the future is not a second Stone Age. Our traditions, our books, our morals, our manners, our films, our speech, our economic organization, everything we have inherited, tells us that to be a Man one must bend Nature to one's will—or other men. This means ecological catastrophe in the first instance and war in the second. To be a Woman, one must be first and foremost a mother and after that a server of Men; this means overpopulation and the perpetuation of the first two disasters. The roles are deadly. The myths that serve them are fatal.

Women cannot write—using the old myths.

But using new ones—?

NOTES

[1] Number three is a version of *The Winter's Tale*; number four the biography of Dylan Thomas, as popularly believed, number five the story of Faust and Marguerite, and number eight a slightly modified version of part of *Day of the Locust*. The others need no explanation.

[2] I am indebted to Linda Finlay of the Philosophy Department of Ithaca College for this formulation and the short discussion that follows it.

[3] I am indebted to Mary Uhl for the observation that Dickens' women are accurately portrayed as long as they are in public (where Dickens himself had many opportunities to observe real women) but entirely unconvincing when they are alone or with other women only.

[4] An overstatement. The plot of *Widowers' Houses* was a gift.

[5] Mary Ellmann, *Thinking About Women*. See the chapter on "Phallic Criticism."

[6] Kate Millett, *Sexual Politics* (New York: Doubleday and Company, 1970), pp. 140-147.

[7] In comparison with the organic integrity of Dickens', I suppose.

[8] In conversation and in a paper unpublished as of this writing.

KATHLEEN CONWAY McGRATH

POPULAR LITERATURE
AS SOCIAL REINFORCEMENT:
THE CASE OF *CHARLOTTE TEMPLE*

Charlotte Temple, by Susanna Rowson, though no longer widely read, was at one time perhaps the most frequently published novel in this country. This paper is, in one sense, an attempt to explain that popularity in terms of Northrop Frye's essay, "Theory of Symbols."

Frye identifies two elements which are useful in approaching literature from certain critical points of view: *recurrent acts* and *statements about what ought to be*. Recurrent acts are those events in the literary work which are common to humanity and which constitute what we think of as being the story line of a work: birth, death, marriage, persecution, etc. Statements about what ought to be constitute the moral precepts to be found in the literary work, or the attitude which the author takes toward the recurrent events dealt with.

Most accounts of why a piece of literature is popular deal, it seems to me, with the popular appeal of the recurrent acts in the work i.e., with the "visceral appeal" of the story line of a work. Thus Leslie Fiedler, in attempting to account for the popularity of *Charlotte Temple*, attributes its appeal to "the story." And Lillie Deming Loshe, in *The Early American Novel*, attributes this novel's popularity to "Mrs. Rowson's taste for sensationalism." I suggest that the popularity of a literary work (*Charlotte Temple* in particular) derives not only from the visceral appeal of that sequence of recurrent events called the story line, but also from the author's ability both 1) to consistently formulate, in statements of what ought to be, the way in which society conceives of itself as a civilized struc-

21

ture, and 2) to identify those forces (human or otherwise) which threaten that civilized structure.

Charolotte Temple, published in 1791, constitutes a slim volume of no more than a few hours' reading. It is subtitled *A Tale of Truth* to indicate the claims of its author that the events chronicled in the novel were derived from real life. Mrs. Rowson's purpose in writing the novel was both moral and social; she begins her Preface with the statement that her book is designed "For the perusal of the young and thoughtless of the fair sex," and she continues throughout the work to address pieces of advice to that audience.

The tale of Charlotte Temple is the story of a young and virtuous British girl of fifteen who is seduced away from her finishing school by the wiles of a certain amoral French teacher (Mme. LaRue) who convinces Charlotte that her attraction toward a young British officer ought to be acted upon instead of ignored. LaRue and this young officer (Montraville) persuade Charlotte to abandon the circle of affectionate and virtuous people who are her friends to accompany the pair to America, where Montraville's commission carries him. He promises to marry Charlotte upon their arrival in the new world; he never makes good this promise. His attraction for another and a treacherous rumor (invented by Belcour, a villainous officer who desires Charlotte in a not-so-sacred way) that Charlotte has been unfaithful to him conspire against Charlotte, who finds herself pregnant and destitute in a foreign land. Turned out of her cottage because she cannot pay the rent (Belcour has witheld funds intended for Charlotte by Montraville) Charlotte wanders in a snow storm to New York, thinking that LaRue (now comfortably installed as Mrs. Crayton, a matron of NY society) will help her. LaRue refuses; Charlotte is given shelter by some of LaRue's servants. She dies shortly after giving birth to a daughter. On her deathbed she is visited by her father, who has come from England to bring her home. Mr. Temple returns instead with Lucy, Charlotte's daughter. As the novel ends Belcour has been killed by Montraville for his treachery toward Charlotte and LaRue, divorced, worn out, sick, and penniless has just expired in a British hospital, where she was placed through the kindness of Mr. Temple.

Admittedly, the story line, or sequence of recurrent acts in the novel is both action packed and tragedy laden—and that fact must have accounted for a good deal of the popularity of the work, which underwent two hundred editions. The story is based upon an event which really is archetypal: an attraction between two people which is not sanctioned by society and which must therefore run its course outside of the structures of society. At least in the beginning of the story, Montraville cannot marry Charlotte because neither of their families would approve a marriage both financially unstable and subject to the consequences of Montraville's military career in a foreign land.

There is a certain amount of "visceral attraction" in other events in the novel, too. Charlotte's plight as Montraville's attention turns from her to another woman constitutes a familiar scene in literature, rendered here all the more moving because of Rowson's insistence upon Charlotte's innocence and helplessness. And the spectacle of LaRue's and Belcour's treachery must have stirred the emotions of Rowson's readers as much as the spectacle of Iago's treachery in another, older literary forum, moved those who witnessed it.

But there is another element to be considered in this accounting: the way in which Rowson consistently reinforces her society's ideas about the value of its institutions and structures. Given the exact same story line, one can imagine numberless different points of view, countless ways of reckoning the *why* of Charlotte's tragedy. It is not hard to imagine a story along similar lines which would berate a society so narrow as to conceive of only one social form for human relationships, so unforgiving as to permit a progress of desperation like that which Charlotte endures. But Mrs. Rowson's imagination is severely limited by the prevailing social norms; she attacks neither the social rigidity of her times nor the prudery which maintained that rigidity; she turns her wrath upon the forces which seduce youngsters away from compliance with the existing social structures. I suggest that it is *because* Rowson reinforces the prevailing social norms that *Charlotte Temple* enjoyed such widespread popularity. I have no doubt that the late eighteenth and nineteenth century readers of *Charlotte Temple* enjoyed the tragic story of Charlotte; they also, I am suggesting, enjoyed being told repeatedly that the social structure in which they were caught up was firmly and rightfully rooted in human nature. Mrs. Rowson gives her readers vast amounts of moral instruction and reinforces the social status quo with her remarks in three general areas: first, the sanctity of the family; second, the sanctity of the virtue of Content; and third, the villainy of certain types of characters who detract from the sanctity of the first two. All three of these areas overlap as is to be expected, since they all derive from one consistent vision of social security with one concomitant set of fears about the dangers to that security.

Rowson presents the life of the family in idyllic tones. This is evident in the novel chiefly in her treatment of Charlotte's parents. When Mr. Temple proposed to Mrs. Temple, he did so in the following words:

We will purchase a little cottage, My Lucy, ". . . and thither with your reverend father we will retire; we will forget there are such things as splendour, profusion and dissipation: we shall have some cows, and you shall be queen of the dairy; in a morning while I look after my garden you shall take a basket on your arm and sally forth to feed your poultry. . . ." (*CT*, p. 55)

This is Rowson's vision of utopia, toward which she would urge all of the youngsters in her society.

Inherent in this idyllic vision of family life are Rowson's fears of 1) irresponsible marriage and 2) marriage contracted under impulsive inclination rather than under "the

precepts of religion and virtue." Rowson surrounds the
meeting of Charlotte and Montraville with stern warnings.
The reader discovers that Montraville's father has warned
his son against irresponsible marriage:

"There is one thing I think it my duty to caution you against; the
precipitancy with which young men frequently rush into matri-
monial engagements, and by their thoughtlessness draw many a deserving woman into scenes of poverty and distress. A soldier has
no business to think of a wife till his rank is such as to place him
above the fear of bringing into the world a train of helpless inno-
cents, heirs only to penury and affliction." (*CT*, pp. 73-4)

And in another place the author addresses herself to "the
young and thoughtless of the fair sex" regarding impulsive
marriage.

The second area in which Rowson reinforces the
social *status quo* comprises her remarks on the preeminence
of the virtue of Content. She is particularly concerned
that women should be content with their lot in life; as she
says in her Preface, she writes "with a mind anxious for the
happiness of that sex whose morals and conduct have so
powerful an influence on mankind in general." She idol-
izes Lucy Temple, Charlotte's mother, because she has
found Content in her marriage. Between what must have
been the harsh social reality of her times and the suffering
individual Rowson interposes her philosophy of Content,
of not expecting too much from life.

Northrop Frye, in the *Anatomy of Criticism*, suggests
that literature in its social aspect tends to identify the obstacles which stand in the way of society's realizing its
dream of itself; "the conception of a garden develops the
conception 'weed', and building a sheepfold makes the
wolf a greater enemy." (p. 105) The final area in which I
see Mrs. Rowson moving to support the social status quo
is in her definition of who the villains are in her society.

Needless to say, the villains in Rowson's scheme of
things are those who would seduce "the young and
thoughtless of the fair sex" away from the holy ground of

the family, away from being Content with the domestic life. There is one passage in *Charlotte Temple* in which it becomes unusually obvious to what extent Rowson is writing as an agent of society desirous of eradicating seducers:

> Gracious heaven! when I think on the miseries that must rend the heart of a doating parent when he sees the darling of his age at first seduced from his protection, and afterwards abandoned by the very wretch whose promises of love decoyed her from the paternal roof; when he sees her poor and wretched, her bosom torn between remorse for her crime and love for her vile betrayer; *my bosom glows with honest indignation, and I wish for power to extirpate those monsters of seduction from the earth.* (italics mine)

In her narrative the monsters of seduction, LaRue and Belcour, come to utter ruin in the last few pages of the work. LaRue's final speech, spoken to Charlotte's mother, who has ministered to LaRue in her last moments, restores the moral order of society:

> "You know not, Madam, what you do; you know not whom you are relieving, or you would curse me in the bitterness of your heart. Come not near me, Madam, I shall contaminate you. I am the viper that stung your peace. I am the woman who turned the poor Charlotte out to perish in the street. Heaven have mercy! I see her now . . . such, such was the fair bud of innocence that my vile arts blasted ere it was half blown." (*CT*, p. 163)

There is, of course, no definitive answer to the question of why *Charlotte Temple* achieved the immense popularity which it did achieve. But the fact that it is no longer "popular"—that is to say, that it enjoyed a historically limited popularity—suggests that its appeal rested more upon its reinforcement of a particular vision of society than upon the universality of the appeal of its recurrent events. There is something very comforting in being reassured that the structures which surround and penetrate one's life are valid structures, structures deeply rooted in human nature. That comfort—which we so seldom experience—is responsible to a large degree for the popularity of *Charlotte Temple*.

From this study of an eighteenth century novel there are certain conclusions useful for the study of popular literature in general. First, and less polemically than what follows, I think that the method which Frye's remarks suggest might be especially useful for studies of popular literature which is dated and no longer popular. In other words, isolating the recurrent events and statements about what ought to be offers the student of popular literature a way of talking about and comparing popular literature of other ages. A comparative study might identify the archetypal events in an older work which have a certain amount of visceral appeal and at the same time analyze the statements of what ought to be in order to define a society's ideas about itself—thus providing the reader with a basis for comparing and differentiating this literature from that of other times.

A second conclusion may answer a question which I can imagine validly rising from what I have written here on *Charlotte Temple*: how can I know that Susanna Rowson was formulating and reinforcing the prevailing social norms of her society? Might she not have been formulating social ideas of her own, or of a small group of people, ideas which conflicted with those of society at large?

I cannot know this for sure, but I suspect that Mrs. Rowson was reinforcing her society's norms for two reasons: first of all, her work was immensely popular *then*; secondly, it is not popular *now*. The conclusion which these facts led to was this: popular literature tends to support society's ideas about itself, and therefore is subject to the same inability to see the full complexity of the truth about its social reality as society is subject to that inability. I would suggest that only literature which sees more about society than society sees about itself can endure the test of time. *Charlotte Temple* does no more than reinforce prevailing social ideas, and because it does no more than that it has passed with the passing of the age it reflects.

SUSAN GORSKY

THE GENTLE DOUBTERS:
IMAGES OF WOMEN IN ENGLISHWOMEN'S
NOVELS, 1840-1920

In spite of the old nursery rhyme, when little girls become grown women they are not uniformly regarded as
being composed of "sugar and spice and everything nice."
Rather, woman has traditionally been seen as either saint
or devil: on the one hand the Virgin Mary, freed from
woman's tainted sexuality, who brings man to God; on the
other Eve, the mother of the human race and the source of
all human woe. We might expect that when women authors create women characters the angels outnumber the
demons, but we might also hope that women could see and
thus describe other women with enough insight to avoid
simple stereotyping. In fact, a survey of nearly one-hundred novels by Englishwomen written between the 1840s
and about 1920 (the ideological center of Victorianism at
one end and the beginnings of Modernism at the other) reveals a greater fulfillment of our expectation than of our
hope, and yet that hope is not fully denied.[1] The angels
do outnumber the demons, but not all of the women characters can be categorized, and the categories themselves are
opened to question.

Most of the characters fit stock roles: the heroines
are blends of angelic grace, saintly virtue, and an occasional
touch of harmless demon for spice; there are relatively few
"bad women" and these are generally the innocent victims
of evil men. Thus these novels, among which are both immediately popular "best-sellers" and enduring "classics"
(as well as the occasional work which crosses the barrier
usually present between these two classifications), generally
present a skewed vision of the members of their sex—a

28

vision which rather than merely projecting reality, limits the options open to woman while enhancing or idealizing her nature. However, all of the women are not stereotyped. Some of the more prominent female characters (especially in the works of George Eliot, Mrs. Gaskell, Charlotte Brontë, and Virginia Woolf) are carefully individualized and realistically portrayed. Of equal importance are those characters who appear to fit the familiar molds and yet through whom those molds are inspected for flaws. Outright rejections of the traditional roles of woman or the received picture of the heroine are rare; rather, the questioning which occurs within the novels is cautious, the disapproval generally subtle. No matter how strongly the author may have disbelieved the wisdom or appropriateness of the tradition, her doubts were expressed gently.

In probing the myths about women and in varying the traditional heroine, the novelists risked alienating their audience which was largely comprised of middle- and upper-class readers who could be expected to share the essentially middle-class assumptions upon which the received feminine ideal was based. Real women—and thus heroines in fiction—were to be obedient, chaste, and pious, to look forward to marriage as their proper goal, and to expect in marriage to see their parents' authority exchanged for that of their husbands. It is probable that such practical reasoning contributed to the widespread conservatism of these novels. Few women novelists of this period are active reformers (at least in their fiction), and their books are generally not the forerunners of social change; however, in the pictures which they present they reveal the problems which women faced, the limitations of the traditional female role, and some alternatives to the currently accepted ideals.

The objection directed at male novelists by the outspoken title character of Charlotte Brontë's *Shirley* is clearly applicable to the majority of the women novelists too:

If men could see us as we really are, they would be a little amazed; but the cleverest, the acutest men are often under an illusion about women . . . their good woman is a queer thing, half doll, half angel; their bad woman almost always a fiend. Then to hear them fall into ecstasies with each other's creations, worshipping the heroine of such a poem—novel—drama, thinking it fine—divine! Fine and divine it may be, but often quite artificial.[2]

While the female characters in these novels are not all heroines or all stereotypes, certain figures with predictable characteristics and behavior appear and reappear, defining the central patterns of womanhood and the roles available to the woman of this era. Continuing a long-established tradition, the woman sees herself as subordinate to man: after all, Mary could lead people to Christ but it is the male God who offers salvation; Eve was led astray not only by feminine curiosity but also by the male Satan; and even though Pandora opened the box which released evil into the world, the box, with its fatal contents, was a gift from Zeus. The drawing-room world created by the women novelists for their largely female audience is scented with roses and filled with fancy-work and ballgowns, but it is a world in which man is supreme. The best hope for the young heroine is marriage with an appropriate man, for the mating-game which leads to marriage is the central adventure of her life and in marriage itself traditionally lies her fulfillment. Here too is the most prevalent plot of these novels, the tracing of a young woman's career through the challenges and obstacles of courtship to the threshold of marriage. The nature of the obstacles and the response of the heroine to them reveal various female stereotypes at work: the Independent Woman must be taught that marriage is best, the Martyr dies when her lover is faithless, the Angel stands by her sweetheart until he is cleared of false charges or inherits an estate and they can marry, the Ingenue learns the value of her rejected suitor. In examining each of these stereotypes, it becomes obvious that changing values and mores which influence the role of woman also affect the definition of a typical member of any group. The ideal girl of 1850 seems rather bland to the 1890s; the Romp of 1910 was a Bad Woman (or nearly so) fifty years earlier. But the categories themselves remain to be choreographed in predictable patterns of plot and to reveal something about the world of women during a period when increasing attention was focused on that steadily changing world.

The typical Victorian heroine is more than pretty, for while she may not be a classic beauty, her face shows animation, intelligence, and character. Her blue or grey eyes always sparkle, twinkle, or shine, and they subtly reveal love she wants to hide, anger she tries to overcome, and merriment she should suppress. Her nose is well-shaped and slender, her lips are rosy, full, round, pouting, or gently curved, and her teeth are invariably white and even. Her complexion is clear and white but not pale, and the color in her cheeks deepens with exercise, excitement, or embarrassment. Her hair is blond or light brown, occasionally darker, but never red, and is smooth, luxuriant, and thick. The rest of her body is modestly ignored, although an occasional white column of a neck or gently rounded arm is seen early in the period, and the relatively low-cut dresses of the turn of the century revealed more of her graceful shoulders and delicate white skin. She is generally slightly taller than average, and is slender and graceful. At the youngest she is twelve or thirteen, at the oldest twenty-seven or eight, but most frequently the heroine is in her late teens, just at the age when a former brotherly or fatherly friend becomes a potential husband.

Her behavior is pre-eminently ladylike, which means that she is gentle, quiet, graceful, subordinate, and restrained. She walks up stairs one at a time, sits peacefully for hours with her "fancywork" (embroidery, worsted, netting, and knitting are four popular, genteel means for filling her many leisure hours), rides a carefully chosen, gentle horse, arranges flowers for the house, practices playing the piano or singing popular little songs faithfully every day, reads selected books and journals (and is especially

partial to romantic fiction—the kind in which she plays a
leading role—and to simple poetry), and varies her day by
making and receiving visits from neighborhood women or—
a far more interesting alternative—receiving visits from men.
In the years leading up to the First World War her dresses
became shorter and the heroine added legs, breasts, and
passions to her attributes. She learned to play tennis and
ride a bicycle, to use a typewriter and do mathematics or
Greek, even to support herself or live alone. A product of
the war and of growing changes in society and in the role
of women, she became a figure increasingly recognizable
as "modern."

Few heroines actually have all of the qualities seen
as standard, but their very differences are defined as departures from the norm. The description of the title character of Mary Braddon's *Vixen* is typical. We are told that
she is not "absolutely beautiful" because

The white skin was powdered with freckles. The rippling hair was
too warm an auburn to escape an occasional unfriendly remark from
captious critics, but it was not red hair for all that. The eyes were
brownest of brown, large, bright, and full of expression. The lips
were full and firmly moulded—lips that could mean any thing, from
melting tenderness to sternest resolve. Such lips, a little parted to
show the whitest, evenest teeth in Hampshire, seemed to Rorie
[the novel's hero and Vixen's future husband] lovely enough to
please the most critical connoisseur of feminine beauty. The nose
was short and straight . . . the chin was round and full and dimpled;
the throat was full and round also—a white column supporting the
tawny head.

While this is long, it is worth quoting in its entirety because
it is typical of the catalogue given with the introduction
to most heroines. Certain features cannot change: a
crooked nose, uneven teeth, or a double chin would be
anathema to heroines. But the experienced reader soon
learns to pick out the more interesting heroines from their
physical description, for they are the ones who, in some
small but important way, vary the stereotype. The innocent, beautiful, delicate, and frequently bland Ingenue

always fits the stereotype: it is she who fulfills Shirley's description of a girl "half doll, half angel." The individualized heroines, those who at least in some degree defy the stock characterization, also defy stock descriptions. Vixen's freckles and not-quite-red hair are warnings of her individuality, a trait which she proves by her behavior and her unusual capacity for passion. Similarly, George Eliot draws attention to Dorothea Brooke's unusual character when she dresses her in ascetically plain clothing, significantly described in the opening paragraph of *Middlemarch*.[3]

Slight deviations from standard behavior also serve as clues to an individualized heroine. In *Wives and Daughters* (Mrs. Elizabeth Gaskell) Molly Gibson's new stepmother reproves her for walking up stairs two at a time, but her stepsister, Cynthia Kirkpatrick, underscores her far greater disregard for the conventions by laughingly admitting that *she* climbs stairs four steps at a time. Vixen likes to ride swiftly and wildly, and once even rides unattended at night to Rorie's home. Music, like painting, needlework, or flower-arranging, is one of the genteel accomplishments of the young woman: it is proper and necessary for a young girl to sing or to play the piano well enough to entertain guests after dinner, but it is improper for her to care too much about her art. Rose Leyburn (Mrs. Humphrey Ward, *Robert Elsmere*) defies the proprieties first by playing the violin, which is not considered a ladylike instrument, and second by being both talented and devoted to music. When Rose's sister scolds her for practicing too long by contrasting her own virtue, Rose's creator suggests the limits both of the artist's pre-occupation and of the alternatives available to a young woman: "I have been attending to my domestic duties, arranging the flowers, mending my pink dress for to-morrow night, and helping to keep mama in good spirits. . . . I should like to know what you've been doing for the good of your kind since dinner." Mrs. Ward's later works confirm her quiet approval of women like Rose and her distaste for the

more paltry—but also traditionally more acceptable—
"domestic duties."

All women are not heroines, and in fact the characterization of the subordinate females in the novels is more
frequently limited to the stereotypes. While the heroine
may also fit a given category, often she is individualized in
at least some small way and occasionally she escapes the
confines of the typical. Still, most of the female characters conform to one of a limited number of categories,
ranging on a scale of feminine virtue from the Angel to
the Bad Woman, with a majority of the heroines rating
considerably higher than the mid-point on the scale. The
most prevalent types are defined below.[4]

ANGELS, SAINTS, AND MARTYRS

The Angel can be of any age, married or single, pretty
or plain. She is above earthly concerns, generous to the
point of self-sacrifice, quiet, forgiving, and capable of absolutely selfless love. Her strength may come from formal
religion or an inner guide. She frequently discovers and
reveals her saintly nature in part as the result of an unhappy experience in love—a broken engagement or the
death of her beloved. Her subservience and self-effacing
love allow her to subordinate her own needs and wishes
to those of her family or the man she loves or even to help
her lover in his relationship with another woman; but displaying the behavior of an Angel does not prove that a
girl is immune to strong feelings.[5]

Sometimes the Angel is rewarded on earth for her
behavior, usually through marriage at the novel's end.
More frequently, however, the angelic woman finds her
only rewards in her own behavior, in its occasional quiet
recognition by others, or in her thoughts of a future life in
heaven. Two instances of women who are finally blessed
by total reconciliation with their husbands reveal their
authors' distaste for the stereotype, as they are led by their
saintliness into the errors of false superiority and intoler-
ance. This is displayed in both Catherine of *Robert Els-*

mere (Ward) and in May Sinclair's *The Helpmate*, but the latter is especially interesting because it reflects the new century's changed attitudes toward sexuality: the asexual, spiritual woman is seen to be abnormal rather than an angelic ideal. The novel is a rare, early study of the power and importance of sexual love. Anne Majendie considers herself a "saint" because she does not leave her husband when she learns he had an affair several years before their marriage, but through contrasts with a number of other women, she is shown to be physically and emotionally cold. She sublimates physical desire and emotional needs into a desperate, possessive maternal passion and substitutes for human warmth a limited and flawed spiritualism. She ultimately denies her husband not only her body but all communion other than that required by politeness. In his extreme frustration, still loving his wife "with his whole soul, with his heart and with his body," Majendie again becomes involved with another woman, who has the "sweetness," "humility," and "love" which Anne lacks but who in turn is missing the complex excitement which his wife so tantalizingly offers Majendie. Three crises occurring in rapid sequence serve to bring to Anne a recognition of Majendie's worth and of what she has done to him, and just before it is too late, a cold woman is taught to love.

While a few of the saintly women, including Sinclair's heroine, vary the stereotype by containing contradictory feelings and unsaintly emotions, most of the Angels are monotonously and unbelievably good. *Daniel Deronda*'s Mirah, *Adam Bede*'s Dinah Morris (both by George Eliot), and Margaret May of *The Daisy Chain* (Charlotte Yonge) are so self-effacing, gentle, and saintly that they become abstractions of an ideal rather than characters who realistically represent human beings. That Dinah is not unfeeling is proven by her relationships with Adam and with Hetty (especially after Adam's loss of Hetty and during the latter's imprisonment and death), but it is not until her turmoil over whether she should marry Adam that she breaks the bonds of the stereotyped Angel and becomes more fully and understandably human.

A special sub-division of the Angel category is the Martyr, of whom there are two kinds. The first is the traditional sufferer who bears the indignities and tortures of her life with the self-sacrificing grace and patient fortitude of a Griselda, and whose life ends in pain or early death. The second, though placed in an identical situation, attempts to fight back against the circumstances or people that have trampled on her. She refuses to destroy herself voluntarily and is sometimes rewarded at the novel's end with a happy marriage. The cause of martyrdom in virtually every instance is a man: male supremacy in law and in tradition could turn a marriage into hideous bondage for a woman, and the double standard in sexual behavior could ruin her life while it left his untainted, except, perhaps, by the faint—and faintly enticing—odor of a rake's reputation.

Like other girls powerless before a tyrannous father, Clara Talboys (Braddon, *Lady Audley's Secret*) expects to find comparative freedom in her proposed marriage. But Milly Barton (Eliot, *Scenes of Clerical Life*) could have warned her about the potential martyrdom of even a seemingly happy marriage, for Milly is enslaved by her devotion to her family, devotion epitomized by her keeping a sewing-box by her bed so that she can darn socks at night when she cannot sleep. Before her seventh pregnancy, which kills her, it is suggested that Milly is too weak to bear the strain of childbirth. But without birth control and with little help from the husband who no longer loves her, she dies at thirty-five of overwork and childbearing. Milly is not unusual, however; her life is typical of the age. Only in the upper classes where nurses, maids, and governesses assumed the bulk of child care could a woman hope to grow into middle age in reasonable health. In the sympathetic portrayal of Milly's life and in the suggestion that her devotion *is* enslavement (at least partly self-induced), George Eliot reveals her anger at the conditions—economic,

social, and psychological—which lead to such a life. Most
of these novels, however, either ignore life after the wedding or provide only a glimpse of the first few years of
marriage, so that we last see the heroine as a young matron,
with one or two children by her side. The later years of
wearying childbearing and the typical large Victorian families are almost totally absent from the chronicles of the
women novelists, except when the subject is such martyrdom as Milly's. In their emphasis upon romance and sentiment, in offering this as an escape, the novelists may also
be criticizing the reality of Victorian maternity and suggesting the alternative of the smaller family of a later
time.[6]

Broken engagements or faithless lovers give many
young women a chance to earn the title of martyr: some
women die for love, some sacrifice their happiness for
others', and a few find subsequent happiness in marriage
with a more suitable man or with the chastened and repentant lover. Other women become martyrs when their husbands leave them, sometimes for another woman, sometimes just before the birth of a child who then may have
to bear the brand of apparent illegitimacy. Loneliness, insanity, and death are common outcomes for the women
left behind, but occasionally the pattern is broken. Some
women threaten to leave their husbands and some actually
do. Yet when such a drastic step is taken, it is seen in
those terms, and the woman who succumbs to the temptation faces social ostracism and possible legal retribution.
The extreme situations which are presented in the novels
reveal clearly where the authors' sympathy lies. Thus,
when Phoebe Fenwick (Ward, *Fenwick's Career*) leaves her
husband for twelve years after he first left her, hid his marriage from his new friends, and courted another woman,
she is seen as the guilty one and her husband as the
wronged spouse. That is, she is so regarded by her husband, their acquaintances, and even by herself, but *not* by
her creator, who concludes the novel by commenting that

in their final reconciliation, both husband and wife have matured.

Women such as Phoebe and the many others like her are seen as martyrs not only to the men who forsake or mistreat them but also to the social tradition and to the law. In Victorian England a woman could not legally leave her husband: she was his property and had no rights exclusive of those he chose to give her. Regardless of his own behavior he could claim their children, force her to live with him, and deprive her of liberty and property as well as of love. However, as the turn of the century approached and passed, women increasingly had more rights and made greater use of the rights they had. They were freer to act on their own, to avoid marriage as the only legitimate mode of life, and to escape from a marriage which proved intolerable. Thus, some alternatives were made available to those who increasingly refused Griselda's fate.

THE CENTER OF THE SCALE: THE ROMANTIC HEROINE FROM INNOCENCE TO INDEPENDENCE

The Ingenue

Generally in her late teens but sometimes even younger, the Ingenue is a frequent figure in the drawing-rooms and country homes of these novels. When she is the heroine, she usually displays enough development to outgrow this classification by the end of the story; however, the Ingenue often sweetly exchanges her father's arm for her husband's with no perceptible change in herself. Innocent, unformed, and naive, often self-effacing and unsure, the Ingenue is at the mercy of the adults—especially the men—who enter her life. In her innocence she has implicit trust in man, who is as likely to lead her into a ruinous affair as to offer her marriage, the only socially acceptable goal.

The extent of the possible naivete is astounding—and sometimes unreal. Girls are regularly duped into secret or false "marriages" and accept without question the frequent absences or total desertion of their "husbands." One young heroine, Undine (Charlotte Braeme, *The World Between Them*), marries a man she barely knows and does not love because the idea of a secret marriage, consummated by a kiss, initially seems like a pleasant adventure and because she cannot figure out how to reject his proposal. This secret marriage leads her into a life of lies, bigamy, discovery, and violent death.

The Ingenue makes a perfect wife, according to many heroes—Victorian and later. The eighteen year old Kate Forster (Braeme, *Married in Haste*) typifies the innocence and value of such a girl. She is content with silent worship: "I was not presumptuous in my love. To live where I should see him, to do all in my power for those he loved, to live loving him, to die breathing his name—I had no greater ambition, no more fervent hope." When her lover declares himself, he is gratified to find he is her first love, for he tells her that "no woman's eyes are ever the same after a lover had looked into their depths!" The double standard, especially rampant in the early years of this period, is encouraged by the frequent large age gaps between the pair: a husband twice his wife's age is not unusual. As a result, what is said about Elsie Vaughan (R. N. Carey, *Mrs. Romney*) could be said about the other Ingenues: she is "only a child-woman," an epithet justified by her typically childlike behavior.[7]

If the child-woman marries before the man has been able "to educate" her (as Elsie's fiance claims necessary), the result can be, as it is for Undine, disastrous. In a rare examination of life after the wedding, *The Semi-Attached Couple* (Emily Eden) displays the problems of adjustment which the Ingenue faces. With the acquaintance of a few weeks' courtship, "carried on solely in a ball-room or at a breakfast," Helen Eskdale marries Lord Teviot, because "she was too young to act for herself" (that is, too young to break the engagement, but *not* too young to marry). After a few months of a rapidly deteriorating relationship they separate (in a socially acceptable way), and during their separation, freed from the fears generated by his passionate love and his anger, Helen begins to recognize and respond to that love. He returns, very ill, and as Helen nurses him back to health she loses her fear of him. Finally, at all of eighteen, she expresses her new maturity, saying, "I was a foolish, spoiled child then, and now I am a happy woman." In nearly one-hundred novels, this is the only one which considers what happens to the sheltered sixteen, seventeen, or eighteen year old when she begins marriage with a man she has known for a few weeks or months in a romantic fairy-land of girlish dreams and crowded dances. It is, perhaps, less disturbing to a sentimental vision to employ the stereotype of the Ingenue and to close the door discreetly behind the newlyweds than to wrestle with the real problems of realistic characters. But, at least some of the novelists, as we have seen, opened the door enough to show the existence of the problems.

The Independent Woman

Not all heroines are quite this young and even some of the young ones are more mature and less naive than is the typical Ingenue. Forced to be the "woman" of the household because of the death of one or both parents, girls not yet twenty accept responsibility for younger brothers and sisters and for a home until they in turn are given shelter by marriage. In the working classes, girls had to display at least a modicum of maturity, for their home responsibilities were greater and they were frequently required to help the family financially. For Mrs. Gaskell's dressmakers, factory and farm girls, work was only a necessity, and one which they hoped would end with marriage; but for some of their contemporaries, work was a symptom and proof of independence.

According to Dinah Mulock, writing *A Woman's Thoughts about Women* in 1858, approximately one-half of the women in England then were forced to be independent, that is, to support themselves in one of the occupations open to women: teaching, acting, singing, painting, and the less acceptable jobs in domestic service, sewing, or selling. The Independent Woman is an increasingly popular—and increasingly powerful—figure in the novels of the period, but it is significant that a very popular plot presents the young woman's recognition of the superiority of marriage (and, explicitly or implicitly, of the man) over any form of feminine independence. In the novels of the late nineteenth century are found several governesses and teachers, a few artists and musicians, some factory and shop workers, a nurse or nurse's aide, and a number of young women who would sympathize with the jobless Shirley and her friend Caroline (Brontë, *Shirley*) when they proclaim their desire for an "occupation" or "career" and search for ways to make satisfying and useful lives for themselves without marriage. But many of these women are ultimately happy to accept what Caroline calls "the ordinary destiny" of woman, "the duties and affections of wife and mother," and those who remain single often do so out of necessity—the death or desertion of their lovers.

The necessary antagonism between marriage and a career is clearly spelled out in several books, and normally even the most independent young woman gracefully capitulates to love at the novel's end. A typical novel concludes with the hero's assumption that his future wife needs neither education nor career. "Can you give up everything for me? . . . Your dream for years has been Girton," says the young man in *A Girton Girl* (Annie Edwards), and the heroine responds, "I desire that you shall guide me. . . . I need no other life, no other wisdom, no other ambition than yours." The smug author concludes that her heroine "had proved herself a very woman after all."[8] Still, not all of the heroines—or their creators—capitulate so easily. Molly Gibson's father wishes to limit her education to the abilities to "sew, and read, and write, and do her sums" and even wonders whether "reading or writing is necessary." He wishes "to keep her a child" and believes too much education can be "rather a diluting of mother-wit." But Molly does not accept these limits, insisting on "French and drawing lessons" and reading "every book that came in her way," including all those that interest her in her father's extensive library (Mrs. Gaskell, *Wives and Daughters*).

Most of the Independent Woman's contemporaries, expecially the men and the older women, would have agreed with the man in the following conversation from Mrs. Ward's *The Mating of Lydia*. Mr. Delorme says that a working woman "can only unsex herself. . . . What, in God's name, has she to do with paying the rent? Let her dance and sing—have a train of lovers—look beautiful!" His hostess replies, "The whole duty of woman . . . for our grandmothers," and he answers, "No: for all time." In 1913, when these words were published, "our grandmothers" would have been among the heroines of the earliest of these novels. By the turn of the century, many more women were forced to be self-supporting and some were devoted to an independent life. In the years before the war, new responsibilities and new freedoms were created for women, who are shown attaining and using greater knowledge, traveling alone or with men, making decisions about business and personal life that a quarter-century earlier would have been made by parents, uncles, or brothers. Still, the independent woman of the early twentieth century, the career woman who either remains single or tries to combine her work with marriage, is seen as an anomaly, with minimal success and only a limited chance for happiness.

While it is not easy, it is less difficult for the unmarried girl to maintain her independence of thought and action than it is for a married woman, according to these novelists. Three women writers, Jane, Nina, and Laura, are contrasted in *The Creators* by May Sinclair, in part to analyze the relative values of career and marriage and the possibility of combining the two. Nina acts out what the other two women give lip service to, the idea that only in a virginal life can intellectual creativity be fully developed. Perhaps the most talented and initially the most successful is Jane, but "married she served a double and divided flame," ultimately becoming incapable of writing. Laura also marries, and she alone is more or less able to balance her career and marriage. Her greatest fluidity and her popular success—but not necessarily her best work—follow her marriage, and with her husband's death she stops writing. Even for these unusually dedicated, talented, and successful women, if they marry, their independent careers must be kept distinctly secondary to their duties as wives. Laura and Jane demonstrate that a woman can be interrupted at her work for any reason, she is dependent upon her husband's tolerance to work at all, and she is pressured by family and society to minimize or better yet to abandon her career.

Perhaps the most independent matron of all these books is Frances Crimsworth (Charlotte Brontë, *The Professor*), whose words sound more amenable to readers a century later than they did to her contemporaries. "Think of my marrying you to be kept by you," she says to her fiance. "I could not do it; and how dull my days would be! . . . I should get depressed and sullen, and you would soon tire of me." Her husband is still clearly her superior, but Frances works with him and later has her own school. She loses none of her femininity, as the traditionalist Mr. Delorme feared a working woman must: "I seemed to possess two wives," the Professor says, the firm, "stately and elegant" directress and the loving, submissive wife and mother.[9] In this way, Charlotte Brontë is able to suggest that a recognition of woman's individual talents and fulfillment of her desires need not lead to radical changes in the established norms: a woman could work, could use her mind, and could enjoy at least an approximation of an independent life without threatening the traditional superior-

ity of the male or the importance of the home. George
Eliot's less positive view of this question takes fully into
account the powerful role of the man involved: only if
her husband cooperates can the wife achieve even as much
independence as Frances does (who, after all, runs her
school with her husband's permission and encouragement).
The title character of Eliot's *Romola* is at least as intelligent and well-educated as Frances, but she is stymied and
frustrated by a husband who cares neither for her nor for
her mind. Even the most independent woman, if she wishes also to be married, is responsible to the whims of her
husband. It took World War I, with its tremendous need
for workers, to open the way to reliance upon and trust in
women: from the changes caused by the war, the conditions were set for the emergence of the twentieth century
career girl who is foreshadowed by some of these Independent Women. But these early characters proved that a woman could display her own ideas and still be a romantic
heroine; she could toy with a profession and remain a
woman. Nonetheless, at least in the nineteenth century
and frequently in the twentieth, she still generally found
her ultimate happiness and ideal career in marriage.

The Romp

From the tomboy through the daring girl who breaks
the minor conventions to the Coquette, the Flirt, and the
Jilt (who is at the very limit of behavior above the Bad
Woman), the Romp frisks around the pages of these novels,
climbing a tree here, scandalizing the neighborhood gossips
there, and breaking men's hearts everywhere. The Coquette can be simply a fun-loving girl, but if she is not careful, she runs the risk of being known as a Flirt, or worse
yet, a Jilt. The codes of behavior were strict, and a nineteenth century girl who walked alone with a young man,
who went unchaperoned on day trips with a man or group
of young people, or who showed a preference for dancing
with a man to whom she is not engaged could expect to
lose her good reputation. For greater transgressions of the

social code, a girl could expect to lose more than this. Because they are seen pelting cherry-tarts in public streets, driving donkey carts, smoking, and going for evening boat rides with men, Prue (Rhoda Broughton, *Dr. Cupid*) and Lenore (Broughton, *"Goodbye, Sweetheart!"*) are regarded as "Bohemians": both girls ultimately die of unrequited love, paying with their lives for their behavior. The actual social code which called for ostracism and the fictitious code which required at least penance (and even death, as in Miss Broughton's more outlandish stories) are questioned by the novelists both through their exaggerations (the deaths of Prue and Lenore) and through more subtle means. Thus Letty Sewell's hypocrisy is mocked by Mrs. Ward in *Sir George Tressady*. Letty flirts with pleasure before her engagement to Sir George (she "had not been afraid to be 'talked about.' Dances, picnics, moonlight walks; the joys of outrageous 'sitting-out,' and hot rivalries with prettier girls; . . . it was all pleasant enough to think of."), but once engaged she develops an "ultra-conservative note." As times change, of course, so do customs, and by early in the twentieth century the heroine can walk alone or with a male companion, and can ride a bicycle and smoke, although the last two still disturb her more conservative acquaintances.

Except for developing the reputation of a Bad Woman, the worst thing a girl could be known as is a "Jilting Jessie" (*Wives and Daughters*). An engagement was formal and binding, and breaking one could leave a permanent stain on a girl's reputation. Still, the Jilt's unbecoming carelessness and insufficient attention to proper behavior are crimes against society which could occasionally be forgiven and which, in any case, were not serious enough to make her an outcast.

THE DEMON

Between the Jilt and the classical Bad Woman lies the Schemer, descendant of Milton's Eve, the wicked stepmother of fairy tales, and the conniving woman of all times.

Perhaps because the women novelists left the portrayal of such unpleasant females to men, this archetypal figure generally plays a subordinate role such as the match-making mother, the girl determined to marry, the unfaithful wife, and one or two wicked stepmothers. Yet the writers are realistic enough to include women whose motives for their evil behavior are judged not fully acceptable by author or reader. Other scheming women present in these books include those who lie about their social or financial status, their backgrounds, or even their feelings to achieve the security of marriage or of social position.[10] If unmarried, the Schemer works to become so. If she is married, she may intrigue against her husband (Rosamond Lydgate in *Middlemarch*), commit murder for her husband (Lady Culmore in Braeme, *Married in Haste*), or keep her marriage secret in order to marry again (Undine in *The World Between Them*). These women all consciously attempt to achieve something; they all use wiles, tricks, or even criminal acts with a direct purpose in mind. But this is not always true of the Bad Woman, who may have earned her reputation through wilful acts but who is equally likely not to have *earned* her reputation at all.

The woman who bears the stigmatic title of Evil without deserving it can be a victim or a martyr. She may be the trusting wife of a secret marriage which has left her with an unexplained child, or she may be the victim of gossip or lies. Of the few Bad Women who earn their reputations (almost never the heroine) most are condemned for sexual freedoms or the mere contemplation of such freedoms as committing adultery, running away with another man, having an illegitimate child, or becoming pregnant before marriage. But two drunkards, one drugaddict, and a few murderers are found among the heroines and incidental women of these novels.

When the "Fallen Woman" is the heroine, she is usually young and innocent, quickly repentant, and thoroughly punished. The title character of Mrs. Gaskell's *Ruth* is betrayed by her trusting innocence as well as by the totally unsympathetic Mr. Bellingham, by society's double standard, and by economic necessity, and she spends her life in penance and service. Even when the novelist displays the reasons for a girl's fall, she is certain to punish her heroine. Few women in these novels can lose their chastity or even their reputations and survive untainted and whole: punishments typically take the form of madness, prison, transportation, or death. Even complete repentance, as in Ruth's case, results in only mixed rewards.

The contrast between *Ruth* at the beginning of the period and *The Immortal Moment* (May Sinclair) at its end reveals a striking change in the freedoms of fiction and a less marked one in social mores. Ruth makes one mistake, goaded by poverty and led by a profligate. Kitty Tailleur too was initially the young victim of a thoughtless man, but unlike Ruth she enters into a series of illicit relationships, and is finally supported by prostitution. Mrs. Gaskell judiciously skips over most of the time when Ruth is with Bellingham (concentrating within that time on Ruth's innocence and her desperation), and focuses instead on the heroine's years of penitential behavior. On the other hand, most of May Sinclair's novel deals with Kitty's existence on the borders of acceptable society, leading up to her engagement to Robert Lucy and the breaking of this engagement when she reveals her past. Kitty tells Robert the truth because she feels that she will not make a fit stepmother for his two daughters. He agrees, but declares that except for the girls he would marry Kitty "tomorrow." Robert's declarations and his sister's support of Kitty suggest a change in the attitudes of at least fictive English society and an increased tolerance on the part of novel readers, but the end of Kitty's story provides a partial sop to Mrs. Grundy's descendants: having vowed neither to return to her "career" nor to be supported (innocently) by Robert, Kitty sees no alternative but death. In her suicide she varies only slightly the usual fate of the fallen woman; yet it is a significant variation for Kitty determines the outcome of her life in a way which blends the usual remorse and humility with courage.

In only one case is a former Bad Woman allowed a full measure of happiness as well as a resurrected conscience, and this exception points to a possible reason for the punishment of the sexually free woman. Recognizing her shortcomings and understanding her husband's attitude towards herself and their forced marriage, Charlotte (Mulock, *Parson Garland's Daughter*) works for the long years he is away to grow into the educated, refined, gentle, graceful, and loving wife he had hoped for. Her reward is his renewed and more mature, complete love and the gift usually reserved for the virtuous girl, a happy marriage and home. To protect and enhance the social tradition—the goal of marriage, the ideal of home—seems part of the purpose of these novels. To show too much sympathy for a Ruth or a Hetty Sorrel (*Adam Bede*) would be to endanger the virtuous woman and the sanctity of marriage. These authors could safely make excuses for the fallen woman to the point of observing and stressing her helplessness, her poverty and innocence, the superior strength, social position, and knowledge of her betrayer. Still, they could not fully condone the fall or give sanction to sexual indiscretions by allowing the indiscreet to prosper, because in so doing they might alienate or undermine the social world for which they wrote and upon which they were financially dependent.

BEYOND THE STEREOTYPES

Two types of characters remain: the players of bit parts who fit a traditional role and those rare individuals who defy simple classification. In the first group are found the selfish, petty old maids; the busy, useful spinsters; the eternal invalids—patient or peevish; the good-natured, virtuous, efficient matrons; the querulous, interfering mothers—and mothers-in-law. In the second group are some of the most important and interesting women of these novels, the few characters who are sufficiently complex to make simple categorizing impossible. Generally the creations of one of the several recognized artists among the novelists surveyed, such women may display traits of one or more typical figures, but they are not defined or limited by the stereotypes. Thus, for example, Maggie Tulliver (George Eliot, *The Mill on the Floss*) is a Romp as a child, Independent in supporting herself, a Martyr to Tom, a self-conscious Saint in her attempted renunciation of all pleasure, and a would-be Angel with an only partially undeserved reputation as a Bad Woman in her relationships with Philip and Stephen. Similarly, Dorothea Brooke (*Middlemarch*) displays touches of the martyr, angel, saint, virtuous girl and matron, independent and even wilful woman. The limitations of looking at stereotypes becomes obvious in such summary characterizations of these well-developed and reasonably complex women or of the few others like them. In each case, something is left out; the characterization is incomplete.

Mrs. Gaskell has created warm, varied, and realistic women in a number of her heroines—Cynthia and Molly (*Wives and Daughters*), Mary Barton (*Mary Barton*), Sylvia (*Sylvia's Lovers*), and especially Margaret Hale (*North and South*). Charlotte Brontë is most successful with Lucy (*Villette*) and next with Shirley, although the slightly masculine, independent woman becomes increasingly prevalent in the later fiction. In the first Catherine Earnshaw (Emily Brontë, *Wuthering Heights*) is a powerful and individualized, though somewhat unreal, variant of the untamed, passionate girl, who is closely related to some of the "Romps" that follow, most notably Braddon's Vixen. George Eliot has the longest list of complex, realistic, and unusual women: Dorothea, Maggie, Romola, and Gwendolen Harleth, all of whom have been mentioned above; but in such characters as Celia Brooke and Rosamond Lydgate (*Middlemarch*), Lucy Deane (*The Mill on the Floss*), Millie Barton and Janet Dempster (*Scenes of Clerical Life*), little Eppie (*Silas Marner*), and Dinah Morris and Hetty Sorrel, she has employed essentially standard figures. In the majority of the novels and especially in those once-popular books which in some ways deserve the lack of attention paid to them in recent years, stock actions and attitudes are consistently presented by women. Most heroines and incidental women alike fill defined and limited roles and are circumscribed by predictable behavior.

In presenting their angels, martyrs, ingenues, and occasional demons, the women novelists were not merely describing what they saw and knew of woman and her role. Rather, with important exceptions, they idealize the woman while limiting her role. However, although they essentially and perhaps surprisingly uphold the conventionally accepted role of woman, they are able subtly and delicately to probe into the tradition. Marriage is consistently shown as the central goal for a young girl. Still, by describing an unhappy marriage or the difficult adjustment which the child-bride must make, they question the validity of that goal for all women and the wisdom of the ideal of absolute innocence; by limiting the average family to two or three children, they suggest an alternative to the cycle of yearly confinements ending in early death. The intelligent and artistic girls are repeatedly taught that marriage is better than independence. Once married, however, they may also learn that men want them to ignore their minds and talents and that men are not necessarily their intellectual superiors. Because of the laws and the social conventions, at this point their knowledge can bring them only pain. Perhaps ninety-five percent of these novels take place at an English country manor or a quiet but exclusive foreign hotel, but enough are set in a mining or factory town with a working-girl heroine to show the illness, exhaustion, and despair of poverty and the miserable conditions of the factories and workshops. Finally, while it is true that virtually every woman who indulges in sexual freedoms is punished in some devastating way, it is also true that the "fallen" woman is presented with sympathetic understanding and with a pointed study of the economic, social, and personal pressures which caused her fall. That the man involved escapes her fate, even though he may have added the sin of desertion, is not accepted lightly, by the author or by the reader.

The women who wrote these novels demonstrated in their own lives that they did not believe in all the social conventions and that they did not accept the notion that a woman must lose her identity and intellect when she married. But the majority of the women for whom they wrote and upon whom they were financially dependent were living in a world which was just beginning to be aware of the limitations and indignities of the contemporary condition of women. The period was one of increasing agitation for women's rights, from Mill's *Subjection of Women* (1869) through the great changes effected by World War I and the granting of voting privileges in 1928. By proceeding with caution and hesitancy to probe the myths, examine the realities, and suggest alternatives, while still supporting the traditional bases of woman's role, these novelists both reflected the questioning going on around them and brought these questions to a wider audience of women who would have been largely unaware of and perhaps inimical to the new currents of thought. Thus they continued a process of probing and thinking which, with the guns of the war and its attendant social changes, exploded the traditional view of woman and her role.

NOTES

[1]Included in the survey are such authors as Dinah Mulock (Craik) and Charlotte Yonge, who were very popular with their contemporaries but are now virtually unread, and others, like George Eliot, Charlotte Brontë, and Virginia Woolf who still earn a warm response from the general public and respect from the critics. Choosing boundary dates necessarily involves a measure of the arbitrary, but the years selected mark significant points in the history of women writers and in their world. The first published novels of the

Brontë sisters appeared in 1847, at a time when Victorian values and ideas were flourishing without the questioning and doubts which later assailed the society and entered fiction; the first novels of Virginia Woolf and Dorothy Richardson—both experimenters and feminists—appeared in 1915, when England was rocked by the First World War and Englishwomen by concomitant changes in society. The years included thus span the development from Victorianism to early Modernism, in the form and concerns of the novel and in the role of women.

2Charlotte Brontë, unlike her heroine, feels that women fare no better at picturing men than men do with women. Cited by Mary A. Ward (Mrs. Humphrey Ward) in her Introduction to *Shirley* (London: John Murray, 1929), xxii.

3Cf. also Maggie Tulliver (Eliot, *The Mill on the Floss*) and Molly Gibson (Gaskell, *Wives and Daughters*) who are both "brown" in complexion and have obstinately curly, dark hair. Mrs. Gaskell's description of a girl with a subordinate role in *Mary Barton* offers a tongue-in-cheek acknowledgement of the necessary attributes of a heroine: "Sally . . . was but a plain, red-haired, freckled girl; never likely, one would have thought, to become a heroine." Thus in a subtle, joking manner, Mrs. Gaskell rejects one of the traditional stereotypes, although her heroines (at least in their physical attributes) bend the mold only slightly.

4Patricia Thomson in *The Victorian Heroine: A Changing Ideal* (London, 1956) discusses the roles available to women in the novel and in the world outside of fiction between 1837 and 1873, studying philanthropists, governesses, educated women, career women, spinsters, prostitutes, and women who question the values and form of marriage and the double standard of sexual behavior. In *All the Happy Endings* (New York, 1956), a study of nineteenth century domestic novels by American women, Helen Waite Papashvily refers without definition to a variety of such stereotypes as "the Coquette, the Belle, the Femme Fatale, the Injured Wife, the Erring Heart," "Folly Repentant," and "Innocence . Accused." A recent book, Hazel Mews' *Frail Vessels* (London, 1969), suggests that the better novelists were able to go beyond "the stock characters of heroine, siren, hoyden, [and] sentimental mother" to present realistic portraits of "new kinds of women . . . in all their variety" (199).

5For examples, see Margaret in Charlotte Yonge's *The Daisy Chain*, Lucy in Charlotte Brontë's *Villette*, Hester in Mrs. Gaskell's *Sylvia's Lovers*, and Eugenie in Mrs. Ward's *Fenwick's Career*. Lucy Snowe's love for Paul Emanuel (*Villette*) is full, robust, and real, but her religious stoicism controls and guides her in love an in the pain of Paul's death. A less realistic and thus less sympathetic "angel" is

Lucy Foster in Mrs. Ward's *Eleanor*. The frequent appelations of "saint" and "beautiful nun" are proven partly true by the actions and attributes of the overdrawn heroine. Surely Lucy is saintlike when she subordinates both pride and passion and agrees to travel with Eleanor (who loves Edward Manisty, the man who in turn loves the innocent Lucy). Lucy first avoids Edward, and later rejects his proposal; but her "maidenly coldness" and "young stiffness" prove to be a cover for a warm and sensitive nature, fully capable of passionate love, as is shown when the dying and penitent Eleanor brings the two lovers together. Mrs. Ward seems to suggest the limitation of stereotyping: Lucy is an "angel" in her ability to so fully subordinate her feelings for another's sake, but she is not another of the unemotional "saints." Furthermore, Lucy will have need of her angelic temperament in her marriage with the egotistic and selfish Manisty.

6A notable exception to this is Charlotte Yonge, in whose unusually popular novels large and happy families are the rule (*The Daisy Chain* and its sequel, for instance, center on a family with eleven children).

7Elsie's fiancé is described as one of those men who "like to educate their wives—at least, discipline them—before they marry them." For men like this, the "child-woman" makes an appropriate wife: she is more in need of and more amenable to such treatment, and she satisfies the man's sense of power while confirming the tradition of masculine superiority. The author's disapproval of this relationship is revealed in such word choices as "discipline" and "child-woman."

8Constance Laurayne (Charlotte Braeme, *The Heiress of Hilldrop*) typifies the temporarily independent girl of the period. Although she successfully supports herself for eight years by painting, when she marries "the world lost a great artist," for as a married woman, "her pictures and drawings now adorn the walls" only of her home, not of any gallery.

9Although this novel was written in 1846, it did not find a publisher for ten years, until Charlotte Brontë's other successes provided a market for *The Professor*. Even more than *Shirley*, this book was considerably ahead of its time. Another interesting independent matron is Lady Maxwell in Mrs. Ward's *Sir George Tressady*. She acts as the social and intellectual equal of the men she works with in her husband's political career, but is forced to return to a more traditional role when her sex becomes a problem: Tressady falls in love with her.

10Such schemers include Julie le Breton in Mrs. Ward's *Lady Rose's Daughter*, Gwendolen Harleth in George Eliot's *Daniel*

Deronda, and Lady Jesmond in Charlotte Braeme's *Fair But False*. In Gwendolen's case, and to a lesser extent in Julie's, the reader sympathizes with the schemer, who is driven to her misbehavior by a mixture of motives—in part by legitimate desperation, in part by pride or aspiration.

CHARLES BLINDERMAN

THE SERVILITY OF DEPENDENCE:
THE DARK LADY IN TROLLOPE

A study of the Dark Lady in the novels of Anthony
Trollope helps define the mode in which the Victorian
woman was stereotyped by society and by literature. Trollope, as one of the most popular writers of his time, played
a commanding role in reinforcing prevailing social and
literary stereotypes. His Dark Lady has ancestors who stole
through Arcadian forests, who were burned at the stake
throughout Renaissance Europe, and who reappear in bad
dreams wielding scissors. Trollope adapted this Dark Lady
archetype to symbolize the Victorian woman liberationist
and her reductio ad absurdum, the Jewess.

Trollope's attitude towards change was conservative.
In *The Belton Estate* one of his characters says:

When any practice has become the fixed rule of the society in which
we live, it is always wise to adhere to that rule, unless it call upon us
to do something that is actually wrong. One should not offend the
prejudices of the world, even if one is quite sure that they are prejudices.[1]

There is always a danger in identifying an author's beliefs
with what his characters say; but on the matter of conservatism in general, and on sexism in particular, Trollope's
own views are often expressed by his characters. For example, Escott's observation and the directives offered in
the two statements quoted are validated by Trollope's
explicit comment in his own voice: He hoped that, "For
the sake of those who are to come after me—both men and
women—I hope that there may be no change in the old established tradition."[2]

The old established tradition was being shaken in

55

Victorian England by many revolutionary movements, among them the reform agitation, the Darwinian upset, and, most frightening because it hit closest to home—its target was not the cloister, but the hearth—the woman's emancipation movement. Michael Goodwin's *Nineteenth Century Opinion* is a useful collection of articles extracted from *The Nineteenth Century* during the last twenty-three years of the Victorian age. The definition of woman that emerges from contributions to a discussion that spans the twenty-three years typifies the stereotype widely held by Victorians, including Trollope. As almost always happens when one discusses sexism, the participants in *The Nineteenth Century* debate consider the primary question of innate capacity. George Romanes suggested with immediate clarity that the reason why there have been no female poets or scientists of any importance is that women lack five ounces of brain. A figure considerably less well known, one Mrs. A. Sutherland Orr, wrote:

Women are intelligent; they are not creative. . . . That men possess the productiveness which is called genius, and that women do not, is the one immutable distinction that is bound up with the intellectual idea of sex.

The point really wasn't whether women do or do not have the innate mental equipment; for even if they do, they still ought not to challenge men in the latter's arenas— the intellectual, the professional, the political life. Such a challenge will, first of all, be detrimental to her looks. Mrs. E. Lynn Linton, in her contribution to the controversy, warned that the consequences of emancipation will be a flat chest, lean hips, a bass voice, and a bearded chin. *The Saturday Review*, condemning the woman who plunges into science by attending Professor Huxley's lectures, brought physical and moral features together in a conventional physiognomic approach by editorializing that such a woman's character, like her face, will become rigid and osseous. More urgent than physical ugliness was moral ugliness. It was obvious to the traditionalists that the Wild

Women, also dubbed the Shrieking Sisterhood, were immoral, for they threatened the integrity of society and of marriage. In woman's hands, wrote Louise Creighton, "rests the keeping of a pure tone in society, of a high standard of morality,"[3] and by living her life nobly and unselfishly, woman could make her contribution to progress of a good sort.

The literary men—such as Carlyle, Tennyson, Ruskin, Kingsley—agreed with these commentators. Literary tradition offered an archetype wonderfully suited to represent the bad women, the suffragettes, the "mad wicked folly" of woman's rights, though no one before Trollope had ever used this archetype for that purpose: the Dark Lady.

A convenient but still significant way of understanding the Dark Lady archetype is through physiognomy. Her physical features are indicative of temperamental features, her dark hair and mysterious eyes in particular revelatory of the darkness within; other physical features identify another value: her white skin, her height, the chiselled features of her face, her lofty poise—these identify her as emotionally as well as physically unembraceable. Characterized by these traits, she appears all over western literature, in earlier ages as merely a foreshadowing, but after the witch-burnings of the Renaissance as a fully created type. That is not a fortuitous consequence, for she is the transformed witch as she appears, for example, in Keats' "La Belle Dame sans Merci," in Coleridge's "Christabel," in Poe's "Ligeia," and throughout Trollope. A careful reading of Trollope's novels uncovers, out of the scores of women characters, many who conform to the Dark Lady stereotype in fundamental physical, emotional, and intellectual features. Of these, four occupy a sub-category of automata (Clementina Golightly, Griselda Grantly, Arabella Trefoil, and Georgiana Wanless), and about twelve are full realizations of the type (Carolina Waddington, Sophia Furnival, Clara van Siever, Julia Brabazon, Josephine de Montmorenci, Lizzie Eustace, Adelaide de Baron,

Lady Mabel Grex, and three who will be looked at in this paper: Signora Neroni, Marie Max Goesler, and Rebecca Loth).

The Dark Lady exists in Trollope's works, fiction and non-fiction, first of all as a stimulant. Lady Mabel Grex of *The Duke's Children* says: "Nothing gives so much zest to admiration as novelty. A republican charmer must be exciting after all the blase habitues of the London drawing room." Another character, Conway Dalrymple, of *The Last Chronicle of Barsetshire*, directs observation to the Dark Lady archetype:

Artists in all ages have sought for higher types of models in painting women who have been violent or criminal, than have sufficed for them in their portraitures of gentleness and virtue. Look at all the Judiths, and the Lucretias, and the Charlotte Cordays; how much finer the women are than the Madonnas and the Saint Cecilias.[4]

Thus, against the advice of a Longman reviewer who didn't approve of *Barchester Towers* because of the presence there of the grotesque Signora Neroni, Trollope kept her anyway. He acknowledged that the Dark Lady Arabella Trefoil would be considered by readers to be "unwomanly, unnatural, turgid,—the creation of a morbid imagination"[5] — but he kept her anyway. The assumption, then, is that despite the lack of critical comment on Trollope's Dark Lady, the archetype does exist in his works; and the thesis is that she exists partially to give zest to admiration, but more importantly for the political purpose of confounding the aspirations of the women's rights movement.

the English type

The ideal Victorian woman, according to the traditionalists, was not merely resigned to being, but delighted in being, wife and mother. One contributor to the *Nineteenth Century* discussion expressed this succinctly: the purpose that women should have in life is "maternity, for which, after all, women primarily exist."[6] Barbara Bodichon has a typical girl ask her mother: "What am I created for? What use am I to be in the world?" And her mother replies: "You must marry one day. Women were made for men. Your use is to bear children, to keep the home comfortable for your husband. The only respectable life for women is in marriage."[7] Trollope agreed with the conventional wisdom.

His British maiden or "little brown girl"—a type that has been recognized in criticism—represents his ideal. In physiognomic terms, the British Maiden's very brownness is an emblem of her usefulness. Her color indicates that she is—and this is the crucial concept—serviceable—the way the Queen was serviceable in having nine children. Trollope describes one of these girls:

There was a pervading brownness about her which left upon those who met her a lasting connection between Lucy Graham and that serviceable, long-enduring colour. . . . A good lasting colour she would call it,—one that did not require to be washed every half-hour. . . .[8]

Of many examples, the following few will illustrate why he liked the little brown girl so much:

from *Castle Richmond* (1860):

With him she could realize all that she had dreamed of a woman's love; and that dream which is so sweet to some women—of woman's subjugation.

from *Cousin Henry* (1879):

Oh, how she loved him! How sweet would it be to submit her pride, her independence, her maiden reticences to such a man as that! How worthy he was of all worship, of all confidence, of all service.

from *The Struggles of Brown, Jones, and Robinson* (1870):

Woman's smile had a charm for him, but no charm equal to the servility of dependence.[9]

For him, nature, the world, circumstances, "the whole

theory of creation," manifest a "higher power's" determination that a radical reconstruction of society aimed at the achievement of woman's rights was vicious as well as hopeless. What he said in his own voice confirms the opinion expressed by his characters who approve of women being subservient: "The necessity of the supremacy of man is as certain to me as the eternity of the soul."[10]

The Dark Lady's appearance and actions announce that she is not subservient and not serviceable. To the British Maiden's pretty intimations of fecundity, the Signora Neroni opposes a sterile and haughty beauty; to the ideal of subjection, she offers a cynicism that ridicules male supremacy.

Without mentioning Trollope at all, Mario Praz captures Trollope's Dark Lady in his comment:

. . . just as the Byronic hero's origin was often said to be mysterious and extremely noble, so, too was the origin of the Fatal Woman. And like the Byronic superman, the super-woman also assumes an attitude of defiance to society.[11]

Ladies, countesses, and various shapes of Signora abound as descriptive titles of Trollope's Dark Lady—for her being noble is both attractive and repelling, another trait that simultaneously arouses male aggression and puts the challenge out of reach. "Sir!" said Dr. Johnson, "in the case of a countess the imagination is more excited!" Trollope's Dark Ladies reject the role assigned to women of wife and mother. Their desire is not to their husbands, but only to themselves. Beautiful, remote, narcissistic, a closed circle into which man wants to break, but cannot, the Dark Lady is competent to be a subversive agent.

She is most defiant on the subject of marriage. Cynical as well as intelligent, she will pierce through what may be considered the fortifications or the facades of society. Marriage excites the Dark Lady to passion, as it does in this appealing argument made by the Signora:

I hate your mawkish sentimentality, Lotte. You know as well as I do in what way husbands and wives generally live together; you know how far the warmth of conjugal affection can withstand the trial of a bad dinner, or a rainy day, or of the least privation which poverty brings with it; you know what freedom a man claims for himself, what slavery he would exact from his wife if he could. And you know also how wives generally obey. Marriage means tyranny on one side, and deceit on the other.[12]

Twenty-five years after *Barchester Towers*, in the 1882 *Kept in the Dark*, Francesca Altifioria, the resident Dark Lady of that late novel, orates about women's rights and insults the little brown girl, Cecilia Holt, for aspiring to wifehood and motherhood. Cecilia is unaffected by her friend's criticism of marriage; she willingly accepts the mastery of the husband: "He had a right to command, a right to be obeyed, a right to be master."[13] Between the two novels, in 1870, legislation was passed which at least allowed wives to possess what they earned—the first Married Women's Property Act, a small but useful step in advancing liberation of women by breaking the servility of dependence. In a recognition of the power-play that inevitably obtains between men and women throughout Trollope's fiction (and elsewhere), Lady Mabel Grex dissolves her affair with Lord Silverbridge; in speaking of the kind of girl Silverbridge should marry, Lady Mabel defines the British Maiden:

In the first place, she should be two years younger, and four years fresher. She should be able not only to like him and love him but to worship him. How well I can see her! She should have fair hair, and bright green-gray eyes with the sweetest complexion, and the prettiest little dimples,—two inches shorter than he,—and the delight of her life should be to hang with two hands on his arm. She should have a feeling that her Silverbridge is an Apollo upon earth. To me he is a rather foolish, but very, very sweet-tempered young man; anything rather than a god.[14]

The Victorian wife, and Trollope's fictional stereotyping of her, finds the fulfillment of her destiny in abnegating certain aspects of her personality. The Dark Lady, on the other hand, replenishes her personality through establishing intellectual, creative, and even—there is a hint of this—sexual superiority over the male; and he wilts under such treatment. In *Is He Popenjoy?*, the Dark Lady representative is given a name that codifies the ultimate threat presented by her and by her real-life suffragette activists in England: she is named Baroness Banmann.

foreigner as Dark Lady

Foreign countries generate women whose self-possession and independence thrilled Trollope in the exotic fictional characters he created. Maria Daquilar, who is Spanish, has a "quiet sustained decision of character" which makes her impervious to brute passion. In Vienna, the girls go to beer halls. The Viennese Dark Lady is Lotta Schmidt, who agrees with the archetype in having jetblack hair, but also in the more significantly defining qualities of being independent, undomestic, of no lasting service.

But perhaps the peculiar characteristic in their faces which most strikes a stranger is a certain look of almost fierce independence, as though they had recognised the necessity, and also acquired the power, of standing alone, and of protecting themselves. I know no young woman by whom the assistance of a man's arm seems to be so seldom required as the young women of Vienna. . . . But overriding everything in her personal appearance, in her form, countenance, and gait, was that singular fierceness of independence, as though she were constantly asserting that she would never submit herself to the inconvenience of feminine softness.[15]

The exquisite self-possession of the American girls makes all of them what Trollope said it made of Winifred Hurtle—and his metaphor is a crucial one—"a witch of a woman." Like Lucinda Roanoke, of *The Eustace Diamonds*, these American girls are characterized by "queenly pride," "unyielding coldness," and "a stern spirit."[16] An Icelandic Bishop's daughter, Thora, is encompassed by one brief and telling observation: she can hold her own with young men and return answers to them "from her own quiver of wit"; the Australian girl, intelligent, self-dependent, is offensive, Trollope tells us, to "old-fashioned" people like himself. All these girls "fear nothing,—neither you nor themselves; and talk with as much freedom as if they were men."[17] There may be a pleasurable frisson in accepting the challenge offered by the Dark Lady; but it is an enterprise fraught with danger to a man's sense of self. His virility hangs in the balance.

the Jewess

The complete Dark Lady is the Jewess. Others besides Trollope have indulged in fantasies leading to the creation of the same hallucination. Hawthorne's Miriam, in her obscurity, timelessness, beauty and intelligence is a typical example. So is Scott's Rebecca. And Lawrence Durrell's Justine, who, "like all amoral people . . . verges on the goddess." The Jewish Dark Lady is a most tempting and dangerous creature for the Christian lover. Lotta Schmidt makes Trollope think of "the tribes of Israel," and we learn more about what that means when, in *The Bertrams*, he notes that Mohammedan women are "apelike" but Jewesses are "glorious specimens of feminine creation." Glorious or not, she stares back when stared at, boldly, defiantly, even scornfully, for there is about her "no feminine softness," no "young shame." She is an exotic, like those Hebrew writers of scripture whom George Bertram discusses in his biblical studies, orientals "with the customary grandiloquence of orientalism, with the poetic exaggeration which, in the East, was the breath of life"—and which in England, witness Disraeli, is the breath of destruction.[31] These and other features of the Dark Lady are seen in two extended portraits of Jewesses— Madame Max Goesler of *Phineas Finn* and Rebecca Loth of *Nina Balatka*.

Madame Max Goesler's origin is mysterious. She is tall, dresses well, and is surpassingly beautiful. Her thick black hair captivates Lady Glencora's child, who calls her "the beautiful lady with the black hair." Her eyes are those of the archetype:

large, of a dark blue colour, and very bright,—and she used them in a manner which is yet hardly common with English women. She seemed to intend that you should know that she employed them to conquer you, looking as a knight may have looked in olden days who entered a chamber with his sword drawn.[18]

But her beauty is fake, her wit superficial. The Jew is often in Trollope's novels a liar and impostor. Madame Max's conversational talents, fluency with languages, and general vivacity are also tinsel.

English country gentlemen are not to be classed among that section of mankind which speaks easily in public, but Jews, I think, may be so classed. The men who speak thus easily and with natural fluency, are also they who learn languages easily. They are men who observe rather than think, who remember rather than create, who may not have great mental powers, but are ever ready with what they have, whose best word is at their command in a moment, and is then serviceable though perhaps incapable of more enduring service.

If it be true, as Cockshut maintains it is, that "Trollope's moral consciousness was dominated by the ideas of sincerity and honesty,"[19] then Trollope's Jew, male or female, is the negation of his ideal; the female, because she brings sexual as well as intellectual prowess to the contest, is the more dangerous.

Trollope was so affected by the contrast between light and dark (character as well as hair) that he used what Lady Glencora said as a model for Lady Laura's opinion (in *Phineas Redux*). Trollope observes about Lady Laura's diatribe that Lady Laura, as a blonde, hated Madame Max because the latter was a brunette. All of which supports Leslie Fiedler's thesis that in the historical treatment of the Dark Lady, is apparent "the Northern European wish to glorify the fair and debase the black."[20]

When we turn to the Dark Lady in her own lair—the

foreign ghetto—we find further amplification of the contention that Trollope identified the Dark Lady with the Jewess. *Nina Balatka* is a love story of Prague, with the Jew Anton Tredelssohn as the man for whom Nina, a Christian, and Rebecca Loth, a Jewess, contend. Nina is an unusual European girl in Trollope's gallery, for she is very like the British Maiden. She feels that love is sacred and worships Anton even though she is worried about damnation for doing so. She has fair hair and gray eyes, is quiet and demure, and looks forward to accepting woman's properly subservient role in life. But the Jewesses of the Prague ghetto, in their outlandish finery and masculine independence, are a nest of Dark Ladies, "tall bright-eyed black-haired girls . . . with something of boldness in their gait and bearing, dressed many of them in white muslin, with bright ribbons and full petticoats." This ghetto is a breeding ground for juvenile temptresses. They become expert at manslaughter by practicing their wiles upon stray gentiles such as Ziska, Nina's Christian suitor.

Rebecca Loth is a female Disraeli in her colorful costume—ruby ribbons, colored boots, jacket with jewelled buttons, heavy gold earrings—and in her intelligence, her wealth, her heritage. No better summary of this paper can be provided than the following passage from the novel; here the Dark Lady is netted and dissected, exhibited in her physical features, temperament, and function as the Jewess:

Rebecca Loth was dark, with large dark-blue eyes and jet-black tresses, which spoke out loud to the beholder of their loveliness. You could not fail to think of her hair and of her eyes, as though they were things almost separate from herself. And she stood like a queen, who knew herself to be a queen, strong on her limbs, wanting no support, somewhat hard withal, with a repellent beauty that seemed to disdain while it courted admiration, and utterly rejected the idea of that caressing assistance which men always love to give and which women often love to receive.[21]

conclusion

Trollope's last novels introduce a note of ambiguity. He had before expressed a little dissatisfaction with the little brown girl—for example, once remarking that her dimples are but fortuitous aids to beauty, and at another time wondering if perambulator-pushing and changing diapers were all there is.

But the hypothesis that Trollope's sexist attitude changed—that he finally saw in the Dark Lady type something of moral worth—is not valid. Trollope approved of the little brown girl because she was not only plump, full-lipped, and fair-haired, but because she knew that her place in life was to be subservient to man, that she was charming insofar as she practiced the servility of dependence. He approved of her foil, the Dark Lady, as a fictional character who lent zest to the novel, but disapproved of this type when it marched down the Strand carrying banners urging the emancipation of women. Perhaps a quick reference to a couple of biographical points will be of some use: Trollope may have been working out a resentment against his own mother, who was a professionally successful woman, and an ambivalent feeling towards his sister-in-law, Theodosia, who was a poetess, musician, singer, linguist, revolutionary—and Jewess. The crucial comment on all this appears in the 1884 novel, *The Land-Leaguers*. Rachel O'Mahoney, an American, an actress, and the Dark Lady representative, is chastized because "she lacks feminine weakness, which of all her gifts is the most valuable to an English woman, till she makes the mistake of bartering it away for women's rights."[22]

NOTES

[1]*The Belton Estate* (Oxford University Press, 1951), pp. 256-57.

[2]*Australia and New Zealand* (Chapman and Hall, 1873, I, 478.

[3]Michael Goodwin, ed., *Nineteenth Century Opinion* (London, 1951), pp. 83-111 in passim.

[4]*The Duke's Children* (Dodd, Mead, n.d.), II, 17; *The Last Chronicle of Barsetshire* (Dodd, Mead, n.d.), I, 362.

5Trollope quoted in Michael Sadlier, *Trollope: A Commentary* (London, 1927), p. 311.

6*Nineteenth Century Opinion*, p. 108.

7E. Roylston Pike, *Pioneers of Social Change* (London, 1963), p. 181.

8*Tales of All Countries* (Chapman and Hall, 1861 and 1863), II, 49.

9*Castle Richmond* (John Lane, 1906), p. 140; *Cousin Henry* (World's Classics, 1929), p. 140; and *The Struggles of Brown, Jones, and Robinson* (Smith, Elder & Co., 1870), p. 48.

10Quoted in Bradford Booth, ed., *The Letters of Anthony Trollope* (Oxford, 1951), No. 45.

11Mario Praz, *The Romantic Agony* (London, 1951), p. 261.

12*Barchester Towers*, p. 121.

13*Kept in the Dark* (Chatto & Windus, 1882), II, 191.

14*The Duke's Children*, I, 209-10.

15*Lotta Schmidt*, p. 322.

16*The Land-Leaguers* (Chatto & Windus, 1884), p. 33; *Rachel Ray*, pp. 82-83; *Hunting Sketches* (Mitchell, 1929), pp. 45-46; and *The Way We Live Now* (Knopf, n.d.), pp. 431, 748.

17*Tales of All Countries*, I, 94; also I, 80; "Iceland," *The Fortnightly Review*, XXIV, N. S. No. 139, p. 179; *Travelling Sketches* (Chapman & Hall, 1866), p. 50; and *Australia and New Zealand*, I, 478.

18*Phineas Finn*, II, 224, 25, 199.

19*Rachel Ray*, 329; A. O. J. Cockshut, *Anthony Trollope: A Critical Study* (1955), p. 189.

20Leslie Fiedler, *Love and Death in the American Novel* (1960), pp. 266-67.

21*Nina Balatka* (World's Classics, 1946), pp. 80, 82-83.

22*The Land-Leaguers*, p. 104.

MADONNA MARSDEN

GENTLE TRUTHS FOR GENTLE READERS:
THE FICTION OF ELIZABETH GOUDGE

Elizabeth Goudge is a kind of phenomenon among contemporary British writers. She began writing in 1934 and presently has about forty-six titles to her credit, many of which have appeared on best-seller lists. Almost every book has had dual publication in both Great Britain and America, and many have appeared in foreign translations. She has been published in regular editions, gift editions, book club editions, and paperbacks. One of her novels was made into a film. Her short stories have appeared in periodicals ranging from *Senior Scholastic* to *Ladies Home Journal.* Selections from her works have been anthologized into "The Best of . . ." kinds of volumes. What is intriguing, however, is that reviewers accord Ms. Goudge less than enthusiastic praise and academicians have totally ignored her, despite her impact on the reading habits of a substantial number of women all over the world.

Obviously any conclusions drawn about the appeal of Elizabeth Goudge would have to include a statement that what she writes must be what a large segment of the public, unconcerned with aesthetic value, wants to hear. Her own estimate of her work is that it is escapist, not true to life, and therefore perhaps inartistic.

I know that happy endings are sometimes inartistic, and certainly, not always true to life, but I can't write any other kind. I am not a serious chronicler of the very terrible contemporary scene, but just a story-teller, and there is so much tragedy about us everywhere today that we surely don't want it in the story books to which we turn when we are ill or unhappy, or can't go to sleep at night. We must escape somewhere.[1]

Ms. Goudge has further assessed her own appeal as largely palliative and visceral.

> I prefer writing about children, dogs, and ordinary men and women in surroundings of natural beauty. My work appeals mostly to the old and the young and those who are ill. The sick tell me my books help them to forget their aches and pains.[2]

A substantial portion of the fiction of Elizabeth Goudge *is* devoted to the escapist and the medicinal. As noted, Ms. Goudge finds herself incapable of writing a novel with an unhappy ending. Because she integrates into this plot structure elements such as distant and remote settings and romanticized historical characters, it is perhaps too easy to dismiss her as simply a huckster of nostalgia, and ignore the paradoxical fact that war, changing ideologies, and breakdowns in myth structures provide the dramatic spine of her work. Almost all of Ms. Goudge's fiction is based on a dialectic between a self-constructed imaginative form which demands a happy ending and a content drawn from a world which does not provide that kind of well-ordered material. And it seems to be her talent for creating character images who illustrate the sacrifice of truth which must be made in exchange for order which captures her audience even more than the romance and the comfort which her novels bring. Particularly the women in Ms. Goudge's novels, then, find themselves pulled between the paradigm which models their happiness around their biology, and their own experiences which indicate that the paradigm may be false. The central problem of the fiction, then, is to reconcile the truth of the individual experience to the truth of the behavioral model —in short, to gently expand the old paradigm to absorb threats to the old truths rather than to invent a new paradigm to handle a new truth.

The cosmos posited by Elizabeth Goudge is one in which there is a definite and hierarchical as well as interconnected order of things. She sees the universe as governed by a plan, and nothing happens which is not a part of that plan. Each person, plant and rock has a definite role to fulfill, and even apparent evil works towards the creation of good. Perhaps the most succinct description of Ms. Goudge's vision of the order of the universe is the following passage from *The Castle on the Hill*. Mr. Birley, an elderly and wise historian, tells the confused and weary heroine of the novel:

> Personal experience and the study of history have taught me to believe in a pattern. . . . And in spite of all that has befallen the world I still believe that the threads of it, ourselves, are held securely in the scheme of things by some great unconquerable spiritual power. Call it what you will—destiny, fate, the first cause, the life stream, God—it does not lose hold of a single thread. In wanton wickedness we may tangle the pattern into what looks like hopeless confusion, but in unwearied patience the power unravels the tangle, reforms the pattern, keeps it moving along to some great goal of order whose nature we cannot even guess at yet. If the threads are not lost, there can be no lasting chaos.[3]

The directing force of this universe, then, allows humanity freedom of will, but it can also direct that freedom to meet its own ends, which always prove to be positive. Confusion is only apparent, rarely real. Chaos, meaninglessness and alienation can occur only when the individual fights the natural order of the paradigm. Ms. Goudge's vision, then is in direct opposition to that of those who would posit that order is the illusion and chaos the reality. In fact, it comes close to the eighteenth-century model of the rationally ordered Great Chain of Being.

But Ms. Goudge expands the rational to also include a tinge of the mystical. The pattern metaphor indicates that the thread which breaks away from the tapestry not only mars the beauty of the tapestry, but also loses its individual meaning. The thread alone simply has no function. In the chain metaphor the link which breaks the chain has simply created two chains. For Ms. Goudge, this metaphor and the happy ending are not possible. Two incomplete paradigms pose, rather than resolve, threats to the established myths.

Within the broad paradigm, there are implications which present a model for the role of woman. This orderly, mystical, purposeful view sees woman's particular biology as the particular governor of her destiny. Therefore, her role is to marry and to produce children. This is what gives a woman her meaning. There is a range of choice for the female character, however, and it is this range which either creates a dialectic and therefore provides the basis for a kind of imaginative literature in which the female can be a central character, or which relegates the female to secondary importance because a larger issue of the paradigm is at stake.

Generally, Ms. Goudge sees the woman in Western culture as faced with five possible choices within this pattern: 1) she can accept the demands of femininity, marry, and live happily ever after; 2) marry, question the demands of femininity and become a rebel who is eventually absorbed back into the value system; 3) reject or be rejected by the demands of femininity, not marry, and be reasonably happy if she finds family surrogates; 4) reject the demands of femininity, not marry, and find happiness through a creative career; 5) reject the system entirely and be damned by her choice. For the purposes of this article, the second kind of heroine provides the most interesting focus for demonstrating the neutralizing and absorbent function of Ms. Goudge's fiction, yet all of these types provide an interesting insight into the very limited role which a woman can play in the literary imagination.

The simple heroine is of little fictional use, since though she may recognize that the female's lot in life is not as interesting or as exciting as the male's, she accepts without question the notion that because her biology governs her destiny, marriage constitutes the whole of her existence, while it is only part of a much broader concept of life for a man. In *Gentian Hill*, for example, Stella, the heroine, knows

. . . by instinct that men do not want women with them all the time; they keep certain compartments in their lives for them, and do not want them overflowing into the wrong ones.[4]

As a result of their attitudes, Stella and the heroines like her are not the center of interest in the novels or short stories in which they appear. The cultural conventions of femininity which they embody offer no paradigmatic conflict upon which the artistic imagination can act. Their basic structure offers no antithesis to the accepted thesis. Their function is subordinated to some larger issue.

The heroine who marries and then finds that wifehood and motherhood do not bring the kind of satisfaction which the paradigm has promised, provides a much more interesting fictional subject, since this type can offer material for a sensitively drawn portrait of the sacrifices which the order and rigidity of the paradigm demand. The truth of her experience vs. the truth of the paradigm offers a dramatic spine which can give this type of character a place of central rather than subordinate purpose in the novel.

Although Ms. Goudge has used this type of heroine in many of her novels, her most interesting creation is Nadine Eliot, a character who appears in the trilogy of the Eliot family, *The Bird in the Tree* (1940), *Pilgrim's Inn* (1948) and *The Heart of the Family* (1953). But this type of heroine is too prevalent in women's fiction to ascribe the creation of her image to the psychic structure of a single author. She has appeared in literature almost from its beginning under such various guises as the "castrating woman," the "unfaithful wife," or just simply "the bitch." Basically, what this type has always represented is a kind of hermaphroditic and therefore taboo blend of male spirit with female body. Intellectually and spiritually, the hermaphrodite heroine has a penis, though physically she is a woman, and should therefore be a receptor rather than an actor. Her tragedy is that she *does* act, and that that action makes her ugly somehow.

The Bird in the Tree was not originally conceived as

the opening novel of a trilogy. The story, however, met with such success that readers demanded to hear more about Nadine; an indication that perhaps this type of heroine is the perfect image of the weaknesses of the myth structure in which she operates, and therefore a creation who has an archetypal appeal despite the critical pronouncements. There is something archetypal about Nadine's quest for a self, a quest which unlike that of the male adventure hero, is somehow turned in on itself.

The Bird in the Tree opens as Nadine's three children are in the care of their grandmother, while their father is stationed in India on assignment for the Foreign Office. Nadine has taken advantage of the freedom which her husband's absence offers her and has moved from the Eliot country estate to London, where she has opened a small antique shop. This taste of freedom has convinced her that she no longer needs George.

Nadine is an embarrassment to her mother-in-law, Lucilla, because she has blotted the family honor through her willing estrangement from George, her open indifference to her children, and her desire to be economically independent. This embarrassment is intensified when Lucilla discovers that Nadine is in love with George's young nephew, David. In an attempt to break up what she considers a highly immoral and almost incestuous affair, Lucilla admits to Nadine that as a young wife she had experienced a similar rebellion against the constraints of her role. In an effort to assert some kind of active control over her life, Lucilla had an affair with a man who seemed to offer her more freedom and excitement than her husband. As they were about to run off together, however, the man realized that his duty to his vocation took precedence over his love for her. Lucilla was angered and shamed, but the experience aided her to perceive her role on a new level of awareness.

A doctor's work is splendidly creative, I thought; building strong bodies and healthy minds; it is more creative even than the work of painter and sculptor, for he deals in flesh and blood and thought, materials that are living. It seemed to me appalling, as I thought it over, that all this should be sacrificed to his passion for a pretty woman. It was every bit as bad as that my work for my husband and children should be sacrificed to my passion for a charming man. The love of a man and woman, I saw, should never be allowed to be an end in itself; it should be the helpmate of their work.[5]

And a bit later, she tells Nadine how she came to be able to put this new awareness to work in her life:

Love at its highest, I thought, like truth at its highest, is a creative thing. Perhaps it is action, not feeling. I was playing the part of a good wife and mother quite successfully in the outward ways, but that, I saw now, was not enough. That was not love. Creative love meant building up by quantities of small actions a habit of service that might become at last a habit of mind and feeling as well as of body. I tried, and I found it did work like that. Feeling can be compelled by action not quite as easily as action by feeling, but far more lastingly.[6]

Lucilla's advice is ludicrous on one plane and yet quite valid on another. In many ways, it resembles a formula for breakthrough to mystical awareness. Buddhists repeat common words until they become meaningless and a new level of consciousness opens up to them. Magicians use the incantation of words to evoke the real substances which they represent. Lucilla has advised Nadine to repeat common acts to achieve the same end.

The novel *Pilgrim's Inn* opens some six years or so after this. George and Nadine have been reconciled, and Nadine has apparently taken Lucilla's advice to heart, for she is now the mother of five-year-old twins. But her actions do not seem to have improved her feelings. The twins are aggressive, exuberant children who compel little but exhaustion from their mother. Realizing that Nadine is still unhappy, Lucilla contrives that George and his family should move to the country where she can keep a watchful eye over the situation. Against Nadine's wishes, they move to an old estate which had once been an inn for pilgrims who were journeying to the nearby monastery. Nadine becomes immersed in refurbishing the inn, finds a nurse to care for the twins, and is leading a fairly happy life until David returns to the country for a visit. Once again Nadine becomes discontented with her life and the flame of her old love for David is rekindled.

An artist who is painting Nadine's portrait notes that something impairs her real beauty from emerging. Some struggle within has, he notes, hardened her mouth and tightened her eyes.

You know or should know, what needs cutting out of your own life. Some quite trivial thing, probably, perhaps no more than some reservation of thought. But it's enough . . . to keep you stewing in your own juice, pulled both ways and getting nowhere. Cut it out, that thought or whatever, and you're free, and probably others, too. We're so bound together in this complicated world that the spiritual condition of each one of us is as catching as the measles.[7]

Nadine has still not reconciled herself spiritually to being a woman. She still is the divided, taboo, and therefore ugly hermaphrodite.

Nadine lets go of David, repeats the outward acts which her femininity demands, and finds that acting like a woman does indeed make her content to be one. She is at peace when she realizes

What a ridiculous fuss she was making about doing what everyone was always doing every day, every hour, every moment of their lives almost: gathering in the divided allegiance, denying it to the one thing, giving it to the other; the choice never really in doubt when to the inner beseeching of the spirit the motive is revealed. It was a process that could not end while the eventual salvation of one's soul was still a possibility, the pain of the effort merely a question of degree, but not differing moment by moment in essence. One lived, and it was so. Accept it and have done.[8]

The situation reaches a happy ending, but the dialectic has really reached no synthesis. The antithesis is simply shown to be false because it has created chaos. The original thesis is preferable apparently because it makes life more orderly. In *The Heart of the Family*, of course, Nadine is no longer a prominent character. She can't be because she no longer offers any imaginative possibilities.

She is now a well-integrated, happy woman.

The fiction of Elizabeth Goudge finds another way to give a female character a prominent position in a novel or short story through the use of another familiar type, the spinster heroine. Once again, this type offers the promise of sustained artistic possibilities because she offers a dialectic between what the paradigm posits as her meaning and her refusal or her inability to embrace it.

Both Dolores Brown of *The Castle on the Hill* and Ada Gillespie, the central character in the story "A Shepherd and A Shepherdess," have found meaning in their lives by finding surrogate ways of fulfilling what the paradigm posits as their functions. Dolores devotes her life to the care of aged parents, and when they die, opens the home she has inherited from them to lonely boarders. Ada, the only girl in a large family, mothers her brothers and then their children. Both of these characters, however, find that when their functions are gone, so are their identities. Dolores is forced to evacuate her English coastal home because it is threatened by wartime invasion. Ada's nieces and nephews grow up and can take care of themselves. And both are lost until they find new substitute families in which their female biology automatically ascribes to them the nurturing function of mothers.

All of the Elizabeth Goudge heroines who find happiness without marriage are historical figures whose talents clearly indicate that they are exceptions to the rule. "Escape for Jane" is based on a true incident in the life of Jane Austen. It focuses on her rejection of marriage and the subsequent nurturance of children in favor of the nurturance of the "dreams" inside her instead. It is interesting to note that her historical reality is what allows her to do this. Her rejection of the conventional feminine road to happiness does not threaten the paradigm, because the reader retrospectively knows that her career was a part of the pattern after all. The decisions of such a heroine do not come into conflict with the truth of the paradigm because they are always retrospective and therefore no threat.

The most tragic of Ms. Goudge's heroines is Mother Skipton, the black witch in the novel *The White Witch*, because she has chosen to reject the paradigm and has no historical truth to mediate her decision. Her unhappiness and her failure as a woman are the results of her urge to gain power over the lives of others. As she herself admits, however, what she thought to be the truth of her own experience was not truth at all. Her failure to preceive this until it is too late is Ms. Goudge's negative variation on the presentation of that larger positive truth.

If souls in Hell were incapable of longing they would not be in Hell. That *is* Hell—longing for what you've thrown away and can never get back. I was a woman who wanted power. Through what stages I passed from white to black witchcraft I need not tell you but they were governed by the passion to possess power over the bodies and souls of men. At last, I liked to kill. But power is a devil who turns round on you at last. You possess it, then it turns and possesses you. Then power becomes powerlessness. I am far too tired now to change my way of life.[9]

What the fiction of Elizabeth Goudge does, then, is to establish that although many women are unhappy in the roles which Western culture demands of them, the fault lies not with the paradigm, but with the individual. The threat which is posed to the social fabric by the fact of woman's discontent with the roles of wifehood and motherhood is absorbed by demonstrating that discontent carries with it the seeds of chaos and destruction. Traditional cultural paradigms, when used as a framework for this type of fiction, serve to reaffirm and reassure us of the truth of our public vision of life as objectively meaningful. Private, threatening visions which contradict this notion are neutralized by their absorption into what is publicly and conventionally considered the larger scheme of things. The fiction of Ms. Goudge absorbs and neutralizes threats to conventional femininity by neutralizing the validity of her heroines' primal, but conventionally masculine urges for quest. Activity, aggression, intellectual curiosity, lead, in almost all cases, to an intensification of unhappiness. Passive persistence in an assigned role, on the other hand, leads to the ability to accept and transcend its limitations.

Finally, then, the appeal of the novels of Elizabeth Goudge seems to rest in their ability to affirm the rightness of humanity's artificial constructs. To have them creates the necessity for sublimation, an exchange of what Freud has called "a threatened external happiness . . . for a permanent internal unhappiness, for the tension of the sense of guilt."[10] But Ms. Goudge can create a dialectic which eliminates even the guilt as a threat. Basically, her novels save us from the embarrassment of having to admit that honest anarchy may be more personally fulfilling than the organized lie. But the organized lie has always managed to find room, through popular culture, for the threats which would expose it. Bloody cultural revolutions are prevented through the bloodless ones which are gradually fought in our mass media every day.

NOTES

[1] This quotation can be found on the book jackets of various novels. I first saw it on the jacket of the American edition of *The Heart of the Family.*

[2] James Leasor, *Author By Profession* (London: Cleaver-Hume, 1952), p. 147.

[3] Elizabeth Goudge, *The Castle on the Hill* (New York: Coward-McCann, 1941), p. 128.

[4] Elizabeth Goudge, *Gentian Hill* (New York: Coward-McCann, 1949), pp. 60-61.

[5] Elizabeth Goudge, *The Bird in the Tree* (New York: Coward-McCann, 1940), p. 246.

[6] *The Bird in the Tree*, pp. 247-248.

[7] Elizabeth Goudge, *Pilgrim's Inn* (New York: Coward-McCann, 1948), pp. 153-154.

[8] *Pilgrim's Inn*, p. 146.

[9] Elizabeth Goudge, *The White Witch* (New York: Coward-McCann, 1958), p. 309.

[10] Sigmund Freud, *Civilization And Its Discontents*, translated and edited by James Strachey (New York: W. W. Norton, 1962), p. 75.

JOANNA RUSS

THE IMAGE OF WOMEN IN SCIENCE FICTION*

Science fiction is *What If* literature. All sorts of definitions have been proposed by people in the field, but they
all contain both The What If and The Serious Explanation;
that is, science fiction shows things not as they characteristically or habitually are but as they might be, and for this
"might be" the author must offer a rational, serious, consistent explanation, one that does not (in Samuel Delany's
phrase) offend against what is known to be known.[1] Science fiction writers can't be experts in all disciplines, but
they ought at least to be up to the level of the *New York
Times* Sunday science page. If the author offers marvels
and does not explain them, or if he explains them playfully
and not seriously, or if the explanation offends against
what the author knows to be true, you are dealing with
fantasy and not science fiction. True, the fields tend to
blur into each other and the borderland is a pleasant and
gleeful place, but generally you can tell where you are. Examples:

J. R. R. Tolkien writes fantasy. He offends against all
sorts of archaeological, geological, paleontological, and linguistic evidence which he probably knows as well as anyone
else does.

Edgar Rice Burroughs wrote science fiction. He explained his marvels seriously and he explained them as well
as he could. At the time he wrote, his stories did in fact
conflict with what was known to be known, but he didn't
know that. He wrote *bad* science fiction.

Ray Bradbury writes both science fiction and fantasy,
often in the same story. He doesn't seem to care.

79

Science fiction comprises a grand variety of common properties: the fourth dimension, hyperspace (whatever that is), the colonization of other worlds, nuclear catastrophe, time travel (now out of fashion), interstellar exploration, mutated supermen, alien races, and so on. The sciences treated range from the "hard" or exact sciences (astronomy, physics) through the life sciences (biology, biochemistry, neurology) through the "soft" or inexact sciences (ethology, ecology, psychology) to disciplines that are still in the descriptive or philosophical stage and may never become exact (history, for example).[2] I would go beyond these last to include what some writers call "para-sciences"—extra-sensory perception, psionics, or even magic—as long as the "discipline" in question is treated as it would have to be if it were real, that is rigorously, logically, and in detail.[3]

Fantasy, says Samuel Delany, treats what cannot happen, science fiction what has not happened.[4] One would think science fiction the perfect literary mode in which to explore (and explode) our assumptions about "innate" values and "natural" social arrangements, in short our ideas about Human Nature, Which Never Changes. Some of this has been done. But speculation about the innate personality differences between men and women, about family structure, about sex, in short about gender roles, does not exist at all.

And Why Not?

What is the image of women in science fiction?

We can begin by dismissing fiction set in the very near future (such as *On the Beach*) but most science fiction is not like this; most science fiction is set far in the future, some of it *very* far in the future, hundreds of thousands of years sometimes. One would think that by then human society, family life, personal relations, child-bearing, in fact anything one can name, would have altered beyond recognition. This is not the case. The more intelligent, literate fiction carries today's values and standards into its future

Galactic Empires. What may politely be called the less sophisticated fiction returns to the past—not even a real past, in most cases, but an idealized and exaggerated past.[5]

Intergalactic Suburbia

In general, the authors who write reasonably sophisticated and literate science fiction (Clarke, Asimov, for choice) see the relations between the sexes as those of present-day, white, middle-class suburbia. Mummy and Daddy may live inside a huge amoeba and Daddy's job may be to test psychedelic drugs or cultivate yeast-vats, but the world inside their heads is the world of Westport and Rahway *and that world is never questioned.* Not that the authors are obvious about it; Fred Pohl's recent satire, *The Age of the Pussyfoot,* is a good case in point.[6] In this witty and imaginative future world, death is reversible, production is completely automated, the world population is enormous, robots do most of the repetitive work, the pharmacopoeia of psychoactive drugs is very, very large, and society has become so complicated that people must carry personal computers to make their everyday decisions for them. I haven't even mentioned the change in people's clothing, in their jobs, their slang, their hobbies, and so on. But if you look more closely at this weird world you find that it practices a laissez-faire capitalism, one even freer than our own; that men make more money than women; that men have the better jobs (the book's heroine is the equivalent of a consumer-research guinea pig); and that children are raised at home by their mothers.

In short, the American middle class with a little window dressing.

In science fiction, speculation about social institutions and individual psychology has always lagged far behind speculation about technology, possibly because technology is easier to understand than people. But this is not the whole story.[7] I have been talking about intelligent, literate science fiction. Concerning this sort of work one might simply speak of a failure of imagination outside the exact sciences, but there are other kinds of science fiction, and when you look at them, something turns up that makes you wonder if failure of imagination is what is at fault.

I ought to make it clear here that American science fiction and British science fiction have evolved very differently and that what I am going to talk about is—in origin—an American phenomenon. In Britain science fiction not only was always respectable, it still is; there is a continuity in the field that the American tradition does not have. British fiction is not, on the whole, better written than American science fiction, but it continues to attract first-rate writers from outside the field (Kipling, Shaw, C. S. Lewis, Orwell, Golding) and it continutes to be reviewed seriously and well.[8] American science fiction developed out of the pulps and stayed outside the tradition of serious literature for at least three decades; it is still not really respectable.[9] American science fiction originated the adventure-story-*cum*-fairy-tale which most people think of (erroneously) as science fiction. It has been called a great many things, most of them uncomplimentary, but the usual name is Space Opera. There are good writers working in this field who do not deserve the public notoriety bred by this kind of science fiction. But their values usually belong to the same imaginative world and they participate in many of the same assumptions.[10] I will not, therefore, name names, but will pick on something inoffensive—think of Flash Gordon and read on.

Down Among The He-Men

If most literate science fiction takes for its gender-role models the ones which actually exist (or are assumed as ideals) in middle-class America, space opera returns to the past for *its* models, and not even the real past, but an idealized and simplified one. These stories are not realistic. They are primitive, sometimes bizarre, and often magnificently bald in their fantasy. Some common themes:

A feudal economic and social structure—usually paired with advanced technology and inadequate to the complexities of a Seventh Century European mud hut.

Women are important as prizes or motives—i.e. we must rescue the heroine or win the hand of the beautiful Princess. Many fairy-tale motifs turn up here.

Active or ambitious women are evil—this literature is chockfull of cruel dowager empresses, sadistic matriarchs, evil ladies maddened by jealousy, domineering villainesses and so on.

Women are supernaturally beautiful—all of them.

Women are weak and/or kept offstage—this genre is full of scientists' beautiful daughters who know just enough to be brought along by Daddy as his research assistant, but not enough to be of any help to anyone.

Women's powers are passive and involuntary—an odd idea that turns up again and again, not only in space opera. If female characters are given abilities, these are often innate abilities which cannot be developed or controlled, *e.g.* clairvoyance, telepathy, hysterical strength, unconscious psi power, eidetic memory, perfect pitch, lightning calculation, or (more baldly) magic. The power is somehow *in* the woman, but she does not really possess it. Often realistic science fiction employs the same device.[11]

The real focus of interest is not on women at all—but on the cosmic rivalries between strong, rugged, virile, he-men. It is no accident that space opera and horse opera bear similar names.[12] Most of the readers of science fiction are male and most of them are young; people seem to quit reading the stuff in their middle twenties.[13] The hard-core readers who form fan clubs and go to conventions are even younger and even more likely to be male. Such readers as I have met (the addicts?) are overwhelmingly likely to be nervous, shy, pleasant boys, sensitive, intelligent, and very awkward with people. They also talk too much. It does not take a clairvoyant to see why such people would be attracted to space opera, with its absence of real women and its tremendous over-rating of the "real he-man." In the

March 1969 issue of *Amazing* one James Koval wrote to the editor as follows:

Your October issue was superb; better than that, it was uniquely original. . . . Why do I think it so worthy of such compliments? Because of the short-stories *Conqueror* and *Mu Panther*, mainly. They were, in every visual and emotional sense, stories about real men whose rugged actions and keen thinking bring back a genuine feeling of masculinity, a thing sorely missed by the long-haired and soft-eyed generation of my time, of which I am a part . . . aiming entertainment at the virile and imaginative male of today is the best kind of business. . . . I sincerely hope you keep your man-versus-animal type format going, especially with stories like *Mu Panther*. That was exceptionally unique.[14]

The editor's response was "GROAN!"

But even if readers are adolescents, the writers are not. I know quite a few grown-up men who should know better, but who nonetheless fall into what I would like to call the he-man ethic. And they do it over and over again. In November, 1968, a speaker at the Philadelphia Science Fiction Convention[15] described the heroes such writers create.

The only real He-Man is Master of the Universe. . . . The real He-Man is invulnerable. He has no weaknesses. Sexually he is super-potent. He does exactly what he pleases, everywhere and at all times. He is absolutely self-sufficient. He depends on nobody, for this would be a weakness. Toward women he is possessive, protective, and patronizing; to men he gives orders. He is never frightened by anything or for any reason; he is never indecisive and he always wins.

In short, masculinity equals power and femininity equals powerlessness. This is a cultural stereotype that can be found in much popular literature, but science fiction writers have no business employing stereotypes, let alone swallowing them goggle-eyed.

Equal Is As Equal Does

In the last decade or so, science fiction has begun to attempt the serious presentation of men and women as equals, usually by showing them at work together. Even a popular television show like *Star Trek* shows a spaceship with a mixed crew;[16] fifteen years ago this was unthinkable. *Forbidden Planet*, a witty and charming film made in the 1950's takes it for granted that the crew of a spaceship will all be red-blooded, crewcut, woman-hungry men, rather like the cast of *South Pacific* before the nurses arrive. And within the memory of living adolescent, John W. Campbell, Jr., the editor of *Analog,* proposed that "nice girls" be sent on spaceships as prostitutes because married women would only clutter everything up with washing and babies. But Campbell is a coelacanth.

At any rate, many recent stories do show a two-sexed world in which women, as well as men, work competently and well. But this is a reflection of present reality, not genuine speculation. And what is most striking about these stories is what they leave out: the characters' personal and erotic relations are not described; child-rearing arrange-ments (to my knowledge) are never described; and the women who appear in these stories are either young and childless or middle-aged, with their children safely grown up. That is, the real problems of a society without gender-role differentiation are not faced. It is my impression that most of these stories are colorless and schematic; the authors want to be progressive, God bless them, but they don't know how. Exceptions:

Mack Reynolds, who also presents a version of future socialism called "the Ultra-Welfare State" (is there a con-nection?). He has written novels about two-sexed societies of which one is a kind of mild gynocracy. He does not describe child-rearing arrangements, though.

Samuel Delany, who often depicts group marriages and communal child-bearing, "triplet" marriages (not polygamy or polyandry, for each person is understood to have sexual relations with the other two) *und so weiter,* all with no differentiation of gender-roles, all with an af-fectionate, East Village, Berkeley-Bohemian air to them, and all with the advanced technology that would make such things work. His people have the rare virtue of fitting the institutions under which they live. Robert Heinlein, who also goes in for odd arrangements (*e.g.* the "line mar-

riage" in *The Moon Is a Harsh Mistress* in which everybody
is married to everybody, but there are seniority rights in
sex) peoples his different societies with individualistic, possessive, competitive, pre-World War-II Americans—just the
people who could not live under the cooperative or communal arrangements he describes. Heinlein, for all his
virtues, seems to me to exemplify science fiction's failure
of imagination in the human sphere. He is superb at work
but out of his element elsewhere. *Stranger in a Strange
Land* seems to me a particular failure. I have heard
Heinlein's women called "Boy Scouts with breasts"—but
the subject takes more discussion than I can give it here.
Alexei Panshin's critical study *Heinlein in Dimension*
undertakes a thorough investigation of Heinlein *vs.* Sex.
Heinlein loses.[17]

Matriarchy

The strangest and most fascinating oddities in science
fiction occur not in the stories that try to abolish differences in gender-roles but in those which attempt to reverse
the roles themselves. Unfortunately, only a handful of
writers have treated this theme seriously. Space opera
abounds, but in space opera the reversal is always cut to the
same pattern.

Into a world of cold, cruel, domineering women who
are openly contemptuous of their cringing, servile men
("gutless" is a favorite word here) arrive (s) men (a man)
from our present world. With a minimum of trouble, these
normal men succeed in overthrowing the matriarchy, which
although strong and warlike, is also completely inefficient.
At this point the now dominant men experience a joyful
return of victorious manhood and the women (after initial
reluctance) declare that they too are much happier. Everything is (to quote S. J. Perelman) leeches and cream.[18]
Two interesting themes occur:

(1) the women are far more vicious, sadistic, *and
openly contemptuous* of the men than comparable domi-

nant men are of comparable subordinate women in the usual space opera.

(2) the women are dominant because they are taller and stronger than the men (!).

Sometimes the story is played out among the members of an alien species modeled on insects or microscopic sea-creatures, so that tiny males are eaten or engulfed by huge females. I remember one in which a tiny male was eaten by a female who was not only forty feet tall but maddened to boot.[19] There are times when science fiction leaves the domain of literature altogether. Least said, soonest mended.

I remember three British accounts of future matriarchies that could be called serious studies. In one the matriarchy is incidental. The society is presented as good because it embodies the traditionally feminine virtues: serenity, tolerance, love, and pacifism.[20] In John Wyndham's "Consider Her Ways" there are no men at all; the society is a static, hierarchical one which (like the first) is good because of its traditionally feminine virtues, which are taken as innate in the female character. There is something about matriarchy that makes science fiction writers think of two things: biological engineering and social insects; whether women are considered naturally chitinous or the softness of the female body is equated with the softness of the "soft" sciences I don't know, but the point is often made that "women are conservative by nature" and from there it seems an easy jump to bees or ants. Science fiction stories often make the point that a matriarchy will be static and hierarchical, like Byzantium or Egypt. (It should be remembered here that the absolute value of progress is one of the commonest shibboleths of science fiction.) The third story I remember—technically it's a "post-Bomb" story—was written by an author whose version of matriarchy sounds like Robert Graves's.[21] The story makes the explicit point that while what is needed is static endurance, the Mother rules; when exploration and initiative again become necessary, the Father will return.

The Great Mother is a real, supernatural character in this tale and the people in it are very real people. The matriarchy—again, the women rule by supernatural knowledge—is vividly realized and there is genuine exploration of what personal relations would be like in such a society. There is a kind of uncompromising horror (the hero is hunted by "the hounds of the Mother"—women whose minds have been taken over by the Magna Mater) which expresses a man's fear of such a world much more effectively than all the maddened, forty-foot-tall male-gulpers ever invented.

So far I've been discussing fiction written by men and largely for men.[22] What about fiction written by women?

Women's Fiction: Potpourri

Most science fiction writers are men, but some are women, and there are more women writing the stuff than there used to be. The women writer's work falls into four rough categories.

(1) *Ladies' magazine fiction*—in which the sweet, gentle, intuitive little heroine solves an interstellar crisis by mending her slip or doing something equally domestic after her big, heroic husband has failed. Zenna Henderson sometimes writes like this. *Fantasy and Science Fiction*, which carries more of this kind of writing than any of the other magazines, once earned a deserved slap over the knuckles from reviewer James Blish.[23]

(2) *Galactic suburbia*—very often written by women. Sometimes the characters are all male, especially if the story is set at work. Most women writing in the field (like so many of the men) write this kind of fiction.

(3) *Space opera*—strange but true. Leigh Brackett is one example. Very rarely the protagonist turns out to be a sword-wielding, muscular, aggressive *woman*—but the he-man ethos of the world does not change, nor do the stereotyped personalities assigned to the secondary characters, particularly the female ones.

(4) *Avant-garde fiction*—part of the recent rapproche-

ment between the most experimental of the science fiction community and the most avant-garde of what is called "the mainstream." This takes us out of the field of science fiction altogether.[24]

In general, stories by women tend to contain more active and lively female characters than do stories by men, and more often than men writers, women writers try to invent worlds in which men and women will be equals. But the usual faults show up just as often. The conventional idea that women are second-class people is a hard idea to shake; and while it is easy enough to show women doing men's work, or active in society, it is in the family scenes and the love scenes that one must look for the author's real freedom from our most destructive prejudices.

An Odd Equality

I would like to close with a few words about *The Left Hand of Darkness*, a fine book that won the Science Fiction Writers of America Nebula Award for 1969 as the best novel of that year.[25] The book was written by a woman and it is about sex—I don't mean copulation; I mean what sexuality identity means to people and what human identity means to them, and what kind of love can cross the barriers of culture and custom. It is a beautifully written book. Ursula K. LeGuin, the author, has imagined a world of human hermaphrodites—an experimental colony abandoned by its creators long ago and rediscovered by other human beings. The adults of this glacial world of Winter go through an oestrus cycle modeled on the human menstrual cycle: every four weeks the individual experiences a few days of sexual potency and obsessive interest in sex during which "he" becomes either male or female. The rest of the time "he" has no sex at all, or rather, only the potential of either. The cycle is involuntary, though it can be affected by drugs, and there is no choice of sex—except that the presence of someone already into the cycle and therefore of one sex will stimulate others in oestrus to become of the opposite sex. You would imagine that such a people's culture and institutions would be very different from ours and so they are; everything is finely realized, from their household implements to their customs to their creation myths. Again, however, (and I'm very sorry to see it), family structure is not fully explained. Worse than that, childrearing is left completely in the dark, although the human author herself is married and the mother of three children. Moreover, there is a human observer on Winter and he is male; and there is a native hero and *he* is male—at least "he" is *masculine in gender, if not in sex.* The native hero has a former spouse who is long-suffering, mild, and gentle, while he himself is fiery, tough, self-sufficient, and proud. There is the Byronesque memory of a past incestuous affair; his lover and sibling is dead. There is an attempted seduction by a kind of Mata Hari *who is female* (so that the hero, of course, becomes male). It is, I must admit, a deficiency in the English language that these people must be called "he" throughout, but put that together with the native hero's personal encounters in the book, the absolute lack of interest in child-raising, the concentration on work, and what you have is a world of men. Thus the great love scene in the book is between two men: the human observer (who is a real man) and the native hero (who is a female man). The scene is nominally homosexual, but I think what lies at the bottom of it (and what has moved men and women readers alike) is that it is a love scene between a man and a woman, with the label "male: high status" pasted on the woman's forehead. Perhaps, with the straitjackets of our gender-roles, with women automatically regarded as second-class, intelligent and active women *feel* as if they were female men or hermaphrodites. Or perhaps the only way a woman (even in a love scene) can be made a man's equal—and the love scene therefore deeply moving—is to make her *nominally* male in gender. Here is the human narrator describing the alien hero:

to ignore the abstraction, to hold fast to the thing. There was in this attitude something feminine, a refusal of the abstract ideal, a submissiveness to the given. . . .[26]

Very conventional, although the story is set far, far in the future and the narrator is supposed to be a trained observer, a kind of anthropologist. Here is the narrator again, describing human women: [he has been asked if they are "like a different species"]:

No. Yes. No, of course not, not really. But the difference is very important, I suppose the most important thing, the heaviest single factor in one's life, is whether one's born male or female. . . . Even where women participate equally with men in the society, they still after all do all the child-bearing *and so most of the child-rearing*. (Italics mine)

[Asked "Are they mentally inferior?"]

I don't know. They don't often seem to turn up mathematicians, or composers of music, or inventors, or abstract thinkers. But it isn't that they're stupid . . .[27]

Let me remind you that this is centuries in the future. And again:

the boy . . . had a girl's quick delicacy in his looks and movements, but no girl could keep so grim a silence as he did . . .[28]

It's the whole difficulty of science fiction, of genuine speculation: how to get away from traditional assumptions which are nothing more than traditional straitjackets.[29] Miss LeGuin seems to be aiming at some kind of equality between the sexes, but she certainly goes the long way around to get it; a whole new biology has to be invented, a whole society, a whole imagined world, so that finally she may bring together two persons of different sexes who will nonetheless be equals.[30]

The title I chose for this essay was "The Image of Women in Science Fiction." I hesitated between that and "Women in Science Fiction" but if I had chosen the latter, there would have been very little to say.

There are plenty of images of women in science fiction.

There are hardly any women.

[1] In conversation and the discussion of "speculative fiction" given at the MLA Seminar on Science Fiction in New York City, December 27, 1968.

[2] Basil Davenport, *Inquiry Into Science Fiction,* Longmans, Green and Co., New York, London, Toronto, 1955, pp. 39 ff.

[3] A recent novel by James Blish, *Black Easter,* published by Doubleday, Garden City, N. Y. in 1968, does exactly this. See in particular the Introduction, pp. 7-8.

[4] Samuel Delany, "About Five Thousand One Hundred and Seventy Five Words," in *Extrapolation: the Newsletter of the Conference on Science-Fiction of the MLA,* ed. Thomas D. Clareson, College of Wooster, Wooster, Ohio, Vol. X, No. 2, May 1969, pp. 61-63.

[5] There have been exceptions, e.g. Olaf Stapledon, George Bernard Shaw. And of course Philip Wylie's *The Disappearance.* Wylie's novel really ranks as a near-future story, though.

[6] Frederik Pohl, *The Age of the Pussyfoot,* Trident Press, New York, 1968.

[7] I don't want to adduce further examples, but most well-known science fiction is of this kind. It suffices to read *Childhood's End,* for example, (Arthur C. Clarke) and ask about the Utopian society of the middle: What do the men do? What do the women do? Who raises the children? And so on.

[8] See William Atheling, Jr. (James Blish) in *The Issue at Hand,* published by Advent Press, Chicago, 1964, pp. 117-119. I ought to make it clear that I am talking here of science fiction as a literary/cultural phenomenon, e.g. nobody can accuse George Bernard Shaw of suffering from the he-man ethos. But Shaw's ventures into science fiction have had little influence on what is written by other people in the field.

[9] The American pioneer was Hugo Gernsback, whose name adorns the yearly fan awards for best novel of the year, best short story, etc. In 1908 the Great Gernsback founded a magazine called *Modern Electrics,* the world's first radio magazine. In 1911 he published a serial of his own begetting called "Ralph 124C41+." Gernsback founded *Amazing Stories* in 1926 and by common consent, real science entered the field with John W. Campbell, Jr., in the late 1930's

[10] Some of the better writers in this genre are Keith Laumer, Gordon Dickson, and Poul Anderson. Most magazine fiction is at least tainted with space opera.

[11] In *Age of the Pussyfoot* the heroine makes her living by

trying out consumer products. She is so ordinary (or statistically extraordinary) that if she likes the products, the majority of the world's consumers will also like them. A prominent character in John Brunner's recent novel, *Stand on Zanzibar*, is a clairvoyante.

[12]Also "soap opera"—the roles of the sexes are reversed.

[13]I would put the ratio of male to female readers at about five to one. It might very well be higher.

[14]I *think* March and I think it was *Amazing*; it is either *Amazing* or *Worlds of If* for 1968 or 1969. Sorry!

[15]Me.

[16]It is noteworthy, however, that the ladies of the crew spend their time as stewardesses and telephone operators.

[17]See Alexei Panshin's *Heinlein in Dimension*, Advent Press, Chicago, 1968, especially Chapter VI.

[18]Entertaining use can be made of this form. Keith Laumer's delightfully tongue-in-cheek "The War With the Yukks" is a case in point. You will now complain that I don't tell you where to find it, but trying to find uncollected stories or novellas is a dreadful task. I don't know where it is. I read it in magazine publication; magazines vanish.

[19]Again, vanished without a trace. It's an oldie and I suspect it appeared in one of Groff Conklin's fat anthologies of The Best S.F. For (fill in year). It was a lovely story.

[20]This one may be American. A Russian (or American) and a Red Chinese, both from our present, are somehow transported into the future. They kill each other at a party in a xenophobic rage which their hostesses find tragic and obsolete. I remember that the ladies in the story shave their heads (that is, the ladies' heads). Not exactly a matriarchy but a semi-reversal of gender-roles occurs in Philip Wylie's *The Disappearance*, a brilliant argument to the effect that gender-roles are learned and can be unlearned.

[21]Again I find myself with distinct memories of the story and none of the author's name. I would appreciate any information. Science fiction is in a dreadful state bibliographically.

[22]This is perhaps too sweeping a statement; Isaac Asimov certainly writes for everybody, to give one example only.. But male readers do outnumber female readers, and there is a definite bias in the field toward what I have called the he-man ethos. I think the generalization can stand as a generalization.

[23]See William Atheling, Jr., (James Blish), *The Issue at Hand*, Advent Press, Chicago, 1964, p. 112.

[24]Carol Emshwiller is a good example. See the *Orbit* series of anthologies edited by Damon Knight (Putman's in hardcover,

Berkley in paperback).

25Ursula K. LeGuin, *The Left Hand of Darkness,* Ace Books, New York, N. Y., 1969 (paperback). As of this writing it has also received the Hugo, a comparable fan award.

26*Ibid.,* p. 201.

27*Ibid.,* p. 223.

28*Ibid.,* p. 281.

29I am too hard on the book; the narrator isn't quite that positive and one could make out a good case that the author is trying to criticize his viewpoint. There is also a technical problem: we are led to equate the human narrator's world (which we never see) with our own, simply because handling *two* unknowns in one novel would present insuperable difficulties. Moreover, Miss LeGuin wishes us to contrast Winter with our own world, not with some hypothetical, different society which would then have to be shown in detail. However, her earlier novel, *City of Illusions,* also published by Ace, is surprisingly close to the space opera, he-man ethos— either anti-feminism or resentment at being feminine, depending on how you look at it.

30There is an old legend (or a new one—I heard it read several years ago on WBAI-FM) concerning Merlin and some sorceress who was his sworn enemy. Each had resolved to destroy the other utterly, but they met and—each not knowing who the other was—fell in love. The problem was solved by Merlin's turning her into him and her turning him into herself. Thus both destroyed and reconstituted in the opposite sex, they lived happily ever after (one assumes). Or as Shaw was supposed to have said, he conceived of his female characters as being himself in different circumstances.

THE INVISIBLE WOMAN

TILLIE OLSEN

SILENCES: WHEN WRITERS DON'T WRITE

The winner of the O. Henry Award for the best American story of 1961 tells out of deep personal experience of the persistent influences that keep a writer from his work. What toll, she asks, is taken during those enforced and unnatural silences that are so much a part of the creative life?

Literary history and the present are dark with silences: some the silences for years by our acknowledged great; some silences hidden; some the ceasing to publish after one work appears; some the never coming to book form at all.

What is it that happens with the creator, to the creative process in that time? What *are* creation's needs for full functioning? Without intention of or pretension to literary scholarship, I have had special need to learn all I could of this over the years, myself so nearly remaining mute and having let writing die over and over again in me.

These are not *natural* silences, what Keats called *agonie ennuyeuse* (the tedious agony), that necessary time for renewal, lying fallow, gestation, in the natural cycle of creation. The silences I speak of here are unnatural; the unnatural thwarting of what struggles to come into being, but cannot. In the old, the obvious parallels: when the seed strikes stone; the soil will not sustain; the spring is false; the time is drought or blight or infestation; the frost comes premature.

The very great have known such silences—Thomas Hardy, Melville, Rimbaud, Gerard Manley Hopkins. They tell us little as to why or how the creative working atrophied and died in them—if it ever did.

"Less and less shrink the visions then vast in me,"
writes Thomas Hardy in his thirty-year ceasing from novels
after the Victorian vileness to his *Jude the Obscure*. ("So
ended his prose contributions to literature, his experiences
having killed all his interest in this form"—the official explanation.) But the great poetry he wrote to the end of his
life was not sufficient to hold, to develop, the vast visions
which for twenty-five years had had scope in novel after
novel. People, situations, interrelationships, landscape—
they cry for this larger life in poem after poem.

It was not visions shrinking with Hopkins, but a different torment. For seven years he kept his religious vow
to refrain from writing poetry, but the poet's eye he could
not shut, nor win "elected silence to beat upon [his]
whorled ear." "I had *long* had haunting my ear the echo of
a poem which now I realized on paper," he writes of the
first poem permitted to end the seven years' silence. But
poetry ("to hoard unheard; be heard, unheeded") could
be only the least and last of his heavy priestly responsibilities. Nineteen poems were all he could produce in his last
nine years—fullness to us, but torment pitched past grief to
him, who felt himself become "time's eunuch, never to
beget."[1]

Silence surrounds Rimbaud's silence. Was there torment of the unwritten; haunting of rhythm, of visions;
anguish at dying powers; the seventeen years after he
abandoned the unendurable literary world? We know only
that the need to write continued into his first years of
vagabondage, and that on his deathbed he spoke again like
a poet-visionary.

Melville's stages to his thirty-year prose silence are
clearest. The presage is in his famous letter to Hawthorne,
as he had to hurry *Moby Dick* to an end:

I am so pulled hither and thither by circumstances. The calm, the
coolness, the silent grass growing mood in which a man ought always
to compose, that can seldom be mine. Dollars damn me. What I
feel most moved to write, that is banned, it will not pay. Yet
altogether, write the other way I cannot. So the result is a final hash.

Reiterated in *Pierre* (Melville himself), writing "that book whose unfathomable cravings drink his blood . . .

when at last the idea obtruded that the wiser and profounder he should grow, the more he lessened his chances for bread.

To have to try final hash; to have one's work met by "drear ignoring"; to be damned by dollars into a Customs House job; to have only occasional weary evenings and Sundays left for writing—

How bitterly did unreplying Pierre feel in his heart that to most of the great works of humanity, their authors had given not weeks and months, not years and years, but their wholly surrendered and dedicated lives.

Is it not understandable why Melville began to burn work, then refused to write it, "immolating" it, "sealing in a fate subdued"? Instead he turned to sporadic poetry, manageable in a time sense, "to nurse through night the ethereal spark" where once had been "flame on flame." A thirty-year night. He was nearly seventy before he could quit the Customs dock and again have full time for writing, start back to prose. "Age, dull tranquilizer," and devastation of "arid years that filed before" to work through before he could restore the creative process. Three years of tryings before he felt capable of beginning *Billy Budd* (the kernel waiting half a century); three years more, the slow, painful, never satisfied writing and rewriting of it.

Kin to these years-long silences are the *hidden* silences; work aborted, deferred, denied—hidden by the work which does come to fruition. Hopkins' last years rightfully belong here, as does Kafka's whole writing life, that of Mallarmé, Olive Schreiner, probably Katherine Anne Porter, and many other contemporary writers.

Censorship silences. Deletions, omissions, abandonment of the medium (as with Thomas Hardy). Self-censorship, like Mark Twain's. Publishers' censorship, refusing subject matter or treatment. Religious, political censorship —sometimes spurring inventiveness—most often (read Dostoevski's letters) a wearing attrition.

The extreme of this: those writers physically silenced by governments. Isaac Babel, the years of imprisonment, what took place in him with what wanted to be written? Or in Oscar Wilde, who was not permitted even a pencil until the last months of his imprisonment?

Other silences. The truly memorable poem, story, or book, then the writer never heard from again. Was one work all the writer had in him, and he respected literature too much to repeat himself? Was there the kind of paralysis psychiatry might have helped? Were the conditions not present for establishing the habits of creativity (a young Colette who lacked a Willy to lock her in her room each day? or other claims, other responsibilities so writing could not be first)? It is an eloquent commentary that this one-book silence is true of most Negro writers; only eleven, these last hundred years, have published more than twice.

There is a prevalent silence I pass by quickly, the absence of creativity where it once had been; the ceasing to create literature, though the books keep coming out, year after year. That suicide of the creative process Hemingway describes so accurately in *The Snows of Kilimanjaro*:

He had destroyed his talent himself—by not using it, by betrayals of himself and what he believed in, by drinking so much that he blunted the edge of his perceptions, by laziness, by sloth, by snobbery, by hook and by crook; selling vitality, trading it for security, for comfort.

No, not Scott Fitzgerald. His not a death of creativity, not silence, but what happens when (his words) there is "the sacrifice of talent, in pieces, to preserve its essential value."

Almost unnoted are the foreground silences, *before* the achievement. (Remember when Emerson hailed Whitman's genius, he guessed correctly, "which yet must have had a long *foreground* for such a start.") George Eliot, Joseph Conrad, Isak Dinesen, Sherwood Anderson, Elizabeth Madox Roberts, A. E. Coppard, Kate Chopin, Angus Wilson, Joyce Cary—all close to, or in their forties before they became writers; Lampedusa, Maria Dermout (*The Ten Thousand Things*), Laura Ingalls Wilder, the "children's writer," in their sixties. Their capacities evident early in the "being one on whom nothing is lost." Not all struggling and anguished, like Anderson, the foreground years; some needing the immobilization of long illness or loss, or the sudden lifting of responsibility to make writing necessary, make writing possible; others waiting circumstances and encouragement (George Eliot, her Henry Lewes; Laura Wilder, a daughter's insistence that she transmute her storytelling gift onto paper).

UNMINED GENIUS

Very close to this last grouping are the silences where the lives never came to writing. Among these, the mute inglorious Miltons: those whose waking hours are all struggle for existence; the barely educated; the illiterate; women. Their silence the silence of centuries as to how life was, is, for most of humanity. Traces of their making, of course, in folk song, lullaby, tales, language itself, jokes, maxims, superstitions, but we know nothing of the creators or how it was with them. In the fantasy of Shakespeare born in deepest Africa (as at least one Shakespeare must have been), was the ritual, the oral storytelling a fulfillment? Or was there restlessness, indefinable yearning, a sense of restriction? Was it as Virginia Woolf in *A Room of One's Own* guesses—about women?

Genius of a sort must have existed among them, as it existed among the working classes, but certainly it never got itself onto paper. When, however, one reads of a woman possessed by the devils, of a wise woman selling herbs, or even a remarkable man who had a remarkable mother, then I think we are on the track of a lost novelist, a suppressed poet, or some Emily Brontë who dashed her brains out on the moor, crazed with the torture her gift had put her to.

Rebecca Harding Davis whose work sleeps in the forgotten (herself as a woman of a century ago so close to remaining mute)[2] also guessed about the silent in that time of the twelve-hour-a-day, six-day work week. She writes of the illiterate ironworker in "Life in the Iron Mills" who sculptured great shapes in the slag, "his fierce thirst for beauty, to know it, to create it, to *be* something other than he is—a passion of pain," *Margaret Howth* in the textile mill:

There were things in the world, that like herself, were marred, did not understand, were hungry to know. . . . Her eyes quicker to see than ours, delicate or grand lines in the homeliest things. . . . Everything she saw or touched, nearer, more human than to you or me. These sights and sounds did not come to her common; she never got used to living as other people do.

She never got used to living as other people do. Was that one of the ways it was?

So some of the silences, incomplete listing of the incomplete, where the need and capacity to create were of a high order.

THE FRIGHTFUL TASK

Now, what *is* the work of creation and the circumstances it demands for full functioning—as told in the journals and notes of the practitioners themselves: Harry James, Katherine Mansfield, Gide, Virginia Woolf; the letters of Flaubert, Rilke, Conrad; Thomas Wolfe's *Story of a Novel,* Valéry's *Course in Poetics.* What do they explain of the silences?

"Constant toil is the law of art, as it is of life," says (and demonstrated) Balzac:

To pass from conception to execution, to produce, to bring the idea to birth, to raise the child laboriously from infancy, to put it nightly to sleep surfeited, to kiss it in the mornings with the hungry heart of a mother, to clean it, to clothe it fifty times over in new garments which it tears and casts away, and yet not revolt against the trials of this agitated life—this unwearying maternal love, this habit of creation —this is execution and its toils.

"Without duties, almost without external communication," Rilke specifices, "unconfined solitude which takes every day like a life, a spaciousness which puts no limit to vision and in the midst of which infinities surround."

Unconfined solitude as Joseph Conrad experienced it:

For twenty months I wrestled with the Lord for my creation . . .
mind and will and conscience engaged to the full, hour after hour,
day after day . . . a lonely struggle in a great isolation from the
world. I suppose I slept and ate the food put before me and talked
connectedly on suitable occasions, but I was never aware of the even
flow of daily life, made easy and noiseless for me by a silent, watchful, tireless affection.

So there is a homely underpinning for it all, the even
flow of daily life made easy and noiseless.

"The terrible law of the artist"—says Henry James—
"the law of fructification, of fertilization. The old, old
lesson of the art of meditation. To woo combinations and
inspirations into being by a depth and continuity of attention and meditation."

"That load, that weight, that gnawing conscience,"
writes Thomas Mann—

That sea which to drink up, that frightful task. . . . The will, the
discipline and self-control to shape a sentence or follow out a hard
train of thought. From the first rhythmical urge of the inward creative force towards the material, towards casting in shape and form,
from that to the thought, the image, the word, the line, what a
struggle, what Gethsemane.

Does it become very clear what Melville's Pierre so
bitterly remarked on, and what literary history bears out,
why most of the great works of humanity have come from
wholly surrendered and dedicated lives? How else sustain
the constant toil, the frightful task, the terrible law, the
continuity? Full self, this means, full time for the work.
(That time for which Emily Dickinson withdrew from the
world.)

But what if there is not that fullness of time, let alone
totality of self? What if the writer, as in some of these
silences, must work regularly at something besides his own
work—as do nearly all in the arts in the United States
today?

I know the theory (kin to starving in the garret makes
great art) that it is this very circumstance which feeds crea-

tivity. I know, too, that for the beginning young, for some who have such need, the job can be valuable access to life they would not otherwise know. A few (I think of the doctors, Chekhov and William Carlos Williams) for special reasons sometimes manage both. But the actuality testifies: substantial creative work demands time, and with rare exceptions only full-time workers have created it. Where the claims of creation cannot be primary, the results are atrophy; unfinished work; minor effort and accomplishment; silences. (Desperation which accounts for the mountains of applications to the foundations for grants—undivided time—in the strange breadline system we have worked out for our artists.)

Twenty years went by on the writing of *Ship of Fools,* while Katherine Anne Porter, who needed only two years, was "trying to get to that table, to that typewriter, away from my jobs of teaching and trooping this country and of keeping house." "Your subconscious needed that time to grow the layers of pearl," she was told. Perhaps, perhaps, but I doubt it. Subterranean forces can make you wait, but they are very finicky about the kind of waiting it has to be. Before they will feed the creator back, they must be fed, passionately fed, what needs to be worked on. "We hold up our desire as one places a magnet over a composite dust from which the particle of iron will suddenly jump up," says Paul Valéry. A receptive waiting, that means, not demands which prevent "an undistracted center of being." And when the response comes, availability to work must be immediate. If not used at once, all may vanish as a dream; worse, future creation be endangered, for only the removal and development of the material frees the forces for further work.

There is a life in which all this is documented: Franz Kafka's. For every one entry from his diaries here, there are fifty others which testify as unbearably to the driven stratagems for time, the work lost (to us), the damage to the creative powers (and the body) of having to deny, interrupt, postpone, put aside, let work die.

"I cannot devote myself completely to my writing," Kafka explains (in 1911). "I could not live by literature, if only, to begin with, because of the slow maturing of my work and its special character." So he worked as an official in a state insurance agency, and wrote when he could.

These two can never be reconciled. . . . If I have written something one evening, I am afire the next day in the office and can bring nothing to completion. Outwardly I fulfill my office duties satisfactorily, not my inner duties however, and every unfulfilled inner duty becomes a misfortune that never leaves. What strength it will necessarily drain me of.

[1911] No matter how little the time or how badly I write, I feel approaching the imminent possibility of great moments which could make me capable of anything. But my being does not have sufficient strength to hold this to the next writing time. During the day the visible world helps me; during the night it cuts me to pieces unhindered. . . . Calling forth such powers which are then not permitted to function.

Which are then not permitted to function.

[1912] When I begin to write after such a long interval, I draw the words as if out of the empty air. If I capture one, then I have just this one alone, and all the toil must begin anew.

[1914] Yesterday for the first time in months, an indisputable ability to do good work. And yet wrote only the first page. Again I realize that everything written down bit by bit rather than all at once in the course of the larger part is inferior, and that the circumstances of my life condemn me to this inferiority.

[1915] My constant attempt by sleeping before dinner to make it possible to continue working [writing] late into the night, senseless. Then at one o'clock can no longer fall asleep at all, the next day at work insupportable, and so I destroy myself.

[1917] Distractedness, weak memory, stupidity. . . . Always this one principal anguish—if I had gone away in 1911 in full possession of all my powers. Not eaten by the strain of keeping down living forces.

Eaten into tuberculosis. By the time he won through to himself and time for writing, his body could live no more. He was forty-one.

I think of Rilke who said: "If I have any responsibility, I mean and desire it to be responsibility for the deepest and innermost essence of the loved reality [writing] to which I am inseparably bound"; and who also said: "Anything alive, that makes demands, arouses in me an infinite capacity to give it its due, the consequences of which completely use me up." These were true with Kafka, too, yet how different their lives. When Rilke wrote that about responsibility, he is explaining why he will not take a job to support his wife and baby, nor live with them (years later will not come to his daughter's wedding nor permit a two-hour honeymoon visit lest it break his solitude where he awaits poetry). The "infinite capacity" is his explanation as to why he cannot even bear to have a dog. Extreme—and justified. He protected his creative powers.

WHAT'S SPECIAL ABOUT WOMEN

Kafka's, Rilke's "infinite capacity" and all else that has been said here of the needs of creation, illuminate women's silence of centuries. I will not repeat what is in Virginia Woolf's *A Room of One's Own,* but talk of this last century and a half in which women have begun to have voice in literature. (It has been less than that time in Eastern Europe, and not yet, in many parts of the world.)

In the last century, of the women whose achievements endure for us in one way or another, nearly all never married (Jane Austen, Emily Brontë, Christina Rossetti, Emily Dickinson, Louisa May Alcott, Sarah Orne Jewett) or married late in their thirties (George Eliot, Elizabeth Barrett Browning, Charlotte Brontë, Olive Schreiner). I can think of only four (George Sand, Harriet Beecher Stowe, Helen Hunt Jackson, and Kate Chopin) who married and had children as young women. All had servants. All but Sand were foreground silences.

In our century, until very recently, it has not been so different. Most did not marry (Lagerlöf, Cather, Glasgow, Gertrude Stein, Sitwell, Gabriela Mistral, Elizabeth Madox Roberts, Charlotte Mew, Welty, Marianne Moore) or, if married, have been childless (Undset, Wharton, Woolf, Katherine Mansfield, H. H. Richardson, Bowen, Dinesen, Porter, Hellman, Dorothy Parker). Colette had one child. If I include Kay Boyle, Pearl Buck, Dorothy Canfield Fisher, that will make a small group who had more than one child. Nearly all had household help.

Am I resaying the moldy theory that women have no need, some say no capacity, to create art, because they can create babies? And the additional proof is precisely that the few women who have created it are nearly all childless? No.

The power and the need to create, over and beyond reproduction, is native in both men and women. Where the gifted among women (*and men*) have remained mute, or have never attained full capacity, it is because of circumstances, inner or outer, which oppose the needs of creation.

Wholly surrendered and dedicated lives; time as needed for the work; totality of self. But women are traditionally trained to place others' needs first, to feel these needs as their own (the "infinite capacity"); their sphere, their satisfaction to be in making it possible for others to use their abilities. This is what Virginia Woolf meant when, already a writer of achievement, she wrote in her diary:

Father's birthday. He would have been 96, 96 yes, today; and could have been 96, like other people one has known; but mercifully was not. His life would have entirely ended mine. What would have happened? No writing, no books;—inconceivable.

It took family deaths to free more than one woman writer into her own development.[3] Emily Dickinson freed herself, denying all the duties expected of a woman of her social position except the closest family ones, and she was fortunate to have a sister, and servants, to share those. How much is revealed of what happened to their own talents in the diaries of those sisters of great men, Dorothy Wordsworth, Alice James.

And where there is no servant or relation to assume the responsibilities of daily living? Listen to Katherine

Mansfield in the early days of her relationship with John Middleton Murry, when they both dreamed of becoming great writers:

The house seems to take up so much time. . . . I mean when I have to clean up twice over or wash up extra unnecessary things. I get frightfully impatient and want to be working [writing]. So often this week you and Gordon have been talking while I washed dishes. Well someone's got to wash dishes and get food. Otherwise "there's nothing in the house but eggs to eat." And after you have gone I walk about with a mind full of ghosts of saucepans and primus stoves and "will there be enough to go around?" And you calling, whatever I am doing, writing, "Tig, isn't there going to be tea? It's five o'clock."

I loathe myself today. This woman who superintends you and rushes about slamming doors and slopping water and shouts "You might at least empty the pail and wash out the tea leaves." O Jack, I wish that you would take me in your arms and kiss my hands and my face and every bit of me and say, "It's all right, you darling thing, I understand."

A long way from Conrad's favorable circumstance for creation: the flow of daily life made easy and noiseless.

And, if in addition to the infinite capacity, to the daily responsibilities, there are children?

Balzac, you remember, described creation in terms of motherhood. Yes, in intelligent passionate motherhood there are similarities, and in more than the toil and patience. The calling upon total capacities; the re-living and new using of the past; the comprehensions; the fascination, absorption, intensity. All almost certain death to creation.

Not because the capacities to create no longer exist, or the need (though for a while, as in any fullness of life, the need may be obscured) but because the circumstances for sustained creation are almost impossible. The need cannot be first. It can have at best, only part self, part time. (Unless someone else does the nurturing. Read Dorothy Fisher's "Babushka Farnham" in *Fables for Parents*.) More than in any human relationship, overwhelmingly more, motherhood means being instantly interruptible, responsive, responsible. Children need one *now* (and remember, in our

society, the family must often be the center for love and
health the outside world is not). The very fact that these
are needs of love, not duty, that one feels them as one's
self; that there is no one else to be responsible for these
needs, gives them primacy. It is distraction, not meditation,
that becomes habitual; interruption, not continuity; spasmodic, not constant toil. The rest has been said here.
Work interrupted, deferred, postponed, makes blockage—
at best, lesser accomplishment. Unused capacities atrophy,
cease to be.

When H. H. Richardson, who wrote the Australian
classic *Ultima Thule,* was asked why she—whose children,
like all her people, were so profoundly written—did not
herself have children, she answered: "There are enough
women to do the childbearing and childrearing. I know of
none who can write my books." I remember thinking
rebelliously, yes, and I know of none who can bear and
rear my children either. But literary history is on her side.
Almost no mothers—as almost no part-time, part-self
persons—have created enduring literature—so far.

A PRIVATE JOURNEY

If I talk now quickly of my own silences—almost presumptuous after what has been told here—it is that the
individual experience may add.

In the twenty years I bore and reared my children,
usually had to work on a job as well, the simplest circumstances for creation did not exist. Nevertheless writing, the
hope of it, was "the air I breathed, so long as I shall breathe
at all." In that hope, there was conscious storing, snatched
reading, beginnings of writing, and always "the secret root-
lets of reconnaisance."

When the youngest of our four was in school, the
beginnings struggled toward endings. This was a time, in
Kafka's words, "like a squirrel in a cage: bliss of movement,
desperation about constriction, craziness of endurance."

Bliss of movement. A full extended family life; the

world of my job (transcriber in a dairy-equipment company); and the writing, which I was somehow able to carry around within me through work, through home. Time on the bus, even when I had to stand, was enough; the stolen moments at work, enough; the deep night hours for as long as I could stay awake, after the kids were in bed, after the household tasks were done, sometimes during. It is no accident that the first work I considered publishable began: "I stand here ironing, and what you asked me moves tormented back and forth with the iron."

In such snatches of time I wrote what I did in those years, but there came a time when this triple life was no longer possible. The fifteen hours of daily realities became too much distraction for the writing. I lost craziness of endurance. What might have been, I don't know, but I asked for, and received, eight months' writing time. There was still full family life, all the household responsibilities, but I did not have to go out on a job. I had continuity, three full days, sometimes more, and it was in those months I made the mysterious turn and became a writing writer.

Then had to return to the world of work, someone else's work, nine hours, five days a week.

This was the time of festering and congestion. For a few months I was able to shield the writing with which I was so full against the demands of jobs on which I had to be competent, through the joys and responsibilities of family. For a few months. Always roused by the writing, always denied. "I could not go to write it down. It convulsed and died in me. I will pay." My work died. What demanded to be written, did not; it seethed, bubbled, clamored, peopled me. At last moved into the hours meant for sleeping. I worked now full time on temporary jobs, a Kelly, a Western Agency girl (girl!), wandering from office to office, always hoping we could manage two, three writing months ahead. Eventually there was time.

I had said: always roused by the writing, always denied. Now, like a woman made frigid, I had to learn response, to trust this possibility for fruition that had not been before. Any interruption dazed and silenced me. It took a long while of surrendering to what I was trying to write, of invoking Henry James's "passion, piety, patience," before I was able to reestablish work.

When again I had to leave the writing, I lost consciousness. A time of anesthesia. There was still an automatic noting that did not stop, but it was as if writing had never been. No fever, no congestion, no festering. I ceased being peopled, slept well and dreamlessly, took a "permanent" job. The few pieces which had been published seemed to have vanished like the not-yet-written. I wrote someone, unsent: "So long they fed each other—my life, the writing; the writing or hope of it, my life—and now they destroy each other." I knew, but did not feel the destruction.

A Ford grant in literature, awarded me on nomination by others, came almost too late. Time granted does not necessarily coincide with time that can be most fully used, as the congested time of fullness would have been. Still, it was two years.

TO GIVE ONE'S ALL

Drowning is not so pitiful as the attempt to rise, says Emily Dickinson. I do not agree, but I know of what she speaks. For a long time I was that emaciated survivor trembling on the beach, unable to rise and walk. Said differently, I could manage only the feeblest, shallowest growth on that devastated soil. Weeds, to be burnt like weeds, or used as compost. When the habits of creation were at last rewon, one book went to the publisher, and I dared to begin my present work. It became my center, engraved on it: "Evil is whatever distracts." (By now, had begun a cost to our family life, to my own participation in life as a human being.) I shall not tell the "rest, residue, and remainder" of what I was "leased, demised, and let unto" when once again I had to leave work at the flood to return to the Time Master, to business-ese and legalese. This most harmful of all my silences has ended, but I am not yet recovered, may still be a one-book instead of a hidden and foreground silence.

NOTES

This article is adapted from a talk entitled "Death of the Creative Process," given at the Radcliffe Institute for Independent Study in 1963. Copyright © 1965 and all rights reserved by Tillie Olsen. Reprinted from *Harper's*, October, 1965. Used by permission of the author. Olsen's "Writers Who Are Women in Our Century—One Out of Twelve," a talk given to the MLA in 1971 and reprinted in *College English*, October, 1972, concerns itself further with circumstances affecting women as writers.

[1] A letter to Bridges, four years before he wrote the poem.

[2] See my afterword on Rebecca Harding Davis in the Feminist Press reprint of her *Life in The Iron Mills* (1973).

[3] Kate Chopin, George Eliot, Helen Hunt Jackson, Elizabeth Gaskell.

SUSAN KOPPELMAN CORNILLON

THE FICTION OF FICTION

For the most part, women in our culture experience themselves and their lives in terms of and in response to masculine centered values and definitions. We are conditioned from earliest infancy to think of ourselves in specific ways by strong social expectations of, reinforcements of, and demands for gender-typed behavior. We internalize that conditioning to such an extent that most of us have little or no sense of our selves apart from the ways we have been conditioned to perceive ourselves in terms of the kinds of genitals we have. Thus, it is true for most of us, that anatomy is destiny—because of our culture's self-fulfilling prophecy that it shall be so.

If I claim that women internalize the male idea of the feminine and create themselves in the shape of that idea, then it would appear to follow that there would be no difference between perceptions of the female by male and by female novelists, and that there would be no difference between the idea of the feminine and the reality of the female. But there *are* differences in both cases. The difference is that in the male culture the idea of the feminine is expressed, defined, and perceived by the male as a *condition of* being female, while for the female it is seen as an *addition to* one's femaleness, as a status to be achieved.[1]

This difference between the idea of the feminine and the reality of the female may be experienced in a number of ways, but for almost every woman this gap is perceived in terms of personal inadequacy . . . because she fails "in the raw" to live up to the culture's image of the feminine. She usually interprets the fact that she does not correspond to the cultural definition of the feminine as an exposure of her failure to be "normal," her failure to be what she is supposed to be, her own falling short—a cause for shame rather than a transcendence of it or a cause for redefining or throwing out received definitions. She is conditioned to see herself at fault, and not the cultural idea. And she is taught to feel shame (guilt, modesty, etc.) for her deviation, enough shame so that she strives to hide and will not discuss her deviation. Because the recognized personal deviations cause too much shame to allow for their revelation to others, women never "blow" their own or each other's "cover stories" of "normal feminity," and they even collaborate in the destruction of their daughters by raising them to be grotesque, half-real schizoids like themselves. Women frequently go to self-crippling, self-denying, self-distorting lengths to force themselves into the mold. They are, in effect, involved in a struggle to "cure" themselves of personhood.

In the fiction of even our most talented women novelists, the writers fail to communicate this secret, usually shame-filled, inner life of women on an overt, artistically self-conscious level. They reinforce female shame by not discussing women's deviation from the cultural myths of what is supposed to be feminine. There are bits and pieces of this kind of reality that slip out occasionally, but there is no detectable pattern to the inclusion of details that tell of this reality. We must seek for this level of reality in their fiction in a manner similar to that applied by psychoanalytic critics who chase Oedipus through Shakespeare, i.e., a belief that the artist is not consciously responsible for all that we can find in the artifact. What I am saying, basically, is that certain types of feelings and experiences common to women in our culture are not represented in our fiction by male or by female novelists, or, if these phenomena are mentioned, it is in a context that reinforces our alienation from ourselves and the mystification of our humanness.[2]

The physical "chores" of a man's life have been invested with symbolic meaning. The novels of recent years are filled with men taking philosophical shits, introspective pisses, transcendental middle aged inventories of wrinkles and flab in front of private mirrors, and engaging in metaphysical masturbation. These things happen in highbrow novels, the ones analyzed in Ph.D. seminars. I've seen papers on the significance of Herzog's excretory functioning. And in middle and low brow novels we have had countless symbolic encounters between man and his mirror with the razor as medium and mediator. Innumerable heroes have shied away from praises or thanks with a diffident, "Well, hell, I have to look myself in the eye when I shave." The simple act of shaving one's face took on all sorts of symbolic overtones; we might call it the "mug in the mirror" motif. It was a moment when a man faced himself, measured himself, took stock.(3) It was a profound moment.

If one is willing to recognize the novel as functioning in our culture as, among other things, an instrument for education and socialization, one can see the kind of service such episodes as the ones mentioned above provide for young males. We are all aware of the agony of adolescence in our culture, the evasive fumblings as we attempt to communicate about our fears and our needs and our anxieties without actually ever mentioning to anyone what they really are; the creation of elaborate private symbologies that enable us to grieve about our pimples, our sexual fantasies, our masturbation, the strange changes happening to our bodies. But boys outgrow this secretiveness soon—because there is a vast wealth of literature for them to stumble on, both great and popular, classical and contemporary, pious and lewd, that assures them that, indeed, they are normal. Or even better, their suffering is portrayed as a prerequisite for maturity, if not a prelude to greatness.

Women, too, have physical "chores" to perform. Among others, women (in order to look "clean" and "neat" and "feminine") must periodically (and for a great many women that period is daily) rid our bodies of all hair considered "not feminine." We must depilate our legs, our armpits, our chests, our chins, cheeks, upper lips and eyebrows. We women must "meet our ugly mugs" in a daily mirror, too. But, typically, this daily confrontation has been invested with no symbolism, no lofty philosophical overtones, no speculative undertones, no theological sidelights.

Women in our culture are expected to prepare their bodies to be socially visible as conventionally attractive—or as near to it as they can get. Simple, but time consuming tasks that we all, male and female, know about, but that not even women write about. And yet these activities that we perform on our bodies (i.e., our selves) so that they (i.e., we) can be attractive, presentable, etc., are, by their very natures, denials of the reality of who and what we are. These duties are disguises, transformations, that we know are only temporary and must be performed again and again, although it is the disguised self and the transformed self that is recognized as the authentic self.

When a woman is still a young girl and cannot yet perform these operations of transformation and disguise without concentration (if she ever can), perhaps she thinks about them, about what they mean, about who she is before and after, but most of all we think about how there must be something wrong with us that we have all this hair to get rid of.

Those of us who recognize our beautified, "transformed" selves as inauthentic representations of our Self inevitably feel alienated from responses to and those responding to our "beauty." There is a certain ironic self-satisfaction to be derived from a successful con job, but it is always accompanied by anxiety that the con will be discovered, and loneliness and a sense of isolation when it isn't.

We don't complain about this sometimes painful,

usually uncomfortable, and always tedious necessity to transform our bodies into something acceptable because we aren't sure that every woman has to do it and none of us wants to be the first to admit her inadequacy. (Does Theda do it? Does Greta do it? Does Rita do it? Does Marilyn do it? Does Raquel do it?) It must surely be that somewhere there is a woman born with glossy lips, purple eyelids, a hairless body, and odorless genitals. And it is she, that one in a billion, that never to be discovered or known, perfect woman, it is she who is normal and not me (or any of my friends). And when you first start to shave your legs, although you do it partly for the thrill of being grown up, all the time that you are scraping that razor across your calf, you are wondering if those first gashes will scar you for life; you are panicking because someone told you that the more often you shave, the faster and thicker the hair will grow, and part of you is horrified to think of the time when you will have to do it twice a day and still have a five o'clock shadow below the knee. You begin to look at older women and you wonder where they find all the time to make themselves even minimally presentable on a day-to-day basis.

And yet, with all this that attaches itself to female leg-shaving slavery, I have never seen any fictional female character either shave or pluck a hair. American fiction is not devoid of reference to female depilation. For instance, in Joyce Carol Oates novel *them*, we can assume that the Wendall women shave from a comment that Loretta, the mother, makes about her difficulties with a welfare worker: "He asked me why *I* needed razor blades, who's in the family to use them, he said. Is there a man in the family not reported? The smart-ass bastard, I don't know if he was kidding or not." However, this oblique reference to female depilation behavior is not intended to bring to our attention anything about women shaving their legs or armpits or whatever; nor is it intended to call to our attention that one of the ways men humiliate women in our society is by referring to their shameful secrets (hairy bodies) in accusing or derogatory manners; rather, the passage is apparently being used to say something about the relationship between the poor and the welfare system, the poor and the more well-off: namely, that the poor are harassed, humiliated, distrusted and confused.

Those of us who mistake our transformed selves for our real Self are destined to a schizoid experiencing of life, destined to perpetual and intensifying disappointment in our situations and in our relationships. We constantly feel cheated and deprived. Our lives are never real to us when we mistake a cultural stereotype for our self.

Let us look again at *them* for an example of this kind of mistake. Early in the book, Oates tells us about Loretta's identifying herself with the cultural myth of femininity, experiencing a sense of commonality with all young females for whom the story is and ever will be "they got married and lived happily ever after." But never once during the thirty years we spend with Loretta do we see her experiencing the discrepancy between the idea of femininity and her sense of self; never once do we see her doubt that that story was meant to be her story. We see her disappointment, at times her anguish and rage, that the dream does not come true for her, but we never see her experience herself as someone other than that ideal of the feminine for whom the dream, that particular romantic Hollywood fairy tale dream is supposed to come true. In fact, so thoroughly does Loretta identify herself with the myth that she perceives everything in her life that does not conform to the myth as not "her life," and weeps, when she is thirty-six years old, has borne four children, won and lost two husbands, at this age and after all this living, none of which she had expected to be "like that," she weeps and says, "What about my life? When is it going to begin?"

This obvious example of female schizoid life[4] serves another purpose for Oates. It would appear that she is using the episode to tell us something about her vision of human destiny, of the human condition and its inevitable tendency towards illusion; and not that she is aware of something special about the female human condition. For instance, when Loretta's son Jules is twelve and her daughter Maureen a year younger, we are given this description of their after-school life:

Then came the hours after school. . . . Maureen . . . would straggle home and Jules would be out for a few hours running loose, until, exhausted and sometimes bloody, he showed up at the house . . . around six.

We are never told why it is that male children are free to "run loose" while female children "straggle home" after school.

It is possible for a writer to present fictionally the kind of sexist child-rearing that Jules and Maureen obviously undergo without allying herself with it. In other words, a writer can portray the unconscious perpetration of socialization on her characters without herself reinforcing the attitudes being internalized by her characters. May Ann Evans, writing *The Mill on the Floss*, filled her pages with evidence of Maggie Tolliver's sexist upbringing without at any time approving of or aligning herself with those attitudes. Miss Evans' ability to separate herself from the attitudes of some of her major characters was greatly facilitated by the kind of structuring common to Victorian fiction, which allowed the writer to step back from her omniscient silent role and address her audience directly. But it was not only this technique that enabled Miss Evans to separate herself from the mistaken notions of her characters. It was a clear-minded knowledge in her own head that, indeed, she did not share those ideas. One is uncertain, while reading the works of Miss Oates, whether or not she does, in fact, separate her own attitudes and opinions on the issue of sex role from her characters.

We are frequently presented with generalizations about the nature of women and the nature of men in which the point of view being expressed is not made explicit. It would appear to be the expanded consciousness of a narrator sharing the point of view of a less articulate character, and, insofar as it is appropriate in the detailing of one's characters to convey their prejudices and misunderstandings of reality, it is appropriate for Oates to include passages such as the following:

Off to themselves, safe and lively, women always talked about men; their eyes and their voices seized hungrily upon men.

and

A woman grows up to take all the shit she can from men, then she breaks down, that's the way it is. . . .

Although it may be appropriate (i.e., in keeping with who Oates has shown them to be) for her characters to express ideas like the above, it is not appropriate for Oates to share them. There is, however, no indication in her books or short stories that she does not fully participate in the myths of our culture about the "basic natures" of men and women. All her women are anatomically determined; all her men have at least an illusion of freedom. No one in Miss Oates' world escapes this gender-role stereotyping—except Miss Oates, who has said in an interview (*Commonweal*, December 5, 1969, p. 308) that her male protagonists are autobiographical, but that she feels no sense of identification with her female characters. And at no time does Miss Oates separate herself from her characters and say, "This sexism, like their racism, their ignorance, their desperations, their inarticulateness, their poverty, is part of their victimization." The sexist attitudes that control (and destroy) their lives might really be manifestations of genetic genderal realities for all that we are allowed to see of their insidious origins.

The second major example of "skillful avoidance or unconsciousness of the specialness of the female condition in our culture" present in a great deal of fiction is evidenced by the peculiar way female sexuality is portrayed. The events of female physical being-in-the-world are mentioned but are accorded no more significance than any other peculiarly female experience or occupation in a culture where significance is derivative of a male value structure.

Turning again to *them*, we see that although two of the major and one of the important minor characters in the book are women, and the author is a woman, we are never permitted to share the experiencing of any of the physical phenomena that are uniquely female. We share only those physical experiences that are in no way gender related and that male authors have already established patterns for the telling about. But the fact is that Maureen and Nadine and, one has reason to believe although it is never made explicit, Loretta (whose sexuality per se is no part of the story and therefore not necessary for us to know about), are frigid. Maureen is not capable of experiencing any sensation when she is engaged in some sort of physical encounter, and Nadine, who is capable of great heights of sexual excitation and arousal, is unable to achieve orgasm.

Maureen has been conditioned to believe that she cannot escape marriage, pregnancy, subjection and submission to male whim. She dreams constantly about escape, about freedom, and finally begins to believe that if she had enough money, she could escape. While she is loitering home after school one day, a man approaches her, and she makes the age old sex-money connection. She begins to "go with men" for money. And when she is with the first man, "Freedom came to her like air from the river, not exactly fresh, but chilly and strong; she was free and she had escaped." But the price she is paying for this freedom is the integrity of her self. Because, as she asserts over and over again, with a sense of awe and confusion, as various men touch and enter her body, she doesn't feel anything at all. She has divorced her sense of self from her physical being.

Her stepfather discovers the money and beats her half to death, presumably because he knows how she got the money, and he keeps it. Although her body recovers from the beating quickly enough, she lies in bed for thirteen months in a catatonic state. And then, one day, she "wakes up." Some ability to live is healed in her, but her will to escape has been destroyed. So now, with as little feeling as when she was whoring, she sets out to secure what she is now willing to accept as the best available to her in this life. Now, she asks only to:

see myself like this: living in a house out of the city, a ranch house or a colonial house, with a fence around the back, a woman working in the kitchen, wearing slacks maybe, a baby in his crib in the baby's room, thin white gauzy curtains, a bedroom for my husband and me, a window in the living-room looking out onto the lawn and the street and the house across the street. Every cell in my body aches for this! My eyes ache for it, the balls of my eyes in their sockets, hungry and aching for this, my God how I want that house and that man, whoever he is.

This reads to me like the end of *1984* when the hero starts yelling, and really means it:

HURRAY FOR BIG BROTHER! LONG LIVE BIG BROTHER!

Maureen perceives her body as an object to be manipulated, as an object that is inevitably subject to men, and as an object she can control only insofar as she can choose the male(s) to whom it shall be subject, by whom it shall be used, and what shall accrue to her as a result of its use. It is a weapon she can aim; an instrument she can perform on, but her physical experiences are not a part of her subjective reality; she cannot apprehend that which happens to her body as that which happens to Maureen Wendall, as part of Maureen's experience. She does not experience herself as being co-extensive with her body. Like her mother, Loretta, her life is lived according to a schizoid modality.

Oates would have us believe that this is somehow a danger of slum life, that Maureen's tragedy is a result of her socio-economic condition. But Maureen has less in common with her own brother Jules than she does with

Nadine, daughter of great wealth and privilege. Both females experience the same brand of ontological insecurity. Nadine tries and fails to communicate her sense of suffering to her lover, Jules, who can't believe that rich people suffer. But one knows that Maureen would be able to understand the fear that Nadine is talking about. What happens to their bodies is a hiatus in their experiencing of life.

Jules lives through his body as well as through his mind. He cannot understand the sufferings of either his sister or of Nadine, both of whom he loves. Maureen does not live through her body, but we do not see her experiencing this estrangement from her body as wrong or abnormal, or as a deviation from her perception and internalization of the idea of the feminine. Nadine, on the other hand, responds to a similar divorce between her self and her body as something horrible.

Nadine is portrayed as having been always strange and eventually, ultimately, mad. Because she is mad we are permitted to get close to her perception of herself. Oates allows Nadine to mention that she is menstruating and to discuss how she feels about it. Oates does a good job of dealing with Nadine's orgasmic frigidity (a topic leaded with guilt and unfortunately totally personalized, i.e., stripped of all political meaning, by our neo-Freudian age), but is still so nervous about dealing with that level of feeling in a woman in terms of how it feels to the woman experiencing it, that she makes the perceiving consciousness Jules'. And then Nadine shoots Jules, an act which does not seem consistent with the character of Nadine as she has been developed through the book. Perhaps only that violent and insane a response to Nadine's own orgasmic frigidity, only that bizarre a denouement, makes Oates feel safe in being so explicit about the agony of Nadine's sexual disappointment. Nadine had to have been mad to have been allowed to express her rage and disappointment about her orgasmic frigidity instead of feeling shame and guilt, all of which she would have had to hide, had she been sane.

This timorousness in describing the existential realities of female life

. . . the various sordid and shocking events of slum life, detailed in other naturalistic works, have been understated here, mainly because of my fear that too much reality would become unbearable.

Unbearable for whom? I would guess unbearable for Miss Oates—a reader can close a book and refuse to contemplate further what becomes unbearable. If Miss Oates finds the sordid realities of slum life too unbearable to record, it would follow that she would find the sordid realities of female life, for females in our culture dwell in the slums of personhood, too unbearable to record also. We see that when "too much" of the "reality" of the condition of women is experienced by her female characters, they have been portrayed as deranged by the experiencing of this reality. This serves a dual purpose for the writer: on the one hand, this insanity serves as a warning to those who might, the author included, examine the reality of the condition of women too closely, and, on the other hand, it serves to divorce these women from all us normal women, so that when we examine the reality of their condition, we are shielded from too great a temptation to identify since they, unlike ourselves, are insane.

This tendency to mask explicit agony with madness is not peculiar to Oates. We see that sexual frigidity in women is almost always dealt with, explored, portrayed as co-existent with madness, homosexuality, "unawakened-ness" (i.e., the implication here being that there is no self-generating female sexuality), or bitchiness (i.e., the implication here being that women derive greater pleasure from withholding from a man the pleasure of sexually satisfying her than they do from being sexually satisfied), or some other form of "unnaturalness" (such as ambition, aggressiveness, creativity, or dissatisfaction with the social/political order she finds herself a part of).

For instance, in Jeanne Rejaunier's *The Beauty Trap*, one of the major female characters is quite explicit about all the failures of technique, the anatomical ignorance, the inconsiderateness, insensitivity, selfishness, ineptness, etc., she has suffered at the hands of men that are no doubt a part of a great many more women's sexual experiences than one would ever guess from a careful reading of all the fiction ever written. But all that this character and the Vassar classics major who runs the stud house have to tell us about female sexual disappointment is undercut by writing that at this point in the book is so bad that the characters become ridiculous and unbelievable. However, the "truth" this woman tells about female experience is even more brutally undercut by her portrayal as an insensitive, greedy, hard woman who discovers at the end of the book that she is a lesbian. The implication of the linking of this type of unpleasant character with unfortunate sexual experiences is that her sexual disappointments are the result of characterological deficiencies rather than sexual politics. The character is created so unsympathetically that readers will be unable to identify with her and at the same time retain any self-esteem.

Women writers seem more willing to take their cues for the portrayal of female sexuality from the latest male psychotherapist or sex manual writer than from their own experiences or the experiences of other women. They are willing enough to present female characters who are sexually unhappy, unfulfilled, disappointed, confused, etc., but the vision of their condition is always filtered through some "attitude" about such "female problems" that exonerated men and isolates woman. Doris Lessing, one of our most highly-praised writers, also tends to mystify female sexuality. In *The Four Gated City*, we are presented with a woman we are encouraged to perceive as insane throughout more than half the book—and accompanying her insanity (we are not told whether this is a result or a symptom of insanity, but that there is a connection between the two is implicit) is frigidity. No matter how much her husband desires her, no matter how long he waits faithfully for her to be "cured" so she can enjoy his embrace she can't stand to have him touch her. The fact that there has already been a child of this marriage would lead us to suspect that the "insane" character has had some unwilling and unpleasant sexual experiences with her husband which we can be sure she did not initiate. And yet despite this evidence of marital rape her husband is portrayed throughout the book as a touching sympathetic person.

In Rona Jaffe's *Away From Home* we find a long and painful account of that kind of female frigidity that arises from a woman's preternaturally extended state of unawakenedness. What this usually means, and means here, is that the "right" man hasn't come into Margie's life yet. She is twenty-five years old and she's never felt "anything" until Mort comes into her life and teaches her to feel. Here we have the old story of woman-as-child, woman-as-student. If we believe what we read in novels, we would never know that "normal" women have sexual feelings without and before the tutelage of the penis.

In the fiction of women writers as well as men writers, female frigidity is always seen as a problem of the individual woman, a personal problem rather than a socio-political problem. The only books I can ever remember reading where there is an attempt to demystify female orgasm are the *Peyton Place* books. Alison spends a weekend with her publisher off at some sort of romantic hide-away and he introduces her to the pleasures of the flesh. She has all along been terribly snowed by him, and when she finally has an orgasm in his bed, she's certain it's love. Then she discovers that he is married and that he thought she knew it and that for him the weekend had a meaning and a value totally different from its meaning for her. She then spends a considerable period of time separating her feelings about sex from her feelings about love, thinking about technique, sexual satisfaction, anatomical ignorance, and good relationships. She is allowed to think all of this through without being portrayed as insane, corrupt, homosexual, or dying of cancer. She is allowed to think it all through and emerges enriched in her understanding of human behavior, human needs, herself, her relationships, and even—taboo of all taboos being broken—her art and her commitment to that art. She emerges from adolescence a strong, sensitive, richly maturing young woman. And you know what the reviewers had to say about all that!

Jessamyn West has written a book, *Leafy Rivers*, in which the major character, a female, is allowed to think about her sex life and reminisce about how she learned about her own anatomy and the techniques for sexual satisfaction and the enrichment of her marital bed adventures. But throughout the whole book, Leafy is lying in a bed, trying to deliver a child who won't come out, being given inaccurate obstetrical directions, and practically dying. One has a sense that the physical torture of the extended labor is somehow a punishment for all that sexual knowledge and pleasure.

Women in fiction only very rarely either deal with (i.e., touch, perform acts upon) their own bodies or experience their bodies directly, unless they are putting the finishing touches on a make-up job or suffering either labor pains or some non-genderally related agony. In fiction female bodies do not belong to females; they are male accessories, male possessions or rejections. Perhaps one of the most significant bits of evidence we have of this state of affairs is the fact that women do not masturbate in fiction. Boys do—we know about the tender narcissistic self-explorations, self-consolations of many a young identity-seeking hero. Old men do—we know what's happening under the hats in the laps of the old men in the front rows of the burlesque shows because we're read about it in fiction. And we even know about the symbolic significance of a middle aged married man's *self-satisfaction*.

It's usually an act of hostility or aggression towards some bitchy female. Or else an act of defiant freedom, an assertion of self-possession. But the closest our young heroine ever gets to self-love is a modest running of her hands over her budding breasts or down the sides of her newly curving body in front of a mirror that tells her that, finally, men will find her desirable. Her appreciation of her physical being is only her anticipation of his potential appreciation.

The invisibility in fiction of the kinds of experiences and realities of women I have been discussing lead to a number of speculations about the kind of people who write fiction, the kinds of pressures they are working under, the schizoid modalities that they work out of.

Many women writers, operating out of the myth of individualism, fail to recognize themselves as members of a discriminated against class or group. Frequently, as was the case with Gertrude Stein, who left the entertainment of the wives and mistresses of the artists who visited her to Alice B. Toklas, separate themselves from other women, thinking of themselves as better than, or different from other women. They identify with men, as we saw Joyce Carol Oates doing earlier. Or they explain away the deviation from the received definition of woman that their writing represents by telling themselves and others that their work isn't something they are serious about. It's just a hobby, they say, or just something they do to earn some badly needed money—both excuses offered time and again by Mary Roberts Rinehart, Faith Baldwin and, I am sure, others. Or else they might say, as do so many, that they aren't "just" women, but persons who are women in whom a young boy is locked up—and it is he who is responsible for the work. Some excuse their unfeminine creativity by explaining it as a baby-substitute. These women don't usually stay around to answer the question of why they don't just have babies instead, unless they are pitiously but triumphantly and definitely sterile. But only rarely and recently have women writers tried to expand the limits of definition or to transcend the definitions altogether.

And when their work fails to be recognized or is criticized harshly, or is recognized only by other women whom the female artists cannot respect because, after all, they are only other women, then the kinds of self-doubt, self-torture they suffer as artists are endless and unanswerable.

There are those female novelists who write about the things that happen in their lives, in their guts, to their bodies as things that happen in their minds. They report on the places that their bodies go as spiritual trips. And when they do this, when they disguise the feeling-location of their reality, they are euphemizing as surely as when they call fucking "sleeping together." This dislocation of feeling and being realities is common in the work of a great many female fiction writers. They would rather be second-rate artists, guilty of sentimentalism, mawkishness, circumlocution, evasiveness, frothiness, anything—rather than open themselves up to the awful charge of "unnatural." They have risked enough by daring to write at all.

Perhaps most tragic are those women writers who do not ever write because they only know how to write about what they know, what is real for them. And what is real for them has never been fictionalized and they are afraid to be the first. They discover about themselves things that violate the cultural notions of "femininity" and they are afraid to expose themselves as "unnatural women."

NOTES

[1]Males suffer similarly from stereotypic mythologies about the nature and essence of masculinity. I do not in this paper intend to depict men as evil victimizers and women as simply victims. Surely it is obvious by now that both men and women are equally enslaved by the Procrustean bed of genderal stereotyping. It is long since that both blacks and whites have come to recognize that racism distorts life, cripples the self, and mystifies reality for whites as well as for blacks. Just so do men and women both wriggle on the end of sexist identity pins. However, as in the case of poor

southern whites who were duped by racist distortions into seeing their "common cause" as one with whites and not as one with poor people, so is it the case with men and sexism. Although we all, men and women, are victimized by the sexist myths of our culture, although we are all puppets, those whose strings make of them potential if not actual lynchers, rapists, *Playboy* executives earning $50,000 a year, etc., tend to be slower to notice let alone protest, their strings, to object to their victimization, than do the puppets being threatened with or actually lynched, raped, sentenced to twelve years of diaper changing, twenty years of typing someone else's letters, etc.

2I will not attempt to deal with the reasons male novelists misrepresent female characters in their work, i.e., create inauthentic females (much has been said about this topic, particularly in relation to the fiction of Hemingway), but I will attempt to deal with this problem in the work of female novelists.

3Such an interpretation sheds a possible new light on the beards so many men are wearing these days. Could it be that they can't face themselves in the mirror any longer?

4For discussion of the relationship between membership in a victimized group, class, or caste, and schizophrenia, see R. D. Laing, *The Divided Self*; Gordon Allport, *The Nature of Prejudice*, chapter nine "Traits Due to Victimization"; Meredith Tax, *Woman and Her Mind*, N.E.F.P.; *The Radical Therapist*, ed. Jerome Agel.

CAROLE ZONIS YEE

WHY AREN'T WE WRITING ABOUT OURSELVES?*

To be Jewish, and a woman, between the ages of, let's say, fifteen and fifty, is not uncommon. And yet it is interesting to observe, as I have recently discovered, that this not uncommon experience seems to be virtually unrecorded in modern fiction or poetry. Sure, we can identify parts of ourselves with some of the fine writing of our sisters—Lessing, Joan Didion, Sylvia Plath, et al.—and share the sense of struggle for female consciousness coming to light more and more as these journals of women's inner selves are published and made available. Nevertheless, there is an inconsistency in seeing that the names of some of the most prominent writers in the women's movement as well as the names of many writers in any women's free newspaper (like *oob*) bear the unmistakable mark of the twelve tribes of Israel, while fictional and poetic representations of Jewish women and their awarenesses are unavailable. Except as the fantasies of Jewish *male* writers, like Malamud, Philip Roth and Saul Bellow. And more, the inconsistency becomes more apparent when we remember that of those academicians teaching literature and writing criticism of literature, many seem to be women and Jewish. And certainly, of the students who ravish and exclaim over modern writings describing their contemporary scene, many are Jewish and women.

Clearly, the modern Jewish woman is *not* just preparing chicken soup in her strict kosher kitchen, saying the blessing over the Sabbath candles, preoccupied with child raising and the Haddassah. No. She is writing articles for the movement, teaching in the highest academies in the

131

land, living in communes, having non-*Yiddishe* babies, and learning the meaning of being a woman and being Jewish on a whole different plane than her grandmother in Poland or on the Lower East Side ever suspected she would have to confront. This modern Jewish woman is active, alive, creative and outspoken. And yet, I repeat, she does not appear to be portraying her struggles and experiences in literary form: novels, plays or poems.

If she wishes to read about and identify with characters in fiction who represent the modern Jewish woman— well, there's Mrs. Portnoy or Brenda Potemkin in Philip Roth. Roth's Jewish women are spoiled and selfish, and they exist to destroy his Jewish male identity. Or there's Helen Bober in Malamud's *The Assistant*, overwrought by deprivation to a bitchy Puritan morality, guided by a latent sensuality in conflict with her "finer mind." In the end, of course, her finer mind wins out and goes to college, but, alas, at the expense of Frank Alpine's masculinity. In other words, if a Jewish woman looks in modern letters for her counterpart, she finds herself portrayed as threatening, destructive, and the keeper of the home with its attendant misery (while impressing upon her men that the world outside is worse!).

I recently read a review of a novel (*An American Girl*, by Patricia Dizenzo) in *Rolling Stone*. The reviewer, Sheila Weller, registered her disappointment with the novel, saying what it was that she expected:

"An American girl in the 1950's, hmmm: one could get a lot of literary mileage out of that. A young female Portnoy, perhaps, collecting autographed glossies of Johnny Ray and plugging herself periodically with a half empty Cutty Sark bottle, then dutifully returning it to the liquor cabinet by cocktail hour." (June 10, 1971, p. 52.)

Weller's remarks made me wonder where are all the Jewish women writers who can tell us the reality of what it feels like to be a woman and Jewish. And I began to imagine characters and plots:

For instance, a young, brilliant, attractive Jewess who sees herself climb to fame and reputation as a university professor, giving speeches at MLA conventions, publishing articles, adored by her students, who is afraid to stay alone at night because women in *her* family are taken better care of than that (and by Jewish husbands, too) and so she makes forbiddingly expensive long distance phone calls all night long. And then begins calling anonymously, the dean of the college, the President of B'nai B'rith, Golda Meir.

Or maybe, a young Jewish Angela Davis, respected for her intelligence and revolutionary zeal, but whose only outlet for her tremendous energy and political genius is to organize Jewish girls at summer camp on the model of the Israeli Women's Army, yearning for a real theatre for her abilities, until when we meet her she is a block parent in Philadelphia, dutifully taking her family to her parents for dinner, every Friday night.

Or a modern Sarah. Devoted mother, wonderful homemaker, good wife who has dreams of love and passion with, of all people, the *goyim* who comes to hang her dining-room drapes, because one time while they measured the window, his hand inadvertently touched her breast and he smiled. And when she lies awake at night, withering under the closeness of her pharmacist husband's body, she knows she's locked in this situation for good, because a nice Jewish girl, a good little *maidel*. . . .

A Jewish woman, no matter how Orthodox, Reform or "assimilated" her home, is taught to believe that her home, children and kitchen are what really matter in this life. Let the world fall apart, like the walls of Babylon, if she can still make a good *knaidlach* there is *always* a future in her children. As long as the dietary laws are followed and the Chanukah candles are lit, God's blessing will fall on the Jews. But above all else, Mama's kitchen must be protected!

But we know that this is no longer the case with many of us. We know that our lives are much more complex,

Americanized and, thank God, rich than Mrs. Portnoy's.
We have discovered other channels for our energy and being
than learning to make jello with suspended peaches and
tyrannizing ourselves and our children. But when we will
begin to express this new life, through novels, films, poetry,
and teach ourselves and each other the meaning of being
a woman and being Jewish, is still an open question.

*From *Off Our Backs*, February-March, 1972. Used by permission.

NINA BAYM

THE WOMEN OF COOPER'S
LEATHERSTOCKING TALES*

"The Women he draws from one model don't vary,"
James Russell Lowell rhymed in *A Fable for Critics*, "All
sappy as maples and flat as a prairie." Estimation of Cooper's seriousness and depth has risen sharply since 1848,
but the view of his women has changed little. The fact
that women are central characters in all the Leatherstocking books is therefore an embarrassment to his critics, who
have contrived various strategies to overlook them. The
leading school of Cooper criticism, focusing on his socio-
political and historical ideas and his instincts for myth-
making,[1] plays down his treatment of women on the
grounds that it represents a genteel, sentimental and trivial
dimension which is not Cooper's fault but the fault of the
genteel, sentimental and trivial women who made up most
of the American reading audience and who had to be satisfied if an author was to sell.[2]
    Freudian analysis, a second major trend in Cooper
criticism, admits women into the core of his work, but
only as projections of the male fears and desires which are
taken to constitute the substance of Cooper's homoerotic
myth of the wilderness.[3] The Freudian criticism, trans-
muting Cooper's universe into its own, has distorted the
meaning of women in the works; the sociopolitical criticism has more simply and deliberately underestimated it.
But to give the women their due importance in the Leatherstocking saga is not automatically to make light of Cooper's achievement. Nor need we claim a skill for Cooper in
feminine portraiture that he obviously did not have, in order to investigate his heroines with seriousness and respect.

135

Might not the neglect of women in his works have been due, at least in some small measure, to the critics' belief that the subject itself was of no importance? I do not in the least wish to deny that Cooper's depiction of women reflects the trivializing and patronizing denigration of the sex which is so marked a feature of 19th century American cultural attitudes.[4] I would argue, however, that the place of women in the Leatherstocking Tales relates directly to Cooper's main themes: contrasting modes of thought as they are brought into play in the establishment of an American civilization. It is not only that the place of women in society is an inseparable part of the social totality—though this is surely true; not only that the way an author places women is a fundamental element in his total vision—though this is true too; it is rather that Cooper himself believes that women are of central social significance. His theme is society, and he defines women as the nexus of social interaction. Therefore women have an important place in his works even when they themselves seem like insignificant beings, or are very crudely drawn by the author.

Cooper's view of society is at once strongly patriarchal in its ethics, and peculiarly anticipatory of some trends in modern anthropological thought in its systematizing.[5] In a basic sense, women are not full members of the societies Cooper depicts; his cultures are composed entirely of males. Women are, however, the chief signs, the language of social communication between males; in the exchange of women among themselves men create ties and bonds, the social structures that are their civilizations. Without women there can be relationships like the friendship of Natty and Chingachgook, profoundly resonant with personal feeling and meaning, and yet entirely without social significance. With women, there are classes, societies, civilization. Though Cooper's women have no power over his men, they are vital for man's civilizations, and thus man has to take them along wherever he goes, and at whatever cost. The chief "statement" of the social language is,

of course, marriage, which is shown in Cooper's Leatherstocking stories as a transaction between males, where the
giving away of women creates a rhetoric of group membership and exclusion. The content of the marriage statement
is deeply conservative: marriage takes place within the
boundaries of the group. Neither extending or modifying
the social structure, it confirms the group's previous membership, and tightens the group's solidarity and exclusive-
ness.

In Cooper's conservative view of society, no person
is a "person" in the romantic or existential sense wherein
he exists for his own ends, and wherein the group's ultimate purpose is to facilitate self-development and fulfillment. On the contrary, the chief "existent" is the group,
and the idea of personhood is only rudimentarily developed. It is largely from a conflict between the social and
romantic senses of "personhood" that a character like
Natty Bumppo draws his continuing strength and interest.
Women, as signs and objects in the society—as the mortar
rather than the bricks of it—are even less persons than men
are, and Cooper's depiction of them is controlled by the
issue of their social use. Marriage rather than love is the
matrix of his "romances," which are not truly romances
because the sentimental interest in the heroine's feelings is
largely absent. Absent, too, is the genteel romancer's guid-
ing faith that marriage is both a personal epiphany and a
social good. Cooper does not dispute this belief; the matter is simply not of interest to him.

Chiefly, Cooper divides women into those who can be
married and those who cannot. One can also distinguish
in his handling of women, as well as in the psychologies of
the women themselves, some vaguely sensed stress between
woman-as-person and woman-as-object. This stress is particularly evident in the contrast between Cora and Alice
Munro (*The Last of the Mohicans*) and between Inez Middleton and Ellen Wade (*The Prairie*). There is no simple
equation between these two aspects of woman's situation

in the Leatherstocking Tales, however. It is not the case, for example, that "persons" are unmarriageable while "objects" are eligible. This is true in the case of the Munro sisters, but an object-woman like Hetty Hutter (*The Deerslayer*) is not marriageable while such persons as Ellen Wade and Mabel Dunham (*The Pathfinder*) are marriageable. Marriageability in fact has little or nothing to do with personhood, since, as suggested, personhood is not a factor recognized in social structure. For this reason attempts to organize Cooper's women according to types, or stereotypes, are more confusing than clarifying.

The Leatherstocking Tales show no particular growth or change in Cooper's views of women, and for efficiency's sake I will take them up in order of the increasing complexity of the depiction of the female situation. *The Pioneers* (1825), possibly because its action is circumscribed by its static setting, possibly because it is the first and least self-conscious of the series, presents its ideas in a particularly elementary form. The heroine, Elizabeth Temple, daughter of Templeton's chief citizen, is a "lady." Unlike many historical members of this class, who achieved a high degree of individuality because of their leisured and cultivated existence, Elizabeth has been designed to embody the type. She has a high degree of moral and aesthetic sensibility and her refinement is exemplified, conventionally enough, in her sensitivity to "sublime" landscape. Her natural generosity and gregariousness have been tempered by an awareness of social distinctions into a generally agreeable and charitable frame of mind. It should not be overlooked, in a historical society where poor health was regularly exhibited, like stigmata, by the bourgeois lady, how insistent Cooper is on the good health and amiability of his heroines regardless of their class status. Though Elizabeth is high-spirited and articulate, the limits of decorum result in a combination of vivacity and shallowness that is, ultimately, profoundly uninteresting. But marriageable girls are not bred to be interesting—that is a quality appropriate for women who must live by their wits; it is precisely the fact about a lady that she does not *have* to depend on her own qualities.

The class hierarchy in Templeton makes Judge Temple and his daughter Elizabeth the only members of the group whose values they are trying to establish in America. Though they have links to an aristocracy on the coast, where Elizabeth has been sent to receive an education suitable to her station, at the fringes of the forest they *are* the aristocracy. Our popular mythology of the rough-hewn pioneer, building his crude dwelling with simple tools and bare hands, is likely to obscure the fact that to Cooper, Judge Temple with his mansion, his architect and his imported trees, is the true pioneer engaged in the most difficult and yet most vital of all pioneering tasks. He is establishing true civilization in the wilderness—that is, himself, his way of life and his values.

Inappropriate as Elizabeth's schooling would appear to be for the difficulties of settlement life, it is part of this pioneering. The survival of a type like her is one test of the ability of high civilization to survive in the wilderness. She is brought up as though she were going to live in a cultivated atmosphere, and her cultivation in a sense imposes such an atmosphere on the frontier. She is brought back from her schooling to grace her father's dwelling as its chief ornament, and to serve him. Far from feeling demeaned by this role of ornamental servant, Elizabeth like all Cooper's daughters takes great pleasure in it. The perfection of the female type at any class level is always one who does willingly what society requires from her. But Elizabeth's purposes are more profound than this: it is her existence that guarantees the formation of an artificial group, a linking of men which is other than the natural family and which, simply because is is *not* natural, is the base of civilization. The linking of men in a common culture is accomplished by women.

Frontier conditions involve, of course, a great scarcity

of eligible suitors, and Cooper invents a most implausible plot to provide one for her. At the same time, the appearance in disguise of the heir to the ousted Tory owner of the estates which are now Temple's makes a certain point. It is Cooper's idea that class lines override political and even religious differences, and the ultimate survival of a class system as such depends on the awareness among aristocrats of this priority. It is proof of Elizabeth's proper breeding that she senses the aristocrat beneath Oliver Edward's pretense of lower-class identity; however, Cooper is at such pains to assure us that Elizabeth, bred as she is, would be incapable of loving a socially unworthy suitor, that he virtually undercuts whatever suspense the disguise plot was intended to create. Because she is a dutiful daughter, however, there is no question of Elizabeth's expressing her love until its consummation in marriage is sanctioned by her father. Filial obedience is the chief requisite quality in a woman whose function is to be given away; in a more general sphere, woman is expected to be dependent on the male sex for direction and decision in her life. In brief, woman is taught to rely on authority, which is embodied in every particular case by the male parent. Insofar as there is any complexity in Elizabeth's situation, it rises from her need to reconcile the incompatible elements of her class-and-caste situation, where she is a member of an inferior sex but a superior class to those males—the disguised Edward Effingham (Oliver Edwards) and the social clown Natty Bumppo—who are perpetually coming to her rescue.

Feminine dependency is acted out in all the Leatherstocking Tales by the rescue of the female from external dangers. Since *The Pioneers* is focused on the threat to civilization posed by the wilderness itself, Elizabeth is saved from such natural hazards as panthers and forest fires. In *The Last of the Mohicans*, second book in the series, Cooper deals at length with the far greater threat posed to a society by competing civilizations, and in this work the women must be saved from the aggressions of members of alien groups. Woman's need for protection does not simply result from her actual physical weakness, though this is the rationalization subscribed to by members of both sexes in this culture. The plain fact is that she is not permitted to protect herself. In return for relinquishing all attempts at independence even to the point of forgoing self-defense, woman has the right to expect the continual protection of men and to demand unremitting vigilance from them on her behalf. Thus there are definitions of both womanhood and manhood implicated in the chivalric code. The hypothesis of woman's feebleness on which the code is based is not tested in the Leatherstocking series. Indian women fend for themselves and do quite well at it; white women appear in the forest so weighted down with the appurtenances of their cultural role—heavy veils, cumbersome and constricting clothing, satin slippers—that self-defense is out of the question. White women are men's burdens, but these burdens are cherished by men whose manhood is predicated on the successful defense of them. Natty Bumppo is as much bound up in this cultural network as the other white males, his celibacy notwithstanding, for he is chiefly valued by civilization for his skill at transporting the feeble ones safely through dangerous or unfamiliar terrain, and this skill is an important source of his pride and self-respect.

In *The Pathfinder* (1840) Cooper adds to a conventional and civilized definition of Natty's manhood by giving him a passionate, though unrequited, love. Because of this romance, the book fits very poorly into the logic of the series as it has been developed in the criticism, and it is generally omitted in critical discussions.[6] It is more responsible, I believe, to take the saga as we find it. In *The Pathfinder* Cooper uses Natty's capacity to experience romantic love as an indication of his civilized sensibility. His love is in part a recognition of superior qualities in the female which his rough and elemental existence might have been supposed to unfit him to perceive—her refinement, delicacy, gentleness, spirituality—all products of civiliza-tion. Cooper stresses this point by giving Mabel Dunham other suitors whose feelings for her are expedient or crude. Romantic love is, moreover, a fiction whereby a weaker and inferior creature is invested with exalted qualities by the transforming imagination of the lover. Romantic love, like the chivalry with which it is associated, is sign of a noble spirit, for it is a courteous pretense by which the stronger being submits his will to the weaker rather than enforcing his will on her. The clear opposite to this is found in the behavior of Indian men to their wives; these strong men simply compel their women to labor for them; they treat them indifferently and discard them if another woman catches their fancy. Such behavior is evidence to Cooper of the over-all lower quality of Indian to western civilization, however admirable certain Indians or certain Indian traits may be. One might sum this all up by saying that the very peculiar position of woman in western soci-ety as the impedestaled feeble one, a position which clearly requires leisure and luxury to support it and is therefore available to very few even in European culture—that posi-tion is for Cooper one of the chief claims to superiority that Europe has over the rest of the world. However in-efficient or absurd these fragile burdens may appear in the wilderness, to alter the position of women would be to modify the civilization to a point where it would no longer be as worthy of preservation or establishment.

For women love has different significance. It is not a sign of magnanimity in her, since she loves the man for traits he really has, and love is a necessity of her nature. As a natural emotion it is not so ennobling as the same emotion is in the man, for whom it is less natural. We might note here two kinds of confusion in Cooper's views about woman. For one thing, he really does not believe that woman's "superior" qualities are finally superior; or at least he believes it only intermittently. More significant is his uncertainty about whether the civilized woman is the natural woman, finally recognized for what she is and given her rightful place as an idol worthy of man's devotion and sacrifice, or whether in contrast she is an artifact, manufactured or cultivated by society as an expression of its high degree of civilization. In any event, when Cooper tries to show that Mabel is a truly noble woman, he avoids these confusions by giving her qualities which transcend her sex: stamina, boldness, resourcefulness, enterprise. In other words, he gives her the virtues of a man.[7] The chief action of the book is her holding of a stockade which her father has unwisely abandoned, against a combined force of Indians, French and traitors, with the help only of Dew-of-June, an Indian woman. (It's a minor point, but worthy of note, that the women cross cultural divisions with bonds of sympathy and liking much more easily than the men do.)

Intrepid behavior of this sort would be unthinkable for a "lady"; it would be equally unthinkable that Natty with his strong sense of social place might permit himself to love a lady. Mabel, therefore, belongs to the lower classes, but she has a refinement above her class which has been created in her by association in childhood (as a "humble companion") with ladies. In her the delicacy of the upper class blends with a yeoman sturdiness, and she might be seen as representing Cooper's attempt to mediate not only between the advantages and disadvantages of "female" qualities, but also between his avowed dedication to aristocracy, and some lurking respect for the American freeman.

The circumstances of Mabel's upbringing have improved but not declassed her; it is a paradox of her refinement that she is above any vulgar aspiration to rise above her circumstances. She cannot marry Natty, however, because he is declassed. The circumstances of his life have put him entirely outside society, and the institution of marriage has therefore no use for him. The purpose of marriage is to perpetuate social groups; only those who are members of a group may marry within it, and since Natty belongs to no group it follows that he may not marry. At a number of points in *The Pathfinder* and again in *The Deerslayer* it is suggested that the appropriate wife for Natty would be an Indian girl. Since race lines are the only ones more firm than class lines, this suggestion functions mainly to emphasize the social irrelevance of Natty Bumppo. His own usually acute self-perceptions fail him when he aspires to Mabel's hand, but this is not so much his fault as the fault of Sgt. Dunham, who has forgotten his class responsibilities when he selected Natty as a son-in-law. The general incompetence of Dunham, who flounders throughout the book and finally bumbles into his own death, points up very sharply a motif which is latent in *The Pioneers* and which is found to some degree in all the Leatherstocking Tales: the motif of the inadequate father. Under the stress conditions, and particularly the isolation, of the frontier, those who are supposed to maintain civilization prove unequal to their obligations. The incompetence of fathers is sharply contrasted on the one hand with the sound social instincts of the young, and on the other with the harmonious functioning of the tribal structures of the Indians.

For Mabel, the dereliction of her father untwines and opposes two moral stands which every daughter must suppose inseparable—the obligation to love and marry appropriately, and the obligation to marry according to one's father's choice. The latter obligation takes precedence, and Mabel prepares therefore to make a match which she rightfully dreads. The death of her father liberates her, but not directly. No woman in the Leatherstocking Tales belongs to herself (Judith Hutter in *The Deerslayer* possibly excepted). Woman is always subject to man's disposition of her, and as Judith Hutter's case shows, the unowned woman is considered by man to be common property. Therefore, when Dunham is killed Mabel is effectively inherited by Natty Bumppo who, as her betrothed, takes over her guardianship. In this position of responsibility Natty's clear sight returns, and he hands Mabel over to Jasper Western, an eligible suitor who has been fretting impatiently in the wings of the story since its opening chapter. This peculiar transaction makes sense only if one recognizes how marriage is an interaction between men where women are simply the exchanged goods.

The Last of the Mohicans (1826) introduces the duality of dark and fair heroines which occurs as well in The Deerslayer and The Prairie. The presence of contrasting heroines, of course, increases the possibilities of complexity in the treatment of women, and as a formal device is found in countless works of 19th and 20th century fiction. So basic is it that it seems almost to be a structural property of the genre quite anterior to any meaning which may be attached to it. It is a pity that this device has been subsumed by Freudian criticism, for its uses are far more various than that theory permits us to see and there are many different kinds of contrasts between heroines for which it is employed. Approaching The Last of the Mohicans along the route laid out by Leslie Fiedler, we may well fail to notice Cooper's special handling of the stereotype. Cora, the dark heroine, is not in any meaningful sense a bad woman. On the contrary she is very good; encomiums to her goodness recur throughout the text. She presents no threat, moreover, to any character in the novel; the pervasive anxiety that the presence of the dark lady is supposed to arouse is entirely absent.[8]

The main point seems to be that in spite of her superior qualities—her kindness, courage, modesty, maturity, thoughtfulness, steadfastness, self-reliance, nobility of soul, resourcefulness and very great beauty—Cora cannot be married. Because her mother was partly black, Cora is hopelessly spoiled. Her "blackness" is not the cause of her many virtues, but is the cause of all these virtues counting for nothing. Cora is well aware of her tragedy, and her sense of fatality gives her a seriousness entirely lacking in Cooper's more fortunate young girls. One such fortunate young girl is her sister Alice, unquestionably the silliest of Cooper's heroines. In Alice the training for uselessness has been carried to an extreme that even Cooper finds amusing. Helpless, dependent and infantile, she is certain to faint whenever any situation of stress arises, so that in her case the concept of woman as package becomes literally expressed. Yet, to Duncan Heyward this is woman as she should be; he is proud to haul his "precious burden" about, he manfully supports her "infantile dependency." It is clear that his sense of manliness is enhanced by her fragility. Yet one should not make the mistake of thinking that he shrinks from Cora because her strength threatens him. He shuns her simply for her impure blood. The girls both represent acceptable, if contrasting, developments of the "lady." Cora's tragedy is not that she is unladylike, but that her exclusion from the prerogatives of her class is gratuitous: blood, not character or breeding, is fate.

In a second significant way her blood affects her history. It determines the nature of her beauty, which is such as to make her attractive to men of other races. Although she herself is untouched by her kind of attractiveness, remaining decorous, pure and chastely in love with Duncan Heyward throughout, it is the source of powerful magnetism to others. Here, indeed, there is meaning to the idea of Cora as threat. She threatens no particular individual, but the whole system of proprieties between men on which civilization rests. A woman of such attraction is more highly charged than is convenient for those who must protect, control and dispose of her. The quotidian transaction of marriage requires a commoner coin. Alice, in this sense, is unquestionably a "better" woman than her sister just because she is so ordinary, so unimpressive. Cora's blackness makes her on the one hand a counterfeit coin which "passes" but is really fraudulent, and on the other a gem too rare and extraordinary for the purposes she is designed to fulfill. She is both below and above her function. Cooper is here reaching for a conclusion which is postulated in many theories of social origins: the idea that there can be no civilization without the repression and control of "female sexuality"; i.e., the capacity of the female to arouse the male. Cooper is very far, however, from acknowledging that women possess sexual drives themselves. Even Judith Hutter, his one bad woman, is motivated in her fall by a desire for finery and a better life rather than by a voluptuous nature. Her attraction to Natty, which goes far to redeem her, consists of an intellectual and spiritual appreciation of his noble qualities.

Judith Hutter is the dark heroine of *The Deerslayer* (1841), a book which at first glance looks like a simple exaggeration of the duality in *The Last of the Mohicans*. Cora's strong-mindedness has been intensified to the point of rebelliousness and bitterness in Judith while Alice's passivity has become feeblemindedness in Hetty. But Cora's leading quality is her purity, Alice's her predictability. In contrast, Judith is lax and Hetty is erratic, so comparisons are misleading. The crucial thing about both Hutter girls is their lack of social position. They are the daughters of an outcast, which is bad enough in terms of their marriage potentiality; but before the book is over we learn that they are in fact the illegitimate daughters of someone unknown, and that Thomas Hutter married their mother after the children were born. Of what society might these girls hope to be a part? Together these girls form a single entity, "the unmarriageable," and they are contrasted to Hist, the Indian maiden whom Chingachgook has come to wed. The capture, rescue and defense of Hist make up the romantic cable of this novel; to center a chivalric romance on either Hutter sister would simply be indecorous. The relationship of Hist and Chingachgook goes far to define the young Indian as a noble savage; chivalric love is particularly ennobling in an Indian.

Of course we cannot overlook the potential romance

between Deerslayer and Judith. Much has been written about this episode, for by concentrating on Natty's rejection of Judith and ignoring his rejection by Mabel, it has been possible to construct a myth of the Leatherstocking which is much more congenial to the 20th century critics' obsession with homoerotic purity than are the actual materials of the saga as Cooper wrote it. But Cooper's own audience, reading the books as they appeared, would recall *The Pathfinder* (published just the year before) and contrast his passion in the one case with his reluctance in the other. Judith, as Natty several times observes, does not know her place, or refuses to accept it. Her love of finery is symptomatic of desires for things which she is not socially entitled to have and therefore ought not to want. Her sexual fall is related to her social dissatisfaction, she went with officers for economic reasons rather than sentimental ones. Moreover, she has given *herself* away, and for selfish purposes. The conservative Natty is attracted by her spirit and beauty but profoundly alienated by her radical willfulness. He is not, D. H. Lawrence notwithstanding, afraid of her. And a modern reader who is not afraid of her might well find her the most interesting of the woman characters: restless, intelligent, experienced, impatient, moody, and yet with keen sensibilities and a sharp appreciation of high moral qualities (this is evidenced by her attraction to Natty, and contrasted with her dull-witted sister's animal impulse toward Hurry Harry), she combines enough qualities to take on the semblance of a rich life. She must surely be the prototype for Hester Prynne and Zenobia. Her decision when Deerslayer turns her down to go off to Scotland and be an officer's mistress puts her in the tradition of Moll Flanders and Becky Sharp—women who manipulate their opportunities in a man's world.

Although Natty does not see it, Cooper certainly recognizes a certain kinship between Judith and his hero. The attraction between them, articulated on her side and denied on his, derives from the fact that after all they *are* members of the same class, those whom Crèvecoeur called offcasts, "a kind of forlorn hope, preceding by ten or twelve years the most respectable army of veterans which come after them." Even in their departures from the sexual norm these two resemble one another; since their initial positions are not identical, sexual freedom in the woman really corresponds to chastity in the male. The union between them is symbolized in that extraordinary transaction wherein Judith gives Natty the rifle—Killdeer—which is to be his magic weapon and which retroactively enriches the whole Leatherstocking legend, for Natty is now seen to owe his potency not merely to his chastity, but also to a woman's gift.

The Prairie (1827) also gives us difficulty when approached by the avenue of the dark/fair stereotype. Two problems in particular confront us. Both Inez, the dark exotic, and Ellen, the homegrown plant, are "good" heroines, so that as in *The Last of the Mohicans* the fundamental dark/fair = bad/good contrast does not hold. Further, although Inez is conventionally foreign and sexual, she is also passive, dependent, artless, girlish and innocent, thereby amalgamating qualities which are stereotypically opposed. Ellen is too strong-willed and independent to be "fair" but also too innocent, honest and open to be "dark." The operational contrast—i.e., that which has results in the story—is between passivity and activity, dependence and independence. The core vision of the aristocratic woman as she who is carried about, she who is transferred among men, is clearly represented in the abducted Inez, who spends virtually the entire novel reclining on her couch within her wheeled tent. The vision is intensified by the concealing draperies and veils which remind us of all the strongly patriarchal cultures that keep their women veiled and secluded. The veils can also be interpreted as wrappings, which refer to the idea of woman as transportable package, as object. Hawthorne's Priscilla, another wrapped package, comes to mind here.

Inez is emotional and extremely attractive, yet physically tiny, mentally childlike and thoroughly dependent on men. Profoundly religious, her religion consists in doing what her priest tells her. She is a complete image of the superrefined, artificial woman bred to be man's object and plaything. In contrast to Cora, whose attractiveness to alien tribes lay in her hint of likeness to them, Inez attracts because she is so unlike anything that primitive men with their untutored, workaday women have ever seen. She is, completely, a work of art, a cultural artifact. The abduction plot in which she figures, preposterous from so many angles, iterates the idea that she is a piece of portable, appraisable property. Yet, if she is perfected woman, she is also overbred: too exquisite, too desirable, to function properly. She requires too much surveillance, takes too great a toll from the culture she is supposed to enhance.

From this point of view she would seem to represent a kind of decadence, not within herself but within the society that has produced her. Some critics feel that in this story Cooper divides the French-Catholic from the English-Protestant strains in the European tradition, and suggests that the one is unsuitable for Americans, the other desirable, But since Cooper unites Inez with great fanfare to the scion of his favorite Anglo-American family, the Effingham-Temples, we cannot accept this interpretation. Whatever decadence Inez represents derives from the aristocratic tradition as a whole. And indeed in this novel Cooper sets the aristocracy alongside of other sorts of social organizations, and at least considers the possibility that another kind of polity might be better for Americans than a rigid class hierarchy. For while Inez is confined to her couch and tent, shut away from the eyes of men, a pearl of great price and yet an existential vacuum, Ellen Wade is very much in evidence, bounding about the prairie like a young antelope, strong, healthy, busy, noisy, sneaking away from the encampment at night to meet her lover, minding the battalion of little Bush children, talking back to men, and—unprecedented behavior for a Cooper heroine—actually brandishing a loaded weapon. Here, most unexpectedly in a Cooper cast of characters, is the "new woman," woman in a democracy, woman as a free spirit.

Ellen is not the only cultural contrast to Inez. Once again Cooper gives us an abused Indian wife, to remind us of the low caliber of Indian culture. Another "new" character is Hester Bush, the only mother in all the Leatherstocking Tales, an impressive, strong woman, full partner to Ishmael Bush. Participating in the group's labors and in the group's decisions, outspoken and strongly emotional, she earns full human status in the clan; the usual comparisons of the Bush group to an Old Testament patriarchy are for this reason in error. It is commonly theorized that the patriarchy emerges in history when questions of property and succession make it imperative that men fully possess the women who are to give them heirs. The unpropertied Bush clan represents a pre-patriarchal form where woman is wife, in contrast to the true patriarchy (Cooper's common social form) where woman is epitomized as the daughter—i.e., Inez. Ellen Wade, neither wife nor daughter, seems to me to represent a post-patriarchal social form, and thus stands not between but in advance of the other two cultural organizations.[9]

The striking fact about Ellen in this view is that she is fatherless and that it doesn't matter. In a democracy, it would seem, people are not subject to their fathers; they are not obliged to perpetuate groups; they define and express themselves, and only the "now" of their existence has import. In the absence of fathers and all that they imply, woman becomes a different sort of human being. Inez and Ellen indeed, seem like members of two different species. Ellen is an entirely new, unprecedented kind of social being. She is the first heiress of all the ages. Her romance with Paul Hover is the only true love story in the whole series, developed with reference to the feelings of the lovers themselves and with almost no concern for external pressures. Paul has followed Ellen onto the prairie to rescue her, but he is not going to deliver her to anybody or to "claim" her as his own. Since Ellen is only nominally under the protection of Ishmael Bush she is really free to go whenever she makes up her mind to do so. Leaving the Bush tribe thus becomes her moral decision—virtually the only moral decision that a woman in the Leatherstocking Tales is called upon to make.

The democracy, then, despite its lack of refinements that requires Ellen to be placed as Inez's attendant, would seem to be the answer to a dark heroine's dilemma. Its conditions take much of the onus away from her because her qualities imply no threat, and this is because no structure exists for her to threaten. Ellen need not conceal her attractiveness, because attractiveness is no longer so highly charged a quality; she is able to be openly affectionate to her suitors, because to be so takes no prerogative away from the male; her origins—the all-important question for establishing any heroine in her patriarchal place—are immaterial. The reduced importance of fathers implies the reduced importance of marriage, and this opens a whole new sort of life for woman, and creates an entirely new sort of woman.

How does Cooper feel about this free woman? Or about Cora, his condemned and yet guiltless dark lady? Or Judith, his brilliant, bitter social castaway? He feels about them, I suspect, much as he does about Natty Bumppo or Chingachgook: ambivalently. Committed to a conservative, stratified view of society; convinced that societies preserved themselves intact or not at all, he had to discard these characters. Yet his imagination peopled the asocial space with them, his more memorable creations. The conception of a flexible social structure evaded him; in every book his rigid hierarchical view of society eclipses the romantic sympathies which he embodied in loners and outcasts. Only in Ellen Wade and Paul Hover do we get a hint

that a liberated human being might be the center of a
viable social order; otherwise, in the Leatherstocking Tales,
order is achieved only at the cost of a social submission
that falls with particular completeness and severity on the
women.

NOTES

[1] The best single work on Cooper in this vein is James Gross-
man, *James Fenimore Cooper* (New York: William Sloane, 1949),
still unsuperseded as a full-length study. Important interpretations
of Cooper as mythologist and historical thinker in the Leatherstocking Tales are to be found in Roy Harvey Pearce, "The Leatherstocking Tales Re-examined" (1947), reprinted in *Historicism Once More*
(Princeton: Princeton Univ. Press, 1969), and *The Savages of America* (Baltimore: Johns Hopkins Press, 1953); Henry Nash Smith,
Virgin Land (Cambridge: Harvard Univ. Press, 1950); R. W. B.
Lewis, *The American Adam* (Chicago: Univ. of Chicago Press,
1955); A. N. Kaul, *American Vision: Actual and Ideal Society in
Nineteenth-Century Fiction* (New Haven: Yale Univ. Press, 1963);
Edwin Fussel, *Frontier: American Literature and the American
West* (Princeton: Princeton Univ. Press, 1965); John Lynen, *The De-
sign of the Present* (New Haven: Yale Univ. Press, 1969).

[2] The facile blaming of female writers and readers for everything wrong with the 19th century American literary situation
would be amusing were it not so seriously and pervasively offered as
scholarly explanation. From Hawthorne to Fiedler, the lady scrib-
bler or the lady reader (box of chocolates by her side) has been a
favorite scapegoat. Investigations of the 19th century literary situation free of sexual prejudice are badly needed.

[3] The chief self-styled Freudian interpretations are those of D.
H. Lawrence, *Studies in Classic American Literature* (New York:
Thomas Seltzer, 1923); Leslie Fiedler, *Love and Death in the Ameri-
can Novel* (New York: Criterion Books, 1960); and Joel Porte, *The
Romance in America* (Middletown, Conn.: Wesleyan Univ. Press,
1969).

[4] The recent proliferation of books about women has added
enormously to our understanding of myth, culture, society and literature, and created a firm base for further work; the field of woman's
history is mostly empty still. A new book by Page Smith, despite
some fatuous chapters on woman's nature, makes a beginning. Smith
asserts that the situation of the American woman deteriorated in the
late 18th and early 19th centuries as a one-class, small-town society

gave way to a stratified urban one, with a corresponding change in values from Puritan to commercial (*Daughters of the Promised Land* [Boston: Little, Brown, 1970], 57-76).

[5]For examples of such thinking, see Claude Levi-Strauss, *Structural Anthropology* (New York: Basic Books, 1963): Robin Fox, *Kinship and Marriage* (Baltimore: Penguin Books, 1967); Jacques Ehrmann, ed., *Structuralism* (Garden City, N. Y.: Double-day Anchor Books, 1970), pp. 31-99.

[6]An exception is Porte's *The Romance in America*, which interprets Natty's proposal to Mabel as a revenge or punishment inflicted on her for her sexual attractiveness by the Puritanical or celibate Natty. This is ingenious, but I think not supported by Cooper's rhetoric, which is conventionally romantic in the extreme.

[7]Tomboy heroines always embody this truth: that the human virtues are masculine ones.

[8]A class of graduate students of both sexes discussing this novel recently agreed unanimously that Cora was a "misfit," not a threat. The main emotion she aroused—insofar as she was felt as a real person at all—was pity.

[9]Henry Nash Smith in his introduction to the Rinehart edition of *The Prairie* sets out a scheme wherein the American continent is seen as recapitulating in reverse the various cultural stages of man. The aristocracy is the highest and most recent, while both the Bush clan and the Indian tribes are versions, bad and good, of the ancient, nomadic tribal system. Paul and Ellen are identified as a transitional structure, but the structure is given no name which suggests that they do not fit the scheme. As I have suggested, the Indians and the Bush group are not strictly comparable; nor do I see any way by which Ellen and Paul are actually conveying or modifying traits of the Bush group so that they will evolve into traits of the Middleton group.

LINDA RAY PRATT

THE ABUSE OF EVE BY THE NEW WORLD ADAM

A number of recent feminist critics have indicated the two dimensional nature of women in the nineteenth-century American novel.[1] Their work leaves little doubt that characterization in the American novel has often denied women the emotional, moral, and intellectual complexity of fully defined human beings, and that the role women have played in the American novel as a whole has been overshadowed by the male heroes. The failure of nineteenth-century American culture to produce women novelists of the stature of Jane Austen or George Eliot is again obvious. The reasons which may explain these facts are not yet so clear. Part of the explanation no doubt lies in the answers offered by such generalized studies as Kate Millett's *Sexual Politics*, or Carolyn Heilbrun's forthcoming *Androgyny: A Literary Essay*. From the standpoint of literary criticism, however, such explanations as "patriarchy" or "anti-androgynous" "male-fantasy" novels,[2] or any of several other offerings, are often unsatisfying and occasionally inaccurate.

Two reasons stand out for the inadequacy of this criticism. First, assumptions regarding the two dimensional nature of women in certain novelists often ignore the fact that the male characters in those novels may suffer the same lack of fully human delineation. This condition is especially true in the nineteenth-century novel where, with the exception of Henry James, characters are often more abstractly symbolic than humanly detailed. Richard Chase, in defining the American novel as a "romance," observes that characters become "somewhat abstract and ideal," "a function of plot," and that the whole work veers freely "toward mythic, allegorical, and symbolistic forms."[3] Critics who slight this general characteristic of American novels and who proceed to criticize the novelists for their "refusal to allow full humanity to women"[4] are less than entirely convincing.

The second shortcoming of some recent criticism is in analyses and interpretations which depart widely from the context of both the understood critical vocabulary, and the controlling worlds of the novels themselves. Such criticism extracts from the novel the image of a two-dimensional woman and then proceeds to measure her by such innovative terminology as "patriarchy" or "anti-androgyny," or even "Galetea." Here the chief thrust of the criticism is to illuminate certain societal attitudes toward women rather than the function of women characters within the context of a specific novel.

As feminist critics of literature, we must now take our new understanding of women back into the works themselves and re-examine the characters within the controlling values of the novel. My paper proposes to look briefly at several major women characters in Cooper, Hawthorne, and James in terms of the ubiquitous Edenic myth which has traditionally been of such importance to our critical thinking about the American novel. My comments are, on this occasion, suggestive rather than detailed, and my purpose is to advance a critical feminist approach to American literature that will reveal more accurately the nature of female characters within the world of the novels, as well as perhaps suggest the attitudes of the authors toward women in nineteenth-century America.

If, as many have suggested, Cooper, Hawthorne, and James are not narrow Edenic ideologues preaching the inviolable innocence of the American Adam, we cannot safely assume that their light-dark women characters represent a rigid dualism of good and evil. Commentary indicates that many readers find Hester Prynne far more attrac-

tively human than any of the men surrounding her; that
Zenobia controls our interest in the end of *The Blithedale
Romance*; that Miriam is singularly more real than any of
her companions in *The Marble Faun*. Even in Cooper,
many find Judith Hutter more vitally alive than the
mythic Leatherstocking, or that Elizabeth Temple is the
most vivacious of *The Pioneers*. James, of course, reserves
the greatest moral triumphs for women and leaves to men
such roles as the naively egotistical Christopher Newmen,
or the bumbling Lambert Strether. So general a response
can hardly be a matter of perversity and eccentricity on the
part of readers. The authors themselves must have some
hand in evoking these feelings for the women characters.

The interpretation of Edenic myth often subverts the
traditional Fortunate Fall, since the fall is necessary preparation for a higher, purer state. Such a subversion of God's
plan makes meaningless whatever virtues an unfallen Adam
may possess, but also robs Eve of any purpose. Cooper
and Hawthorne use the pure and impure women to represent the pre- and post-lapsarian Eve. The pre-lapsarian Eve can
never enter the world of experience and be humanized by
worldly contact. Even the maternal role is ruled out since,
as Hawthorne tells us, innocence dies of a blood stain. The
pre-lapsarian Eve is necessarily a static and abstract companion to the unfallen Adam. The post-lapsarian Eve has
been humanized by the experience of evil, but she is rejected by the Adamic hero who must protect his innocence. She is further ostracised by a society absorbed in
its own Edenic illusions. Woman, in this circumstance, is
damned if she doesn't and damned if she does, since the
unfallen Adam can have no use for her except as he constantly reaffirms his own static and abstract nature through
a perpetual rejection of her knowledge.

Viewed in the mythic context which dominates these
novels, the women characters who are post-lapsarian Eves
often emerge as the most human figures of all. The role of
women in Cooper, Hawthorne, and James appears to be in-

extricably bound by the degree to which the novelist is imprisoned by Edenic myth. Thus, the freer the novelist is from the attractions of Edenic innocence, the greater the measure of human status afforded the women characters. James, who most completely rejects the appeal of an Adamic American, creates the kind of fully defined woman who most nearly approaches the level of Eliot's Dorothea Brook. The escape from the Garden into the fallen world means woman's release from symbolic abstraction into the condition of humanity.

Fenimore Cooper's Natty Bumppo is perhaps the clearest archetypal American Adam, but Natty can only retain his innocence through retaining his literal virginity. Cooper's conception of Natty is not without its ambiguities and ironies, however. David Noble has argued that "the Leatherstocking tales are an allegorical attack on the American Adam. . . ."[5] "Allegorical" may imply too conscious a purpose and design, but certainly such novels as *The Deerslayer* illustrate many ironic qualifications as to the value of Edenic innocence. The pale, simple-minded Hetty Hutter and the brunette, mysterious Judith represent the pre-lapsarian and the post-lapsarian Eve. Although Natty's judgments are clear and firm, Cooper's attitude is more complex. Hetty is "gentle," "feminine," "right-feeling," and "sinless," but she is also "feeble-minded" to the point of being destructive. Her simple-minded charm endangers the lives of those around her and ultimately causes her own death. In contrast is Judith, who, although she is beautiful, intelligent, spirited, and morally complex, knows too much of the material and social world to be acceptable to Deerslayer. Noble calls her "the American Eve":

She too is her father's daughter, not the child of nature. Hutter has fled his past as a pirate, but this frontier body of water has not washed away his sinfulness which has been inherited by his beautiful daughter.[6]

In the terms used by R. W. B. Lewis in *The American*

Adam, Judith exists in time, in place, and in experience.[7] To maintain his Adamic nature, Natty must escape her seductions into the world of virgin men and virgin land. Ironically, the sexual celibacy which Natty imposes on himself is the key to maintaining his special variety of manhood. In refusing Judith's proposal of marriage, Natty justifies his isolate life of warrior as "both manful and honorable."[8] The anti-life values of war, isolation, and sexual denial become the elements of the definition of ultimate manhood.

Nina Baym has said that "Cooper divides women into those who can be married and those who cannot,"[9] but Natty exists outside both circles. The truth is that Natty cannot marry any woman if he is to retain his Adamic identity. Natty's refusal to consummate the union of Adam with a fallen Eve destroys the conventional pattern of moral progress in the fortunate fall. Natty is doomed to the perpetual flight from his own humanity, and Judith is left with no acceptable function. Without the companionship of a fallen Adam, Judith's moral meaning is lost and the purpose of her existence frustrated. Her fate is the debasement of her sexual love.

Natty's innocence is, in fact, analogous to the arrested development of the pre-lapsarian Eve. Hetty and Natty share the virtues of simplicity, honesty, and goodness, but their virtues leave them unable to cope with the life of the world. Lewis accuses Hetty of "a self-delusive helplessness; a half-witted conviction of universal goodness, which exposes her to every physical and moral danger and also kills her."[10] Yet in *The Pioneers* Natty, too, seems helpless and simple. Only through the helpfulness of such worldly-wise figures as Judge Temple does the aging Adam survive to seek yet another Edenic frontier. In *The Prairie* the octogenarian Natty is so far removed from the life of men as to dwell alone in the empty hills without even a roof over his head. His "Pup" is his closest companion, and his "adopted" Indian son his nearest human relation.[11]

This unnamed Natty is the apotheosis of the mythic, iso-late Adam. Only in such a woman as Judith, who fought against self-delusion and sought the life of the world, does Cooper achieve a human character.

Women in Hawthorne are the source of an even more intense contradiction, and they have been the subject of numerous critical interpretations.[12] Hawthorne reserves the "higher innocence" for his post-lapsarian Eves, but the pre-lapsarian figures are the only ones who find happiness. Perhaps because of Hawthorne's responses to the attraction of naive innocence, the Hildas and Priscillas find joy in life, although the Miriams and Zenobias earn the higher inno-cence. Hawthorne's intellectual understanding of the For-tunate Fall is explicit. He writes in *The Marble Faun*:

> Is sin, then—which we deem such a dreadful blackness in the Universe—is it, like Sorrow, merely an element of human education, through which we struggle to a higher and purer state than we could otherwise have attained? Did Adam fall, that we might ultimately rise to a far loftier paradise than his?[13]

The figures of Hilda and Miriam in *The Marble Faun* are Hawthorne's most direct treatment of the pale-dark dichotomy within the terms of the fortunate fall. Hilda, a New England paleface who dresses in white, lives in a dove tower above the ancient corruption of Rome. Miriam, of mysterious origin, dark, and with a secret sorrow, "had great apparent freedom of intercourse; her manners were so far from evincing shyness that it seemed easy to become acquainted with her, and not difficult to develop a casual acquaintance into intimacy" (p. 21). Hilda's insistence on maintaining her innocence comes, however, at the cost of her human compassion. When, literally after the fall of the Capuchin, Miriam comes to Hilda for comfort, she is re-jected. She asks for Hilda's compassion and friendship on the basis of her womanhood:

> "I am a woman, as I was yesterday; endowed with the same truth of nature, the same warmth of heart, the same genuine and earnest love, which you have always known in me." (p. 208)

Hilda rejects Miriam in order to preserve her white-robed innocence, but the rejection places Hilda outside humanity and in the ironic "innocence" that, in its mercilessness, is the worst of sins. The inhuman cruelty of Hilda's compromised innocence is exemplified by her white-black domino costume in the carnival scene which closes the book. Although Kenyon earlier argued for "a mixture of good . . . in things evil," Hilda's insistence on "only one right and one wrong" (p. 383, 384) frustrates the wisdom he might have won from knowing the fallen Miriam. As a weak and unsure Adam, Kenyon disavows belief in the fortunate fall and turns to his pre-lapsarian Eve to guide him back to the Edenic world: "Were you my guide, my counselor, my inmost friend, with that white wisdom which clothes you as a celestial garment, all would go well. Oh, Hilda, guide me home!" (p. 461). Hawthorne's distaste for Kenyon is amusingly obvious when, in the midst of the carnival gaity, Kenyon is struck with a cauliflower; Miriam's accusation is, however, the more serious one: "You are yourself unkind, (though you little think how much so,) . . ." (p. 447).

The moral and intellectual transformation possible through embracing the post-lapsarian Eve is evident in the case of Donatello. Prior to committing his life to his love for Miriam, Donatello was a charmingly innocent and simple-minded pet. His passion for Eve "kindled him into a man; it . . . developed within him an intelligence" (p. 172). The murder of the Capuchin weds a now fallen Adam and Eve in a stance that is both guilty and heroic, agonizing and rapturous. The journey to higher innocence is a movement back to the original self, but with the depth and experience that defines soul and makes sense of human suffering.[14] For Miriam, it brings a release from the empty loneliness of her mysterious and isolating past. Her passions, not the stereotyped moral blandness of Hilda, prove to be the redemptive force for both herself and her Adamic companion. The extent to which society rejects the fallen pair is a measure of its lack of wisdom and compassion, a theme Hawthorne develops more emphatically in *The Scarlet Letter.*

In *The Blithedale Romance* Hawthorne's subject is the fate of the post-lapsarian Eve whose Adam refuses the saving embrace. The judgment against Zenobia is that she is a woman, and "womanliness incarnated" is sacrificed before the "monster self" of a self-deceptive Adam. As Nina Baym says, "She is a depiction of the eternal feminine as earthy, maternal, domestic, natural, sensual, brilliant, loving, and demanding, and is described mainly in images of softness, radiance, warmth, and health, none of which are even slightly ambivalent or ambiguous in their emotional import."[15] Henry James calls her "the nearest approach that Hawthorne has made to the complete creation of a *person.*"[16] Yet her fate is to be flung away as "a broken tool" by Hollingsworth, or to be transformed from a woman "into a work of art" by the frightened eye of Coverdale.

Zenobia's dark, exotic beauty arouses Coverdale's imagination to visions of a nude, sensual Eve, and this Eve-like influence is in contrast, he says, to most of the other women "now-a-days, and in this country, who [do not] impress us as being women at all; their sex fades away, and goes for nothing. . . ."[17] Unlike her paler sisters, Zenobia has intellect, candor, courage, and "a certain warm and rich characteristic, which seems, for the most part, to have been refined away out of the feminine system" (p. 17). At one point Coverdale tells us that her presence revealed the others as "grown-up men and women" who "were making a play-day of the years that were given us to live in" (p. 21).

In the eyes of Coverdale, who later claims to have secretly loved the pale and sickly Priscilla,[18] Zenobia's "womanly frankness" suggests something not "maiden-like." Her "unconstrained" manner hints at knowledge of the flesh. He theorizes, "Zenobia has lived and loved! There is no folded petal, no latent dew-drop, in this perfectly developed rose!" (p. 47). Sexual experience, the loss of virginity, is the basis for a judgment of evil against Zenobia. Although Coverdale acknowledges such an interpretation as "masculine grossness," he nevertheless feels himself "defrauded" by the suspicion. Certainly an experienced Eve gives the lie to an Adamic illusion of innocence. Apparently unsure of his own identity, Coverdale is "nervous" about Zenobia's suspected "knowledge," and he wishes to escape her presence and her attraction. Priscilla's visits to his bedchamber are much less disquieting.

For Coverdale and Hollingsworth, the escape from the post-lapsarian Eve is through devotion to the pre-lapsarian Eve. Priscilla lacks "earthly substance," and her smile is compared to a "baby's first one" (p. 73). Hawthorne further stresses her deceptive sense of Edenic innocence through the comparison to a "butterfly at play in a flickering bit of sunshine, and mistaking it for a broad and eternal summer" (pp. 74-75). Her "poor but decent gown" is "made high in the neck," and in a footrace, her "peculiar charm . . . was the weakness and irregularity with which she ran" (p. 73). As Judith Montgomery notes, Coverdale admires Priscilla "for ineptness, a propensity for falling down when she runs, for hesitancy in her speech, for pale delicacy and adoration."[19] Her life "full of trifles" is a refuge from the secret knowledge which an embrace of Zenobia might impart. Yet in a world of men seeking escape from knowledge, Priscilla is a powerful force. According to Nina Baym, Priscilla, despite her apparent fragility, "is not helpless in a battle against Zenobia. Men will fight to the death to defend her as a slave. In this sense, both the men in the story are on her side, and Zenobia succeeds only in aligning the men against her."[20]

Priscilla's unworldly love saves Hollingsworth's self-image and restores his sense of Adamic innocence after the accusations of Zenobia, though it is an ironic salvation. Hollingsworth sags under Zenobia's charge of "Self, self, self! . . . your disguise is a self-deception" (p. 218). Con-

fronted with the "ruin" of his heart, Hollingsworth turns
to Priscilla for both revenge and support. He seeks to in-
jure Zenobia when, in "the abased and tremulous tone of
a man whose faith in himself was shaken," he "spoke those
two words," "Priscilla . . . come" (p. 219). As a true unfallen Eve, Priscilla rejects the possibility of evil in her
Adam, and her undiscriminating love restores to Hollingsworth some reassurance of his innocence: "Her engrossing
love made it all clear. Hollingsworth could have no fault.
That was the one principle at the centre of the universe"
(p. 220). Coverdale had, for a moment, thought that Priscilla might fail Hollingsworth, and in fact she does. Hollingsworth's concept of Adamic identity is now totally dependent on Priscilla's reassurance, and that dependency
"casts out his own vitality"[21] and his integrity. The irony
of the unfallen Eve is that her "guardian" powers stand
between the now childlike Hollingsworth and his true manhood, which is dependent on acceptance of his humanity.

As a rejected post-lapsarian Eve, Zenobia no longer
has any function or any arena in the world. Three interpretations of her suicide are offered as an attempt to explain her life. Coverdale first thinks her suicide is logical
because "Everything had failed her—prosperity in the
world's sense, for her opulence was gone—the heart's prosperity, in love" (p. 239). Westervelt criticized her because
"She had life's summer all before her, and a hundred
varieties of brilliant success. . . . How forcibly she might
have wrought upon the world, either directly in her own
person, or by her influence upon some man, or a series of
men, of controlling genius!" (p. 240). Coverdale argues
against Westervelt's theory on the basis that it left nothing
to satisfy Zenobia's heart, yet he, too, admits that it is "a
miserable wrong" that she should die "because Love had
gone against her":

It is nonsense, and a miserable wrong—the result, like so many others,
of masculine egotism—that the success or failure of woman's existence should be made to depend wholly on the affections, and on one

species of affection, while man has such a multitude of other chances, that this seems but an incident. For its own sake, if it will do no more, the world should throw open all its avenues to the passport of a woman's bleeding heart. (p. 241)

As usual, Coverdale has only a half-truth. Certainly the very existence of a fallen Eve depends "on one species of affection," but Hawthorne's novels repeatedly suggest that man's existence is equally dependent on his ability to offer that affection. Coverdale is wrong when he claims that men have a multitude of other chances, as the cases of Hollingsworth, Coverdale, Kenyon, Donatello, and Dimmesdale must illustrate. None of the Adamic figures were ever truly innocent, and none can ever achieve an Edenic state; all they accomplish in rejecting such post-lapsarian Eves as Zenobia, Miriam, and Hester is their own damnation.

In refusing the reality of women who are touched by the world, these false Adams condemn themselves to a life of self-deception and moral infancy. Their lives become a series of repeated refusals of the truth, for though dead, the truth of the Zenobias is "still hovering about the spot and haunting it" (p. 228). Thus, Kenyon, who conceives the obvious lessons in the fall, rejects such wisdom for the life of a washed-out artist with a simpleton wife; Hollingsworth, fleeing the accusations of Zenobia, wrecks his heart and spends his life in "self distrustful weakness" by the side of the "puny" Priscilla; and Coverdale, who refuses the truth of his heart, falsely explains the "emptiness" of a life that has come to "an idle pass" with the absurd illusion that he was in love with Priscilla. The burden of moral timidity and intellectual shallowness must be carried on the shoulders of the men in Hawthorne's work, not the women whose extraordinary beauty, wisdom, and vitality are finally inadequate to shake the men from their fearful dependence on the male illusion.

The character of Isabel Archer in Henry James' *The Portrait of a Lady* combines the pre- and post-lapsarian Eve figures in the full configuration of the elements of Adamic myth. James' novels are nineteenth-century America's most sophisticated literary rejection of the appeal of Edenic innocence. Many critics have identified Isabel as Eve-like,[22] but the *schema* becomes confused in the second half of the story. The difficulties in interpretation climax in Isabel's refusal of Caspar in order to return to her loveless husband in Rome. If viewed in the perspective of the dual nature of Eve, Isabel's conduct is rational and intelligent. Her choice is analogous to that made by Miriam in *The Marble Faun*, and wise beyond the capabilities of the unsophisticated Judith Hutter or the undisciplined Zenobia. As the post-lapsarian Eve, Isabel's rejection of Caspar, the "American Adam," frees her to grow while it incapacitates him in a static illusion. Her qualified acceptance of the role of wife to Osmond, who is "convention itself," imposes on the fallen world the knowledge of sin and redemptive wisdom which is the essential function of Eve.[23] The reader is not told just what Isabel expects to do in Rome, other than the immediate matter of Pansy, but we are wrong to assume that the open-ended plot means that she has no extended purpose. The "straight path" is the path out of the garden (literally, Gardencourt) into the world of experience where she will exercise her identity in a world dominated by a man who finds her vision "a personal offence."[24] Isabel's final choice rejects both the role of pre-lapsarian Eve which the Adamic Caspar wishes her to play, and the strictures of obedient effacement which her husband demands.

The crucial problem of interpretation in the novel revolves around Isabel's refusal of Caspar and the immediacy of her return to Rome. Numerous critics, mostly male, have interpreted Isabel's actions as sexual fear of Caspar's "hard manhood." According to this theory, she escapes his sexuality in the "sterile dilettantism" of Osmond.[25] Few critics who discuss Isabel's sexual fears point out the violent possessiveness of Caspar's "hard manhood." Some then proceed to belittle Isabel for her distaste for his passion. Perhaps it is significant that Dorothea Krook is one of the few critics who have argued that Isabel's fear is of Caspar's violence, and that her sexual repression is a matter of preserving herself until she could surrender herself to the right person.[26]

Caspar is, of course, the American Adam operating outside time, space, and experience. He mistakenly tells Isabel that "We've nothing to do with all that [the world]; we're quite out of it; we look at things as they are" (II, 434). Tossing aside her experience and connections of the last four years, he tells her, "you've nothing to consider" (II, 434). Caspar's proffered moral justification for deserting her husband to live with him is indulgent: "a woman deliberately made to suffer is justified in anything in life—in going down into the streets if that will help her!" (II, 434). His rationale virtually suggests that the pain of life in the world justifies a private morality to protect one's emotional ease. Such a position approximates Hilda's rejection of Miriam in order to wear back to God her white robe of inhuman innocence. In terms of the myth, Caspar urges Isabel to return to a pre-lapsarian state where "The world is all before us. . . ."[27]

Wearied with the burden of the current crisis, Isabel is momentarily attracted to the promises of Caspar. The "help" she sees in his offer is, however, an escape from life analogous to that promised by death: "she believed just then that to let him take her in his arms would be the next best thing to her dying" (II, 435). The "rapture" which she momentarily feels is far more suicidal than sexual. Caspar's "lightning" kiss is in essence a death embrace, for he wishes to obliterate Isabel's life and purpose in an act of total possession. Perhaps even more than Osmond, Caspar desires to rob her of her personality and make her "all for one's self" (II, 79). It is "each aggressive fact of his face, his figure, his presence, justified of its intense identity and made one with this act of possession" that displeases her in his "hard manhood." Isabel's instincts in rejecting Caspar are those of survival, instincts "deeper than any appetite for renunciation" (II, 392). Isabel had already "recognized . . . the quick vague shadow of a long future," "that life would be her business for a long time to come" (II, 393). Her rejection of Caspar is the rejection of the illusion of Eden.

Isabel's return to Rome has struck many readers as prideful self-emolation of the ultimate "Emersonian self-culture."[28] Yet if she is to make any meaning out of her life, her fall from innocence to wisdom must move her back into the world of experience.[29] That means the world of Osmond. Although she had earlier refused "to publish" her mistake, to judge her return as an act of pride denies that Isabel has learned anything from such later events as the revelation of Madame Merle's true involvement in her life and of the source of her fortune, the death of Ralph, and the banishment of Pansy. Noble argues that she returns "in order to sustain her invulnerability in a hostile world. The preservation of her marriage means the preservation of her innocence."[30] The opposite seems more likely since the return to Rome is *to* the hostile world of immense evil to be encountered on a daily basis.

Social freedom from Osmond is no more possible for Isabel than Caspar's naive promise that "The world is all before us. . . ." Yet her understanding of Osmond's nature and of her own egotistical deception frees her from Osmond's moral and spiritual influence. Even he has seen "that she could after all dispense with him" (II, 201), at least as the law of her existence. Osmond's objection to her "had been the whole thing—her character, the way she felt, the way she judged" (II, 195), and she had at first tried to play the part he prescribed. Her unwillingness to continue as an obedient agent for Osmond is illustrated in her refusal to further promote the Warburton-Pansy affair, and by her defiant trip to England. Isabel's insistence on identity was never truly squelched, as she herself explains, "she was, after all, herself—she couldn't help that; and now

there was no use pretending . . ." (II, 190). To project
her actions upon returning to Rome as anything but an
elaboration of her insistence upon her moral and intellectual integrity subverts the logic and consistency of her
established character.

Her journey to England is a "start" toward full acceptance of her life. In England the pride which earlier prevented her from publishing her error is stripped away.
When she greets Bantling in London with praise for his
kindness, "It seemed to her she should never again feel a
superficial embarrassment" (II, 395). With Ralph, she
loses "all her shame, all wish to hide things" (II, 413). Together they can look at the truth of her life, and it momentarily stupifies her. Ironically it is Caspar who is the cata-
lyst in defining a path for Isabel. He breaks in upon her
during a moment of "singular absence of purpose" in the
same garden where she had once held his love letter while
rejecting Warburton's proposal. Caspar offers her the new
Eden where the two of them alone and unbound "can do
absolutely as we please" (II, 435). The impossibility of
his proposal clarifies for Isabel the rigorous path of moral
responsibility and human ties in which she must walk. With
wisdom as unappreciated as that of Zenobia and Hester,
Isabel nevertheless insists on pursuing her post-lapsarian
purpose in a world of confounded Adams.

In the figure of Isabel Archer James rejects the limits
imposed on women by such Americans as Cooper and Hawthorne. More than any other major nineteenth-century
American author, James denied the validity of American
innocence. Uncommitted to the preservation of innocence
and unambiguous as to the educational value of sin, James
has no necessity to force women into pre- and post-lapsarian dichotomies. His women characters are more fully human because they are less abstract and less symbolic.
Freed from the static world of the Edenic frontier, his
women characters may grow morally and intellectually into a triumphant realization of self and purpose that is de-

void of subservience to men. The very corruption of Adam becomes evident in his attempt to contain Eve.

The example of James offers some suggestions as to why women in English novels of the nineteenth century were generally so much more prominent and sophisticated in character development than in American novels of the same period. Nothing about European society supported Edenic myth as a viable interpretation of the culture, and the English novelist was unhampered by an emotional or moral need to reassert the Adamic innocence of characters existing outside time and place. Women in English novels, excepting the Bronte heroines, are a part of society, not an abstraction in a rigid moral and symbolic drama. The problem of women in English novels is suggested by the case of Dorothea Brook of *Middlemarch*, who tried to find a fuller role in a society which had no interest in or use for her talents. That, of course, was not an easy path, but a woman struggling to find a place in a real world had more humanity, flexibility, and potential than a woman struggling to find a real existence in the unyielding trap of a fanatic masculine myth.

Perhaps, too, the American devotion to Adamism suggests some reasons why nineteenth century America did not produce great women writers of the stature of Austen or Eliot. The cultural pursuit of innocence demanded of American women precluded knowledge of the ways of the world. Ignorance was a virtue in a woman, and as the novels suggest, departure from a pre-lapsarian mould was an unacceptable moral, social, and sexual role. The "damned women scribblers" who did write generally used their fiction as an extension of woman's accepted role—as the moral vessel, the protector of wisdom, the dispenser of sweet idealism. The American woman's authorial gifts, when directed at truth and realism, became a matter of immorality, a threat to the great cultural illusion.

This glancing look at the treatment of women in three of our major nineteenth-century novelists suggests that the writers themselves may not have been truly so callous to the plight of women in American society. Certainly James was not taken in by America's chief delusion, and such vital characters as Judith Hutter, Zenobia, Hester, and Miriam are evidence that neither Cooper nor Hawthorne was a consistent advocate of the Adamic stance. Part of the responsibility for stereotyping dark and light women as good and evil instead of as persons must lie with the readers and critics who are themselves influenced by the myth. As critics at last breaking free from the misunderstandings about women, our task is a major re-reading and re-evaluation of our literature in the light of social and sexual realities. My hunch is that such an effort will reveal that women characters often surpass the so-called heroes in moral complexity and human veracity. Such a study might prove, too, that America's writers have been, in fact, wiser and more compassionate than some of their critics.

NOTES

[1] For example, Carolyn Heilbrun, "The Masculine Wilderness of the American Novel," *Saturday Review* (Jan. 29, 1972), pp. 41-44. This article is based on her forthcoming book, *Androgyny: A Literary Essay*; Judith H. Montgomery, "The American Galetea," *CE* 32 (May 1971), 890-899, says, "It must be recognized that in fiction, as frequently in life, woman is taken to be feminine first and human second; that the definition of what is feminine depends upon man's idealization or disparagement of woman; and that the heroine is judged most frequently as she fulfills or betrays that idealization" (p. 899). Wendy Martin, "Seduced and Abandoned in the New World, 1970: The Fallen Woman in American Fiction," *Woman in Sexist Society* (New York: Basic Books, 1971), rpt. in *The American Sisterhood: Writings of the Feminist Movement From Colonial Times to the Present*, Wendy Martin, ed. (New York: Harper Row, 1972), 257-272, also examines several of the major nineteenth-century American heroines within the context of the Edenic myth. She sees woman as the traditional Eve, a "frail creature." These novels "perpetuate the archetype of the fallen woman, thereby conditioning women to accept their inferior status . . ." (p. 260). My argument for the superior humanity of these heroines suggests the

opposite. Nina Baym's "Hawthorne's Women: The Tyranny of Social Myths," *Centennial Review* 15 (Summer 1971), 250-272, and "The Women of Cooper's Leatherstocking Tales," *AQ* 23 (December 1971), 696-709, are of interest. More generalized studies relating to this subject include Mary Ellmann, *Thinking About Women* (New York: Harcourt, 1968); Annis Pratt, "The New Feminist Criticism," *CE* 32 (May 1971), 872-878; and Hortense Calisher, "No Important Woman Writer," *Mademoiselle* (February 1970); rpt. *Women's Liberation and Literature*, Elaine Showalter, ed., (New York: Harcourt, 1971), pp. 223-230.

2The two terms are from Kate Millett, *Sexual Politics* (New York: Doubleday, 1970), and Heilbrun.

3Richard Chase, *The American Novel and Its Tradition* (Garden City: Doubleday Anchor, 1957), p. 13.

4Heilbrun, p. 41.

5David W. Noble, *The Eternal Adam and the New World Garden* (New York: George Braziller, 1968), p. 6.

6Noble, p. 10.

7R. W. B. Lewis, *The American Adam* (Chicago: University of Chicago Press, 1955, Phoenix Book, 1958).

8James Fenimore Cooper, *The Deerslayer* (New York: Kelmscott Society, 1896), p. 563.

9Baym, "The Women of Cooper's Leatherstocking Tales," p. 698.

10Lewis, p. 105.

11Natty's desire to "adopt" Hard-Heart is itself an interesting variation from his normal chosen isolation. Hard-Heart may represent to Natty his own idealized self—brave, skillful, uncivilized, noble, strong, *et al.*,—while being sufficiently removed by the barriers of race, religion, culture and extremity of age from the true closeness of a father-son relationship. Another interesting variation in *The Prairie* involves the two women; the married Inez is totally desexed as the idol of innocence and pure beauty, while the unmarried Ellen is allowed vitality and passion. Although Middleton and Inez are long married, Cooper suggests that the immediacy of the kidnapping and the persistent companionship of Ellen as her bedfellow have preserved Inez's virginity. Although Middleton is properly married, only the wild men, Hard-Heart and Mahtoree, are tainted with lustful thoughts.

12Perhaps the best is Baym's "Hawthorne's Women: The Tyranny of Social Myths." Other studies include Frederic I. Carpenter, "Puritans Prefer Blondes: The Heroines of Melville and Hawthorne," *NEQ* 9 (June 1936), 253-272; Gloria C. Erlich, "Deadly Innocence: Hawthorne's Dark Women," *NEQ* 41 (1968), 163-179; Virginia

Ogden Birdsall, "Hawthorne's Fair-Haired Maidens: The Fading Light," *PMLA* 75 (June 1960), 250-256; Allan and Barbara Lefcowitz, "Some Rents in the Veil: New Light on Priscilla and Zenobia in *The Blithedale Romance*," *NCF* 21 (1966), 263-275; Morton Cronin, "Hawthorne on Romantic Love and the Status of Women," *PMLA* 69 (March 1954), 89-98; Neal Frank Doubleday, "Hawthorne's Hester and Feminism," *PMLA* 54 (1939), 825-829; Philip Rahv, "The Dark Lady of Salem," *PR* 8 (Sept-Oct. 1941), 362-382, rpt. *Image and Idea* (Norfolk, Conn.: New Directions, 1949), pp. 22-42. Two other articles by Baym are also interesting in this regard: *"The Blithedale Romance*: A Radical Reading," *JEGP* 67 (1968), 545-569; and "The Head, the Heart, and the Unpardonable Sin," *NEQ* 40 (1967), 31-47.

[13]Nathaniel Hawthorne, *The Marble Faun* IV (Athens: Ohio State University Press, Centenary Edition, 1968), 460. Subsequent quotes from this edition are noted in the text.

[14]Erlich argues that Miriam's change is due to the fact that "Woman's love is aroused through the harm she does to man" (p. 174). Baym believes that Hawthorne connects women with love and freedom, but that "When the hero, unable to cope with the condition of freedom that woman represents, repudiates her, he is *really* repudiating a part of himself projected onto her and defined as 'other.' This is self mutilation." ("Hawthorne's Women," p. 257).

[15]Baym, *"The Blithedale Romance*: A Radical Reading," p. 553.

[16]Henry James, *Hawthorne* (New York: Macmillan, 1887), p. 134.

[17]Hawthorne, *The Blithedale Romance*, III (Athens: Ohio State University Press, Centenary Edition, 1964), 17. Subsequent quotes from this edition are noted in the text.

[18]Rahv, *Image and Idea*, says, "It is evident on every page that the only genuine relationship is that of Coverdale to Zenobia," an emotion Coverdale "displaces" (p. 37).

[19]Montgomery, p. 892.

[20]Baym, *"The Blithedale Romance*: A Radical Reading," p. 567.

[21]Baym, *"The Blithedale Romance*: A Radical Reading," p. 568. In her article "Hawthorne's Women: The Tyranny of Social Myths," she adds, "The lifetime service of woman is required to hold together the shattered male ego. . . . But by subjugating the women to patriarchal values—by employing Priscilla to nurse Hollingsworth instead of Zenobia to be his companion—man perpetuates the neuroses which these values have created" (pp. 264-265).

[22]Chase speaks of her "Eve-like innocence," (p. 124), as

does R. W. Stallman, *The Houses that James Built* (East Lansing: Michigan State University Press, 1961); Richard Poirier says of her return to Rome, "there is nothing in her act which holds the promise, as does Adam and Eve's, of eventual happiness through suffering," *The Comic Sense of Henry James* (New York: Oxford University Press, 1960), p. 246. Lyall H. Powers, "*The Portrait of a Lady*: 'The Eternal Mystery of Things,' " *NCF* 14 (September 1959), 143-155, deals with the novel in terms of the fortunate fall.

23Powers says she is to "confront the evil of the world, to work at the redemption of that evil . . ." (p. 153).

24James, *The Portrait of a Lady* (New York: Charles Scribner's Sons, 1908) II, 195. Subsequent quotes from this edition are noted in the text.

25Peter Buitenhuis, "Introduction" to *Twentieth Century Interpretations of The Portrait of A Lady* (Englewood Cliffs: Prentice-Hall, 1968), p. 12; Tony Tanner, "The Fearful Self," *CQ* 7 (Autumn, 1965), 205-219; Poirier, 244-245; Leon Edel, "Preface," *The Novels and Tales of Henry James*, Vol. 5 (London: The Bodley Head, 1968); Oscar Cargill, *The Novels of Henry James* (New York: Macmillan, 1961), pp. 105-106; F. O. Matthiessen, *Henry James: The Major Phase* (New York: Oxford University Press, 1944), pp. 179-180.

26Dorothea Krook, *The Ordeal of Consciousness In Henry James* (New York: Cambridge University Press, 1962), pp. 357-369.

27As noted by virtually everyone, an echo from Milton's *Paradise Lost*.

28Chase, p. 134.

29See n. 23.

30Noble, p. 96.

JOHANNA LEUCHTER

SEX ROLES IN THREE OF
HERMANN HESSE'S NOVELS

In the three novels under consideration, *Siddhartha, The Journey to the East,* and *Magister Ludi,* traditional sex roles prevail. In *Siddhartha* Kamala becomes a benefactress of the pilgrims of Gotama after Siddhartha shows her the "Enlightened Path." In *The Journey to the East* H. H. is searching for Princess Fatima; she is the principal female in this Hesse novel. Like *The Journey to the East,* female characters are almost totally absent from *Magister Ludi.* Women are not admitted to the elite spiritual Order which serves as the governing body for the institution of Castalia.

In *Siddhartha* only males are seekers of "the Way" and "Enlightened Ones," and all the females are treated in a sensual/sexual manner. Siddhartha courts and wins Kamala in order to learn about love. They come to grow together, and they come to understand each other well. Once Siddhartha says to Kamala, " 'You are like me; you are different from other people. You are Kamala and no one else, and within you there is a stillness and sanctuary to which you can retreat at any time and be yourself, just as I can. Few people have that capacity and yet everyone could have it.' "[1] This quotation shows that Siddhartha understands Kamala well, and that he sounds relatively wise in discussing their spiritual natures compared to Kamala and her statement: " 'You are the best lover that I have had.' "[2] Traditionally in literature male characters are more intellectual than female characters.

After Siddhartha leaves, Kamala changes her way of life.

One day, when very many people were making a pilgrimage to the dying Buddha, Kamala, once the most beautiful of courtesans, was

175

also on her way. She had long retired from her previous way of life, had presented her garden to Gotana's monks, taking refuge in his teachings, and belonged to the women and benefactresses attached to the pilgrims.[3]

Hesse does not explain the change in Kamala's way of life, nor does he explain how she makes her living after the change. In Indian culture women are not considered to have worth, and so Kamala could not have become a first-rate true follower of Gotama. In this respect Hesse is true to Indian culture; important women characters searching for the Path would not have fitted in with Indian culture. There are nunneries for the women seeking enlightenment; however, they are not thought of as highly as are the monks and their monastaries.

Contrasted to *Siddhartha* in which Kamala plays a fairly important role, *Journey to the East* mentions a woman about five times. The goal of H. H.'s journey is to see Princess Fatima. As H. H. relates meeting other groups of other people on the journey, he describes a woman he meets in the following words: "I met and loved Ninon, known as 'the foreigner.' Dark eyes gleamed beneath her black hair. She was jealous of Fatima, the princess of my dreams, and yet she was probably Fatima herself without my knowing it."[4] All the other journeyers H. H. describes are men, and they are all described by explaining what their goals are on the journey or what they do that differentiates them from the others, e.g., reciting poetry. Ninon is not described in this manner; she is described only in the ways she relates and appears to H. H. It must have been flattering for H. H. to have Ninon jealous of Princess Fatima.

From reading *Journey to the East* one might come to the conclusion that women seeking the Spiritual are rare, or else that very few women exist. Sex and romantic love are not very important in *Journey to the East*; perhaps this is one reason why Hesse almost completely excludes women from the novel. Many times in literature women are found in only romantic and/or sexual contexts. Hesse is limited in his vision of potential for life in women in *Journey to the East.*

Women are also almost completely excluded from *Magister Ludi.* As previously mentioned, women are absent from the Order that governs Castalia. Furthermore, members of the Order are required to be bachelors, but they are not required to be celibate. "The daughters of the citizenry"[5] in the province look upon Castalian students and scholars as desirable lovers. Since the Castalians have no money, they "make their repayment by giving more of themselves than others would."[6] One assumption behind this statement is that men need money to repay women for their company; another is that most men do not give much of themselves in regular love relationships—perhaps this is true. Occasionally an elite student would marry, thereby giving up Castalia and membership in the Order. "But these few, rare cases of apostasy in the history of the schools and of the Order amount to little more than a curiosity."[7]

Father Jacobus, a Catholic scholar, remarks to Knecht, the main character in *Magister Ludi,* about history and seizing the historical moment in saying: " 'The corporal who becomes a dictator overnight, or the courtesan who for a while controls the good or ill humor of a ruler of the world, are favorite figures of such historians' (who believe a mark of greatness is the ability to divine and seize upon a historical moment.)"[8] In this statement, Hesse assumes that a woman's path to power lies through her influence upon a man in power, i.e., a woman can wield only secondary and derived power.

The principal interest of *Magister Ludi* is the life of Joseph Knecht, and the only woman who is mentioned in the book with whom Knecht has personal contact is the wife of his friend Designoris. In the discussion about whether to send the son, Tito, to Castalia to be educated, "Tito's mother took a lively part." When the decision is negative, she concludes, "with a painful smile, that in any case she would not have been able to part with her child, since he was all that made her life worth living."[9] Hesse assumes that a woman's ultimate fulfillment is through her son; nothing in her own life makes life worth living. Hesse is not sensitive to the causes of impoverishment of women, i.e., the vacuum in which they live.

A secondary part of the novel is the posthumous writing of Joseph Knecht. It principally consists of lives Joseph Knecht wrote in his free years between school and his membership in the Order. The most interesting of these lives as far as sex roles are concerned is one entitled, "The Rainmaker" which begins with the following paragraph:

> It was many thousands of years ago, when women ruled. In tribe and family, mothers and grandmothers were revered and obeyed. Much more was made of the birth of a girl than of a boy.[10]

Hesse does not live up to the beginning of this story. "The Rainmaker" enforces the sex roles of Hesse's own culture; the characters in this story do not personify the sex roles one would expect in a matriarchy. A girl from the Village gets lost while picking berries, and "the young men were sent out"[11] to search. In a matriarchy with the women being more highly respected and revered than the men, it seems that if a child gets lost, women would be sent to search for the missing child rather than the young men. When Knecht, the main character who later becomes a Rainmaker, desires to marry Ada, he arranges it with her father; Ada is not consulted at all about her marriage wishes. Later when they are married and when they have children, one night the stars appear to be falling, and Knecht says to Ada,

> 'Let the children sleep; I don't want them to see this, do you hear?' he whispered intensely. 'Don't let any of them come out, not even Turu. And you yourself stay inside.'[12]

Knecht is protecting his wife and children. In this culture

what right would a man have in protecting a woman and in telling her what to do?

When Hesse uses the word "man" in "The Rainmaker," it is not evident whether it should be assumed that he means males or persons in general:

In those times of calamity and universal anxiety it became apparent that a man is the more useful, the more his life and thinking is turned toward matters of the spirit, matters that go beyond the personal realm, the more he had learned to venerate, observe, worship, serve, and sacrifice. [13]

It is also interesting to note that the title tribal mother (the most respected and revered position in the Village) is not capitalized in the story, while Rainmaker (which is a male profession) is capitalized. "The Rainmaker" is the most obviously sexist literary piece among the ones under consideration. Hesse does not follow through his beginning assumptions to the end of the story; and the basis of the story is *not* the overthrow of a matriarchal system in favor of a partiarchal one.

Every person is a reflection of her/his own culture. Hesse is no exception. He transcends many of the prevalent ideas of his culture and time, but he does not transcend sexual roles as they exist in his culture even in a literary piece that purports to concern itself with a matriarchy. There are no women in these three of Hesse's novels truly searching for a Spiritual Way. Outside of romance, sex, love, and motherhood Hesse has no female characters in these novels.

Hesse employs sexist language; few people think that questioning sexist language is important; however, I do. Children have difficulty learning that when adults use words such as *man, men, mankind, chairman, fellow* they mean person(s)—sex unspecified. The title page to the first section of *Magister Ludi* says, "The Glass Bead Game: A General Introduction to the History for the Layman." All of Hesse's sexism could be passed off by saying that he is reflecting only the culture of the locale and period of time in which the novel takes place exept for *Magister Ludi* which takes place in the future. Especially in futuristic fiction I think it is important for the author to realize that it is not human nature for women to be restricted to mistress, wife, and/or mother roles.

NOTES

1Hermann Hesse, *Siddhartha*. (New York: New Directions Publishing Company, 1951), p. 58.

2*Ibid.*, p. 59.   3*Ibid.*, p. 90.

4Hermann Hesse, *The Journey to the East*, New York: Farrar, Straus & Giroux, 1969), p. 24.

5Hermann Hesse, *Magister Ludi*, (New York: Bantam Books, Inc., 1970), p. 98. The words "daughters of the citizenry" may perhaps connote that these young women belong to the citizens and do not have a separate and equal identity among the citizens; Hesse might have used the words "the young women in the province."

6*Ibid.*, p. 98.   7*Ibid.*, p. 98.
8*Ibid.*, pp. 151-152.   9*Ibid.*, pp. 303-304.
10*Ibid.*, p. 413.   11*Ibid.*, p. 416.
12*Ibid.*, p. 443.   13*Ibid.*, p. 431.

THE WOMAN AS HERO

ELLEN MORGAN

HUMANBECOMING: FORM & FOCUS IN
THE NEO-FEMINIST NOVEL*

Three new forms, or rather, three recastings of old
forms, are beginning to reflect in literature the influence of
neo-feminism—the bildungsroman, the historical novel, and
the propaganda novel.

Woman as neo-feminism conceives of her is a creature
in the process of becoming, struggling to throw off her
conditioning, the psychology of oppression. She is pitting
herself against her patriarchal culture and its institutions.
She is teaching herself how to play the game of sexual
politics on her own terms, and the stakes are her personhood and humanity. In short, her story in this period of
transition is the story of an education, of a coming to consciousness and a subsequent development of self and search
for authenticity, of rebellion and resolution. Her task is
the integration of all of her parts which have been discon-
nected as she has faced the fragmentation attendant upon
her socialization, a socialization which has prepared her to
play many contradictory roles all with reference to men
and male institutions.

Neither the psychological nor the sociological novel is
a form adequate to express the neo-feminist conception of
woman, for she is not only a psyche, but a political being;
not only a product and victim of her culture, but also a
personal being who transcends it. The stream-of-consciousness novel, with its tendency to equate reality and value
with consciousness cannot sufficiently express her experience, which is political and social as well as personal and
psychological.

According to Thrall, Hibbard and Holman who list it

under "apprenticeship novel," the bildungsroman is

a novel which recounts the youth and young manhood of a sensitive protagonist who is attempting to learn the nature of the world, discover its meaning and pattern, and acquire a philosophy of life and "the art of living." Goethe's *Wilhelm Meister* is the archetypal apprenticeship novel; noted examples in English are Samuel Butler's *The Way of All Flesh,* James Joyce's *A Portrait of the Artist as a Young Man,* Somerset Maugham's *Of Human Bondage,* and Thomas Wolfe's *Look Homeward, Angel.*[1]

The bildungsroman is a male affair. Of course that is not entirely true; we have had Dorothy Richardson's *Pilgrimage* for example, and there have been other works which could be classified as female novels of apprenticeship, if one accepts for this description novels in which the apprenticeship is generally for marriage and motherhood. But by and large the bildungsroman *has* been a male form because women have tended to be viewed traditionally as static rather than dynamic, as instances of a femaleness considered essential rather than existential. Women matured physically, at which point they were ripe for being loved. Then they deteriorated physically, at which point they either disappeared from sight in the novel or became stereotypes. Once physically mature, they were thought to have reached the peaks of their potential and development, which were defined in physical rather than spiritual, intellectual, or emotional terms. In works such as Dorothy Richardson's *Pilgrimage* the potential for interior growth is strangely handled; prior to the neo-feminist movement, the female protagonists who did grow as selves were generally halted and defeated before they reached transcendent selfhood. They committed suicide or died; they compromised by marrying and devoting themselves to sympathetic men; they went mad or into some kind of retreat and seclusion from the world. They grew up to a point, and then, as one woman was heard to say at a women and literature section of the 1970 meeting of the Modern Language Association, they "grew down."

Neo-feminists write stories of defeat, for the

psychology of oppression is not conquered and women are in a period of transition in which the future is uncertain and largely unimaginable. There are female protagonists who "grow down," who run into insuperable opposition and do not succeed in understanding and transcending their condition as women. There are those whose stories end with the doubt, uncertainty, and inconclusiveness which are the experience of many women in this era. But the thrust of neo-feminism is toward change and futurity. The single most absorbing consideration and obsessive need of the neo-feminist woman is to envision what authentic self-hood would be for her and how she might move toward and achieve it. Because there is such yearning among neo-feminists for the creation of the free self, such longing to break out and assert individual potency, many neo-feminist artists are primarily concerned not with documenting the effects of oppression or detailing the chaos and confused-ness women are facing as they organize themselves for struggle; they are primarily concerned with the imaginative construction of images of transcendence and authenticity for women.

Thus the female bildungsroman appears to be be-coming the most salient form for literature influenced by neo-feminism. The novel of apprenticeship is admirably suited to express the emergence of women from cultural conditioning into struggle with institutional forces, their progress toward the goal of full personhood, and the effort to restructure their lives and society according to their own vision of meaning and right living.

As for the historical novel, it seems inevitable that neo-feminists will revive it because, as blacks have said, without one's history one does not know one's name. Un-avoidably, some neo-feminist writers are concerned with giving women back their history in a new form. There is evident in many stories an effort to convey the quality of life lived by most women and the strengths with which they met oppression. Emphasis is given to their ingenuity and courage, and perhaps most importantly to the female culture—including art and metaphor and rebellion and the homely wit and wisdom which characterized it and set it off from the dominant culture. Women who have never or rarely been heard of emerge as heroines for different reasons than either women or men have been granted heroic status before; simple historical prominence, possession of power or beauty do not determine those chosen for depiction. The focus reflects neo-feminist consciousness that power, beauty, fame are not the wellsprings or housing of dignity and worth, that the dignity and value of a person are to be found in the degree of inner growth achieved, in compassion, in the affirmation and acting out of humanistic values over and against the specifics of one's condition. Already neo-feminist journals are full of stories about women who have no claim to fame. Perhaps they are the grandmothers and great-grandmothers of the writers, who heard their stories passed down in family legend. Perhaps they are the often maligned and over-shadowed wives, mistresses, mothers, or sisters of men of historical prominence. Someone, for instance, will certainly soon reconstruct the life of Xanthippe, wife of Socrates and heretofore described as the quintessential shrew. Attention is already being given to Wordsworth's sister, who furnished much material to her brother and devoted her life to him, never developing her own very considerable talents to the full. Some composers of music and other prominent men such as Freud had sisters whose talents were sacrificed to the education and comfort and egos of their brothers. Because the need to identify and take pride in their lost heroines and to set their failures fully in the context of their situations as women is so great among neo-feminists, these figures are being unearthed and revived.

Recasting of the historical novel, then, appears to be becoming another offshoot of neo-feminist influence on literature. It offers to neo-feminist writer and reader alike the opportunity to reconstruct the lives of their forebears and to avail themselves of their example and their strength in the building of the contemporary woman's selfhood. Most significantly of all it enables living women to view women's past in their own terms, thus clearing away that part of women's conditioning which has resulted from the focus of history on exclusively male pursuits and the concomitant diminishing of women as ancillary to the progress of civilization.

A few words need to be said about the third recast form in which neo-feminist influence is surfacing. The propaganda novel seems to be an unavoidable corollary to most social movements of any scope. Neo-feminist journals are full of writing—poems and plays and some short stories—the content of which is propagandistic, that is, writing in which message is more important than, and emphasized to the detriment of, form and/or language. Neo-feminists are understandably eager to proselytize. Myrna Lamb's play *But What Have You Done for Me Lately?*, Una Stannard's novel *The New Pamela,* and other such works are primarily valuable as message.

They function to encourage women to break out of their conditioning. They teach something valid about the human condition, and make it seem unwise to go along with prevailing critical judgments of propaganda as a low-born and unworthy step-sister to literature. For propagandistic writing can share what is perhaps the most important characteristic of art—magnitude of conception, even if it lacks magnitude in form and language. Much of neo-feminist writing, as much of all writing, falls into this category of the propagandistic. The capacity to teach and to delight which some of this work has would suggest that critical standards which deny literary legitimacy and value to these two kinds of writing may be inadequate tools for their evaluation.

But although movements such as neo-feminism are particularly inclined to produce polemical writing, and although it will be a long time before neo-feminists will gain any distance from their material, their sexual identities being so significant in patriarchal culture and so problematic, their natural inclination toward polemic should not be thought to imply that neo-feminist writing is, or will be, primarily of this type. Where there is passion, there is the need for form, for containment and refining. Obviously, to use Ellison's *Invisible Man* as just one case in point, passionate consciousness of oppression does not preclude the creation of art.

Taking an overview of neo-feminist influence on form, the internal form of neo-feminist work is controlled by the dynamic of struggle. Time, place, pattern, rhythm and plot are functions of the meeting of women with the forces aligned against them. Where there are tightness and compression, they reflect the pressure and constriction of these forces. Where there is looseness, disorder, chaos they reflect women's sense of disorientation, their feeling that they are between two worlds.

There are very few neo-feminist novels yet published, if one defines the neo-feminist novel as a work written during and influenced directly by the current women's liberation movement. Neo-feminist journals are bulging with poetry and short stories and plays in this category but novels take longer to write, and therefore, as one would expect, neo-feminist influence is taking longer to find expression in this form. I have been able to locate only two novels to date which are neo-feminist by this strict definition; one is the aforementioned *The New Pamela*, which I shall not discuss in depth. While it is ideologically neo-feminist on many levels, protesting many sex-role stereotypes and gestures and suggesting a new sexual ethic, it was written prior to the movement's coalescing around certain crucial issues such as the solidarity of women with each other, the strong bias against classism, and the emphasis on the soundness and health of many attributes traditionally considered "feminine." It sets forth almost in tract form some of the major neo-feminist grievances but does not reflect enough of the development of neo-feminist thought to be a good illustration of the way the movement is likely to influence literature from now on. The other novel is truly neo-feminist in every sense and I believe it is the first such work to have emerged to date from the American movement. It was written by Alix Kates Shulman, active in the movement for several years in New York, and is called *Memoirs of an Ex-Prom Queen.*

However, it is not a myth that artists frequently anticipate new sensibilities and are able to express, even if in fragmentary form, the substance and mood of cultural change before they come into mass consciousness. Together with this fact is the fact that the central ideas of the current movement are not new and both these ideas and the feelings of rebellion which women have long had were available to women writers before the movement. So it is not surprising to find that prior to the movement, some novels were written by women who independently had come to many of the conclusions now openly being expressed. The surprise is that these women should have documented their perceptions at a time when they were virtually alone in their willingness to challenge accepted mores and assumptions, and at a time when they were subject to castigation for doing so. In addition there are novels written very recently whose authors do not identify with neo-feminism but who yet reveal on some levels their ideological solidarity with it.

So before the Shulman novel is discussed, two novels which are neo-feminist in this looser sense of the term will be considered. They cannot be omitted from any consideration of literary neo-feminism and when there are a larger number of strictly movement-influenced novels in published form, these precursors and sister-works will be seen to belong fundamentally to the same category of work and to be likewise discrete from other literature.

Virginia Woolfe's *Orlando* and June Arnold's *Applesauce* are fantastic rather than realistic novels although each is a bildungsroman. It is next to impossible for a realistic novel to be written which defies the sex-role system, for society everywhere upholds this system, and social realities are staples of the realistic novel.

Orlando is the story of a person who starts out as a young male living in the age of Queen Elizabeth I. He becomes female towards the end of the seventeenth century, and lives as a female until the end of the story in the year 1928, when Orlando is thirty-six years old and Virginia Woolf published the book. Orlando's life thus spans about three and a half centuries. As a young man he tries to be a poet; as a women she succeeds as one. As a man Orlando fathers three children. As a women she bears a son. The tale is full of social comedy and satire, particularly of Victorian prudery. Woolf does not make many direct hits at the sex-role system as an arbitrary division; instead, through descriptions of Orlando's feelings, she attacks indirectly. She does, however, protest the sexism expressed by some of the great figures of the centuries in which Orlando lives and the disadvantages the sex-role system entails for women. And by not concentrating on Orlando's maternity any more than on his paternity, or making her marriage to Shelmardine any more prominent than his love affairs and barely more so than his marriage. Woolf protests some of the important conventions which have been used to confine women to functions of their sex role.

When, on page ninety, Orlando is found to have changed into a woman, Woolf writes:

Orlando had become a woman—there is no denying it. But in every other respect, Orlando remained precisely as he had been. The change of sex, though it altered their future, did nothing whatever to alter their identity. Their faces remained, as their portraits prove, practically the same. His memory—but in future we must, for convention's sake, say "her" for "his," and "she" for "he"—her memory, then, went back through all the events of her past life without encountering any obstacle.[2]

We see Woolf insisting that sex is not a fundamental component of identity except insofar as it affects a person's outward destiny. Even looks are not as sexually distinct as is supposed—that is, as Woolf points out later, until sex-role behavior and clothing are brought in. The passage also questions the linguistic conventions with which the sexes are separated.

Woolf also shows the connection between the arbitrary sex-role system and women's dependence, and between the enforcement of the system by men and their power. Orlando soon realizes that her body is a thing independent of personality now that she is a woman. She must keep it covered because men react to her physical presence rather than to her as a total person. She realizes she can no longer swear, use physical force, insult or defy men, lead an army, prance along on a horse, or do most of the things she was accustomed to doing as a man and is still entirely capable of doing. "All I can do," she says, "once I set foot on English soil, is to pour out tea, and ask my lords how they like it" (103).

Orlando cannot do things she is perfectly capable of doing as a woman and must be content with trifles. On the other hand, this oppression results in freeing women from some power struggles and inhumanities.

Orlando sees just how much disadvantage for women is involved in the system, and she rejects it. "If," Woolf writes, "it meant conventionality, meant slavery, meant deceit, meant denying her love, fettering her limbs, pursing her lips, and restraining her tongue" then she would set sail for the land of the gipsies (106-107), who had no such system. Orlando discovers as a woman she cannot hold property; she cannot walk out alone. Stunted and bound at every turn she reacts with rebellion, resorting to comfortable male gestures, male clothing, and male activities whenever possible throughout the rest of the story. Woolf comments:

She had, it seems, no difficulty in sustaining the different parts, for her sex changed far more frequently than those who have worn only one set of clothing can conceive; nor can there be any doubt that she reaped a twofold harvest by this device; the pleasures of life were increased and its experiences multiplied. From the probity of breeches she turned to the seductiveness of petticoats and enjoyed the love of both sexes equally (144).

She challenges the entire heterosexual sex-role system. Orlando fits neither the female nor the male stereotype, Woolf is saying. The qualities ascribed to females and males are indeed different and show up in the sexes in different proportions because of the role-structure; but each human being is naturally, underneath, inclined to traits of both kinds, with one set predominating at any given time, combined with some of the other.

In conclusion, *Orlando* is important as a neo-feminist work because it shows that Woolf emphatically believed selfhood is not a matter of gender, although the sex-roles stereotypes of a particular time and culture are clearly shown to affect the individual's ability to develop and express selfhood. But more importantly, by the end of the book, one has some positive notion of authentic selfhood as Woolf conceived it. Orlando excapes the sex-role system by learning to express in her actions, gestures, writing, and love relationships the whole of her personality rather than only that part of her self which is sanctioned as within the female role by her time and milieu. As it unfolds, her life becomes the life of a mind the fundamental characteristic of which is its sovereignty. It is a mind which learns to judge and evaluate the myriad sensibilities and modes of thought to which it has been exposed, and which throws off the constraints of sex-roles as it breaks through those of time and culture. Orlando lives centuries and reaches only the age of thirty-six just as he-she encompasses both sexes because authentic selfhood as Woolf defines it is not a function of time, culture, gender, role. These things, rather, are functions of the self, when it, as in Orlando's case, has become primary, free, and transcendent, the final arbiter and standard.

June Arnold's *Applesauce* (think of apple blossoms, then of the firm, ripe fruit which takes their place—and then of what is done to the fruit to make applesauce of it) is a brilliant first novel by a woman who became active in the neo-feminist movement. In a letter she wrote to me dated 14 January 1970 she said, "I think I am much surer now (after Liberation consciousness) than I was when I wrote the book as to how central feminism was to the story." From the same letter I quote the author's conception of the book:

. . . it is about the impossibility of being a woman: a female child born Liza Durach tries on three "feminine" roles . . . sexmate, intellectual, earth mother, killing off each "self" successively as they fail her needs and ending up finally as a man "self." The man-self is called Gus which is the name she called her husband (. . . he changes personalities as she changes "selves") . . . this is supposed to mean that she chose as husband a man into whom she could project her husband-ideal, her "self" which needed male embodiment. I explain it to you because reviewers understood the book in Freudian terms and it meant as an experience in womanness . . .

Applesauce is a predominantly psychological novel although also the story of an education which is as much political as psychological. It is in many senses a *tour de force*, containing the kind of poetry which sometimes startles a reader into new sensations and a new perspective. It is especially distinctive for its extreme sensitivity and clairvoyance in the depiction of children and the child-parent relationship.

Liza Durach, the heroine, moves through several metamorphoses. She is Eloise, the round, sensual woman who is Gus' first wife. Then she becomes his second, Rebecca, the intellectual who studies at Rice University and has trouble integrating her intellectual life with her femaleness and maternity. Rebecca feels that women doing graduate work at men's schools "begin to wonder whether they're really women at all!"[3] They must compete with men and it is confusing when they are expected to do essentially sexless work while playing the "feminine" role. Then she becomes Gus' third wife, Lila, the fertile, all-accepting mother who finds emptiness at her core. Finally she becomes Gus himself, her male counterpart who throughout the book has been building a room inside his/her own room, a place in which to "burst"—to escape the walls which constrict him/her. When the first three inadequate role-selves have died, Gus finds "he" no longer needs this room because it is really "nothing." Between the killing off of the role-self and the time when a real self will emerge there is a limbo of nullity. Ultimately the real self is born. Gus shouts "I AM LIZA!" (240) and the book ends.

What did June Arnold mean when she said the book was about the "impossibility of being a woman"? The plot line I have just sketched tells us that self and role are enemies. At least the roles which are sanctioned for women are enemies to selfhood. None of them includes all of Liza, and she must throw them all off before she can come home to herself. Before this can happen she must also open up to the side of herself which is composed of traits sanctioned only for men—she must release herself not only from female roles but from femaleness as an identity, in order to arrive at her humanity.

There are some rather explicit passages in the book which deal with this concept of androgyny. Like Virginia Woolf, Arnold notices how the natural self is often almost sexless until decked out in the accoutrements of sex-role.

It is as Rebecca, the intellectual, that Liza first articulates the androgynous concept of selfhood. She points out that we all have desires for both freedom ("male") and security and protection ("female") and that we are all trying to gain both for ourselves (139). In the middle of this thought sequence she finds a coral snake threatening her children and kills it, but she is distressed to find that the ("male") force she is exhibiting is psychologically only available for her to use because she is using it to fulfill the traditional role of mother protective of children, a female role.

An awareness of conditioning is also present in the book. As a young girl Liza is told she is too little to run with her dog in the streets. As she grows older she is suddenly too big to do the same thing because "the other thing might happen" (29). Her real self yearns for freedom but is caught in the compulsory sex-role system.

Arnold also deals with the theme of the alienation of women from their physical selves caused by men's attitudes toward them as primarily sexual beings. As Liza is growing up she becomes embarrassed about her developing breasts, which boys stare at until she feels, "So that was who she was. Judy Two-Breast." (Girlie—she had been girlie before, as if she were only her sex") (31). It was as if she were nothing, as if aside from her breasts she had disappeared.

Later in her life, as Rebecca, she stands naked on a beach at night, enjoying the solitude and freedom. But men seem to be everywhere. She "stood . . . helplessly enveloped in the fact of her own sex" (151). She feels "reduced by fear to cunt and that is all" (152), and attempts to commit suicide.

Liza in all her incarnations discovers that Gus wants her on his own terms. He wants Eloise "soft inside . . . to give herself to him, to melt into him in yielding trust" but she rebels by being "as defiant as a block of granite" (44).

Men in this book are concerned with maintaining power, and sex becomes a weapon which Gus and his wives use against each other. Rebecca fights Gus's desire to treat her sexuality on his terms, as a function of his needs and prerogatives. She is insulted at his egoistic belief that she has consented to play the role of his prey.

Liza exhibits ambivalence in all her incarnations toward her children. Even in her role of earth-mother, she both loves and hates them, refusing to play up to the image of serene and all-fulfilled maternity which is patriarchal culture's ideal of woman as mother.

Rebecca is much troubled by the conflict between what a mother is supposed to be and what she is—a woman primarily interested in her own intellectual development and fulfillment. Motherhood is not enough for Liza, even in her earth-mother incarnation, Lila.

Finally, unable to fill the emptiness inside her and desperate, she decides she wants another child. She, like Gus, is caught up in the stereotype; despite the evidence of her own emotions, she still believes this is the answer to her needs. Shortly thereafter, however, she begins to show signs of incipient madness. She lies in bed for hours, unable to cope. She is lying in bed when a hurricane hits; she has not gathered the children to safety. Her son is killed in the storm. Lila goes through three years of psychological torture and guilt. The male psychologist insists to Gus that unconsciously she had wished the child's death; he does not grasp the desperation which made her unable to cope with her emotions and care for the children at the time of the storm. Lila has another child. Then she dies. The attempt to fulfill herself in the role of earth-mother has failed. There follow the "Gus" period, the period of emptiness between Liza's having thrown off all roles including the male, and, at last, the emergence of Liza, her real self.

This book is important as a neo-feminist work for a number of reasons. Like *Orlando* it seeks to cross the barriers which language and stereotype set up. It shows woman in rebellion against the confinement of arbitrary sex-roles. Its style and form reflect the chaos and uncertainty which confront the woman who seeks to find her humanity in a culture organized by the role system. Like *Orlando*, it expands the horizons of characterization by presenting an androgynous character who will not conform to stereotype. Much more heatedly than Woolf, Arnold expresses the rage and frustration of women with their condition.

Liza is another "victorious" heroine. Like Orlando, she gains her victory by experiencing and rejecting the role-self in favor of the authentic self. Of course Orlando's real self is more fully expressed than Liza's—we can see what the real Orlando is like from Woolf's descriptions of her behavior in many situations. Liza's real self is only just born on the last page of *Applesauce*. All we really know is what she is not—a sex object, pure intellectual, or earth-mother, and we know what she had to do in order to arrive at her own birth—reject all roles. It remains a mystery how this newborn self will develop, how it will think and behave and feel and what choices will define its textures and contours.

Nevertheless, like *Orlando*, *Applesauce* is an extraordinarily valuable work in neo-feminist terms. It is the only neo-feminist novel I have found besides *Orlando* and the Shulman book in which the heroine "grows up" and actually arrives at a transcendent, authentic selfhood.

Alix Kates Shulman's *Memoirs of an Ex-Prom Queen* is a novelistic rendering of neo-feminist ideology, cultural analysis, and consciousness. As the experiences of the heroine, Sasha Davis, unfold, one notes that the patriarchal institutional mechanisms which neo-feminists have identified are shown as they function to oppress. The book deals with most of the ways in which patriarchal culture oppresses women.

And yet the work is very far from being a propaganda novel. It is well-written, artistically and aesthetically sound. One is sure that the author has fully assimilated neo-feminist ideology and analysis; they have become part of her equipment for perceiving reality, and are thoroughly integrated into the story. Neo-feminist consciousness informs the novel as light informs a painting, rather than appearing as subject matter.

This novel is something of a cross between a bildungsroman and an historical novel. It is the story of Sasha's education and of her reaching toward self-affirmation. But it is also the story of an era and an ethos in women's terms, a record of what women's lives and culture were like during a period of time which ends before the neo-feminist movement begins. Sasha was five in mid-Depresssion, in high school during the second world war, and as the book ends, she is past thirty, so the period spans roughly the years 1930-1960. The book has both a psychological and a political dimension, depicting Sasha's thoughts and feelings in relation to the cultural forces and institutions which affect her. Its structure is not chronological but organized by association of earlier experiences with later, conditioning with its consequences, reality with insights into its meaning.

A discussion of *Memoirs* can be organized in terms of each of the three ideas central to neo-feminism. Under the heading "conditioning" would come Sasha's memories of her training in the female role. "Once I started school," she says, "I learned I would have to choose between hair ribbons and trees, and that if I chose trees I'd have to fight for them. The trees, like the hills, belonged to the boys" (20).

The reason the girls succumbed to this restriction of their movements was that as they attempted to cross the barrier the boys punished them. If a girl was spotted in their territory, Sasha explains, the boys felt perfectly free to do any number of sadistic things to her.

Early descriptions of conditioning backed up by force point to two of the major themes of the book—the hostility which runs from men to women and is manifest in the various types of force men exert on women, and the emphasis on physical appearance which forms the chief preoccupation of women denied by force any other way to make an imprint and control their own destinies.

Sasha starts out with a very healthy attitude toward beauty. "There was a hummingbird in the hollyhocks behind our house," she remembers, "the most delicate, lovely thing I had ever seen; I wanted to be like her" (20). But soon there comes an awareness that looks are saleable, and, moreover, that they are her only means to win any of the power and status available to women. Beauty is female economics.

The emphasis on beauty implies alienation from her own selfhood. She does not want to be loved for her nose, but for herself. The night she becomes queen of the prom, she is paraded before the male judges like a piece of meat. Even her first husband tells her he married her because she was both intelligent and beautiful and he could never love a girl who was not both.

Sasha's relationship with her second husband ends when he finds her new haircut a disaster. "Christ, Willy," she cries, "It's just *hair*! It'll grow in again!" (274) But he has let her know that her beauty is lessened and that his view of her beauty is the basis of any power he grants her in the relationship. Rather than submit to powerlessness, she leaves him.

Reinforcing the notions of her own helplessness, worthlessness and the importance of beauty for women are also the philosophers and other writers Sasha reads in college. There is Emerson, who made grand statements about self-reliance, never giving her any useful advice about what to do when the meat chef at the hotel at which she was a waitress attempted rape. There are the German philosophers who make lofty pronouncements about procreation without ever considering what childbirth does to a woman's body and beauty. There is Schopenhauer with his anti-feminism, and Spinoza and Nietzsche. There are the psychologists like Watson, as well as those in the practice of psychotherapy and psychoanalysis, one of whom Sasha approaches for a cure for frigidity. He notices her desire for self-determination and freedom, her desire to be the queen on the chessboard, and tells her the problem will be solved if only she will surrender to her husband, forget the independence, and become a "real woman."

The hostility and force and emphasis on beauty as power are related to sexual politics, the second idea central to neo-feminism and to this book, because what is implicit is that the relationship between the sexes is power structured. But the nature of this relationship is primarily evident in Sasha's discovery of the economics and role structure of marriage and child raising, in the gestures of power and dominance to which she is exposed, in the economic discrimination she experiences, in the sexual relationship itself, and in the way women are induced to see each other as rivals because successful competition for male approbation is crucial to their status.

Sasha's first husband is an academic. She has chosen him because her first love is philosophy and he gives her credit for being serious about it. She feels that she must marry, and Frank at least will, she thinks, make some room for her career beside his own. They agree that they will alternate working to support each other so each can pursue studies but it is Sasha who ends up taking menial jobs all along and having to forego her own intellectual pursuits.

She makes a further discovery about the economics of female-male relations when she loses a lover; he is poor, and she supports them both. Unable to accept the same economic dependence women traditionally have had to accept, he begins to quarrel and the relationship is soon ruined.

Before her first marriage she had fallen in love with a professor at college, to find that she was jeopardizing his job and thereby his wife's and children's economic security. Sasha at length finds herself in the same bind with her second husband. With two children she cannot afford to cross him in any way because she cannot survive economically without him.

Those are the economics of female-male relationships as Sasha perceives them. Then there are the roles within marriage. In her parents' home, the entire domestic burden fell on her mother, and the pattern is repeated in her two marriages. In her first she cooks and does the dishes while the men talk shop or Frank alone studies. Any discontent Sasha feels she tries to hide, for she has been conditioned to believe confronting a man with "her" problems is wrong, a waste of his working time, which is more valuable than her own time.

In her second marriage Sasha finds herself suddenly

having two children, mainly because every other avenue of "advancement" seems closed and because her husband expects her to have them. She feels totally unprepared to cope—none of the books except the sexist Spock one say anything practical about child care, and she is ashamed to be caught reading magazine articles on the subject, for such articles are held in contempt by society. Child care is not discussed nor taught in schools. She loves her children, but the necessity to take complete responsibility for them, with Willy always absent at work or elsewhere, and her constant preoccupation with them, alienate her husband. The work is never-ending, and there is not time for her studies. ". . . When my child was born," she says, "my fate slipped through my fingers into the bay. I was hers now" (244).

Besides the role structure inside marriage, there is the power relationship between the sexes as it expresses itself in countless gestures of force and dominance. Frank is apt to take her arm commandingly and "guide" her when she walks with him. Joey kisses her by first trapping her with a hand against the wall. Jan, the meat chef at the hotel, refuses to give her the meat platters unless she will agree to go out with him. She is only able to prevent being raped by him by crying and telling him she is a virgin, playing submissive to his dominance and appealing to his charity. Men on the streets whistle. "I know," she says, "it was supposed to be flattering . . . but it was not . . . it was annoying . . . it was a humiliating assault" (111) which makes women walk like blacks in white neighborhoods, eyes to the ground. Even her employers are inclined to pat her "kindly" on the rear in token of her place and status.

Females tend to regard each other as competitors and rivals and do not trust one another easily. Status depends on male approbation. Sasha realizes that her looks will separate her from other women because they make her a serious rival and threat to them.

As a wife, Sasha herself feels threatened by other women. She must surpass Willy's secretaries and the other women in his life away from home in looks and willingness to please. So she hides her housewife's fatigue, does exercises, and pretends that her life is as glamorous as the single women pretend theirs is. One result of this lack of trust and communication among women is that when each woman reaches the point of having children she has not been warned what to expect of her husband or of her new life with its duties and economic and emotional vulnerabilities.

It is perhaps in the sexual relationship itself that sexual politics are most evident. Each of Sasha's sexual relationships is exploitative of her personhood in some way. Joey tortures her—she feels desire for him but is afraid to sleep with him because she may lose her reputation.

All the relationships are games and exploitation. The boys come to her house, ostensibly to study with her but their objective is conquest. With Willy she must play games and lie so he will have a chance to pursue her. In Europe she meets a boy whose father has sent him there to "get laid"—boys are taught to regard females as prey. And none of them takes any responsibility for satisfying the woman sexually. All are out to, as Willy puts it, "enjoy" Sasha. As a wife she is still not immune—she must submit whether she feels like it or not so as to avoid being deserted by her husband.

After many such experiences, Sasha tells Roxanne, the one woman she trusts, "I wouldn't mind living the rest of my life without sex" (209). There seems to be no way for a woman to avoid being demeaned, used, frustrated if she expresses sexual desire and acts upon it. The relations between the sexes are corrupted by the power struggle. Sadly, it is not really in the interest of either sex to trust the other, for they have been conditioned into having divergent interests. Reciprocity is lacking because mutuality of interests is lacking, and respect is made unlikely because females are held in contempt. Women in turn are forced to view men in terms of financial and status security, and thus to do violence to men's personhood.

The third idea central to neo-feminism and to this book is the humanity of women. *Memoirs* is not only the story of Sasha's conditioning into the female role and her many defeats and retreats in the face of sexual politics. It is an account of her rebellion and the beginnings of self-affirmation.

From her earliest years Sasha has shown the desire to come out from under the weight of male power she feels holding her down. She invents a game in which she picks out formidable-looking strange men and stares them down. She wants "to beat the boys at their own vile game. I would rather hate them than fear them; best of all I would make them fear me" (53).

Sasha learns in school to "keep my knowledge and ambitions to myself" (52). In her seminars at Columbia graduate school she is made to feel "either . . . an interloper or an anomaly . . . no one ever listened," she says, "to a single word I said without grinning" (164). She feels "intimidated and stupid" and stops participating. But at least she chooses deliberately for a husband a man who seems to take her mind seriously. Viewing work as purpose she at last comes to fulfill her need for meaning in her life by becoming an author and writing her own story.

Her rebelliousness and will to come to full personhood are most apparent from her leaving both husbands, and from her choice, after leaving Willy, of the independent and self-defining Roxanne as a companion and model. Frank represents respectability and security—she is somebody with him—the wife of an "important" man. In leaving him for Willy she is taking a first step toward fulfilling her own needs, affirming herself. It is true that she needs Willy for security; but it is equally true that she has chosen the lesser of two evils. At least Willy genuinely pleases her.

She has elected to consider her own needs more important than anyone else's; she has ceased viewing herself as rightfully a function of the needs of a man who fails to satisfy any of her own deepest needs.

When Sasha leaves Willy, the step is much more significant. With two children, she is daring to set off on her own despite all the discrimination and humiliation women without men face, and despite the fact that there is no man there to provide the financial or emotional security she has been conditioned to need.

Memoirs of an Ex-Prom Queen is important as probably the first neo-feminist novel to come directly out of the influence of the current movement. It is also important because, unlike *Orlando*, or *Applesauce*, it is a realistic novel. As such it can stand as a model for other neo-feminist works whose authors wish to portray not only the condition of women and their responses to this condition but also the actual possibilities for struggling to achieve authentic selfhood. Sasha is a realistic heroine who ultimately grows up rather than being defeated. She is a new type of female character—neither an exception to the rule nor a typical heroine of stereotype. She embodies the human potential of the woman who, if more intelligent than the average, is yet not separated off from her sex either by extraordinary circumstance or by the possession of qualities not characteristic of many women.

Of course, like Liza Durach, Sasha Davis is only born to personhood as the book closes. We do not know how or whether she will survive or how she will conduct herself as a "free woman." We have yet to be given a realistic novel in which a heroine shows us what it is like to live as a free and fully human female being in a partiarchal society. That heroine, it seems to me, will be the final product of neo-feminist influence on literature.

NOTES

[1]I have used this term to refer to the current upsurge of feminist activity and analysis—the women's liberation movement—which surfaced in the 1960's, and to distinguish this movement from the waves of feminism which preceded it. Idealogically, the current movement differs from earlier feminist movements in at least one crucial respect. Feminists have long advocated equal rights for women, and to some extent they have always challenged the sex-role system and patriarchal institutions which support this system. But never before has the feminist movement *as a body* challenged the idea that biology is responsible for most or all psychological differences between women and men. Neo-feminists tend to hold sex-role conditioning and differential experiences responsible for such differences. Thus neo-feminists are suggesting that the human personality is essentially androgynous.

[2]William Flint Thrall, Addison Hibbard, and C. Hugh Holman, *A Handbook to Literature*, revised, (Odyssey Press, N. Y., 1960), p. 31.

[3]Virginia Woolf, *Orlando* (New American Library, N. Y., 1960), pp. 90-91.

[4]June Arnold, *Applesauce* (McGraw-Hill Book Co., N. Y., 1966), p. 116.

*Adapted from an unpublished dissertation, University of Pennsylvania, 1972. Used by permission.

JOHN CORNILLON

A CASE FOR VIOLET STRANGE

As fans of Anna Katherine Green's mysteries picked up her latest book in 1915, *The Golden Slipper and Other Problems for Violet Strange*, they may have asked themselves as you are asking, "Who is Violet Strange?"

They were familiar with Ebenezer Gryce, the detective hero Ms. Green had created for her first novel, *The Leavenworth Case*,[1] published in 1878, more than a decade earlier than Doyle's Sherlock Holmes; with Amelia Butterworth of Grammercy Park, Gryce's friend and amateur colleague; Sweetwater, Gryce's youthful companion and ambitious protegé; and Jinny, Sweetwater's enthusiastic and energetic assistant. These characters, functioning individually and as a group, had gained an impressive following among mystery novel readers as Ms. Green detailed their triumphs through a succession of books. But occasionally she veered from the path of sure success to experiment with a new character. Such was the case with *The Golden Slipper*.

Violet is introduced to us right from the beginning of the book as a character about whom seeming belies being. When she is pointed out to a new client, he responds, "That yon silly little chit, whose father I know, whose fortune I know, who is seen everywhere, and who is called one of the season's belles is an agent of yours!"[2]

The contradiction is too much and the client bursts out, "It's hard to associate intellectuality with such quaintness of expression." (p. 2) She is variously referred to as "inconsequent," "infantile," and "that airy little being."

This kind of apparent "feminine" personality haunts

the work of Green. Again and again we meet seemingly brainless ninnies, bits of fluff, featherbrains, comic characters, female fools and clowns.[3] Veronica Moore, the victim in *The Filigree Ball*, is just such a character, well-known society belle who writes of herself, "I was light as Thistledown and blown by every breeze."[4] The image of mental and emotional lightness and airiness inhabiting a diminutive body combine in conveying a picture of insubstantiality and insignificance.

We see in this image a demythologized version of the upper class white woman, so popular in Southern fiction, whose physical insubstantiality signified her spiritual transcendence of and disassociation from the world of matter and materialistic motives. But in the works of A. K. G. insubstantiality has come to mean not so much a spiritual transcendence of the material as a social and emotional alienation from what is meaningful and true. It was becoming increasingly obvious to women of the late nineteenth and early twentieth century what it really meant to be sequestered away from the material world of economic survival and to be kept pure for the contemplation of "higher things." It often meant social irrelevance, historical invisibility, and economic powerlessness. It meant being intellectually condescended to because the actors in "the man's world" often considered those "higher things" to be nothing more than superstitious and pious dreams on the one hand and sentimental and romantic fancies on the other, just what one would expect of a woman's inferior and undisciplined mind. Excluded from society's economic and vocational life and given little else to intellectually focus upon other than the realms of religion and art, it was indeed unkind to then turn around and label those religious predilictions as superstitious and those artistic interests as sentimental. For the less well-to-do being saved from the rigors of the workaday world usually meant bearing and raising a number of children, shopping, cooking, cleaning, washing, ironing, sewing, canning, etc., etc., i.e., doing all these tasks of the worker in the domestic factory with no economic control of the means of production. So the myth of the materially uncorrupted woman was in A.K.G.'s time an outworn, formulaic tool that existed primarily to justify the continued oppression of women. As the myth became increasingly transparent, the nobility with which it once had been imbued became increasingly replaced by bitterness, frustration, and self-parody.

It was this vein of malaise pervading female society that A.K.G. was tapping and giving expression to in her creation of Violet Strange. For, although Violet upholds the myth in public by conforming to the role expected of a young woman of her station in life, it is a hollow act, and in secret she lives a life in defiance of those role expectations. "From time immemorial," Allport writes, "slaves have hidden their true feelings behind a facade. . . . Rebellion and aggression would certainly be met by fierce punishment. . . . By agreeing with her "adversary" she "escapes being conspicuous . . . and quietly leads" her "life in two compartments."[5] But Violet's life is not so quiet. She has gone a step farther than merely surviving an oppressive situation. She is working towards a goal. And her means are as liberating for herself and others as are her ends. The mask that serves to safeguard personal integrity serves in Violet's case to disguise social resistance and noncomformity as well.

A.K.G. represents society generally and fathers specifically, Violet's in particular, as being the repressive factors in Violet's life. When Violet speaks to her employer, we are told by the author that "the extreme carelessness of Miss Strange's tone would have been fatal to her socially; but then she never would have used it socially. This they both knew." (p. 64) Society in the larger sense oppresses by its constant inability to *see* her for who she is, but instead to only see the stereotype she is expected to be: "Who would dream that back of this display of

mingled childishness and audacity there lay hidden purpose, intellect, and a keen knowledge of human nature?
Not the two men who listened to this seemingly irresponsible chatter. To them she was a child to be humored
and humor her they did." (p. 82) There is ironic satisfaction in this last phrase, because Violet is capitalizing on
their blind objectification of her to pump them for information.

The fathers of three young people are presented in
the book. All of them are portrayed as rigid, repressive,
and domineering. Violet's own father is presented as follows: "Though she was his favorite child Peter Strange was
known to be quite capable of cutting her off with a shilling, once his closed, prejudiced mind conceived it to be
his duty. And that he would so interpret the situation,
if he ever came to learn the secret of his daughter's fits of
abstraction and the sly bank account she was slowly accu-
mulating." (p. 185)

The secret that lies behind the facade of Violet
Strange's public image is the fact that she is an agent in
the employ of a detective agency.[6] Throughout the
book, Violet affects a dislike for her work. She claims
she is only working because she needs the money; but the
reason for the need is a secret that is not revealed until the
last story or "problem" in the collection. In "Violet's
Own" we learn her story.

In childhood Violet and her brother Arthur were
cared for by an elder sister named Theresa. (Their mother
died during their infancy.) One night when Violet was
about seven, she woke up and heard . . . "My father talking to my sister. . . . She in supplication and he in a tem-
pest of wrath which knew no bounds." (p. 13)

The infuriated father, having discovered Theresa
speaking to someone from her window, raves that she has
disgraced him, the family, and herself. "Was it not
enough that you should refuse to marry the good man
I picked out for you, that you should stoop to this low-

down scoundrel—this—" (p. 408) (an impoverished, Italian singing master).

Theresa interrupts her father, "I love him! I love him! . . . And I am going to marry him," . . . (p. 408).

The father answers in a paroxysm of frustrated rage which Violet reports as having "left scorched places in my memory that will never be eradicated" (p. 408).

The next morning her sister-mother, for so does Violet refer to Theresa, is gone. The children are informed by their father that neither their sister's name nor anything referring to her were to be mentioned in that house again. "Heed me," the father said, "or you go too" (p. 412).

In the days that followed all photographs of Theresa were destroyed, her name was cut out from the leaves of books. Presents she had given the children were surreptitiously taken away. Her piano was removed and her music burnt, until no vestige of her beloved presence remained.

Shortly before the story opens, Violet happens upon her sister by chance. Theresa, however, moves in order to elude her sister and prevent any suffering on her account. Violet goes to the detective who later becomes her employer, and, in the process of tracing her sister, discovers her own remarkable gifts of detection. Theresa's husband has just died, leaving her in the poverty in which they had always lived. Violet wishes to help, but Theresa will not accept anything even indirectly from Peter Strange, preferring impoverished self-sufficiency to charity.

Violet's course of action becomes clear to her however one day when she overhears her sister sing and realizes that Theresa has a "grand voice . . . the voice of a great artist" (p. 423). "All she needed was a year with some great maestro in the foreign atmosphere of art. But this meant money, not hundreds but thousands" (p. 423). Violet ponders the problem and concludes that "if in some way I could earn the money, she might be induced to take it. . . . If she had capabilities in one way, I had them in another" (p. 424). The capabilities to which she refers in herself are the intellectual abilities required by detection, or her powers of "ratiocination." The detective has from the beginning been the symbol of reason and intellect par excellence.

Abstracting the plot from a feminist perspective we see Violet Strange breaking away from absolute dependence upon the patriarch and gaining economic independence by getting a job and starting her own bank account. She is motivated to do this out of a desire to help her sister-mother whom the patriarch has disowned, disinherited, and sought to render invisible in punishment for her refusal to comply with his patriarchal will and for the temerity she displayed by exercising her own will.

In her effort to aid Theresa, Violet performs the following liberating acts: (1) she earns money; (2) she earns the money by using her mind; (3) she helps her sister-mother, a rebel against the patriarch and by extension the patriarchal order, making herself an accomplice to that rebellion; (4) she helps her sister not by finding her a man but by helping her to develop her own artistry and self-sufficiency; and (5) she helps her sister achieve public recognition, putting an end to the obscurity and public invisibility imposed upon her by her father. The book concludes with Violet commenting that Theresa has gained "that place in the world to which her love and genius entitle her" (p. 425).

It is this sense of, and sensitivity to, sisterhood among women that we see expressed throughout these stories. While it is to help her own blood sister that Violet Strange becomes a detective, in the course of her work she greatly aids those who are her sisters because they share the political condition of women in a patriarchal society. In eight out of nine stories, the principal people she helps are women. In the one exception she meets and helps the man whom she will later marry.

The book opens with the story of five young women who, because of their affection for one another, call them-

selves the Inseparables. Despite the threats to the existence of the group imposed by a lover and a father, threats
of romantic exclusivity and patriarchal possessiveness respectively, the group, with the help of Violet Strange,
survives.

In the next story, Violet helps a woman whose
husband and child have been killed, leaving the wife penniless, the life insurance company refusing to pay since the
coroner has ruled her husband's death a suicide. The woman calls Violet Strange in to prove it was murder. In
the course of the investigation the woman reveals she had
had an argument with her husband about childcare: "He
said there was no need of its crying so; that if I gave it the
proper attention it would not keep neighbours and himself
awake half the night. And I—I got angry and insisted that
I did the best I could; that the child was naturally fretful
and that if he wasn't satisfied with my way of looking
after it, he might try his." (p. 52) Whereupon he growled
at her and she fled the room to sleep in the spare room.
The author comments, "It is not difficult to see that she
had no very keen regrets for her husband personally. But
then he was not a very estimable man nor in any respect
her equal" (p. 53).

Violet discovers in the third story who was responsible for committing a particularly brutal murder of a
solitary old woman. The case is solved by the testimony
of another elderly woman.

Violet Strange meets Roger Upjohn, the man she will
marry, in the fourth story. Such a love interest is a firmly
entrenched convention in the popular novel of that day
and this. But the man she and the author choose, as well
as the marital relationship implied by such a choice, is not
conventional. He is described as follows: "though a de-
generate in some aspects, lacking the domineering presence, the strong mental qualities, and inflexible character
of his progenitors . . . , he yet had gifts and attractions of
his own" (p. 104). In the course of the story we see that

he has overcome his degeneracy, but he does not lose his other qualities. He is neither domineering, inflexible, nor too strongly willed, qualities which mean that he neither has the strength nor inclination to prevent Violet from doing what she wants to do. He is a man who has been married before and has a child for whom he has cared since his wife was murdered. He has been ostracised by high society because of the scandal surrounding her death; he has been humanized by suffering and has few romantic illusions about marriage or parenthood. In marrying him, Violet is not about to give up the freedom she has tasted in stepping outside the prescribed confines of the female social role of her day. She will marry wisely; she has chosen a man of egalitarian temperament, who has experienced and accepted his outcast status, more loyal than he is strong-willed, a good ally in what one assumes will be Violet's continued flouting of feminine convention.

In the fifth story, a woman whom Violet is helping explains her extreme aversion to nicely bound books: "There is a reason for my prejudice. I was not always rich. . . . when I was first married . . . I was so poor then that I frequently went hungry, and what was worse saw my little daughter cry for food. And why? Because my husband was a bibliomaniac. He would spend on fine editions what would have kept the family comfortable."

"O life! life!" the author concludes, "how fast Violet was learning it!" (p. 167)

Both "The House of Clocks" and "The Doctor, His Wife, and the Clock" deal with the irrational jealousies and hatred born of a possessive and exclusive romantic love. In contrast to this is the conclusion of Violet's own declaration of love to Roger: "Such a union as ours must be hallowed, because we have so many persons to make happy besides ourselves!" (p. 406)

The second to last story, "Missing Page Thirteen," focuses simply on the hatred that the institution of marriage can breed. This hatred is epitomized by a sword duel to the death between a husband and wife for, in the words of one of the partners, "What would either's life be worth with the other alive and happy in the world" (p. 393).

Anna Katherine Green has used these stories to expose many of the ways women are oppressed by society's laws, conventions, attitudes and institutions. Violet Strange, both as a sister and a detective, has struggled against the oppression of women. The collection is liberating in its depiction of both means and ends. Violet becomes independent, self-confident, and triumphant. And Theresa, despite her defiance of the patriarchal order neither repents nor is destroyed, but instead achieves happiness, wealth, fame, and love. The love she finds is the love experienced in the reunited community of sisters and brother from which Pater Peter had sought to have her expelled. Although the popular novels of a later day might have, in a more "liberal" vein, accorded her happiness, it would have been a happiness that resulted from the salvation effected by some heroic Prince Charming. But, to see her come to a happy end with no repentance through the machinations of no man, but by virture of her own efforts and the aid of her sister is to say the least unusual. It is a pleasure to read in a mass culture novel of sisterhood triumphing over patriarchy. Sisterhood is indeed powerful!

NOTES

[1] This book enjoyed a tremendous success, selling over a million copies. Unmentioned in academic literary criticism, and virtually ignored even in discussions of the detective novel genre, *Publisher's Weekly* the publishing industry's trade journal had this to say at the time of her death in 1935: "While the writing of mystery stories began with Poe, the writing of mystery stories of a popular appeal might be said to have begun with 'The Leavenworth Case.' " (April 27, 1935, "Godmother of Mystery Stories.")

[2] Anna Katharine Green, *The Golden Slipper and Other Problems for Violet Strange* (G. P. Putnam's Sons, 1915), p. 1. All further references to this book will be indicated in the body of the text.

[3] In Gordon Allport's chapter "Traits due to Victimization" he

lists "Clowning" as one of these traits: "If the master wants to be amused, the slave sometimes obligingly plays the clown." That quality that keeps the oppressive class amused, and therefore benign, keeps the oppressive class off-guard by making it underestimate the intelligence of the oppressed; but mostly serving to make the oppressed look harmless and inconsequential and not threatening.

[4] *The Filigree Ball* (The Bobbs-Merrill Company, 1903), p. 381.

[5] Gordon Allport, *The Nature of Prejudice* (N.Y., 1948), Chpt. 9.

[6] Asked what made a good mystery Anna Katharine Green responded: "The essentials are first of all an interesting plot with a new twist—a queer turn that has never been attempted." (*Publisher's Weekly*, April 27, 1935.) In the Violet Strange collection she introduces several "firsts," for her writing at least, which were later to be used by other mystery writers. She creates a female detective hero. That hero has a dual identity. She is often introduced to a case by mysteriously receiving a packet of information which contains all the pertinent data, a technique that has been used with great audience success in the *Mission Impossible* series.

NAN BAUER MAGLIN

FICTIONAL FEMINISTS
IN *THE BOSTONIANS* AND *THE ODD WOMEN*

As women are rediscovering our history, we should also rediscover our literature. Although not written by women, Henry James' *The Bostonians* and George Gissing's *The Odd Women* are about women, women who were concerned about the feminist struggles of their times. There are very few well-known fictional portraits of feminists, women who struggled personally and politically against the stereotypical sex roles. Most of us have been raised on novels that portrayed women in traditionally male-dependent relationships. Heroines have either struggled to find suitable husbands, as in Jane Austen's *Emma,* or to find a meaningful life within the confines of a stultifying marriage, as in George Eliot's *Middlemarch*—in other words, the heroism of these women consisted of fighting within the limits of the system to get the most (or the best) for themselves that the system permitted.

The Bostonians and *The Odd Women* are two full-length novels dealing with feminism in the late nineteenth century which are readily available. The two books have many similarities. *The Bostonians,* published serially in 1885-86 and as a book in 1886, chronicles the struggle for women's emancipation, specifically the struggle for the vote, during the 1870's in New England (primarily Boston). *The Odd Women,* an English novel published in 1893, focuses upon the struggle of women in London around 1890 to redefine themselves as educated persons who work rather than as adjuncts to men. In *The Bostonians,* Olive Chancellor, an aristocrat, and her convert and companion, Verena Tarrant, daughter of a mesmeric healer of little means, lead the movement to gain the vote. While in *The*

Odd Women, Mary Barfoot, a lady with a substantial independent income, and her friend and assistant, Rhoda Nunn, an outspoken woman who worked for her own living, found a school to train women to be autonomous.

In both books we see a pair of women struggling together not only politically and ideologically but struggling also to create between themselves a significant personal relationship. It is interesting to note that both authors chose to create their "pairs" by drawing from different socioeconomic classes. Their finances create a kind of dependency in the relationships that leads the women to ape traditional male-female roles to some degree in their relationships with each other.

In both books there is the proverbial male who comes to conquer. Southern gentleman Basil Ransom, in *The Bostonians,* is the standard bearer for the belief that a woman's place is at the bottom and "the bottom is a better place"[1] for "the use of a truly amiable woman is to make some honest man happy."[2] And it is his goal to save Verena from the "pernicious forces"[3] of feminism and put her back in her rightful place, namely, as an ornament on his mansion's porch. And in *The Odd Women* it is Everard Barfoot, Mary's worldly cousin, who speaks to Rhoda Nunn with a sweet mouth and a forked tongue. He convinces Rhoda (and himself in some measure) that as a reformer he embraces the ideal of the liberated woman while at the same time he semiconsciously plots to prove that men are always on top.

Because of the parallels between these two books it is interesting to speculate about whether Gissing knew about James' *The Bostonians* before he wrote *The Odd Women.* We can presume, at least, that Gissing must have been aware of the numerous English reviews of James' book in 1886, all of which raised the issue of women's roles in society which he was to take up in his novel in 1892.

This should not be taken to mean that the similarities between the two novels can be attributed simply to the direct influence of *The Bostonians* on the writing of *The*

Odd Women. The similarities also have to do with literary convention, but more importantly, the novels reflect the similar state of feminism in Britain and America. In both countries, the movement was generally led by upper and middle class women. Both movements dealt with the role and rights of women, focusing on marriage, the vote, and education.

Both authors were consciously interested in writing socially relevant novels. James writes in his diary on April 8, 1883:

> The scene of the story is laid in Boston and its neighbourhood; it relates an episode connected with the so-called "woman's movement." The characters who figure in it are for the most part persons of the radical reforming type, who are especially interested in the emancipation of women, giving them the suffrage, releasing them from bondage, co-educating them with men, etc. They regard this as the great question of the day—the most urgent and sacred reform. . . . There are to be several other characters whom I have not mentioned —types of radical agitators—and as many little pictures as I can introduce of the woman's rights agitation. . . . The subject is strong and good, with a large rich interest. The relation of the two girls should be a study of one of those friendships between women which are so common in New England. The whole thing as local, as American, as possible, and as full of Boston: an attempt to show that I *can* write an American story.[4]

Gissing was more consistently a political writer than James. He had focused on the question of women's rights both before and after writing *The Odd Women.* For example, *Denzil Quarrier* (1892) and *The Emancipated* (1897) explore the marriage bond/bind, education for women, and female suffrage. Gissing wrote in 1880 that his aim in fiction was to "bring home to people the ghastly condition (material, mental, and moral) of our poor classes, to show the hideous injustice of our whole system of society, to give light upon the plan of altering it."[5]

In any case, because of their similarity *The Bostonians* and *The Odd Women* make an excellently relevant field for comparison of the pro- and anti-feminist attitudes of the time. In the anti-feminist *The Bostonians,* Verena succumbs to her dashing suitor, while in the pro-feminist *The Odd Women,* Rhoda does not. The difference lies not only in the outcome of the story but in the attitude of the authors towards independent women, the women's movement, and women in general. James' attitude is that of disgust and mockery (perhaps with the exception of women in their "proper" place); Gissing's attitude is one of support and concern for women striking out on their own.

To Henry James these women who fight for equality and the vote are most definitely odd! James implies that they are sick, perverted, and weird. Throughout the book Olive Chancellor is depicted as a morbid woman out to seek vengeance upon men as scapegoats for her personal sickness. The name Olive is probably meant to suggest a person who is drab and decidedly unsweet. As James draws her, Olive's white skin is pulled tightly across her prison-like face; her features are sharp and cold; her eyes are green ice; she has absolutely no figure; she is devoid of laughter. "She was so essentially celibate that . . . she appeared old."[6]

James' description of Olive is only a reflection of the epithets that were thrown at feminists at the time that James was writing. In her book, *The Ideas of the Woman Suffrage Movement, 1890-1920,* Aileen S. Kraditor writes:

The suffragists, declared the [opponents of feminism], were a small minority of women, and humanity was fortunate that they were, for if they were to achieve their goal, women would become large-handed, big-footed, flat-chested, and thin-lipped. The qualities of emotionalism and sensitivity which disqualified most women for the political life became, when thrown into the political arena, the unlovely traits of the shrew.[7]

Similarly, in *The Bostonians,* Basil envisions fair Verena being transformed by the movement into a "screamer."[8]

Olive is a caricature; she is portrayed as a fanatic. She feels that because women have been wronged for centuries it is now men's turn to be oppressed by women. Worse, James attempts to make us focus on what he implies is

Olive's personal mental sickness rather than on the cause of women which she espouses. Nevertheless, Olive feels the oppression of women to her very marrow:

The unhappiness of women! The voice of their silent suffering was always in her ears, the ocean of tears that they had shed from the beginning of time seemed to pour through her own eyes. Ages of oppression had rolled over them; uncounted millions had lived only to be tortured, to be crucified. They were her sisters, they were her own, and the day of their delivery had dawned. This was the only sacred cause; this was the great, the just revolution. It must triumph, it must sweep everything before it; it must exact from the other, the brutal, blood-stained, ravening race, the last particle of expiation![9]

Olive tutors and trains Verena so that she can use Verena's speaking ability for the women's movement. Initially, she wins Verena's promise never to marry for:

No man that I have ever seen cares a straw in his heart for what we are trying to accomplish. They hate it; they scorn it; they will try to stamp it out whenever they can. Oh yes, I know there are men who pretend to care for it; but they are not really men, and I wouldn't be sure even of them! Any man that one would look at—with him, as a matter of course, it is war upon us to the knife.[10]

Besides seeing Olive as an archetypal "castrating bitch," James strongly implies that she is a latent lesbian who has hypnotized naive Verena for her own "perverted" purposes. Leon Edel, however, claims that James was not consciously portraying a lesbian relationship, but, rather, that in James' time, Bostonian morality considered an intense, non-homosexual relationship between two women to be improper.[11] James' sister, Alice James, was at the time James wrote *The Bostonians* and for some years thereafter, having an intense relationship with Katherine Loring.

James seeks to discredit the women's movement by portraying a feminist leader as an "odd" woman. In other words, James attempts to brand the women's movement with the charge of "lesbianism" or perhaps only "intense relationshipism"—either way, obviously an effective tactic in puritanical nineteenth century America. Despite James' own view of the matter, we can still be moved by Olive's love for Verena when she begs Verena, "Don't fail me, or I shall die."[12] Because we are not circumscribed by James' sense of Victorian propriety, we can legitimately respond to the relationship between Olive and Verena in a way that James never intended.

James further seeks to defame the women's movement by portraying the women who work with Olive as dull and unsociable misfits. They are mediums, vegetarians, and elderly ex-Abolitionists. James' description of Miss Birdseye, an elderly veteran of several reform campaigns, was immediately recognized by his Aunt Kate, James Russell Lowell, and his brother, William James, to be that of Elizabeth Peabody, Nathaniel Hawthorne's sister-in-law, a well-known figure in the Boston reform movements. They objected to his caricatured portrait of her, and James admitted that Miss Peabody had crossed his mind in his first musings on the character although he hadn't seen Miss Peabody for twenty years. In later installments of the originally serialized novel, James tried to give more "dignity" to Miss Birdseye in response to these reactions, yet it must be seen that his opening portrait of Miss Birdseye is not so much an attack on Miss Peabody as on women who are politically dedicated:

She had a sad, soft, pale face, which (and it was the effect of her whole head) looked as if it had been soaked, blurred, and made vague by exposure to some slow dissolvent. The long practice of philanthropy had not given accent to her features; it had rubbed out their transitions, their meanings. The waves of sympathy, of enthusiasm, had wrought upon them in the same way in which the waves of time finally modify the surface of old marble busts, gradually washing away their sharpness, their details. . . . She belonged to the Short-Skirts League, as a matter of course; for she belonged to any and every league that had been founded for almost any purpose whatever. This did not prevent her being a confused, entangled, inconsequent, discursive old woman, whose charity began at home and ended nowhere, whose credulity kept pace with it, and who knew less about her fellow-creatures, if possible, after fifty years of humanitary zeal, than on the day she had gone into the field to testify against the iniquity of most arrangements.[13]

In James' scheme of values, the pinnacle of virtue is
good taste, refinement, and social grace. Precisely because
the feminists of his novel have dedicated themselves to a
social cause they are, in James' eyes, unrefined and grace-
less.

Because of its concentration on the Olive—Verena—
Basil triangle and on the sexual and emotional aspects of
women in the suffrage movement, *The Bostonians* gives us
an idea of the intense feelings (especially the fears) evoked
by the movement. However, James gives us very little
background information on the political context of nineteenth century feminism. Some of his references, nonetheless, do take us out of the triangle and into history. For
example, James' reference to a struggle in the "feminine
camp" centering around two "imperial women," Olive
Chancellor and Mrs. Farrinder, is probably reference to a
split in the women's movement, of which there were many.

Two organizations had emerged from a national convention of the women's movement in 1869: the National
Woman Suffrage Association based in New York and the
American Woman Suffrage Association based in Boston.
The AWSA, the more conservative of the two factions, attempted to concentrate on one issue, suffrage. It appealed
to upper and middle class women, used tactics that were
calculated to win over influential men in the establishment,
and concentrated on getting the laws changed state by state
rather than federally. The AWSA was willing to defer the
struggle for women's suffrage until after Black suffrage was
won. The NWSA worked for the vote but saw the necessity
to struggle on many fronts, especially against the institution of marriage. The NWSA, according to Susan Reverby,
"concerned itself with the conditions of working women,
but even it separated labor and women's demands."[14]

Mrs. Farrinder was not at all interested in women
from the working class, being the leader of the upper class
"ladies of Roxbury." Olive, on the other hand, supposedly
was interested in working class women:

She had long been preoccupied with the romance of the people. She had an immense desire to know intimately some *very* poor girl. This might seem one of the most accessible of pleasures; but, in point of fact, she had not found it so. There were two or three pale shop-maidens whose acquaintance she had sought; but they had seemed afraid of her, and the attempt had come to nothing. She took them more tragically than they took themselves; they couldn't make out what she wanted them to do, and they always ended by being odiously mixed up with Charlie. Charlie was a young man in a white overcoat and a paper collar; it was for him, in the last analysis, that they cared much the most. They cared far more about Charlie than about the ballot.[15]

Thus, we see James once again confusing politics and personal relationships. Olive's movement, as he describes it, was no more working class oriented than Mrs. Farrinder's faction, despite James' own view of the matter. In any case, James never gets around to dealing with the essential lines of difference that divided the women's movement of his time.

At the end of James' novel Verena is "rescued" from the supposed double evil of feminism and lesbianism by the chivalrous Basil Ransom. James has the threat to home and family defeated in the end. Like the antisuffragists of his time, James rightly viewed feminism as a challenge to the social order. In 1867, Senator Williams of Oregon declared:

The woman who undertakes to put her sex in an adversary position to man, who undertakes by the use of some independent political power to contend and fight against man, displays a spirit which would, if able, convert all the now harmonious elements of society into a state of war, and make every home a hell on earth.[16]

And in 1887, Senator Brown of Georgia intoned:

For my part I want when I go to my home—when I turn from the arena where man contends with man for what we call the prizes of this paltry world—I want to go back, not to the embrace of some female ward politician, but to the earnest loving look and touch of a true woman.[17]

James' character Basil Ransom thinks about the world in terms very similar to those of the good Senators. James describes Basil's attitude towards women thusly: "He admitted their rights; these consisted in a standing claim to the generosity and tenderness of the stronger race."[18] To be sure, James' mockery does not fail to fall upon Basil and his marriage to Verena, yet clearly James chooses to align himself with the forces of *Kinde, Kuche, Kirche.* He presents us with a picture of the feminists of his time as seen from the point of view of the movement's opponents.

Unfortunately for Henry James, the American critics whom he might have expected to applaud his efforts to uphold the banner of male chauvinism seem to have missed his point completely. Many reviewers took offense at the title *The Bostonians.* They felt that James had offended the honor and name of Boston, almost as if he had written a contemporary version of *Peyton Place. Literary World, The Catholic World, The Independent,* and *The Critic* all wrote the novel off as a dull and dismal failure.[19] Both *The Dial* and a later review in *Literary World* emphatically declared that the characters were abnormal and reflective of no one. In the words of *Literary World:*

> Mr. James is probably thought by the English fairly to represent some phases of American life in his careful and highly elaborated novels; but we protest that the advanced women and their men associates, as typified by the Tarrants and others, have an atrociously exaggerated importance attached to them. The types, the class, the cause, are not worth the space they occupy.[20]

For somewhat opposite reasons *The Woman's Tribune* did not think the characters reflected reality in an accurate way, either.[21] *The Nation* gave James one of his best American reviews, although that, too, can at best be characterized as mixed praise.[22]

None of the American reviewers concentrated on the social and political issues that the novel takes off from. They apparently felt that the best way to deal with the feminist movement was to ignore it.

The English reviewers at least realized that the subject of women's suffrage was a valid issue and they were keen enough to understand that James was on their side, i.e., against feminism. *The Academy* understood the novel's moral to be that "all schemes must ultimately fail which seek to uncreate the woman God has made, and to reconstitute her as another kind of being," and, therefore, felt the resolution of Verena's marriage to Basil to be right and proper.[23]

By contrast, George Gissing's aim, six years later in *The Odd Women*, was to show just how unnatural and confining the sphere assigned to women by society actually was. He takes the "odd" women, women in rebellion against the social order, seriously—that is, he knows these women are heroic and deals with them as such. In the novel, "odd" also literally refers to about a half million more English women than men who will never be married. Working class women in the late 1800's usually had to work and upper class women generally had more leisure time than at earlier points in history. According to Ensor, among the "educated and better-to-do sections of society" there "developed a large body of leisured unmarried women—unmarried because the oversea employment of upper-class Englishmen entailed by imperial expansion had seriously upset the balances of the sexes in those levels at home, and leisured, because so few paid employments were open to them and it was still the tradition that ladies should be maintained by their families."[24] These leisured, upper class women, together with women from the middle class are the characters of Gissing's novel.

Gissing develops a plot in which Rhoda Nunn and Mary Barfoot, convinced "that whatever man could do, woman could do equally well,"[25] set up a school to train women for new social roles. As Mary Barfoot declares:

We live in a time of warfare, of revolt. If woman is no longer to be womanish, but a human being of powers and responsibilities, she must become militant, defiant. She must push her claims to the extremity. . . .

The old types of womanly perfection are no longer helpful to us. . . . We have to ask ourselves, What course of training will wake women up, make them conscious of their souls, startle them into healthy activity?

It must be something new, something free from the reproach of womanliness. I don't care whether we crowd out the men or not. I don't care *what* results, if only women are made strong and self reliant and nobly independent! . . . Most likely we shall have a revolution in the social order greater than any that yet seems possible. Let it come, and let *us* help it coming. . . .

So, if you like to put it in this way, we are working for the advantage of men as well as for our own. Let the responsibility for disorder rest on those who have made us despise our old selves. At any cost—at any cost—we will free ourselves from the heritage of weakness and contempt![26]

Despite the heroic terms in which Mary Barfoot defends their lives and declares their goals, in her eyes—and more especially in Rhoda Nunn's—the struggle is not for the great mass of women. Rhoda feels no solidarity with women of the lower class, although she was a working woman herself—even if a privileged one. She was a teacher, a cashier in a large shop, and later a shorthand writer. Now comfortably ensconced in Miss Barfoot's school, Rhoda has no interest in the poorer classes or the "ragged regiment," as she calls them. A student at the Great Portland Street School, Winifred Haven, sums up their view of the matter in these words: "I really don't think . . . that there can be any solidarity of ladies with servant girls."[27] This elitist bias and the tendency to blame women themselves rather than the socioeconomic system for their wretched position can be considered a flaw in the novel, yet it is unfortunately an accurate reflection of part of the feminist movement of that time.

The Odd Women was written during a time when the suffrage movement was in a period of ebb. The suffrage movement had declined due to a variety of political difficulties. It was not until the early 1900's that the movement for the vote was revitalized by Mrs. Emmeline Pankhurst and her two daughters, Christabel and Sylvia. In the 1890's there was no organized mass movement for women's rights in England, but there were a number of struggles going on around feminist issues such as legal rights for women, protective legislation for women workers, liberalization of the marriage and divorce laws, and education for women.

Thus, Gissing's emphasis on education as a means for women to advance their position in society reflects an aspect of the struggles that were actually going on at the time. Under pressure from prominent women, a Royal Commission investigated the education of female children and young women in 1867. The Commission's report revealed the limited extent and stereotypical nature of women's education. From then on, women like Gissing's Rhoda Nunn and Mary Barfoot—most prominently, Dorothea Beale—were active in improving the existing educational system for women and in establishing separate institutions for women.

Gissing's Booker T. Washington-like emphasis on self-help as the primary method for women to improve their status in society as opposed to the building of a mass movement that would struggle against the prevailing powers and for social change is reflective both of the time the novel is set in and of Gissing's own politics. In 1881 Gissing joined a society whose purpose was to educate the working class about socialism. By 1892 he was still speaking positively about the "social revolution in progress" but also affirming his faith in a natural "aristocracy of brains."[28] This ambivalence of political allegiances led Gissing into all sorts of contradictions. In 1888 he heard Louise Michel, heroine of the Paris Commune, speak on "Le Rôle des Femmes dans l'Humanité" at the Salle des Conférences in Paris. He confided the following to his diary:

I had expected to see a face with more refinement in it; she looks painfully like a fishwife. Dressed with excessive plainness in black and wearing an ugly bonnet. Much fluency, of course, and signs of intellect. Demanded absolute equality of women with men in education and rights.[29]

Gissing's class and sexist bias are revealed by the way he

pays more attention to how Louise Michel looked than to what she said. It is hard to determine whether Gissing's general attitude of contempt for Michel stems from the way she looked, the fact that she was a woman from the working class, or the fact that she was a revolutionist.

Gissing's political outlook is made very explicit in *The Odd Women.* Mary Barfoot "did not seek to become known as the leader of a 'movement',"[30] although both she and Rhoda Nunn acknowledge that there are two great movements of their time: the movement for the emancipation of their sex and the movement for the emancipation of the working class. They did not, however, consider these movements to be very effective. Rather, they believed their "quiet work" of training women for new pursuits such as being pharmaceutical chemists, running a bookseller's shop, and being clerks was "probably more effectual than the public career of women who propagandize for female emancipation."[31]

Despite these ideological deficiencies, the novel makes a close examination of the areas of conflict inherent in the institution of marriage in a rather cogent fashion. (Perhaps the fact that Gissing suffered through two miserable marriages had something to do with his success in this area.) Rhoda maintains " 'that the vast majority of women lead a vain and miserable life because they *do* marry.' "[32] Later, she goes on to say, "I would have girls taught that marriage is a thing to be avoided rather than hoped for. I would teach them that for the majority of women marriage means disgrace.' " And when her suitor, Everard Barfoot asks what she means, she replies, " 'Because the majority of men are without a sense of honor. To be bound to them in wedlock is shame and misery.' "[33] She suggests that when women value themselves a marriage of equality might be feasible.

Yet living one's ideology is difficult as Rhoda discovers when Everard Barfoot endeavors like Basil Ransom to prove that there is no such thing as an independent woman. Everard almost succeeds; he brings Rhoda to the point of asking for a legal marriage. He almost succeeds because he is persistent (Everard is a play on words implying that he is always arduous). Rhoda had deceived herself—she had lived like a nun, denying her emotional and sexual needs. Everard's attentions temporarily overwhelmed her precisely because she had never before acknowledged this side of her being. Rhoda, however, finally rejects marriage partially because she sees herself slipping back into a male-dependent role. She re-establishes herself as an independent woman, stronger and more perceptive. That is, she re-establishes her commitment to her self and to her vision of the new woman and to the political and educational work necessary to create the new woman.

Another major figure in *The Odd Women*, Monica Madden, does fall into the marriage trap. She marries an elderly, well-heeled gentleman, Edmund Widdowson, in order to escape the oppressive life of a "shop girl." Although *The Odd Women*, like *The Bostonians*, takes no special notice of the problems of working women, at least Gissing does give us a glimpse of the world of shop women through his portrait of Monica. Monica lived and worked in a drapery establishment. Along with many other women she slept in the establishment's dormitory. She worked from early morning to late at night, thirteen and a half hours a day, six days a week. During Christmas week the women worked until one in the morning. The women were given twenty minutes for each meal, although they were often called into the shop before the allotted time was up and never got a chance to eat. Women would faint on the job. The bosses gave them brandy to keep them going. Since the women were not allowed to sit while working, a common problem was varicose veins. Monica often lost all feeling in her feet. On Sunday, the women were not allowed to remain in the dormitory to rest, but were forced to wander the city. And if their "book of takings" wasn't very good, they would be peremptorily fired.

But from one form of oppression, Monica goes right into another. Widdowson, insane with jealousy and obsessed with his male privileges and status, is described by Gissing as thinking of himself in the following manner: "He himself represented the guardian male, the wife-proprietor, who from the dawn of civilization has taken the abundant care that woman shall not outgrow her nonage."[34] He seeks to chain Monica to the home. Monica is destroyed by her struggle against her new captivity, finally dying in childbirth.

Widdowson is not merely a fanatic. He represents the accepted attitude of a man towards women in Victorian England. The legal right of married women to leave the house against their husband's wishes or to "slam the door" permanently as Monica did in the effort to escape her captivity had been granted to women only shortly before The Odd Women was written. "The wife's refusal to return to her home was no longer regarded as an offence punishable with imprisonment, and the law deprived the husband of his right to confine a wife who refused to live with him. The husband was no longer permitted to deprive his wife by testament of the guardianship of her children."[35] This is not to say that the law ceased to favor the husband's patriarchal rights—and what the law didn't enforce, social convention did.

Monica's struggle looks melodramatic unless one retains a view of the social background against which her personal struggle took place. Grounds for divorce on the part of a woman were few and hard to prove. According to an 1857 English law, a woman was entitled to divorce her husband on the grounds of "incest, rape, bigamy with a married woman, an unnatural offence, or adultery accompanied by cruelty or desertion."[36] In 1878 an addition was made allowing a woman to separate from (but not divorce) her husband if he committed an aggravated assault upon her. No further reforms of the divorce and separation laws were made until 1909. Monica's reason for leaving her husband—mental cruelty—was by no means a grounds for either divorce or separation during the time in which *The Odd Women* took place.

Widdowson was bitter about "the fact that he had wedded a woman who irresistibly proved to him her claims as a human being."[37] He loved her, after his fashion, but his male chauvinism was so all-consuming that he was unable to view her as an autonomous human being:

Never had it occurred to Widdowson that a wife remains an individual, with rights and obligations independent of her wifely condition. Everything he said presupposed his own supremacy; he took for granted that it was his to direct, hers to be guided. A display of energy, purpose, ambition, on Monica's part, which had no reference to domestic pursuits, would have gravely troubled him; at once he would have set himself to subdue, with all gentleness, impulses so inimical to his idea of the married state.[38]

When Monica makes her final break with Widdowson, he considers two alternatives, either "carrying her by main force to an upper room and there locking her in" or killing her: "Only by homicide can a man maintain his dignity in a situation of this kind."[39] He does neither. He is too weak, too drained by Monica's defiance of his male chauvinism.

Every marriage but one in the novel results in tragedy. However, those women who do not marry fare no better. Monica's sisters, educated to be ornaments, are left penniless; they have no survival skills. They do survive, although shakily, on money provided by Monica's husband and by virtue of the encouragement provided by Rhoda Nunn and Mary Barfoot. Eventually, they decide to establish a school of their own. When Monica dies they are left to raise her baby daughter, a symbol of the new woman. Rhoda's final words to them in the book concern the infant. She says, "Make a brave woman of her."[40]

Others who don't marry in *The Odd Women* are the women of the Bevis family—a mother and three daughters.

Their only means of support is income of Mrs. Bevis' son—again the recurrent dependency on a male. As a result he is forced to abandon his creative talents as a musician in order to earn money as a wine merchant. The Bevis women have been so brought up that they are merely frivolous, empty-headed, and decorous; they have no conception of their own oppression or the oppressive situation of their male bread-winner.

Like Henry James, Gissing also portrays an intimate relationship between two feminists: Rhoda Nunn and Mary Barfoot. Both writers pull back from fully exploring the women's feelings for each other, but Gissing does not mock them or suggest that there is something unhealthy in the alliance of two women fighting a common cause. Rather he shows the real day-to-day problems of being women without men, trying to live together with other women, trying to forge new roles and images for women. One of the problems they encounter is jealousy. Mary Barfoot secretly cared for her cousin Everard, but in contrast to the way Henry James depicts Olive's clutching reaction to Verena's involvement with Ransom, Mary manages to suppress her feelings in order to allow Rhoda to work out her feelings for Everard in her own way. In another instance, Mary's concern about a "wayward girl" who eventually commits suicide and Rhoda's indifference to her almost lead to their separation. However, Rhoda apologizes for her hard ways and Mary agrees to "kiss and be friends."[41]

Since feminism was not exactly the English critics' most agreeable topic, Gissing's reception was not overwhelming among them. Most reviewers simply ignored the book. *The Athenaeum*, an English publication, acknowledged that Gissing's book reflected real problems in English society and dealt with them realistically.[42] The American *Nation* praised the book, somewhat ironically, for honoring "old maids" but felt that Gissing played into the hands of "the conservators of morals" by his "intemperance of partisanship" in displaying the wreck of marriages and the vision of *"union libre."*[43] The English *Spectator* expressed interest in the issues raised in the novel and then turned around and suggested that "perhaps the wisest, and certainly the easiest course of procedure, [would be] to regard *The Odd Women* as a novel pure and simple, rather than as a contribution to the discussion of one of the most difficult of social questions."[44]

The generally poor reception which both James and Gissing got for their novels dealing with the topic of feminism—for *The Bostonians* the reviews were negative, while *The Odd Women* was virtually ignored—showed that in the latter part of the nineteenth century polite literary society found the topic of women's emancipation too painful to contemplate. James was so discouraged by the experience that he ceased writing fiction about American society until his last years. One wonders how many other writers, male and especially female, were also discouraged from taking up this most controversial of topics. Only a small number of other novels have ever been written about the feminist movement. For example, and most interestingly, *Ann Vickers* by Sinclair Lewis tells the story of a woman who in the course of her unconventional career becomes an organizer in the Ohio of 1912 for the suffrage movement. Some other feminist-oriented novels include *The Women's Conquest of New York* by Thomas Janvier Allibone (1894), *The Closed Door* by Hannah Julia Price (1913), *Rebel Women* by Evelyn Sharp (1916), *Banner Bearers* by Oreola Harskell (1920), *For Rent—One Pedestal* (1917) by Marjorie Shuler, and *The Sturdy Oak* (1917), a composite novel by fourteen American authors.

In any case, the least that can be said for both *The Odd Women* and *The Bostonians* is that they give us considerable insight into the women's issues and new life styles of their period. Both Basil Ransom and Edmund Widdowson give us a clear picture of the anti-feminist, male chauvinist attitudes of the day. The novels present us with a fairly accurate portrait of the upper and middle class nature of the leadership of the movement for women's emancipation. Most important, despite James' hostility to feminism and Gissing's cautious support, both novels convey a sense of the excitement, the passion and the power of the feminist movement in the late 1800's.

NOTES

[1]Henry James, *The Bostonians* (New York: The Modern Library, 1956), p. 91.

[2]James, p. 244.   [3]James, p. 253.

[4]*The Notebooks of Henry James*, ed. F. O. Matthiessen and Kenneth B. Murdock (New York: Oxford University Press, 1947), pp. 46-47.

[5]*Letters of George Gissing*, ed. Algernon and Ellen Gissing (New York: Houghton Mifflin Company, 1927), p. 83.

[6]James, p. 18.

[7]Aileen S. Kraditor, *The Ideas of the Woman Suffrage Movement 1890-1900* (New York: Columbia University Press, 1965), pp. 36-37.

[8]James, p. 66.   [9]James, pp. 37-38.

[10]James, p. 139.

[11]Leon Edel, *Henry James: The Middle Years* (New York: J. B. Lippincott Company, 1962), p. 140.

[12]James, p. 141.   [13]James, pp. 26-27.

[14]Susan Reverby, "The Labor and Suffrage Movements: A View of Working Class Women in the Twentieth Century" in *Liberation Now*, ed. Deborah Babcox and Madeline Belkin (New York: Dell Publishing Co., Inc., 1971), p. 96. See also, Eleanor Flexner, *Century of Struggle* (New York: Atheneuam, 1970), pp. 217 & 247; Kraditor, pp. 147, 259-261; and Debby Woodroofe, "American Feminism 1848-1920," in *International Socialist Review*, XXXII (March 1971). "The Relation of the Woman Suffrage Movement to the Labor Question" reprinted from *The Woman's Tribune* of Beatrice, Nebraska in the *Woman's Union Journal*, the Organ of the Women's Protective and Provident League of London, pleads with the suffrage movement to support working class women especially in their fight for an eight hour day and on their picket lines: "This year brings us an opportunity of retrieving ourselves from the charge, now only too well founded, of representing the interests of the women of the property holding class, and leaving our sisters of the wage earning majority to take care of themselves." XI (June 1886).

[15]James, p. 35; see also pp. 165-167.

[16]Flexner, p. 148.   [17]Flexner, p. 175.

[18]James, p. 198.

[19]*Literary World*, XVII (April 17, 1886), p. 137. *The Catholic World*, XLIII (April 1886), p. 130. *The Independent*, XXXVIII (April 22, 1886), p. 495. *The Critic*, VIII (April 17, 1886), p. 198.

[20]*Literary World*, XVII (June 12, 1886), p. 198. *The Dial*, VII (May 1886), p. 14.

[21]*The Woman's Tribune*, III (February 1886); also (December 1885).

[22]*The Nation*, XLII (May 13, 1886), p. 407.

[23]*The Academy*, XXIX (March 6, 1886), p. 162. *The British Quarterly Review*, LXXXIII (April 1886), p. 481 also understood the moral of *The Bostonians*: "Mr. Henry James has here written an amusing book—full of characters and points, whose aim is to justify the life of women in the sphere most natural to it—the sphere of home and family influence, and to show how much it lost alike to her and to the world whenever she makes any attempt to pass beyond it."

[24]C. K. Ensor, *England 1870-1914* (London: Oxford University Press, 1960), p. 339.

[25]George Gissing, *The Odd Women* (New York: W. W. Norton and Company, 1971), p. 54.

[26]Gissing, pp. 135-137. *The Women's Union Journal*, XV (Dec. 15, 1890), has an article entitled "Character in Women and How to Educate It" which sounds similar to Mary Barfoot, except this is directed to working class women: "Miss Foley suggested that for women who were breadwinners and standing on their own footing in the battle of life, it was surely better to add to their womanliness those manly virtues by which men in like circumstance become strong and worthy."

[27]Gissing, p. 53.

[28]*Letters of George Gissing*, pp. 96, 327.

[29]*Letters of George Gissing*, p. 225.

[30]Gissing, p. 54.   [31]Gissing, p. 54.

[32]Gissing, p. 59.   [33]Gissing, p. 99.

[34]Gissing, p. 197.

[35]Elié Halévy, *The Rule of Democracy 1905-1914* (London: Ernest Benn Limited, 1961), p. 497. Other fiction from that period besides *The Odd Women* reflects the woman's revolt from the home; e.g., Ibsen's *A Doll House* (1889), H. G. Wells' *Ann Veronica* (1909), G. B. Shaw's *Mrs. Warren's Profession* (1905) and Sarah Grand's *The Heavenly Twins* (1901).

36Halévy, p. 492. 37Gissing, p. 197.
38Gissing, p. 152. 39Gissing, pp. 251-252.
40Gissing, p. 356. 41Gissing, p. 137.
42The *Athenaeum*, No. 3422 (May 27, 1893), p. 66.
43The *Nation*, LVII (July 13, 1893), pp. 31-32.
44The *Spectator*, LXX (May 27, 1893), p. 707.

JUDITH LITTLE

HEROISM IN *TO THE LIGHTHOUSE*

Too often in literature, as in life, the person who acts, suffers, achieves, and learns, is a man. In fiction, the man is the hero; in life, the man is the human being. In both literature and everyday reality, the woman is the protector, the encourager, or the destroyer, of the man's ambitions; she is the "heroine." An unusually perceptive Victorian heroine is Mrs. Ramsey in Virginia Woolf's novel *To The Lighthouse*. Mrs. Ramsey's central position in the novel, and her courageous self-knowledge almost qualify her as "hero." Nevertheless, she must falsify her own perceptions and desires in order to fulfill the prescribed role of "other" —as mere landscape to Mr. Ramsey's postured heroism.

In Section XI of "The Window" Mrs. Ramsey becomes "herself, by herself" as she meets the third and longest beam from the lighthouse; she perceives a contradiction in her values. As she looks at the light, she tries to locate the insincerity in the thought which has just risen in her mind: "We are in the hands of the Lord." This thought seems foreign to her clearest perception of things:

She had been trapped into saying something she did not mean. She looked up over her knitting and met the third stroke and it seemed to her like her own eyes meeting her own eyes, searching as she alone could search into her mind and her heart, purifying out of existence that lie, any lie. She praised herself in praising the light, without vanity, for she was stern, she was searching, she was beautiful like that light.[1]

This moment of vision for Mrs. Ramsey is a startling moment of vision for the reader as well, for we see, perhaps even more clearly than she does, the violent incongruity between her self-knowledge, at this moment, and the actions which she continually directs toward the supposed happiness of others.

In the first place, her relationship to her husband absolutely forbids her to be stern, forbids her to speak the truth, and almost forbids her to perceive it. Also, she has considerable vanity, as she herself suspects. And her capacity for "searching" is restricted to moments such as these, for her husband prefers a "vagueness" in women's minds, and her society's expectations regarding human relationships restrain and simplify her sensitivity to others into conventional solutions and explanations: Paul and Minta must marry, as everybody must; Charles Tansley will survive in the world because he has "his work"; children go through "stages." Although Mrs. Ramsey conducts an elaborate, even imaginative, social symphony, she herself rightly suspects that there is more motion than music to it.

She is not entirely content, for instance, after her exhausting effort to reassure her husband that he is a success in the eyes of the world, and especially in the eyes of his wife. Her son James realizes, standing between her knees, that the reassuring, fertile, sympathetic atmosphere which she creates with her knitting, her conversation, and her laughter costs his mother a tremendous effort; he resents his father for demanding such a sacrifice from her. But Mrs. Ramsey is willing to exhaust her own ego if that is what is necessary to secure her husband in his:

So boasting of her capacity to surround and protect, there was scarcely a shell of herself left for her to know herself by; all was so lavished and spent; and James, as he stood stiff between her knees, felt her rise in a rosy-flowered fruit tree laid with leaves and dancing boughs into which the beak of brass, the arid scimitar of his father, the egotistical man, plunged and smote, demanding sympathy (60).

The irony here is that Mr. Ramsey has demanded and obtained for himself what he denied to his son; Mr. Ramsey has been soothed "like a child," the author remarks in the next sentence; he has received the sustaining assurance of an illusory hope, whereas he would not allow his wife to comfort James with the hope of a trip to the lighthouse. Mr. Ramsey insists that his children confront the "facts," however disappointing, but he cannot himself face the knowledge that his achievements have been moderate instead of spectacular. He insists on truth for his children, but allows himself the comfort of a lie.

Mrs. Ramsey's awareness of her own contribution to this lie disturbs the satisfaction which she would otherwise feel in having so successfully protected her husband from his own fears. She returns to the story which she is reading to James, Grimm's tale of a rather dependent husband in "The Fisherman's Wife," and she tries to understand her discontent:

She did not like, even for a second, to feel finer than her husband; and further, could not bear not being entirely sure, when she spoke to him, of the truth of what she said (61).

It is this element of falsity which continues to trouble her. She recognizes not only a falsity in her relationship with other people, but a certain amount of vanity as well:

For her own self-satisfaction was it that she wished so instinctively to help, to give, that people might say of her, "O Mrs. Ramsey! dear Mrs. Ramsey . . . Mrs. Ramsey, of course!" and need her and send for her and admire her? (65)

The implied answer seems to be "Yes," but the self-seeking is certainly understandable; by knitting stockings for the tubercular boy at the lighthouse, by arranging marriages, by running errands in town for her guests, and by transforming the dinner which culminates Part I of the novel into a celebration of human solidarity and happiness, Mrs. Ramsey is able to regain something of the "self" which she is so continually being asked to sacrifice to the vanity of others. Her own vanity requests that her name be on somebody's tongue occasionally; her husband's vanity requests that she build an elaborate, protective lie around him occasionally.

Mrs. Ramsey's self-knowledge is not really contradictory, although it seems to be so. On the one hand, she recognizes in herself lies and vanity; and yet, as she meets the third stroke of light, she affirms that there is nothing false or vain in her at all. The reasons for her apparent doubleness become clearer as she tries to discover the source of her insincere thought about being in "the hands of the Lord." She knows that "with her mind she had always seized the fact that there is no reason, order, justice: but suffering, death, the poor." And while she muses on the "treachery" of the world and the impermanence of happiness, her face becomes uncharacteristically stern. Her husband sees this and is distressed by "the sternness at the heart of her beauty," because it makes her aloof from him; he is not needed to protect her (98-99). Their relationship depends to a great extent on a code of responses which they both adhere to most of the time. She must protect him, but he must feel that it is he who protects her. She must not presume to see the harsher aspects of life. For if she did see them, how could he trust and believe the illusory world of hope which he from time to time asks her to build around him? In other words, if he allowed her the sternness which he reserves only for his own self-dramatized heroism, he would have no retreat from this heroic sternness. For him, Mrs. Ramsey must be something which she is not; and for this reason, Mrs. Ramsey recognizes the beam of light as "so much her, yet so little her" (99). The lies and the vanity belong to her role as wife of Mr. Ramsey; they do not belong to her.

Mrs. Ramsey senses the implicit request of her husband as he again passes the window; she calls to him, knowing that he will not call to her: "he wished, she knew, to protect her" (100). Her relationship to him depends on his feeling that she is in his protective hands, and it is likely that this relationship has something to do with her thought, "We are in the hands of the Lord." She knows that the thought is insincere, but it came readily, out of habit—the habit of responding to her husband in the same way.

After we have seen Mrs. Ramsey confront so simply and beautifully the revealing third stroke of light, her subsequent conversation with her husband as they walk together seems especially artificial and sad. And yet, it serves for them the same purpose that remarks about the weather serve for casual strangers; it makes them feel that they are meeting each other, even though they are not. They agree that children go through stages, that Charles Tansley would be an unsuitable match for their daughter, Prue, and they disagree about the importance of their son's getting a scholarship. But this disagreement is something customary: "They disagreed always about this, but it did not matter. She liked him to believe in scholarships, and he liked her to be proud of Andrew whatever he did" (103). To depart from these customary roles, or even to threaten to depart from them, causes pain and embarrassment:

He did not like to see her look so sad, he said. Only wool gathering, she protested, flushing a little. They both felt uncomfortable, as if they did not know whether to go on or go back. She had been reading fairy tales to James, she said. No, they could not share that; they could not say that (104).

The irony is extreme; they cannot share what they *do share*: the knowledge of a world which, in their eyes, tends to deal rather harshly with human hopes and endeavors. Both of them see this. And both are capable of searching themselves, of casting aside vanity and self-deceit; Mr. Ramsey recognizes that his books will not be remembered for long, and Mrs. Ramsey can perceive the element of self-interest in her efforts to arrange for everybody's happiness. Both are intelligent, courageous human beings; but both pretend that all the intelligence and courage belong only to Mr. Ramsey.

Here are two people who see the same world, but because one is a man, and the other is a woman and a wife, they must pretend to see the world differently. And the kind of world they see is a rather brutal one, as Virginia

Woolf portrays it—a world in which a death is described casually in a participial phrase while the main thrust of the sentence tells of something else, a world in which a son is blown up between brackets while pages of night, wind, and years nearly overwhelm the brief achievement of human unity, sharing, and happiness which Mrs. Ramsey's dinner celebrates. True, both Mr. Ramsey and his wife arrive at the lighthouse—which is at least a symbol of clear-sighted knowledge about oneself and the world, although this aspect does not exhaust such a fertile symbol. Mr. Ramsey is finally able to cast aside his self-dramatization as he approaches the lighthouse near the end of the novel, and Mrs. Ramsey is freed briefly of her mask as she looks at the third stroke of light. But they could have seen this truth together; instead, as Mrs. Ramsey realizes, "They could not share that."

The role of the hero is reserved for Mr. Ramsey, as the role of the hero in literature generally is reserved for the man; the woman, the "heroine," must then protect him from the rather large burdens of his extravagant fortitude. If the heroism, the courage and strength, were shared in the first place neither the suffering nor the sympathy would need to be built on lies or vanity. Men and women, as companions in a real world instead of play-actors in a fantastic one, would probably find that there is enough real suffering and real sympathy to suffice everyone.

NOTE

[1] Virginia Woolf, *To The Lighthouse* (New York: Harcourt, Brace and World, 1927), pp. 95-97. Further references are indicated by page number in parentheses in the text.

DAWN HOLT ANDERSON

MAY SARTON'S WOMEN

Women in fiction, like women in our culture, usually find, and sometimes lose, their identity in institutionalized relationships such as marriage and motherhood, waiting to see what their men and their children will demand them to be. If they break out of these molds, they usually turn to the business world, a world defined by males, to find their success. Few writers provide women with any models for relationships or ways of life and work outside those which have been codified and sanctified over the years. May Sarton's work, however, is resplendent with new models. Her women characters are alone, forging thoughtful and meaningful lives for themselves, not waiting to be defined in terms of a mate or a nine to five job. Miss Sarton examines valid relationships that women can form, especially with other women, which are outside the usual relationships available to them—women talking, playing and creating together meaningfully. She deals with woman's work and the necessity of integrating womanhood, the total self, into that work so it can become a source of joy and fulfillment. The women who are main characters in three of Miss Sarton's novels establish their own identity by breaking through the molds of standard relationships for women to form new and regenerative ones with others. They rely on themselves as sources of strength, and make full use of their talents in their work.

Two of the novels, *Joanna and Ulysses* and *The Small Room*, begin with the breakup of a standard relationship for women. Joanna has become a mother to her father and a prisoner in her home. She has worked in an office, kept the house going and nursed her father for years. Now at thirty she is breaking the mold for a month's holiday, to paint. Lucy Winter, in *The Small Room*, is also leaving an institutionalized relationship; her engagement is broken. She is on her way to the woman's college where she has taken her first teaching job. Both women must forge new relationships in which to grow. Both must face their aloneness, begin to define themselves as solitary entities, and to find new relationships which will enrich their lives.

In a third novel, *Mrs. Stevens Hears the Mermaids Singing*, Hilary Stevens, a seventy year old writer, reviews her life for two young interviewers. The important relationships for her have each been short lived but intense. Her story is a series of comings together and partings. For most of her life she has lived alone; the best in her has been drawn forth by the brief relationships she has formed with others. In this novel, Miss Sarton dramatizes the great importance of woman's relationships as means to fertilize her creative powers. The seeds of Hilary's creative works, books of poetry and two novels, have blossomed through a variety of personal relationships. Her three year marriage, the only institutionalized relationship Hilary entered, resulted in no writing at all. Marriage was a shelter, a safety to her, a long holiday from herself. Selfhood was "submerged in the great primal darkness" (p. 39) of union. Once when she allowed her husband, Adrian, to see her inner powers, he admonished her for her intensity. "You take everything so hard, Hilary. . . ." (p. 41) The other important relationships in her life have been "instruments of revelation," "epiphanies," (p. 97) for her. In her governess, Phillipa, in an understanding friend, Willa, and even in memories of her long dead mother, Hilary perceives, though only briefly, the passionate inner selves which they submerged in order to function in the culturally acceptable roles as job holders, proper wives and mothers. From moments of intimate contact, Hilary learns to develop rather than to hide the powerful personality within her.

From Phillipa she first learns to direct her emotions, specifically her "crush" on the governess, into works of art rather than to expend them futilely in self pity. Through the deep friendship she forms with Willa, Hilary develops a tight control over her own feelings in her poetry. Willa is a woman who entertains frequently. She listens and questions, drawing from her guests their best thoughts and revealing their talents. Her own inner life is never revealed at these gatherings. From memories of her own mother, a woman who shunned any show of intense passion or thought, Hilary senses that she, like her daughter, was meant to be an artist. But to fit the institutionalized roles of wife and mother, she forced herself to reject her own inner life.

One summer Hilary rents the house of a now dead woman. She comes to know the woman whose peace of mind is reflected in her home. Hilary senses the importance of creating surroundings which will mirror one's own inner life, as much to remind herself of her identity as to reveal herself to visitors. Hilary buys a home, and lovingly tends her garden, her cat and turtles, creating peace and order in her home as in a poem. Miss Sarton comments that "no man would have done that." (p. 148)

Another relationship Hilary forms reveals two important points which Miss Sarton repeatedly makes: first that intense friendships between women bring forth their creativity, and that sexual relationships are not nearly so valuable to individual growth as the culture assumes them to be. Hilary deeply loves her friend Dorothea, a woman with a scientific, "anti-mystic" approach to life. Her cynical and statistical views are the opposite of Hilary's; they operate from different spheres. What matters most to Hilary matters not at all to Dorothea. While their friendship remains just that, Hilary learns to cut her poetry to the sparest, writing sharp, clear lines. But when the women live together in a homosexual relationship, once more Hilary's poetry stops. She is content to make curtains, arrange flowers and stay close to home. Miss Sarton indicates that living with others in sexual relationships is debilitating to personal growth. At best, as in the marriage of Hilary and Adrian, creativity goes to sleep. At worst, as with Dorothea, love becomes a "devastating, destructive rage," demanding so much psychic energy that the truly creative talents wither.

In *Joanna and Ulysses,* Joanna, like Hilary, is an artist. On her vacation island she develops her talents to their fullest after forming a warm attachment with a donkey which she buys to save him from the brutal beatings of his driver. Her tenderness, pity and concern for all things has long been scorned by her father as a woman's foolishness. The men on the island, whose livelihood comes from driving donkeys for the tourists and their luggage, feel the same scorn for Joanna's caring. They can never come to terms with her motives for buying the sorely misused donkey, nor understand her matelessness. The donkey, which she names Ulysses, becomes a symbol for the natural, sensual self, the joy that has been locked away in Joanna. Their relationship, like the human ones Miss Sarton portrays, is not always easy or free from the annoyances and demands which any contact makes on an individual. When Joanna is eager to paint, Ulysses munches the precious flowers of a neighbor or wants to be fed or to play. But she learns to leave the donkey tethered when she paints. She returns to him when her work is done, and is enriched by his joy. Freedom to retreat from any relationship, to turn to solitude[1] and to work, is a necessary aspect of the life styles which Miss Sarton presents.

The contacts in these novels have all the drawbacks of real relationships; yet they enrich the characters and draw forth their inner resources. The donkey's delight in the simplest pleasures, in eating or in a friendly nuzzling, reminds Joanna that tensions are not necessary, that a truly simple life based on fulfilling basic needs, can bring joy. Joanna forms a relationship with a pet, as does Hilary

Stevens. Miss Sarton indicates that some relationship with the natural world—with animals or with the soil—is necessary for drawing out the natural in the self.

At home Joanna's painting has been quite amateurish; her inner self has been long submerged. And at first on her holiday she limits herself, portraying only tiny crannies, small portions of the lovely village where she stays. However, during the holiday, she gives freely of her tenderness and concern, releasing the traits that even she has come to scorn as foolish. She accepts herself and the fact that for her caring and for her solitude she may seem odd to those around her. In accepting these parts of her personality and life style, she becomes more herself and as a result is able to see and thus to paint the essence of the whole village.

On her arrival home, Joanna must hide Ulysses in the basement or her father will send him away. She is again hiding her inner self. But her painting has become real and her talent is recognizable. Her father and others admire her work. Her self esteem grows, so that when Ulysses is discovered she is able to give him to a donkey driver; the relationship ends. Joanna can carry on her work with a new dignity.

Miss Sarton repeats this pattern of life, of a woman alone, learning through her relationships with others to make full use of her own creative talents, in *The Small Room*. Lucy Winter leaves her lover and must, like Joanna, accept her aloneness and forge new relationships. As she comes to Appleton College, she studies the models of established relationships around her. There is the marriage of a delightfully cynical New Englander, Jack, and a passionate and powerful Italian woman, Maria. There is the long-standing friendship of two older women: Caryl Cope, academic genius and star teacher at Appleton, and Olive Hunt, a trustee of the college whose strength and power is money. There is Jennifer Finch, a wise and gracious teacher who is "owned" by her aging mother, and Hallie Summerson who lives alone and has made a warm home in which to entertain her friends and colleagues. All these women except Maria Beveridge live without men. Their relationships are explored, and some of them rent asunder, in the dramatic question of the novel. This question is to define the most valid relationship between teacher and student. It becomes a question that not only Lucy, but the whole college must answer when Jane Seaman, Caryl Cope's most brilliant protege plagarizes an article. Forced to produce more and more by her own desire for approval, and by Caryl's eagerness to develop her intellect, Jane is pushed to cheating. By recognition of her own guilt in Jane's troubles, Caryl comes to feel that the education process must involve more than developing the academic aspect of a person. Her admission that Jane may have come to her for understanding and not just for books, causes a final rift in her friendship with Olive who has steadfastly refused to vote that the college hire a psychiatrist as part of its faculty. Miss Sarton suggests that it is the intelligence of the aging Caryl which allows her to change her views and accept the education of the total person, while Olive, who has relied on her wealth rather than on her inner resources, is set in her character mold and so demands only academic excellence from the students.

Like Olive, Jack Beveridge insists on academic excellence as the only standard for a good education. But Maria, by the instinct of her passionate nature, recognizes Jane's inner torment and the need to deal with the totality of the student, her psychic and emotional as well as intellectual needs. Their marriage almost ends in divorce.

As Lucy tries to find her own answer to what constitutes a good education, all of the women meet again and again, at parties, on walks, on campus. Their conversations are not trivial but real and valid. They question the nature of excellence and of justice. They are women interrelating, concerned with their work and with each other. Jack Beveridge refers to the price of excellence. But Maria and the others insist on the joy of excellence. They see that fulfillment, not sacrifice, is the companion of excellence.

The college's decision to hire a psychiatrist, thus to administer to the total person, is mirrored in Lucy's development as a teacher. By allowing herself to form a relationship of kindly understanding with Pippa, a dramatic and sentimental student, Lucy draws out the girl's academic talents. Miss Sarton presents models of women who have established unions outside the institutionalized ones generally approved for them. She makes more joy, a richer more intense life a possibility for women. Through *The Small Room*, Miss Sarton indicates that long standing relationships such as marriage and the life long friendship between the two older women are debilitating. The briefer relationships such as those with students and colleagues retain the brilliance and intensity of a first love and enrich the individuals who form them far more than do those lasting ones the culture sanctions.

As in the other novels, Miss Sarton insists that meaningful relationships bring fruition to the creativity in the individual. Through her relationships with her colleagues, Lucy grows as a teacher. She begins, uncertain of her goals and methods, but by experiencing the problems of teaching and by contact with the people like Caryl and Hallie who hold opposite points of view about their work, Lucy is able to find her own most creative path as a teacher. Before *The Small Room* begins, Lucy has worked to earn a Ph.D. Her motivation is not academic or intellectual; it is done simply to be near her fiance while he finishes medical school. When she doesn't marry, but instead enters a profession, she must feel out the path between academic commitment and emotional commitment that will fulfill her own as well as her students' total needs. In one conference with a freshman comp student, Lucy asks the girl to rewrite a confused sentence. When she senses the panic in the girl, she allows her to revise later in her own room. Lucy wonders if she has been too easy; shouldn't she have insisted on excellence at the moment? But as the college

determines to add psychiatric services to its other offerings, as Caryl Cope recognizes that she has turned her back
on Jane's emotional needs, Lucy learns to accept her own
sensitive, human response to students as a necessary part
of her self as a teacher.

None of the valuable relationships in Miss Sarton's
books are of lifelong duration such as marriage and motherhood. All begin, enrich and then end. Each individual,
like Joanna and her donkey, becomes strong enough to go
on to solitude, and to his or her own work. Hilary chooses
to live alone, enjoying the brief but intense relationships
which come and go in her life. Joanna remains in the
house with her father, but her inner life and her painting
are rich enough that she can live at peace with herself.
Lucy decides to stay at Appleton, to regard teaching as her
profession and, presumably, to live alone as do Caryl and
Hallie.

Again and again Miss Sarton sets forth models of
women who recognize their need for solitude in order to
establish their own identity. They reject the roles that
society has sanctioned for them. They do not wait to find
themselves by finding a man to urge or shelter them. They
accept themselves as entities; they interrelate with others
in short term encounters from which they are free to return to solitude. From the interaction and from the times
of solitude, they are able to develop their own powers to
the fullest.

NOTE

[1]This idea was derived from an unpublished paper by Susan
Koppelman Cornillon

FEMINIST AESTHETICS

FLORENCE HOWE

FEMINISM AND LITERATURE*

The connections between feminism and literature are deep and abiding, if only because literature has been one of the few vocations open to women. The century that saw what Ian Watt calls *The Rise of the Novel* also saw numbers of women for the first time writing and publishing books. At about the same time that Jane Austen was beginning to conceal from her father and his congregation the fact that she was attempting novels, Mary Wollstonecraft was writing the first feminist tract. Inspired by the prose of Tom Paine and by the ideals of the French and American revolutions, Wollstonecraft in 1791 questioned whether half the human race were to be denied liberty, equality and fraternity. More than fifty years later, across the Atlantic, another woman writer, Margaret Fuller, tried again. *Woman in the Nineteenth Century*, like Wollstonecraft's *A Vindication of the Rights of Women*, was a book ahead of its time. Both volumes have suffered similar fates: they shocked and irritated contemporary readers; and except for a small feminist following, they disappeared from general view. Both volumes have been derided, treated condescendingly, or ignored, respectively, by historians, literary critics, and publishers. Indeed, until late last year, *Woman in the Nineteenth Century* was unavailable in the U. S. as a volume in paperback. Because they were feminists as well as writers, moreover, both women have suffered extraordinary abuse or neglect, both as subjects of biographies and as writers.

In our own century, two novelists—Virginia Woolf

*This essay first appeared in *Soundings: An Interdisciplinary Journal,* Winter 1972, pp. 369-389.

and Simone de Beauvoir—have illumined our consciousness perhaps more brightly than any other feminists. They have had longer and perhaps happier lives and wider audiences than Wollstonecraft and Fuller. Yet, of course, compared to male contemporaries or to non-feminist women writers, they have been treated shabbily. Their feminist works—*A Room of One's Own* (1928); *Three Guineas* (1938); and *The Second Sex* (1949)—bewildered or irritated reviewers much as had the earlier tracts. For all four women, the feminist books were "natural" ones to produce: they, like most women with time to read, were consummate readers; but they were also writers and reviewers, journalists and literary critics when most women were wives and mothers.

In their feminist volumes, Wollstonecraft, Fuller, Woolf, and de Beauvoir make connections between their lives and their work. While their books may be described as feminist tracts or ideological treatises, they are also something else. They are *apologias*: justifications or explanations of their own lives and work. They explain the states of their minds: their perceptions about the social attitudes of men towards women, not only but including intellectual women like themselves; their understanding of the ways in which women learn to be women; their attitudes towards each other. And of course, their volumes are "personal" as well as philosophical or ideological: sometimes they are "emotional," shrill, angry, or even embarrassingly intimate. These exceptional women—and their lives do distinguish them from the mass of women who were born when they were—are trying both to explain their own lives and those forces that control most women's lives.

That may seem to be a simple and rather harmless idea, but it is not. Traditionally, a man's life is his work; a woman's life is her man. That a woman's life might have connections with her work is a revolutionary idea in that it might—indeed, must—lead her to examine and question her place as woman in the social order. The idea may be especially revolutionary when it is not simply in the head of *a* Wollstonecraft, *a* Fuller, *a* Woolf, *a* de Beauvoir, but an idea in all our heads.

I want to begin to demonstrate the power of that idea by tracing the discontinuities between my own life and work. I use my life because it is an ordinary one and because I have been mainly not a writer but a teacher of literature. I begin with autobiography because it is there, in our consciousness about our lives, that the connection between feminism and literature begins. That we learn from lives is, of course, a fundamental assumption of literature and of its teacher-critics.

I

When I was seven, my grandfather, a dispossessed orthodox Rabbi from Gallilee, decided to teach me Hebrew and Yiddish. He was growing old, he said, and he had to teach a grandchild before he died. My brother was only four, and so he had no choice but to begin with me. Each day after school, as I brought my books to the kitchen table, my Zaida, a pale, thin man with a scholar's stoop, would mutter, as if to comfort himself, "Because she is a girl, I am wasting my time. Ach, but I must teach someone. There is no one else." I would pretend not to hear; I never responded to his remarks, certainly I never thought of challenging or even questioning his statements. Yet I have always remembered those words, along with the only compliments he ever offered: at the close of most lessons, he'd say, sometimes grudgingly, other times cheerfully, "For a girl she's not bad." Of course I was "not bad": I never failed *to learn the lesson.* And he'd tell me to study twice as hard for the next lesson—and as long. And I would. I would always learn the lesson. By the time of his death, three years later, he had taught me to read and write Hebrew and Yiddish; but at his death, all such lessons ceased for me. Since girls were not considered by orthodox Jews to be teachable or worth teaching, I escaped, and happily, I should add, from the torments of Hebrew lessons that my brother was forced to endure.

I forgot the Hebrew and Yiddish as quickly as possible, but not the atmosphere surrounding those lessons from my Zaida. I was a slavish student through high school, college and graduate school. I did what I was told, I followed the lines laid out by the teacher, I *learned the lesson*, whatever it was.

The lesson that orthodox Jewry had taught me was extreme only in its frankness. One could say that I knew early where I stood. Other young girls and women, even today, get the same message disguised or indirectly, in the American way. The lesson is simplicity itself; there are rewards for good women students, but to get them they must keep their place. Education prepares women well for submission or stupidity.

My college major was English literature, and my heroes were male: Shakespeare, Chaucer, Wordsworth, then Swift, Shaw and Yeats. I cannot remember reading a woman writer during the four years at Hunter College, although it was a woman's college then and although three of my five most influential teachers were women. I have realized only recently how unusual it was to have had several strong women teachers. It was they who encouraged me to try to go to graduate school, where, in my first year at Smith College, I continued to study Shakespeare, Chaucer, Swift.

I should say something more about those women as models. While I admired them, I did not want to be like them. They were spinsters; even a Dean I loved at Hunter was a spinster. I could not connect them with the women I read of in fiction; or the women men wrote poems about. Nor could I connect them with my mother or other mothers I knew. They were some strange form of being: neither male nor female. Or so I thought in my ignorance.

In 1951 I came to the University of Wisconsin as a graduate student and teaching assistant. I loved teaching from the first and the desire to teach kept me at graduate school. I studied hard, got all A's in my courses, at least in part because I did what I was told and *learned the lesson*, but in my deepest feelings, I was at graduate school only as a means to an end–teaching. Teaching, but never with the assumption that I would be a professor. For example, when a male teaching assistant in a Tennyson seminar turned his term paper into an "article" for publication, I marveled and applauded his daring, but never imagined doing the same. In my free time, I didn't write articles. I gave potato pancake parties! When male teaching assistants talked about where they might apply for jobs, I tuned out of the conversation: I would go where my husband went and look for a job when I got there–probably part-time and/or at the last minute. Let me be perfectly clear: I was not discontented. On the contrary, I have always described those three years at Wisconsin as among the happiest of my life. I was very nearly completely without what we now call "consciousness."

An anecdote may help to clarify what I was like at twenty-two. Towards the end of my first year at Wisconsin I read George Eliot's *Middlemarch*. In the novel, the heroine Dorothea, a very bright, sane, human young woman approximately my age then, chooses to marry a dusty old professor. She reasons thus: I must marry, that's all a woman can do; but I'd like to do something really useful with my life; so why not marry a man whose work is important and, since I am intelligent, put myself at his service; then I'd be part of something important and useful. Not a bad rationale; perhaps one familiar to all of you. When I was twenty-two, I thought Dorothea was a fool; not because of her rationale, however, but because she had made so poor a choice. Her husband was a pathetic drudge, without either common sense or genius. What was wrong with Dorothea, I thought then, was that she hadn't found herself a *bright* and *young* man to serve. I would not make her mistake: I could recognize dullness; I would seek the bright young man. And I did. That is, for more than the first ten years of my post-graduate life—from 1950 to 1963, I did not take myself seriously as an intellectual woman, I could not think of myself as a potential professor. In spite of all my school and college honors, in spite of eight years of hard study, what I wanted was to marry a professor, to be a professor's wife, to cook a professor's dinners, entertain his students, bear and raise his children, type his manuscripts, inspire his great critical books.

By late '63, when my ex-husband was about to move from Baltimore to Berkeley, I chose not to go with him. I remember seeing myself in the glass doors of Van Meter Hall one morning after I had made that decision and thinking, "You are a professor. No, you are *the* professor." And then rather melodramatically, perhaps, "The professor's wife is dead." I felt more frightened than glad. I didn't know what it meant to be a professor other than to be like a man. And I was sensible enough even then to know I wasn't a man.

In the summer of 1964 I went to Mississippi to teach in a freedom school. I date this experience as the turning point in my life. In Mississippi, I continued to teach mostly women students, but they were black and poor, not white and middle-class. In Mississippi I learned a few new things about teaching—only one of which I'll mention here. The subject of the summer was liberation: Freedom Summer it was called, and for many of us, teachers and students, it was just that. To liberate oneself—and no one else can do it for you—you need not only the belief in the value and possibility of freedom—without that nothing else is possible; but you need also an understanding of those social forces that have oppressed you. Without such knowledge powerful enough to include the means of change, freedom or consciousness is meaningless—head-stuff only. And in Mississippi, the aim of Freedom Summer and Freedom School was to change the consciousness of students *and* the social and material conditions of their lives. A phrase that has become trivialized through its misuse was not stale then: teachers and students were "agents of change" in Mississippi. We moved from the classroom into the streets and back again to our books. The education of that summer changed lives, revolutionized people. And it was meant to.

When I returned to Goucher in the fall of '64, it was with reluctance. Until the leap in my own consciousness occurred. Why had those Mississippi students been better writers than Goucher undergraduates? Why had teaching in Mississippi been a living experience rather than the plastering of the living with dead culture? It was not simply a question of curriculum, though there was that. It was more a matter of purpose. How could I expect women who thought of themselves and other women as inferior to write well or to live out their education? Mary McCarthy's *The Group* had caught the experience of college women who learn quickly enough to leave their ideals back in those ivy halls. I had lived that life myself. College and study is one thing; the life of a woman another. But it had taken Mississippi to make clear to me the need for a new connection: between learning and life. Black students needed to feel and love blackness, to want liberation enough to struggle, even die for it. Maybe it would have to be the same for women.

But how does one *love* "being a woman"? You all know the words of pop songs on the subject. In the words of the women's movement, such songs tell us to love "being a sex object." What is there in life for women beyond pleasing one's grandfather, father, or husband? And looking forward to caring for children? What is there for women to love?

Though I had been a teacher for more than a decade, I could not answer those questions in 1964. But I could continue *to ask the questions* of myself, my students, and the books we read together during the next five or six years.

II

When I returned from Mississippi in 1964, therefore, I began very tentatively and timidly to learn to teach what people now call "consciousness-raising," and of course my own consciousness was growing at the same time. Before I turn to the classroom and the reading I was doing, let me emphasize that political consciousness about my own life and the lives of black people preceded my efforts to change my classroom. We all know women (and some men, too) today who are changing their classrooms because of the women's movement. I want to emphasize the line of that educational development because I regard it as healthy not only for women and literary criticism but for education generally, and for social change. It makes sense to me that the classroom should function in response to real needs and questions of students and teachers; and on the other hand that out of the classroom should flow some lively literary and aesthetic debate rooted in the lives and understandings of women.

Beginning in 1964, I felt the need to read all books anew, though I did not change the syllabus of my litera-ture courses, and though they continued to include mainly male writers. (In a freshman writing course, I was more daring: I turned to women writers and to the subject of female identity. But I have written elsewhere of that course.[2]) I will choose two examples from that reading—Joyce and Lawrence—because they are well known and hence will allow me to move rapidly to conclusions.

One of the few literary judgments I can take some pleasure in today is my early response to Joyce. Except for *Dubliners*, I remember feeling bored by his books, though I regret never having the courage until recently to admit to my views. I regret also that I assumed the bore-dom to be a failure of taste—after all, who was I, a mere woman student, to judge that god Joyce? I could not even argue his vulgarity, as Virginia Woolf had, for my origins were as lower-class as his. No, I must be incorrect, I used to think.

But rereading *The Portrait of the Artist as a Young Man* for the fifth or so time in '67 or '68, I noted the places that interested me. One was the opening chapter; another Stephen's epiphany on the beach, just before he makes his decision to abandon family, church, and nation. I focussed on the vision as Joyce gives it to us:

A girl stood before him in midstream, alone and still, gazing out to sea. She seemed like one whom magic had changed into the likeness of a strange and beautiful seabird. Her long slender bare legs were delicate as a crane's and pure save where an emerald trail of seaweed had fashioned itself as a sign upon the flesh. Her thighs, fuller and softhued as ivory, were bared almost to the hips, where the white fringes of her drawers were like feathering of soft white down. Her slateblue skirts were kilted boldly about her waist and dovetailed behind her. Her bosom was as a bird's, soft and slight, slight and soft, as the breast of some darkplumaged dove. But her long fair hair was girlish: and girlish, and touched with the wonder of mortal beauty, her face.[3]

Why, I asked myself, should a young Catholic Irish-man look at a young girl on the beach and think not of loving or marrying her (or of other things) but rather of flying away—of rising as a "hawklike man" and evading family, church, nation? I had never asked the question before, nor had it been asked of me. The socialization of women, and the conventions of the classroom, not to mention the sanctity of Joyce, combine to prepare women to ask few questions. We are, moreover, accustomed to being contemplated as objects of men's visions. We usually accept such contemplation, sometimes even gratefully. There is, after all, "The Solitary Reaper," a source of lovely inspiration for Wordsworth, or Daisy Fay for Jay Gatsby. Is Joyce's Stephen not enjoying that sort of experience? Perhaps, but perhaps not.

The ambivalence of the passage is remarkable: the girl is both "mortal" and a "magic" bird. And yet not a bird, not the sort of bird one imagines flying over vast spaces at all, but a "seabird," like a crane, a species imagistically without motion or power: cranes are fragile and still; they pose; they barely breathe. And yet, even as a magical, delicate object/bird, the girl exists for Stephen/Joyce in moral terms, again ambivalent ones: she is not altogether "pure"—a piece of vegetation besmirches her, beautifully to be sure—it is a piece of the "emerald" isle itself (or its waters); more than that, there is the word "boldly" used to describe the manner in which she had managed her skirts, pulled back to reveal "flesh" and "thighs, fuller" than those of any crane in life or art, as well as "the white fringes of her drawers" which remind Stephen again of a bird, but this time of the feathers, "down"—used to stuff bed-pillows. Stephen's eyes linger on the girl's "bosom," and here again, cranes won't do, since they can hardly be said to have them. "Her bosom was as a bird's, soft and slight, slight and soft, as the breast of some darkplumaged dove." The repetition and inversion suggest Stephen's watching the girl take several breaths: her breasts are mortal ones as are, finally, her "girlish"— twice repeated too—hair and face. Here she is woman, not bird at all. And yet Stephen doesn't approach her.

He stares at her for some time, we are told, and she tries to stare back, "without shame or wantonness." "Long, long she suffered his gaze," but she cuts off first and begins to wiggle her toe in the water. There is one final clue to her mortality: "a faint flame trembled on her cheek." And then Stephen's exclamation of "profane joy" —"Heavenly God." He has had his vision. What is this girlish woman for Stephen? Why does the youthful male artist have to see a *girl*, not a bird or a young man in order to make his decision, to know that he must split from his family, church, nation? to feel "the riot of his blood"?

He has felt his power, or one could say his *difference*. Here is a woman he doesn't know whose beauty attracts him, whose sexuality pushes through his attempt to view her as object. What might she mean to him? A few moments of carnal bliss? Marriage and a family, *his* family? Ugh. Unless, of course, she is a bird, an aesthetic image. But he can only half manage that. Psychologically and

sociologically, of course, a woman can't fly away—it is
Stephen who will fly, Stephen the artist. What the experience confirms for Stephen is his maleness, his energy, "the
riot of his blood" sends him flying—away from the girl. He
even takes the measure of maleness against the girl's biological potential as a woman: "Her image had passed into
his soul for ever," Joyce reports to us, and a few sentences
on, then Stephen, too, will be able "to recreate life out of
life." Not as a biological woman, but as an artist, an image-
maker.

What can we learn from the study of a brief paragraph,
a few pages? It would be possible to demonstrate, at greater length, the manner in which the scene we have been describing functions in several other respects as pivotal in the
novel. To understand Stephen's inability to relate humanly to a young girl is also, of course, to understand the attitudes he was taught by Catholicism, by his class and
national background. The ambivalence towards the young
girl is at once a combination of his earlier idealistic view of
women and his experience with a prostitute as well as his
way of moving past that to declaim himself a man and an
artist. We do not wish him otherwise. But to see the scene
and the novel with this point of view is also to make
specific the maleness of Joyce's view—rather than its al-
leged universality.

Of course, I had come to my view—one I can label
"feminist"—through questions and assumptions I have thus
far taken for granted, or noted only indirectly. At the beginning of this paper, for example, I mentioned the names
of women artists and the titles of their feminist books. I
had come to read Joyce this time with the consciousness of
women's lives, artists and others, my own included. According to the maleness of such views as Joyce's, women
are land-bound. The artist can fly and create, even in
motion. We women are of the earth, we are the earth, we
are the earth-mother. Even in birthing—read Faulkner—we
are passive. The male artist, whether he is Stephen or
Joyce or someone else, must conceive his power, or his dif-

ference from women, must take his measure against them, must finally define the two sexes as different species, active and passive, master and servant. Defenders of Joyce might argue that he is but representing social reality as he knows it; indeed, I would agree. But I should add at once that Joyce's vision of reality is specifically male-centered. Perhaps he should have been more precise about his title: Portrait of *an* Artist, not Portrait of *the* Artist as a Young Man. But of course Joyce was neither reformer nor visionary.

Unlike Joyce, D. H. Lawrence was both reformer and visionary. When I first read *Sons and Lovers,* I was not bored. I was a young woman and I thought I was in the presence of a god. I wept openly at Mrs. Morel's death in that novel, and I marveled that Lawrence could know so much about people, could be so enlightened about sexual relationships. For once I was prepared to quarrel with Virginia Woolf's taste, and I remember feeling, several years later, when I first read de Beauvior or Lawrence, that she was a bit "excessive" in her views. I did not understand why she should "dislike" him so.

Lawrence's popularity has continued unabated from my student days until now, and for several reasons. For one thing, Lawrence helped to liberate parts of the western world from a Christian/Puritan ethic that regarded sexuality as unclean, and we owe him gratitude on that score, especially since women have for centuries been regarded as the prime source of that uncleanliness. In Laurentian fact, without blood-knowledge, that is without the consciousness of one's deepest bodily functions, *man* is merely a dying or a dead machine. And Lawrence certainly has left us a body of writing that honestly and convincingly portrays sexual man. But not woman. Not that I didn't believe Lawrence when I first read him. I did, and many women do. But I don't now.

Lawrence's "love ethic" calls for something he names "star-equilibrium." That is, man and woman, in an intellectual/sexual relationship ought to meet as separate individuals with separate identities, in an ideal balanced orbit. They ought not to melt into one another or merge into conventional marriage: that notion conveys the obliteration of one by the other. Equilibrium, a delicate balance between conscious individuals: not a sentimental blurring of identities into a married couple. As theory, "star-equilibrium" is very appealing, especially to women seeking equality in relations with men. But it is also a snare and a delusion, since if it functions at all (and it does only rarely even in Laurentian settings) it functions never on levels beyond the personal: women are wives and men are writers, thinkers, coal miners, farmers, or other workers of the world.

When we look at Lawrence's novels, it is always man who instructs woman and it is always woman who winds up in service to a man. If she does not, if she is intrepid enough to decide against marriage, to say no to a man, she is dealt with harshly. If she is an artist like Gudrun in *Women in Love,* then she is death-dealing. If she is a would-be intellectual like Hermione in *Women in Love,* if she attempts to think as Birkin does—and Hermione does do that—she is told off for not being womanly enough. Or if she turns to teaching, as Miriam does in *Sons and Lovers,* after being educated by Paul Morel, her male teacher warns her that while work may be all a man needs, work can be for a woman only a small part of her life. A woman, a Laurentian woman at least, needs a man, needs marriage and a monogamous heterosexual relationship to be complete.

It is not that Lawrence is insensitive to the pressures on women, to the boredom and frustration of his own mother for example, as depicted in Mrs. Morel in *Sons and Lovers.* Indeed, he is extraordinarily sensitive. That is precisely why it is also important to note how his maleness, his male ego-centricity, operates in conjunction with his sensitivity and social awareness. A clear case has to do with Lawrence's attitudes towards homosexuality. Birkin, in

Women in Love, longs for a similar star-equilibrium-like relationship with a man and justifies the need for male relationships, even playing suggestively with the notion of a homosexual relationship with Gerald. But nothing disgusts the Puritan in Làwrence more than *female* homosexuals. And as a matter of fact, though *Women in Love* begins with a close relationship between two sisters, the novel effects their alienation from each other. A married woman, Lawrence insists in this novel and in others, does not need even a blood-sister; she ought to be content with her husband's friendship and love, period. Remember Swift's injunction to the young woman just married to have nothing to do with other women? Lawrence seems to be warning women similarly: don't trust other women. Your husband will provide what you need, at least if he is sexually virile.

A student once came to me with a plan for an honors thesis on Lawrence's view of women. First she would look at all the women characters alone; then she would look at them in relation to men. Wickedly, I said, "Go and outline the first part, and let me see it before you begin part two." She returned in a week, bewildered. "I can't find a woman who exists alone—can you help me?" She asked. And I admitted to my wickedness. In a Laurentian world we women exist by prescription in relation to men—or we are doomed, damned, and dismissed. It is not only that his male view is partisan; it is a partial view and leaves much of our lives untouched.

The questions I put to Joyce's and to Lawrence's work may be put to most male writers. Conclusions might also be similar: Lawrence's view is partial; Joyce writes of and for only male artists. In several hundred women's studies courses in literature this year, students are searching for images of women or classifying the stereotypes they find—the bitch-goddess, the earth-mother, the patient housewife, the fallen woman.[4] This is not, perhaps I should add, an effort to damage the reputations of male writers; that's not the point. A more interesting literary question is involved. Wendy Martin, a professor at Queens College who teaches a course called "The Feminine Mystique in American Fiction," puts it this way:

Since there are few women (in fact, no women) in American fiction whose lives are self-actualizing (i.e. who have identities which are not totally dependent on men), we will attempt to analyze the social, economic, and literary reasons why women are presented as passive creatures rather than human beings who lead challenging or even risk-taking lives.[5]

Wendy Martin could not have stated that thesis without another vision of female life apart from the one in the fiction most of us have read. Indeed, she follows her thesis with a hint of that vision for her students:

In our discussion, we will contrast the lives of fictional heroines with the lives of Elizabeth Cady Stanton, Fanny Wright, Amelia Earhart, Margaret Fuller and their twentieth-century counterparts in an effort to determine why, ever since the first best-seller was written by Susanna Rowson in 1798, American fiction has not reflected the lives of women as they really are or could be.

In another essay, I have written about the "reality principle"—that children's books ought to reflect at least the truth of our lives: women do work and men are fathers as well as workers.[6] Professor Martin's synthesis of American fiction—that it "has not reflected the lives of women as they really are or could be"—leads us to basic questions about the nature and purpose of literature.

It is terribly puzzling, even to someone as old as I, let alone to young students, to read a group of novels or poems and discover oneself nowhere in sight. For especially with regard to women, literature is very conservative, even reactionary. Mostly, fiction has reported the condition of domestic life: the excitement of the pre-marital romance, mainly, and the dullness of woman's lot afterwards. As Ian Watt has put it, fiction was usefully directed to support the socialization of women; it has done its job well thus far. But from a feminist's point of view, literature has a significant social function for the future.

III

One of the social functions of literature occurs in the classroom, and it is to that place that I want now to turn. In a recent and still unpublished essay, Nancy Hoffman, a professor at Portland State University, describes her work as a "social" act:

> For those of us who are teachers, reading poetry is not only, or even primarily, a private act, but a social one. We give poems to our students because we know the poems and the students, because *in the public sorting out of a poem, we participate in a communal, often unacknowledged, process of sifting through our lives.*[7]

One of my students at Goucher once described as her purpose for reading fiction "to know what to do with my life." We read to change ourselves and others. Sometimes it is the students who are inspired with vision, sometimes the teacher.

I want to begin with a classroom experience that involved the consciousness of young black high school students participating in an experimental N.D.E.A. Institute in the summer of 1965. They were allegedly non-readers, but they read with attention, even fascination, Richard Wright's novel of 1940, *Native Son.* As you know, the hero of Wright's novel, Bigger Thomas, kills two women: first a white woman accidentally and then later a black woman he has loved. The deaths come relatively early in the novel and Wright focusses attention thus on the aftermath, especially on Bigger's and others' reactions to the murders. Bigger's lawyer, Max, an enlightened Communist of the thirties, defends him admirably, and in the last pages of the novel visits him before his death. Max takes as his last responsibility an attempt to make Bigger understand why he is going to die. He talks mainly about the hatred that the rich and the poor feel for each other, minimizing the racial aspect of the conflict. He concludes by saying, "But . . . on both sides men want to live; men are fighting for life. ·Who will win? Well, the side that feels life most, the side with the most humanity and the most men. That's

why . . . y-you've got to b-believe in yourself, Bigger . . ."

Bigger's response in the next page and half turns Max
from a compassionate, intellectual do-gooder into a man
whose "eyes," Wright tells us, "were full of terror." What
does Bigger say to frighten Max? Here is some of it:

Aw, I reckon I believe in myself . . . (and then) . . . When I think
about what you say I kind of feel what I wanted. It makes me feel
I was kind of right . . . I ain't trying to forgive nobody and I ain't
asking for nobody to forgive me. I ain't going to cry. They
wouldn't let me live and I killed. Maybe it ain't fair to kill, and I
reckon I really didn't want to kill . . . It must've been pretty deep
in me to make me kill!. . .

What I killed for must've been good! . . . It must have been good!
When a man kills, it's for something . . .

and then the most crucial line of all:

I didn't know I was really alive in this world until I felt things hard
enough to kill for 'em . . ."[8]

We had had four days of interesting but not especially
focussed discussion of the novel. On the fifth day, the
last, I summarized some of what the students had been saying and asked a final question:

But why at the end does the kind, white man, who has tried to help
him, now feel terror? . . . you've been saying that what Bigger
wanted was "to feel like a person" . . . At the end of the hour
yesterday, we talked about this. We read what he said. We were
all a little shaken about that: he said that if he did it, it must be
good. Were these murders good, then? And why is Max in terror?[9]

Here are two responses from black sixteen-year old students:

Luke: I believe that Bigger didn't feel like he was a man until he
killed that woman. And Max knew that other Negroes held the
same frustration within them and that they wouldn't be human,
wouldn't feel like people—like men and women—until they killed.
That released the frustrations. And that's why Max felt terrified.

Valerie: I think Max felt terror because he saw something in Bigger
that maybe would be in a lot of Negroes and it scared him . . . If
Bigger is just one of many, then maybe there'll be many killings

. . . And it scared him, because it won't be just one person, but a lot of people.

None of these students had read Fanon; most of them had read little else of what we call literature. They were Biggers with a difference: like him, they had felt social refusals, some very immediately. During the course of the summer two black students had tried to get haircuts in a shopping center close to the campus, and they had been refused. Unlike Bigger, these students had other courses of action—they organized a picket line. Unlike him, too, they could generalize about their condition and his. They had words to explain the relationship between being "Negro"—this was 1965 and no one was saying "black"—and growing up in a world hostile to Negroes. As another student, Howard, put it, "Bigger does represent the Negro population" and "Bigger is just a symbol of how fear grows up in the Negroes."

To possess their history, their cultural selves, without fear or embarrassment, this was the accomplishment of those black students in 1965. They could read Wright's novel with skills that few literary critics have managed, at least in part because they were beginning to recognize their own historical and cultural tradition. After all, Bigger comes out of a well-hidden but nevertheless real enough history of armed black rebellion against slave masters. That such history remains hidden from Bigger is an added irony, even as his violence has embarrassed or frightened many readers of Wright's novel. But these students, engaged in their own modest struggle and at the beginning of their own self-consciousness, took him as their brother: life and art knew no bounds in their reading and in the classroom.

When I returned to this novel last year in a large class of women students, they accepted my lecture on the novel's conclusion without question. Many of them had read Fanon (first published in English in 1966), and besides it was 1971 and they were accustomed to the idea of

racial hatred, even openly expressed. It was a very different atmosphere from 1965, when all the adults in the
room, including me (my teaching that summer was observed daily by about twenty high school teachers and
other visitors) were startled by the students' open statements about racial hatred and fear.

But I asked some new questions that had come out of
my recent reading and thinking: why had Bigger not killed
any of the men, black or white, in the novel, but rather
two *women*? If killing is what might make him feel "free,"
why did he have to kill a woman? Why not a man? He
had had opportunities to kill several men, either in anger
or in cold rage. Why had he not done so? I offered two
"clues":

1. When Bessie guesses that Bigger has killed Mary—she is the only
person to guess the truth about that—she says next, "If you killed
her, you'll kill *me*." (italics Wright's) Bigger tries to reassure her by
reminding her of Mary's skin color, but Bessie remains unconvinced.
"That don't make it right," she says.[10]

2. When Max is questioning Bigger about why he killed Mary, he
asks, "But what had she done to you? You say you had just met
her." Bigger tries to explain that she hadn't done anything, but she
had made him "feel like a dog." And then, Wright tells us:

His voice trailed off in a plaintive whimper. He licked his lips. He
was caught in a net of vague, associative memory: he saw an image
of his little sister, Vera, sitting on the edge of a chair crying because
he had shamed her. . . .[11]

In both instances, sex matters more than race. Bessie
seems to be saying that even though Mary was white, and
I am black, if you killed one woman, you'll kill another.
Your loyalties won't hold to your race where women are
concerned. And Bigger's "associative memory" leaps to
connect his feelings towards Mary with those towards his
own sister.

I can't do much more with these details, and I stirred
little or nothing in my students by citing them (at least
there were no lively responses at the time). But it is intriguing to consider whether Wright might have been alert

to the possibility that sexual identification was sharper even than racial. Is sisterhood that powerful? Did Wright guess this or know it? The vision is probably more terrifying than most of us can manage, even with our feminist consciousness.

An equally terrifying novel has had quite another effect on groups of women students. For the past four years, I have included Kate Chopin's *The Awakening* in my courses. Before this year, my students were young, ordinary college freshmen, and we read the novel early in the first term, sometimes before anything else. Perhaps I should pause to describe the novel, for although Chopin is having something of a vogue these days, women writers are, unfortunately, not as well known as their brothers. In this novel, a young woman in her late twenties, married to a successful New Orleans businessman and the mother of two young children, learns to swim during a summer holiday and finds herself awakened to life and to her own sexuality. Partly it is the sea, partly a young man she takes more seriously than he takes her. The novel was dynamite in 1899—the St. Louis *Republic* said it was "too strong drink for moral babes and should be labeled 'poison.' "[12] And it is still dynamite in the classroom today.

For Edna discovers that she is not a "mother-woman." Indeed, she sends her children to her in-laws, refuses her social responsibilities as the wife of a businessman on the rise, and moves, alone, to a cottage where she may be free to see her own friends and to paint. She even has a brief and not especially rewarding sexual affair. But then the man she loves returns: she leaves him briefly to attend to her friend's difficult childbirth; and when she returns to find him gone for good, she despairs. Shortly thereafter she returns to the scene of her original "awakening," undresses on the beach, and naked, swims out to her death. Her awakening, thus, leads directly to her suicide. Consciousness kills her, and so it might still kill women who feel as Edna does.

Young freshman students several years ago (and for several years in a row) had little sympathy for Edna, and no empathy. They charged her with "selfishness," with being a bad mother, and an extremely poor "manager." Why couldn't she divide her time between her children and her own interests? they queried. And if she could not, perhaps the "happiest" ending possible was suicide. After all, death put her out of her misery. There was always at least one student, however, who argued that the novel was really saying something else entirely. It was about "waste"—for example, "the waste of a person's life who just woke up too late to do anything to change her life." At twenty-eight. Too late.

And the novel supports this view well. Edna's awakening tells her that she has no existence apart from her children, her husband, or other men. And without "existence," there is no point in living. If she is not a mistress or a wife and mother, if she is unwilling to be a mistress or a wife and mother, what is she? Is she doomed to be nothing? Chopin says of Edna, near the very end of the novel, that "there was no one thing on earth that she desired."[13] To want nothing is to feel utterly hopeless—indeed suicidal.

It is the political story of many women. This is not a beautiful and idyllic novel—though one male critic has called it that. It is the tormented struggle of a woman alone, without either a woman's movement or a social theory. She knows her feelings: she suspects herself of "selfishness." Indeed she judges herself most harshly and finds herself wanting, and dies in despair, a wasted life. Or at least that was what I thought.

This year at Old Westbury, I read the novel again, this time in the company of sixteen women mostly my own age, a few older, a few younger, and most with one to eight children, and all from extremely varied backgrounds. And the class exploded as only rare classes do. As was customary, each student had prepared a brief "position paper" on one of several questions. But the central issue was clearly the suicide, and the first student who read her paper set the tone by declaring, "I don't believe it. I don't believe she killed herself. She couldn't. No one could who had been through that much and knew that much. The ending is a mistake."

Few people agreed with her, or with each other, but the papers wove variations on a sense of outrage about the suicide. Somehow, it cheated them; they were not going to accept it as finite, decisive. One woman read it as a new birth, not death at all, but a deliberate move back to the beginning, to the womb and the source of all life, the sea. Most, like this student, were pushing beyond the novel's plot to the novelist's whole canvas. They liked Chopin's view of women, especially that she made room for mothers, for good marriages, and yet gave heart, they thought, to those women who might want other lives entirely.

I listened through the evening and did not argue my views. Occasionally I asked a question or for further explanation. Or I refereed their debates. Mainly I felt awed by the energy and vibrancy the novel had evoked in all of them. Some chord had been struck that touched their lives as it had not touched my younger students or me. I too had come to consciousness late, but I had never despaired, and perhaps I accepted too readily the possibility that some, like Edna, might do so. Perhaps I was wrong.

It is certainly arguable that, like black students who saw themselves as Biggers with a difference, these women recognized their relationship to Edna and drew strength, not despair, from it. Their lives *would* be different from hers: they were grateful to Chopin for drawing the picture that made theirs plain.

The current *possession* by women of literature by women writers is a phenomenon novel in my lifetime, and perhaps in general. I can remember when women students were annoyed with my syllabus because it contained mostly "lady writers." But now there are not enough Kate Chopins to satisfy. And when Tillie Olsen, whose stories

we had read at the beginning of the year, was to visit the
class, the anticipation was greater than anything I have
known. Nor did the excitement abate when it was clear
that Olsen was not very different in age, appearance, or
speech from most of the members of the class. Indeed, the
temperature rose.

Her visit inspired a communal supper, to which many
of the women brought (unannounced) a daughter (one, a
daughter-in-law). Several mothers introduced themselves
and their daughters by saying, "This is my daughter. After
I had read 'I Stand Here Ironing,' I gave it to her to read,
and she wanted to meet you too." Again, for those of
you who don't know this story, it is of a working mother's
reflections about her eldest daughter, now a high school
student whose teacher has sent a worried note home about
her. There are no men in the story. The themes—poverty,
a young girl's life, and a mother's anxious love—are rare in
literature. The language is simple and moves with the
rhythms of the mundane ironing board. Yet its language
is the poetry of speech perfectly caught.

I cannot describe that evening: the circle of chairs,
the people on the floor, the quiet voice that read "Tell Me
A Riddle," a story I won't describe but urge you to read.
Like *Sons and Lovers*, which is the only story I know in
English as good as "Tell Me A Riddle," the story contains
the slow death of a strong woman. But unlike Lawrence's
story, there is more here than pathos and waste. Surprisingly, there is both humor and courage in the life of an immigrant woman who might have been a revolutionary leader or a poet but was "only" a wife and mother. It was impossible to talk about the story that had moved us to tears.
But we could ask about the writer, "Tell us, Tillie," the
students asked, "how you came to be a writer." "Who encouraged you?" "What made you decide you could do it?"
Some of the women asking the questions were her age.
How could she not tell them about her life? Especially
since her life was like theirs. Indeed, her life, she said, was

in the stories. She had written "I Stand Here Ironing" on the ironing board, in between chores. She knew that immigrant woman. Her life was in those stories and we must not be embarrassed to announce that we recognize the life as our own.

Before I close I want to mention two directions for the future. First, I hope that we are going to discover anew and find among ourselves and encourage among our children and students many more Kate Chopins and Tillie Olsens. Let me name some we are reading already: Tess Slesinger, Christina Stead, Harriette Arnow, Toni Morrison, Rebecca Harding Davis, Agnes Smedley, Paule Marshall, Olive Schreiner, Elizabeth Madox Roberts. And I have confined myself to fiction: a list of poets might be longer still. Second, I hope that we are going to write anew the history of our past and especially the biography of our lives. The Feminist Press,[14] with which I am associated, has begun part of that gigantic task: to restore our past; to answer the questions, how does one love being a woman? what is there in life for women? what do women want? Margaret Fuller, the first American to write a feminist tract, tried one answer that you may enjoy:

It is not the transient breath of poetic incense that women want; each can receive that from a lover. It is not life-long sway; it needs but to become a coquette, a shrew, or a good cook, to be sure of that. It is not money, nor notoriety, nor the badges of authority which men have appropriated to themselves . . . it is for that which is the birthright of every being capable of receiving it,—the freedom, the religious, the intelligent freedom of the universe to use its means, to learn its secret, as far as Nature has enabled them, with God alone for their guide and judge.

Ye cannot believe it, men; but the only reason why women ever assume what is more appropriate to you, is because you prevent them from finding out what is fit for themselves. Were they free, were they wise fully to develop the strength and beauty of Woman; they would never wish to be men, or man-like. . . .

Tremble not before the free man, but before the slave who has chains to break.[15]

NOTES

[1]An early version of this paper formed the basis of a lecture given at the University of Wisconsin in October of 1970.

[2]See "Identity and Expression: A Writing Course for Women." *College English*, May, 1971, pp. 863-871. Reprinted in *A Case for Equity* by the National Coucil of Teachers of English, 1971.

[3]London: Jonathan Cape, 1916, p. 195.

[4]See *The New Guide to Current Female Studies,* ed. Carol Ahlum and Florence Howe, available from The Feminist Press, Box 334, Old Westbury, N. Y. 11568. Also for syllabi and bibliographies, *Female Studies I, II. III*: for essavs on the teaching of literature, *Female Studies IV, V,* and *VI.*

[5]*Female Studies II*, ed. Florence Howe, p. 33.

[6]"Sexual Stereotypes Start Early," *Saturday Review,* October 16, 1971.

[7]"The Will to Change: Women's Poetry and Patterns of Progression," probably will appear in an issue of *College English* later this year—1972.

[8]New York: New American Library, 1950, pp. 390-391.

[9]All the classes were taped. My comments and questions and the students' responses that follow are from one of the tapes.

[10]Wright, *op. cit.*, p. 168.

[11]*Ibid.*, p. 324.

[12]Kenneth Eble, Introduction to Kate Chopin, *The Awakening*, New York: Capricorn, 1964, p. v.

[13]Chopin, *op cit.*, p. 300.

[14]For further information, write to SUNY/College at Old Westbury, Box 334, Old Westbury, New York 11568.

[15]*Woman in the Nineteenth Century*, New York: W. W. Norton & Company, Inc., 1971, pp. 62-63.

MODERNISM AND HISTORY *

I

The exponents and the detractors of modernism are in surprising accord about what makes a work of art or criticism "modernist." For Clement Greenberg, to whom the term is a measure of quality, "the essence of modernism lies . . . in the use of the characteristic methods of a discipline to criticize the discipline itself, not in order to subvert it, but in order to entrench it more firmly in its area of competence."[1] Both aspects of this definition—the centripetal nature of modernism and its almost complete identification of criticism with art—are recognized in Louis Kampf's less respectful analysis: "One of the principal reasons for the dominance of criticism . . . is the disintegration of any firm notion of artistic form. . . . The act of esthetic perception has turned into criticism, but a criticism almost entirely concerned with defining the object and our perception of it: in short, epistemology."[2]

Whether it is invoked evangelically or pejoratively, "modernism" suggests an overriding emphasis on the autonomy of the work of art and its formal characteristics, on the permanence of modal change, and on the independence of critical judgment. The peculiar term "modernism" embodies in itself some of the problems presented by this constellation of ideas. It is a period designation whose suffix connotes at once a style and a creed. "Modern" would describe any work produced in the last hundred years or so; addition of the suffix "ism," however, implies a school or tendency, to which only certain of those works belong. The effect of this—both conceptually and semantically—is to detach culture from history, so that modernism becomes a critical stance for works of art from all periods. The work of art is isolated not only from tradition but from those considerations of content, patronage, and audience that brought it into being. Moreover, because of the integration of criticism into modernist culture, the critic is presumed to possess a consciousness equally free of the demands and limitations of history.[3]

In recent years, there have been a number of attempts to re-situate the work of art in its history.[4] These efforts have been based on assumptions about the relevance of subject matter to form and of social or psychological environment to cultural production. They have pleaded with critics to add "contextual" considerations to their formal analyses and apply "flexible approaches" when investigating the art of the past. In reality, they have all been extensions of the maxim that circumstances alter cases; nonetheless, they have implicitly accepted *certain* social and material circumstances as the norm, others as exceptions. Despite its greater attention to the "history of ideas," such criticism still denies certain concrete properties to the work of art or its point of view. Its underlying assumptions are that *if* art has a race, it is white; *if* it has a sex, it is male; *if* it has a class, it is the ruling one. But these matters are almost never part of the "social context" we are urged to examine. When we consider the critic, the situation is clearer, for here is someone to whom we may safely attribute a race, a sex, a class. The problem is whether and to what extent these various memberships inform consciousness.

*   *   *   *   *

For this [Swiss] village, even were it incomparably more remote and incredibly more primitive, is the West, the West onto which I have been so strangely grafted. These people cannot be, from the point of view of power, strangers anywhere in the world; they have made the modern world, in effect, even if they do not know it. The most illiterate among them is related, in a way that I am ñot, to Dante, Shakespeare, Michelangelo, Aeschylus, da

Vinci, Rembrandt, and Racine; the cathedral at Chartres says something to them which it cannot say to me, as indeed would New York's Empire State Building, should anyone here ever see it. Out of their hymns and dances come Beethoven and Bach. Go back a few centuries and they are in their full glory—but I am in Africa, watching the conquerors arrive.

James Baldwin

*　　*　　*　　*　　*

"It is obvious that good art has no sex" So *Art News* tells me.[5] So I have learned to agree. But reading the categorical statement takes me back to my old, "naive" responses. I already had my Master's in art history when my husband and I spent a summer in Europe. One afternoon, at the Alte Pinakothek in Munich, we stopped in front of Boucher's *Reclining Girl*. She is lying on her belly, naked, her elbows supporting the upper part of her rosy body and her legs spread wide apart. My husband looked for a moment and observed with mock pedantry, "Ah yes, a nude of the turn-her-over-and-fuck-her school." But *I* didn't want to turn her over and fuck her. Nor did I want to compete with her candid sexuality. What I felt was her exposure and vulnerability—and I felt that I shared them. We were both supposed to believe that this portrait of a teenaged mistress of Louis XV "is a triumph of simple and memorable design, and shows Boucher's delight in the sheer painting of flesh."[6] As I progressed through graduate school, even such contradictory judgments as this began to come naturally to me, too.

Anonymous

*　　*　　*　　*　　*

I reached the point of thinking you were right, and that your culture was the true one. Perhaps we . . . were still dreaming with a simplicity you had left behind centuries ago. Perhaps our dream of a language that everyone could read, made of plain words, was nothing but a fantasy ahead of its time. By a hair I missed becoming one of you. Like those children of the poor who change their race when they go up to the university.

Schoolboys of Barbiana

*   *   *   *   *

For a long time I have been obsessed with the emotional
possibilities of baroque architecture. I have traveled, gotten grants,
studied, looked and looked—and I have been deeply moved. But
at whose expense were my sensibilities deepened by the experience
of Rome? And why is the joy of a refined esthetic emotionally
available to me—a middle-class academic, an intellecutal—but not to
others? When I last stood in the Piazza Navona, watching my fellow
tourists more than Bernini's fountains, I hardly dared think of the
crimes, the human suffering, which made both the scene and my
being there possible. I stood surrounded by priceless objects—and
I valued them. Yet I hate the economic system which has invested
finely chiseled stone with a price. Our esthetics are rooted in sur-
plus value.

Louis Kampf

*   *   *   *   *

The passages above reflect some of the ways that race,
class, and sex may be present in a work of art or the critical response to it.[7] Far from representing "special cases"
requiring "flexible approaches," these elements are the
very basis of our experience, seeking recognition in the
work of art that is supposed to express it and the criticism
that is meant to interpret it.

II

To be conscious of race, class or sex with respect to high
culture is to be conscious, first of all, of exclusion. The
black, the woman, the worker and peasant are all forced to
acknowledge the existence of a mainstream, self-proclaimed
as the whole of "culture," in which they do not—or do not
fully—participate. But "exclusion" is not in itself a critical
position; to be the Other is, by definition, to be the element that is *not* the subject, defined only in relation to it

and only negatively. For each of the excluded groups, the extent and the nature of its exclusion differ and dictate a different criticism and different cultural alternatives.

Racial exclusion presents the clearest case. In terms of both cultural heritage and social environment, the black person is excluded from white culture.[8] The black confronts a body of art that does not acknowledge his or her existence or experience and that appears richly (or smugly) self-sufficient. In the selection cited, Baldwin sees himself as the outsider in white Western culture, unable, whatever his gifts and education, to "pass" and assimilate into it. Even the folk art of European peasants is part of the tradition that shuts him out, while the folk art of his own people is alien to it. Yet Baldwin accepts the claim of supremacy that Western culture makes for itself; he invokes the great names of European culture with despair at his own incapacity to realize their works completely.

Through this very exclusion, however, the black has another possibility: to reject the white man's culture and create one that reflects and speaks to the black condition. Where Baldwin mentions Africa only to recall the shame of the conquered, other blacks see African civilization as a source of tradition and pride for an autonomous black American culture. It must be understood, however, that it is not Africa Baldwin is ashamed of, but defeat and powerlessness. He does not deprecate tribal music and dance when he sees that Bach's music evolved from its European counterpart. But because the "glory" of past European centuries was expressed in imperial ventures as well as in great art, the most important thing Baldwin knows about his African forebears was that they were victims of European conquest. He does not seek to reconstruct their folk music because the fact of enslavement has made it irrelevant to him.

Baldwin's views in that early essay were not definitive, and they are not at issue here. However, his stress on the cultural significance of oppression raises questions

about the extent to which a black American is ever free to
say, "That culture is Whitey's thing; I've got my own."
Albeit gently, Baldwin brings up the issue of power in the
discussion of culture. The two issues are linked in Baldwin's contrast between his situation as the first black man
to appear in a Swiss village and that of the first white in an
African one:

The white man takes the astonishment as tribute, for he arrives to
conquer and convert the natives, whose inferiority in relation to
himself is not even to be questioned; whereas I, without a thought
of conquest, find myself among a people whose culture controls me,
has even, in a sense, created me, people who have cost me more in
anguish and rage than they will ever know, who yet do not even
know of my existence.[9]

The black who takes part in a separate black culture is still
living in the midst of a society dominated by whites. To
ignore that fact in black art would be to falsify the black
experience in America. An art that made this black experience its subject and built from there would clearly be
sacrificing autonomy in the modernist sense of esthetic in-
violability. But it could be a force for real autonomy in
that real world where experience takes place.

At least, nobody doubts the reality of racial exclusion.
Those whose exclusion from the cultural tradition is based
on sex or class have a more ambiguous problem of consciousness. Obviously, none of the three categories is discrete, and a single individual possesses all three characteristics. The white woman may share all the tastes and concerns of the bourgeoisie if she is born or marries into it.
In this country particularly, such a woman is eagerly wel-
comed into the cultural world in the role of consumer—
as collector, appreciator, patron, enthusiast, and "pre-
server." Her experience is not wholly excluded from the
world of art, because she does participate in the experience
of her class and also because she has learned to interpret
that experience the way the dominant culture does. Or to
feel a proportionate guilt and inadequacy should she fail
to do so.

Nonetheless, most of us have some moment when we wonder what *Beatrice* thought about Dante's sacred and profane loves, or like the episode of the Boucher nude, when our vision is neither hypocritically neuter nor second-hand male. At such moments, it is impossible to deny that the critical mind (as formed in our society) has a gender and that the truth, viewed from this perspective, is more nearly the reverse of what one has been taught. The white woman's response to her exclusion as a woman may be epitomized as, "That's not the way it is; my reality is the opposite."

Such moments are rare, however, and until a woman accepts a consistently feminist position, they are accompanied by discomfort and embarrassment. These feelings often result in her acceptance of critics' undervaluing art that does express her own reality. In any event, it is not so much a separate culture that can come out of this consciousness, as a separate point of view, for both artist and critic.

It must appear almost superfluous to insist that high culture is a ruling class preoccupation. After all, historians of art and literature learn as a matter of course about court intrigues and patterns of patronage, royal favorites and discriminating prelates, when they study a given period or school. We take it for granted that the social milieu of art includes courts and counting houses, cathedrals and drawing rooms, but we do not acknowledge that these are rather exclusive environments.

Obviously, it is difficult to acknowledge that Western art and criticism exclude certain classes from participation without admitting that a class system exists. The past is less trouble: of course they had social classes back then, but our sophistication demands tolerance; oppressors and victims are equally dead, and anyway how could one study the cultural history of that vast majority who did not leave enduring monuments? In discussing the present, however, and especially in matters of culture, it is crude to mention exploiting and exploited classes. The cultural euphemism for the working class is the "less well-educated." The onus is thus placed on the individual rather than on social conditions, and the real causes and effects are implicitly reversed. Whereas, in reality, people have less education because they are working class, the euphemistic formulation implies that they are working class because they have less education. Lack of education explains, for instance, why some people do not go to museums even when admission is free. In short, certain people do not have access to culture because they are uncultured.

The Schoolboys of Barbiana are able to articulate a position that cuts through egalitarian pretenses and the mystique of "education." Their view may be formulated as: "That's *your* culture, Teacher; real life is over here." We shall be referring rather frequently to the *Letter to a Teacher* because it is a rare expression of working class exclusion from bourgeois culture and a self-conscious alternative to it. The Barbiana letters are unique in the totality with which they reject bourgeois culture. For those who lack the rigorous sense of class that informs their critique, some partial accommodation is possible. As long as one does not insist that real life—and hence artistic truth—is elsewhere, as long as one accepts the assumptions of high culture, one is welcome to partake of it. In fact, the elements of "our" cultural tradition are packaged in museums and anthologies for easy access on the part of those willing to receive it on its own terms. The semantics of this acculturation process are revealing: a working-class person acquiring "culture" is said to be concerned with "self-improvement" and is coming in contact with "the finer things," with "spiritual values."[10] Such a person is certainly not becoming bourgeois; but is assimilating part of bourgeois ideology instead of struggling against it on the grounds that unreality means untruth. That person is rejecting what the working class *knows* to be true and, in this sense, "changing race." At present, most working people do not have the confidence in the validity of their own experience from which cultural alternatives could develop. Nor are the irrelevancies of art attractive enough to co-opt them. So they remain outside of culture, unable even to define its function in the system that oppresses them.

III

The problem for cultural theory is to determine the significance of the exclusions based on class, race, and sex and the critique to which they give rise. For the modernist, this is not difficult, for he can take refuge in his formalist concerns, secure in his conviction that other matters are irrelevant. But those who concede that art has social and ideological content may try to find a place for considerations of race, class, and sex. They will probably be quick to distinguish two distinct cases: works in which those elements are acknowledged in the subject, and those where they are not. With its characteristic flexibility, contextual criticism occasionally expands its vocabulary of special cases to allow for a female point of view where sexuality is the subject, a black point of view where race is, a non-elite point of view where class is. It is useful to explore such instances before broaching the knottier question of whether they constitute critical "exceptions" or demand a whole new "rule."

Sexuality is a central issue in much of Western art and literature, and women have often been prominent among the consumers of culture; nevertheless, criticism has rarely recognized that their experience might make women interpret art differently from men. "We, men, women and Ph.D.s, have always read . . . [literature] as men."[11] This is true because criticism has denied the existence of a gender point of view or, where it has acknowledged it, dismissed the female one as peculiar, marginal, and subjective.

The dominant tendency denies that men and women have separate ways of perceiving sexual content in art. In the case of the visual media, formal analysis often goes a step further and tries to ignore the *existence* of sexual content. It is probable, for example, that the patrons and purchasers of painted female nudes invested in them at least partially because they enjoyed looking at naked women. But today only a naive or exceptionally candid man admits that facet of his appreciation of a Titian, a Rubens or a Boucher. The masterpieces of Western painting are not, after all, supposed to serve the same function as the Playmate of the Month. We are expected to look at the nude as an exercise in form and design, much as Levey does for half of the description cited earlier of the Boucher nude. The sexual element is to be admitted only in cant phrases like "Boucher's delight in the sheer painting of flesh." Painters like Boucher and Rubens inspire an entire lexicon of euphemism in which words like "sensuous" and "delight" take on a curiously alienated, unfleshly quality.

In less overt instances of sensuous delight, one is supposed to ignore the sexual implications of female nudity. The study of life-drawing, for example, has become a traditional part of an art student's training, and no sexual construction is to be placed on this attention to the nude. Yet at precisely the time when an art "curriculum" was being formalized and the non-sexual aspect of the body touted, a double standard was at work. As Linda Nochlin documents in a recent article, female art students were not normally allowed to draw from an undraped model, regardless of the model's sex or even that of their classmates.[12] Nochlin's thesis has to do with the inequality of technical opportunity for men and women prevalent in art until quite recently. But she does not underline the bland hypocrisy that could uphold the sexual neutrality of the nude and at the same time bar women from learning to draw it on account of its sexual content.

Nowadays, we have progressed so far into formalism as to be shocked at such an attitude. Male and female art students may work side by side, drawing from the same

nude model, because both are expected to look at her in
the same asexual way. But what of the woman art student
who rejects the alienation from her own body inherent in
that way of seeing? Or the female critic who knows what
a particular nude may symbolize or what heights of color
and brushwork were involved in painting it—and who yet
sees that she is looking at the nude from inside just another
such symbol? And her counterpart in literature, who has
learned to identify with the persistent masculine "I" that
echoes through Western poetry, when she finds that she
has allied herself with a convention that violates her own
responses?

The obvious fact is that when sex is the subject we are
not learning the whole truth if we hear only from the sex
that has consistently dominated "our" culture and its
ideology. The full significance of the Boucher nude eludes
anyone who talks about tactile values or simple and meaningful design quite as much as it does someone who merely
wishes to turn the original over and fuck her. Identifying
the subject as one of Louis XV's mistresses, Levey, parenthetically flippant, adds "little as that particularizes her."
At this point, we are presumably supposed to smile at the
delightfully sensuous monarch who, in addition to a series
of official mistresses, had his own whorehouse of adolescent girls—so many, indeed, that they are hard for history
to enumerate or distinguish.[13] The "unparticularized"
girl is just one more object for sensual delectation, along
with the smoky fragrance from the large censer, the velvet
cushions and the silken draperies, as she lies there so suggestively that only the unimaginative would see the need
to turn her over. To be reminded of Sade and Laclos is
perhaps overly impressionistic. But to call that girl a
victim is merely to state a fact. An empathetic response
to that aspect of the picture may be subjective, but it is
no more so than insistence on seeing her as part of a
pleasing pattern or an obscene titillation. And it comes
closer to what the picture really is.[14]

When we use expressions like "the truth" and "what it really is," we are suggesting that the work of art inhabits a world where it not only reflects but influences values, ideas, and action. That it exists, in short, in the same world that we do and belongs, as we do, to history. It is evident, for example, that literature reflects and codifies prevailing ideologies about sexual love. And it is equally clear that it becomes part of that ideology and exerts influence upon society, on the way people conduct and interpret their lives. Reading a love poem, then, is not merely an excursion into the poet's subjectivity, but rather an exploration of the culture that reader and writer share. Now the lover in that lyric, the "I" who speaks to us, is almost always a man. He presents certain ideas—conventional or eccentric—about what he feels, how his lady treats him, what she and her sex are like. There is only one active element in the poem, one person whose thoughts and sentiments are realized for us. It is his point of view and not that of the passive partner that the reader perforce adopts. For any individual woman reader to do this means acceptance of a certain psychic distortion and alienation. More important, in her acceptance, such a reader is also acquiescing to the poem's entry into and continued effect upon the culture in which she is living her own life.

The factors of race and class present a generally similar situation: modernist criticism does its best to deny that they ever really are the subject of art, but once their critical vision is admitted, it transforms the entire experience. It used to be fashionable, for instance, to read black novelists as if their use of race was archetypal, a symbol of that isolation and alienation that is supposed to be universal to the human condition.[15] But today, race is usually acknowledged as a subject of art made by blacks and whites.

Once again, as with women, the subject group's lack of objectivity is thought to invalidate its criticism of such art. If blacks complain that black people are almost totally absent from European and American painting except in subordinate roles, the counter-argument claims that depicting black pages or maidservants in Western painting only reflects the life of the court or the courtesan as it was; it is misplaced sensitivity, and anachronistic to boot, for blacks to be offended by it. Objections to the perpetual servant role assigned to blacks on the screen were long dismissed on the same grounds. With the introduction of films providing a wider range of black types, there should have come some recognition of how the old servant stereotype was not only realistic but implicitly normative. It thus had its effect on the society *outside* the film.

The "over-sensitivity" of those who are slighted is a biased position, to be sure, but so is acceptance of their subordination. Both authors of this article were educated in a school system that had its own Index of reading matter offensive to one ethnic group or another. *Huckleberry Finn,* for instance, was excised from the curriculum not even because of racism but because of a racist epithet. And many "classics" were forbidden because they reflected anti-Semitic attitudes. As Jewish adolescents who had enjoyed such prohibited works as *The Merchant of Venice* outside of school, we felt this merely demonstrated the folly of censorship. In later years, however, we have talked with people of an older generation who vividly remember the sense of injury aroused by some of those works. One mother of a friend spoke of having read *Ivanhoe* as a book-loving girl and being deeply hurt by the character and fate of Rebecca. Although far from supporting the censorship of such books, we have stopped shaking our heads at these readers' lack of historical tolerance and begun to consider what it means. Anti-Semitism was never a material force in our lives, so it was possible for us to accept the attitudes in Shakespeare and Scott as "the way they felt then" and proceed to the real point of the work. But as recently as a generation before our own, American Jews had undergone real anti-Semitic experiences as well as reading about them.

Their response, therefore, had validity in their culture and at that point in history. Tolerance would have implied acquiescence in their own oppression as well as that in the book.

It is difficult to speak intelligibly about class in a society where a mechanical egalitarianism, driven by "education," is supposed to prevail. Although many people recognize and castigate the pop-sociological jargon about poverty, with its talk of cultural deprivation, under-privilege, and the like, the similar rhetoric of class equality seems to escape them. The realities of a class-stratified system (and the potential for struggle within it) are disguised by such phrases as "Middle American," "lower middle class," and "blue collar middle class."[16] Even to use the term "working class" is to label oneself and, in some circles, to discredit whatever else one says. All this makes it hard to identify and discuss class as the explicit subject of recent art or literature. Its presence is generally acknowledged, however, in the study of past centuries, when the bourgeoisie was the class struggling for recognition and power.

An instructive instance is the Renaissance *topos* about true nobility, a convention that harks back to the time of Dante and his contemporaries of the *dolce stil nuovo*. These highly educated young men of bourgeois origin were understandably preoccupied with the question of their own status. For themselves and their audience, they needed to justify and facilitate the "success" of those who won it through personal endeavor rather than aristocratic lineage. In highly abstract poems, they persistently explore the problem of whether aristocracy is a matter of birth or personal attributes; deciding, inevitably, on the latter, they proceed to consider what personal qualities and experiences make a natural gentleman (and "born lover"), someone possessed of "the gentle heart." Throughout the Renaissance, the issue was to be reopened in poetry, drama, and theoretical dialogues of all sorts, with advice and assis-

tance being proferred from all sides to those attempting
to make good without an aristocratic background. To be
sure, there also was a "blood-will-tell" or "you-can't-keep-
a-true-born-prince-under-a-bushel" tradition, but it merely
stated the converse, that aristocrats did have true nobility,
never that the quality was restricted to them. In the novel,
which was to be the bourgeois literary form *par excellence*,
the theme remained a central statement.

Ironically, though perhaps not surprisingly, the same
assertions about class and the individual that expressed the
aspirations of a bourgeoisie rising against the aristocracy
now serve to consolidate and preserve its power against in-
cursions by the proletariat. Although only one element in
the system of bourgeois ideology, these ideas reinforce the
claim to dominance of the ruling class. The notion that
certain people, whatever their class origin, have the personal
qualities necessary to success, and that such success is actually attainable, simultaneously justifies retention of a hierarchy and places blame on the individual for failing to rise
in it. Once the bourgeoisie is in control, even the strongest
anti-aristocratic statements in bourgeois literature become
an instrument of domination and a weapon of reaction in
the class struggle.[17]

IV

Where the subject matter of art has explicit race, sex or
class content, this content must be understood and experienced to the full extent that it participates in meaning.
But what about works of art whose subject matter seems
only peripherally, if at all, involved with questions of race,
class or sex? Are those works not immune to the critical
approaches we have been suggesting? We would answer
that they are not.

Monet's water-lily paintings provide an example of
apparently neutral subject matter. Canvas after canvas
shows the surface of a water-lily pond; Monet explores, in
the course of several decades, the possibilities of reflection,

light, color, brushwork, texture, pictorial structure, and
format (from easel painting to total environment). With
true insight, critics point to "the apparent dissociation of
colour and brushwork from object"; they observe that
"image and paint surface [seem] to exist on separate levels
of perception"; and they suggest that "Nature, prodded by
an eye obsessed with the most naive kind of exactness, responded in the end with textures of color that could be
managed on canvas only by involving the autonomous
laws of the medium—which is to say that Nature became
the springboard for an almost abstract art."[18] What possible class or race content could be integral to the experience of these paintings? The Schoolboys of Barbiana
would tell us immediately: "Monet's water-lily paintings
are part of *your* culture, Teacher."

Monet's painting belongs to the Western tradition of
high art in its capitalist phase. Ernst Fischer observed that
"the feature common to all significant artists and writers
in the capitalist world is their inability to come to terms
with the social reality that surrounds them . . . Only under capitalism has *all* art above a certain level of mediocrity
always been an art of protest, criticism, and revolt."[19] The
somewhat contradictory development of Monet's style
from his earlier to his later works exemplifies this. In the
1870s, the Impressionists sought to create a new vision of
the world: a new modern form to correspond to a modern subject matter. They did not realize that the bourgeois
society for which they created the new style was bound to
reject them:

The bourgeoisie . . . has left remaining no other nexus between man
and man than naked self-interest, than callous "cash payment."
. . . The bourgeoisie has stripped of its halo every occupation hitherto honoured and looked up to with reverent awe. It has converted
the physician, the lawyer, the priest, the poet, the man of science,
into its paid wage-labourers.[20]

Such a bourgeoisie could not but regard the paintings of
the Impressionists as strange and useless artifacts, or even

recognize the threatening implications of the new style. The artist—become, like everyone else, a wage-laborer— was thus bound to be "unemployed," for he was either useless in the "factory," or a danger to it.[21] In the course of the nineteenth century, he was thrust out of the productive processes of society; he became part of the lumpen-proletariat; the "bohemian" artist was born. The crisis in the Impressionist movement in the 1880's and the subsequent development of various new kinds of painting occurred at a time of intense labor struggles in Europe and America; the social crisis undoubtedly influenced the need artists felt for change, especially for generating new styles in the last decade of the century.[22]

Monet's late painting style was in part a response to society's rejection of early Impressionism. Moving away from the recurrent nineteenth century dream of a modern art for the modern public, it represents a withdrawal into lonely individualism, into a fragmented world of intensely felt sensations, into the minute analysis of private experience, and even, in the huge water-lily friezes, into the attempted construction of an alternate environment as a means to reunite the self with the world.[23] From here, as the critics cited above observed, it is but a short step to abstract art.

No matter how painful and how lonely an artist's existence might have been, the Schoolboys of Barbiana would understand what a luxury it is to be able to withdraw from the realities of bourgeois society. They know well that it could hardly be worse than the pressures created when "a worker stays by his stamping machine eight hours a day, in constant fear of losing his arm."[24] Many artists of the late nineteenth and twentieth centuries tried, at great personal cost, to withdraw, yet in the end they created an art for the bourgeoisie: a happy, decorative art, shimmering with light and color; or an anguished art, full of private pain; or a scientific, rigorous art, as "required" by modern times. Whether abstract or not, all

such art has a definite class basis in that it is an art of
leisure, decoration, and escape, available only to one small
sector of society. To the extent that it is an "expression of
spiritual values," "a portrayal of the inner landscape," etc.,
the values and landscapes were and remain basically those
of that sector. Monet's water-lily paintings speak to the
alienation of the artist and his bourgeois audience. That
we can at best place Monet's art in parallel with the contemporary social upheavals testifies to its successful isolation; those groups whose social identity excludes them
from the world of high culture are excluded as well from
the world of the water-lilies.

Certain types of genre painting present additional
examples of art that is supposedly free of potential race,
class, or sexual reference. Representations of domestic
interiors and "everyday" objects, painted with intense involvement in the material reality of the subject, appear
sporadically in the course of the history of Western art.
Their appearance tends to coincide with periods in which
the patrons and buyers of art had a special involvement,
themselves, with the material reality of objects. The vast
trade network and the prosperous urban life of Roman
antiquity must be seen as the social background not only
for the *Satyricon* of Petronius, but also for still-life, landscape, seascape, and genre scenes in Roman art. Similarly,
the development at the end of the Middle Ages of international trade and a large "middle" class of merchants,
craftsmen, and entrepreneurs, corresponds to the appearance, particularly in fifteenth century Northern painting,
of a meticulous interest in the tangibility of material objects. Not until the seventeenth century in Holland, however, does this interest achieve sufficient independent validity to be expressed in a vast production of paintings geared
to it; the acceptability of still-life, genre, etc., as autonomous subject matter is established.

This brief survey suggests the presence of a class content in such painting, content whose relevance is well estab-

lished in historical discussions of art. What is less generally
recognized is the existence of a gender point of view in still-
life and domestic-interior paintings.

The vision of the Dutch genre painters who produced
for the seventeenth century art market was, more than
that of any painters before them, unobscured by veils of
"spiritual" illusion. When they took the domestic environment as subject, it became an explicitly material collection
of tangible objects. Far from discovering that "there is
great painting without an important subject-matter,"[25] the
Dutch painters realized in their works the very deep significance of material objects for the daily experience of the
rising mercantile class: objects had at last been established
as simple commodities to be manufactured and sold by
the bourgeoisie on the market. The production of articles
for direct use (rather than exchange on the market) was on
the wane, and the future lay in the hands of the burghers.
The artists sold them paintings that lovingly celebrated objects in their new essence as exchangeable commodities and
as private property. The peculiarly insistent clarity, the
urgent involvement with physical texture, and the ever-
present intensity of the naturalism in these paintings force
us again and again to confront the objects as material possessions. The buyers of the paintings identified themselves
with the unseen burghers who owned the objects represented in them; both buyer and "owner" were of course men,
normally with families. The objects burst gloriously forth
from the canvas out at us, and we realize that they are to
be felt as *our* possessions, *our* conquests of reality. Yet
they are merely household objects and environments—the
conquests we have made are those of the male burgher who
heads the household. The "neutral" observer has not only
a class but a sex—he is a man.

In the course of the seventeenth century, the nature
of the burgher's family was changing. Women and children
had traditionally been useful, if severely subordinated, contributors to the participation of the family in production

and consumption; now, in the bourgeois sectors of society, they were more and more transformed into unsentimentalized private property. Women and children were becoming, *without illusion*, merely wives to be acquired, offspring to be produced, daughters to be exchanged—in short, they were becoming commodities. Their very existence as human beings was beginning to be called into question. In this context, the nature of the placing of women and children in scenes of domestic interiors becomes clearer. Strangely immobilized, they often participate in the paintings not as modest caretakers of the household goods, but as passive objects, part of the inventory. At the extreme we have Vermeer, frequently and intelligently described as an artist who, "though we look in vain for a still life by his hand, was perhaps the greatest still-life painter of all time."[26] In other words, women, children, objects, and their domestic environments were clearly seen and depicted in their social reality as material possessions, the itemization of accumulated wealth that validated the experience of the burgher.

Two hundred years later, the reduction in art of people, especially women, to the status of objects was complete. Both in the drawing class and in finished works of art, the human body was, although sometimes ambiguously, denied its actual life and sexuality. The ballet dancers, hairdressers, and "keyhole" nudes in Degas' paintings are the distant cousins of the women in the seventeenth century Dutch interiors. By the nineteenth century, however, they had become even more dehumanized; no longer the private possessions of one bourgeois, they were manipulated like puppets and fragmented into their constituent parts. Degas wrote in his notebook:

Of a dancer do either the arms or the legs or the back. Do the shoes —the hands—of the hairdresser—the badly cut coiffure . . . bare feet in dance action, etc., etc.

Do every kind of worn object placed, accompanied in such a way that they have the life of the man or the woman; corsets which have just been taken off, for example—and which keep the form of the body, etc., etc.[27]

The women have become objects, while the objects can only grasp at life.

The seventeenth century Dutch interiors and the nineteenth century Degas dancers, hairdressers or nudes are unusually clear examples of paintings in which the living existence and sexuality of the women portrayed have been eroded. To the extent that we reconstruct the original male-dominated context in which the paintings were produced, we are justified in discussing the women as more or less inanimate objects. Yet here, as with the Boucher nude, the female observer's point of view produces a different response. In these paintings, she identifies not with the invisible possessor but with the objects possessed, not with the voyeur but with the women seen through the keyhole. She recognizes her own predecessors, women who, like her, tended to be more *things* than *people* to the men who observed and lived with them. The reality of her experience and of her response is part of what these paintings mean.

In literature, even modernist criticism has been unable to convince many readers that ideas are irrelevant. Our problem is less to demonstrate that literature does convey ideas than to show that those ideas have a class origin and a class function. What we mean when we say that an idea is bourgeois is that it arises out of the circumstances of the present ruling class and that it helps in some way to justify or perpetuate the hegemony of that class.

It is not difficult, from our present point in history, to see how certain ideas served to bolster past societies controlled by a monarch or an aristocracy. In such a system, ideas about natural hierarchy, order, and divine sanction clearly shored up the dominant institutions. Literature that expressed and promulgated these ideas can be readily identified, its social function traced. The current ruling class, the bourgeoisie, derives its power from a different system of production and profit. The old myths of aristocracy did not meet the needs of the new ruling class, which could not claim legitimacy from a permanent hierarchy, a fixed social and moral order, or divine will. A new set of ideas, those evolved during the bourgeoisie's struggle for supremacy, had to be codified. It was and continues to be the function of bourgeois culture to express those ideas in new art, of criticism to "discover" them in existing monuments.

In our remarks about bourgeois definitions of "nobility," we chose an example that had to do specifically with the subject of class; most elements of the ideology we call bourgeois are not so direct. They have to do, rather, with fixed categories in "human nature" and "the human condition" that emphasize what is ideal, absolute, and private over what is material, fluid, and collective. According to bourgeois literature, the important events of history are the events of inner history. Suffering is portrayed as a personal struggle, experienced by the individual in isolation. Alienation becomes a heroic disease, for which there is no social remedy. Irony masks resignation to a situation one cannot alter or control. The human situation is seen as static, with certain external forms varying but the eternal anguish remaining. Every political system is perceived to set some small group into power, so that changing the identity of the group will not affect our "real" (that is, private) lives. If the work of literature does not make these notions sufficiently explicit, the critic helps to locate them in their context of "universals."[28]

Thus simply expressed, the elements of bourgeois ideology have a clear role in maintaining the status quo. Arising out of a system that functions through corporate competition for profits, the ideas of the bourgeoisie imply the ultimate powerlessness of the individual, the futility of public action, and the necessity of despair.

V

What we are aiming at is not just a better way to read

poetry or look at pictures, but a way to understand our
own experience as historical beings. In this we are going
beyond the customary frontiers of criticism—certainly of
modernist criticism. We are suggesting that the work of
art exists in a real, rather than ideal, world, and that the
critic is not an ahistorical being—lacking gender, race, and
class—any more than the artist, the patron, or the public.
Blindness to the race, sex, or class content in art brutally
reveals the extent to which consciousness is affected by
circumstances: "Consciousness is . . . from the very beginning a social product, and remains so as long as men
exist at all."[29]

What are the consequences of asserting that the
critic is a human being who exists in history, and that
consciousness comes out of real life? It is a sad fact that
anyone wishing to answer this question and elaborate such
a position is forced each time to review the same fundamental concepts. Circumstances and real life in the United
States have produced a situation in which the precise use
of such categories as "capitalism," "bourgeois," "exploitation," or even the mere citation of Marx, too often produces in the reader a sudden inability to understand. What
is even more frustrating is the reader's stubborn innocence
of the nature and sources of that inability, and the constant refusal to evaluate it.[30] Still, times are changing,
and obstinacy may eventually be overcome by endurance
—we begin at what we believe to be the beginning.[31]

Criticism based on the view of consciousness developed in this paper is still rare. It differs from "contextual"
and "social history" approaches in that it goes beyond the
mere placing of the work against the background in a sort
of silhouette arrangement. It refuses to isolate the work of
art as something distinct from its social environment;
instead it recognizes that the work is itself a part of that
environment and functions in it.

Modernism, by contrast, seeks to intensify isolation.
It forces the work of art, the artist, the critic, and the

audience outside of history. Modernism denies us the possibility of understanding ourselves as *agents* in the material world, for all has been removed to an abstract world of ideas, where interactions can be minimized or emptied of meaning and real consequences. Less than ever are we able to interpret the world—much less change it.

As the twentieth century advances, art increasingly participates in the maintenance of bourgeois ideology; its main vehicle, both in criticism and in art, is modernism. "Great" art and literature enter the curriculum of working class and black high schools and of two-year colleges. They appear in modernist guise, stripped of their full historical meaning and transported to the timeless realm of universals. By teaching art and literature in this way, the educational system tries to do to the students what it has done to the subjects: it implicitly denies them their own full historical identity and instead suggests that they too are isolated, unconnected, and powerless. Art has been forced to support and critics have up to now perpetuated this ideological mystification. The Schoolboys of Barbiana resist it; our task is to replace it!

NOTES

[1] Clement Greenberg, "Modernist Painting," *Arts Yearbook*, IV (1961), 103.

[2] Louis Kampf; "The Permanence of Modernism," *On Modernism: The Prospects for Literature and Freedom* (Cambridge, Massachusetts, 1967), pp. 6, 8.

[3] "To impute a position or a line to a critic is to want, in effect, to limit his freedom. For a precious freedom lies in the very

involuntariness of esthetic judging: the freedom to be surprised, taken aback, have your expectations confounded, the freedom to be inconsistent and to like anything in art so long as it is good—the freedom, in short, to let art (*sic*) stay open." Clement Greenberg, "Complaints of an Art Critic," *Artforum*, VI, 2 (October 1967), 38.

[4]In art historical theory, these include: Erwin Panofsky "The History of Art as a Humanistic Discipline," 1940, and "Iconology: an Introduction to the Study of Renaissance Art," 1939, both in *Meaning in the Visual Arts* (Garden City, New York, 1955), pp. 1-54; F. Antal, "Remarks on the Method of Art History," *Burlington Magazine*, XCI (1949), 49-52, 73-75, reprinted in Frederick Antal, *Classicism and Romanticism* (New York, 1966), pp. 175-89; Otto Pacht, "Panofsky's 'Early Netherlandish Painting'—II," *Burlington Magazine*, XCVIII (1956), 275-77; Arnold Hauser, *The Philosophy of Art History* (New York, 1959), pp. 13-15, 119-276; James Ackerman, "Western Art History," in *Art and Archaeology, The Princeton Studies: Humanistic Scholarship in America* (Englewood Cliffs, New Jersey, 1963); Jan Bialostocki, Review of *The Shape of Time* by George Kubler, *Art Bulletin*, XLVII (1965), 135-39; Lise Vogel, "Flexibility Versus Formalism," *Art Journal*, XXVII (1968), 271-278; "Symposium: The State of Art History," *American Art Journal* III (1971), 83-104, see especially E. H. Gombrich, "A Plea for Pluralism," 83-87 and Victor Lasareff, "Many Directions . . . No Synthesis," 101-104. Presumably because of the nature of the medium, formalist criticism has never been as influential in the study of literature as it has in the visual arts. Nor does the controversy retain the vitality it has in art history, where it is still very much alive. In literature, the paradoxical tendency has been to admit certain formalist insights and techniques, applying them particularly to the teaching of undergraduates, while the graduate schools teach, and a substantial part of the profession practices, historical criticism. Some articles that parallel the methodological discussion in art history are: Douglas Bush, "The New Criticism: Some Old-Fashioned Queries," PMLA, LXIV, 2 (Supplement, Part 2, 1949), 13-21; Robert Gorham Davis, "The New Criticism and the Democratic Tradition," *American Scholar*, XIX, 1 (Winter 1949-50), 9-19; Robert Gorham Davis, *et al*, "American Scholar Forum: The New Criticism," *American Scholar*, XX, 1 (Winter 1950-51), 86-104 and 2 (Spring 1951), 218-231; Randall Jarrell, "The Age of Criticism," *Partisan Review*, XIX, 2 (1952), 185-201; Randall Stewart, "New Critic and Old Scholar," *College English*, XV, 2 (1953), 105-110; Frederick A. Pottle, "The New Critics and the Historical Method," *Yale Review*, XLIII, 1 (1953), 14-23; Alexander E. Jones, "The Poet as Victim," *College English*, XVI, 3 (December 1954), 167-71. Only recently, however,

with the growth of a self-conscious radical movement in the profession, has a full critique of literary formalism been possible.

[5] *Art News,* LXIX, 9 (January 1971), 60.

[6] Michael Levey, *A Concise History of Painting from Giotto to Cezanne* (New York, 1962), p. 218.

[7] The passages cited are: James Baldwin, "Stranger in the Village," *Notes of a Native Son* (Boston, 1955), p. 165; private communication from a female colleague, August, 1971; The Schoolboys of Barbiana, *Letter to a Teacher* (New York, 1970), p. 128; Louis Kampf, "Notes Toward a Radical Culture," in *The New Left,* comp. Priscilla Long (Boston, 1969), p. 434.

[8] Throughout this essay, we have had in mind the cultural situation of the black person in the United States. The vast majority of the world is "non-white" and the cultural problem is somewhat different for colonialized peoples. Frantz Fanon has described the complexities of this consciousness; for example, he recommends "the following experiment. . . . Attend showings of a Tarzan film in the Antilles and in Europe. In the Antilles, the young Negro identifies himself *de facto* with Tarzan against the Negroes. This is much more difficult for him in a European theater, for the rest of the audience, which is white automatically identifies him with the savages on the screen. It is a conclusive experience. The Negro learns that one is not black without problems. A documentary film on Africa produces similar reactions when it is shown in a French city and in Fort-de-France. I will go farther and say that Bushmen and Zulus arouse even more laughter among the young Antilleans. It would be interesting to show how in this instance the reactional exaggeration betrays a hint of recognition. In France a Negro who sees this documentary is virtually petrified. There he has no more hope of flight: He is at once Antillean, Bushman, and Zulu. . . . Quite literally I can say without any risk of error that the Antillean who goes to France in order to convince himself that he is white will find his real face there." Frantz Fanon, *Black Skin, White Masks* 1952 (New York, 1967), pp. 152-153, n. n. 15-16.

[9] James Baldwin, p. 164.

[10] "As Jan Myrdal has observed, spiritual values are the ideology of the ruling class." Louis Kampf, "Notes," p. 427.

[11] Carolyn Heilbrun, "Millett's *Sexual Politics:* A Year Later," *Aphra,* II, 3 (Summer 1971), 39.

[12] Linda Nochlin, "Why Are There No Great Women Artists?" *Art News,* LXIX, 9 (January 1971), 23ff. See especially pp. 32-36.

[13] The subject of this painting is frequently identified as Miss O'Murphy. Levey is not alone, however, in associating her with her anonymous sisters of the King's seraglio, always so ironically labelled

his "mistresses."

14For a discussion of feminist viewpoint in criticism of literature, see Lillian S. Robinson, "Dwelling in Decencies: Radical Criticism and the Feminist Perspective," *College English*, XXXII, 8 (May 1971), 879-889. It should be clear that it is not we who are inventing a gender point of view for hitherto neutral criticism. Rather, we are adding the viewpoint of the feminine gender. Useful analyses of the male point of view as it has dominated criticism may be found in Mary Ellmann, *Thinking About Women* (New York, 1968) and Carol Ohmann, "Emily Bronte in the Hands of Male Critics," in the issue of *College English* cited earlier in this note, pp. 906-913.

15See, for example, Ellin Horowitz, "The Rebirth of the Artist," in *On Contemporary Literature*, comp. Richard Kostelanetz (New York, 1964), p. 337.

16This grotesquerie occurs in the Literary Guild account of K. B. Gilden's *Between the Hills and the Sea* (New York, 1971). Even in describing a novel about trade union struggles, it appears that blurb-writers are unable to acknowledge that its protagonists are members of the working class.

17None of these observations is novel. But most commentators situate the class event parallel to the literary one, rather than relating them causally. The "rise of Puritanism," for instance, is *related* to the rise of the middle class and to individualism, but the causality is, if anything, normally reversed.

18George Heard Hamilton, *Painting and Sculpture in Europe 1880-1940* (Baltimore, 1967), p. 18; Clement Greenberg, *Art and Culture* (Boston, 1961), pp. 43, 42.

19Ernst Fischer, *The Necessity of Art* (Baltimore, 1963), pp. 101-102.

20Karl Marx and Frederick Engels, *Manifesto of the Communist Party* in their *Selected Works in One Volume* (New York, 1968), pp. 37-38.

21The comparative acceptability of "avant-garde" art and artists to the bourgeoisie in the middle of the twentieth century corresponds to a more advanced stage of capitalism, one requiring for its survival a much stronger dose of ideological mystification throughout society.

22For some brief references to this correlation between events in society and in art (perceived as one of art with "extra-artistic" factors), see Hamilton, cited above in note 18, p. 41, or John Rewald, *The History of Impressionism* (New York, 1961), pp. 467-8, 481. The relative success of Monet's painting does not make him immune from feeling the impact of the social crisis.

[23]See the discussion by Fischer, p. 75.

[24]The Schoolboys of Barbiana, p. 82. The Schoolboys are here comparing the pressures endured by teachers to those industrial workers undergo: "We read . . . that your teaching hours are 'enough to drain the psychophysical capacities of any normal human being.' A worker stays by his stamping machine eight hours a day, in constant fear of losing his arm. You would not dare say this sort of thing in his presence."

[25]E. H. Gombrich, *The Story of Art* (London, 1950), p. 323. We cite here an easily accessible popularization of the widespread, and characteristically modernist, notion that "the Dutch specialists . . . ended by proving that the subject-matter was of secondary importance."

[26]A typical observation about Vermeer; the example cited here is Vitale Bloch, in *Burlington Magazine*, XCIV (July 1952), 108. The "rehabilitation" of Vermeer as one of the masters of painting occurred, interestingly enough, only within the last hundred years, that is, under modernism.

[27]Cited in Linda Nochlin, *Impressionism and Post-Impressionism 1874-1904* (Englewood Cliffs, New Jersey, 1966), p. 63.

[28]We have deliberately reduced an entire tradition to its simplest components; in so doing, we do not feel we are vulgarizing it any more than its own devotees.

[29]Karl Marx and Frederick Engels, *The German Ideology* (New York, 1947), p. 19. For a bibliography of Marxist approaches to aesthetics in English see Lee Baxandall, *Marxism and Aesthetics: A Selective Annotated Bibliography* (New York, 1968). See also the even more recent re-publications, translations, and discussions of the work of Georg Lukacs, Max Raphael, Ernst Fischer, *et al.*

As female readers of Marx and Engels who believe in the validity of our own gender point of view, we find ourselves brought to a full stop each time they use the words "man" or "men" to mean human beings of both sexes. It is clear that they accepted the sexist conventions of the German language as unquestioningly as our own male colleagues do those of our language.

[30]"None of us is to blame for our exposure to certain training, including a conditioned revulsion to the rhetoric of class warfare. We are at fault only if we insist—in the face of all evidence—that the realm of the mind is above that struggle, that it is some abstract Agora where ideas duel gracefully among themselves, all unconscious of whose interests they serve." Robinson, *op. cit.*, p. 880.

[31]Our understanding of the relationship between ideas and (

material conditions, that is, of the nature of the formation of consciousness, is materialist and dialectical. Marx and Engels formulated this analysis of history in *The German Ideology*:

The first premise of all human existence. and therefore of all history [is] that men must be in a position to live in order to be able to "make history." But life involves before everything else eating and drinking, a habitation, clothing and many other things. The first historical act is thus the production of the means to satisfy these needs, the production of material life itself. (p. 16)

Consciousness is grounded in these material factors; as the famous phrase goes, "life is not determined by consciousness, but consciousness by life." (p. 15) Some fifteen years later, in the "Preface to *A Contribution to the Critique of Political Economy*" (1859), Marx formulated these ideas in a soberer and more solid form:

In the social production of their life, men enter into definite relations that are indispensable and independent of their will, relations of production which correspond to a definite stage of development of their material productive forces. The sum total of these relations of production constitutes the economic structure of society, the real foundation, on which rises a legal and political superstructure and to which correspond definite forms of social consciousness. The mode of production of material life conditions the social, political and intellectual life process in general. In is not the consciousness of men that determines their being, but, on the contrary, their social being that determines their consciousness. (Marx and Engels, *Selected Works*, p. 182)

In a letter to Joseph Bloch—September 21, 1890—written towards the end of his life, Engels restated with great emphasis that "according to the materialist conception of history, *the ultimately* determining element in history is the production and reproduction of real life. More than this neither Marx nor I have ever asserted." (Karl Marx and Frederick Engels, *Selected Correspondence* [Moscow, 1965], p. 417). His insistence evidently grew out of impatience with simplistic distortions of his and Marx's formulation of the relationship between consciousness and material conditions.

Whose "consciousness" is incorporated into works of art?

"The class which has the means of material production at its disposal, has control at the same time over the means of mental production, so that thereby, generally speaking, the ideas of those who lack the means of mental production are subject to it." (*The German Ideology*, p. 39)

How, *precisely*, does the ruling class manage to produce and distribute ideas? And what about the ideas of the other classes? Marx and Engels only occasionally hint at the answers to these questions. They describe ideology as it functions to preserve a ruling class:

"One part [of the ruling class] appears as the thinkers of the class (its active, conceptive ideologists, who make the perfecting of the illusion of the class about itself their chief source of livelihood), while the others' attitude to these ideas and illusions is more passive and receptive, because they are in reality the active members of this class and have less time to make up illusions and ideas about themselves." (*The German Ideology*, p. 40)

On the problem of the ideas of other classes, they observe that "the existence of revolutionary ideas in a particular period presupposes the existence of a revolutionary class." These views provide cultural criticism with a point of departure; they barely begin to answer our specific questions.

Marxists have traditionally considered the material basis to be the "economic structure" cited by Marx, all else forming part of the superstructure. We would like to suggest that the concept of the base must be extended to include sexual identity; as Engels says, "The *ultimately* determining element in history is the production of real life." This is no mere play on words. Throughout their writings, Marx and Engels approach this conclusion without ever actually reaching it. For example, in *The German Ideology*, they uneasily cite reproduction as one of several coequal determining factors at the origin of historical development (p. 17), and the uncertainties of Engels' formulations in his *Origin of the Family, Private Property and the State* are obvious. In any case, the reproduction of human labor-power is universally acknowledged to be an aspect of production; what must be elaborated is the meaning and consequences of this fact for Marxist theory and strategy. We intend to explore this question in another place.

*From *New Literary History*, Vol. 3, No. 1, Autumn 1971, pp. 177-197. Used by permission.

NANCY BURR EVANS

THE VALUE AND PERIL FOR WOMEN
OF READING WOMEN WRITERS

For too long I have been intimidated in my reading of
literature by the authority traditionally ascribed to male
professors by sex and by role. Women have been trained
to respond to literature as faceless, sexless students, to
write about it without introducing the forbidden first person and in a terminology which is foreign to our everyday,
human language. And for the most part, we have been discussing the works of male authors, which is not an evil in
itself, but which is certainly wrong when it is the *only*
group of books we read or come to know.

More than once I questioned the value of reading literature which either in its subject or by the way in which
it was approached in class had little or was not allowed to
have significance in terms of my own experience. Yet
knowing that something was drastically amiss in my study
of literature, I continued to turn out classic term papers as
prescribed. I did this in part I now realize because I was
then very concerned about grades, that great force of conservatism, and because I felt I could not overcome, if indeed I ever had the right to challenge, the ominous pres-
tige fortressing the English department establishment.

It was not until my senior year at college that I finally
found it impossible to fulfill my student obligations and
imperative to respect my own. And ironically enough it
was *Hamlet*, the play most excavated by scholars in search
of Ph.D.'s, over which my split with tradition came. Having been extremely affected by the similarities between
Hamlet's thinking-out of his problems and my own process,
I could not sublimate this response at the expense of writ-

ing an acceptable objective paper. Having decided, coura-
geously, I then thought, to discuss my emotional responses
within the paper, I found myself immediately justifying my
decision in a hastily attached introduction and conclusion.
The tight-fisted influence of my traditional English major
upbringing betrayed itself; I was self-conscious about doing
what I thought should be most basic and natural: relating
literature to life.

The sources which motivated me, almost demanded
me, to discuss my emotional responses to *Hamlet* were
essentially the same ones which later assured me, in fact
confirmed me of the rightness of my decision. The sources
were three women writers. In the first place, it was Sylvia
Plath in *The Bell Jar* and in the second, it was Virginia
Woolf in an essay entitled, "How Should One Read a
Book?," included in *The Second Common Reader* and,
most recently, Nancy Hoffman in "A Class of Our Own."

Having read Sylvia Plath's *The Bell Jar* for the first
time when her description of her breakdown between
junior and senior years at Smith seemed to be more my
diary than her novel, I found myself at one with the novelist, making little or no distinction between reader and narrator. Reading the book set off a succession of shivers as
I saw my own experiences mirrored in articulated form,
some of which are familiar to many of us: needing to
shed the old self but afraid of losing it; and having nothing to replace it; the disillusionment with *Mademoiselle*
which I had myself experienced at a tea with pink-rose-
printed napkins given in honor of college board members;
the feeling that words have suddenly lost all meaning. All
these experiences had been Plath's in the 1950's and now
were mine in the 1970's. Certainly many male heroes had
passed through some of these same sensations, but it was
the discovery of a female hero, a woman like myself, which
was of importance.

It was so rare to come across a female hero like Esther
Greenwood—in fact, she was the first such hero in my read-

ing experience—that I quite understandably, I think, over-reacted to the identification. With relief and not a small bit of egoism, I grabbed hold of the book by making it do for me what I wanted, which was to give shape to, to give a *raison d'etre* for my anxieties, but most of all to give me a sense that I was not alone in my feelings. And it is this last point which is so crucial in grasping the very real function of women writers for women themselves. For although I was an English major and had read a substantial number of books, I had not met a female protagonist quite like Esther Greenwood before. (Franny in J. D. Salinger's *Franny and Zooey* had been the closest approximation of a real contemporary college woman before Esther.) As a result, the literary value of the book was secondary in comparison to the inestimable value, at that particular point in my life, of meeting a character next to whom I no longer felt so alienated.

Where else, for example, could a woman read so vividly, however simply, about the perplexing duality of self, the schism between the smiling, enthusiastic public self and the serious, critical private self, for which many of us have felt personally guilty and embarrassed? What had previously been viewed as an individual neurosis to be shamefully concealed was through *The Bell Jar* placed in a larger and more proper context. No longer was I alone or wholly responsible for my ambivalent and sometimes seemingly hypocritical feelings. I, like Esther Greenwood, was a victim of a socialization of dancing classes, Girl Scouts, junior proms and motherly advice. Buddy Willard's mother, for example, is quick to recite to Esther: "What a man is is an arrow into the future and what a woman is is the place the arrow shoots off from. . . ."[1] But contrary to the dictum of Mrs. Willard, the stereotype of the American devoted mother and wife, Esther, the would-be all-American girl, asserts: "The last thing I wanted was infinite security and to be the place an arrow shoots off from. I wanted change and excitement and to shoot off in all directions myself, like the colored arrows from a Fourth of July rocket."[2] And, so did I.

Sylvia Plath in *The Bell Jar* had provided me with what Jane O'Reilly described as "one of those rare felicitous moments . . . when two similar confessions of supposed madness . . . result in a comforting sensation of sanity."[3] And that certainly is worth something. But it is not enough to end there. Too many women do end precisely there in a comfort which is at best illusory and temporary and it is then, I believe, the peril of reading women writers begins.

It is exhilarating to share commonality, even if it is one in madness or imagined madness, and it is liberating to be reassured that one is not wholly responsible for a destiny not quite to one's liking. Yet having found someone with whom to identify it is then not a far step removed to become parasitically dependent upon that person to define and vindicate oneself. An identification through mutual oppression as women which should initially lead to an awakening and then to action can quite conveniently be manipulated to become a comfort, an excuse not only for societal ills but personal ones as well. It is this dead-end response to the reading of women writers against which I caution. For the reading of women writers can be destructive, pathetically counter productive if not tempered with critical judgment.

I, for example, in my first reading of *The Bell Jar*, made few distinctions between literature, where anything imaginable is possible, and reality, where qualifications and limits exist. I read egocentrically, looking primarily for those ideas and descriptions which most resembled myself or the self I imagined I was to be. Consequently I picked out what could be of most value to myself and left the rest of the work at the wayside.

There was, however, a positive result from having become so involved in my reading of *The Bell Jar*. It led me to reconsider my approach to literature. Having recog-

nized the obvious weaknesses of my emulating Sylvia
Plath at her most self-destructive and self-gratiating, I was
now able to see the ludicrousness, in fact, the impossibility,
of continuing to separate my personal and intellectual self.
That the two had to be separated was a fact of which I was
constantly reminded by my male professors, but a fact
which I nevertheless found difficult to understand let alone
support. And it was precisely this division of self which
was to a great extent responsible for Esther's breakdown.
To remain under the strictures of most literature courses
was only to widen and accentuate the gap. And, again, it
was a woman writer, Virginia Woolf in "How Should One
Read a Book?," who encouraged me in my belief that reading was more than a cerebral affair.

As in my reading of *The Bell Jar*, I was again dumb-
founded by the number of similarities between a woman
writer's opinion and my own. Woolf emphasized and
warned against the destructive influence of critics and professors who didactically tell us what to read and what
value to place upon what is read. And yet at the same
time she hastened to caution that if we are to enjoy freedom in reading we must learn to control ourselves, by
which she meant we must strike a balance between resist-
ing and giving way to our personal responses. Woolf notes:
"We learn through feeling; we cannot suppress our own
idiosyncrasy without impoverishing it. But as time goes on
perhaps we can train our taste; perhaps we can make it submit to some control."[4]

To submit my feelings to control, not to be smoth-
ered but to be placed in a richer perspective, is what I did
in a semester tutorial on Plath which grew out of my first
reading of *The Bell Jar*. It is because I have now both analyzed her work and been allowed to feel it that the social
implications have been allowed to arise. *The Bell Jar* is no
longer comfortable reading. It certainly has helped me to
better understand many of my own problems and to avoid
some of the mistakes which Plath made. But most impor-

tantly, it has made me more intolerant of the discrimination against women and more dedicated to working against it. In this case, literature made more vivid and palpable an oppression I felt in everyday life.

Nancy Hoffman's "A Class of Our Own" further reinforced my belief that one must feel as well as understand literature if it is to affect us. Hoffman says:

to make a separation between personal and intellectual life, emotion and reason is to destroy a human, to make her a microcosm of our fragmented society by denying her the 'direct sensuous apprehension of thought' or its counterpart—the rational apprehension of emotion.[5]

Hoffman speaks of the disadvantages of a divided self, emphasizing the dangers of either a strictly rational or an overly emotional response.

In reading Woolf and Hoffman, I was encouraged to continue to express and to practice what I considered the healthiest and most vital approach to the reading of literature. I felt a healthy sense of community with other women and now could look back on Sylvia Plath's *The Bell Jar* and learn from her tragedy rather than repeat it. The reading of some women writers' literature can be so vividly reflective of our own experiences that it can be terrifying and interpreted only as a confirmation of the anxieties we have always felt. And, of course, we are not used to seeing our real selves depicted in literature because real women are a rare commodity in literature. So it literally *is* a shock to see someone like ourselves in the pages of fiction.

I imagine, then, that most women, as I did, will have to go through a period of personal fascination with the self they discover through women writers and rightly so. It is an enlightenment; it is as if we are seeing ourselves naked for the first time, really seeing ourselves and discovering our own bodies. Once we have become accustomed to seeing ourselves in literature by reading more novels by women, a bit of the lustre will wear off. We will become more critical of what we read; we will recognize, for example, the faults of Esther Greenwood as well as her positive characteristics and we will perhaps discover that *The Bell Jar*, after a few more readings, is not as great a book as we first imagined.

We will no longer be overwhelmed by encountering a female hero who speaks directly to us nor will we, I hope, become indifferent. We will instead learn from our experiences and those of female heroes so that we may hopefully change the quality of those experiences. In other words, I no longer find satisfaction in imagining that Esther Greenwood and I are the same kind of woman; I want to make sure that there are no more Esthers. And one of the best ways to accomplish this is to allow and encourage women to feel and understand the literature of women writers. Seeing one's self staring out from a book makes it extremely difficult to avoid facing one's problems and after encountering women heroes uncannily similar to ourselves a number of times, we finally have to act. Women's literature felt and learned can effect social change even if it is as small a step as finally writing a term paper on what you want, the way you want, or as great a stride as the determination "to shoot off in all directions myself, like the colored arrows from a Fourth of July rocket."

NOTES

[1]Plath, Sylvia, *The Bell Jar* (New York: Harper & Row, 1971), p. 83.

[2]*Ibid.*, p. 98.

[3]O'Reilly, Jane, "How to Get Control of Your Time (and Your Life), *New York* Magazine, Vo. 5, No. 3, Jan. 17, 1972, p. 24.

[4]Woolf, Virginia, *The Second Common Reader* (New York: Harcourt, Brace & World, Inc., 1960), p. 243.

[5]Hoffman, Nancy, "A Class of Our Own," an unpublished article, p. 12.

FRAYA KATZ-STOKER

THE OTHER CRITICISM:
FEMINISM vs. FORMALISM

The young have the unfortunate tendency of feeling that history is born with them. As we grow older experience begins to feel like a walk down a road of mirrors. We see everything twice; the present is perceived both directly and reflected through the past, that picture of events which existed before we got there. This rediscovery of the past as we move into the future has a certain Alice in Wonderland quality which can be disorienting, but it is this particular process which truly educates us to our contiguity with past history.

With the birth of the 1970's, literary criticism has awakened from a hypnotic trance which was self-induced shortly after the Russo-German pact and the outbreak of war in 1939. Those of us who have taken our literary training during the last two decades are seeing for the first time the emergence of a criticism based on "thought as thought ought to be, passing always in dialectic movement between knowing and being, between dream and outer reality."[1] Formalism, that great block of aesthetic ice, is breaking up and the cold fantasy of "pure" and isolated cerebration that created it is melting away. The heat of social conflict, cultural confusion, and emotional frustration is finally penetrating academia and, despite the powerful refrigeration apparatuses of English departments everywhere, is making fluid the rigid notions of Literature beautifully preserved in a crystal cube, touching no one and nothing.

Several critical articles by established male academicians and the sudden flowering of books and essays by women demonstrate our quickening return to consciousness. For those of us who came to the study of literature during the long sleep, the process of discovering literary criticism on *both* sides of the fifties has been a profound revelation. And so it always is when solutions to present problems are indicated by similar situations and solutions rescued from the past. The recovery becomes a bitter process as we expose the real reasons that led our immediate predecessors to abandon a fruitful direction for a relatively barren sidetrack. The eerie sense of walking on mirrors is balanced by a healthy sense of outrage at what our teachers and the critics put over on us. It wasn't that they forbade us to read certain writers or even that the books were unavailable. It was more subtle than that. Certain writers and certain ideas were treated as if they were nonexistent, even though they should have been an integral part of a balanced literary education. An atmosphere was created in which one was taught to treat and teach literature as if it were unattached to anything else in the world. The words *literature, poetry* and *art* conjure up images of bubbles floating in a cloudless, Platonic sky, and MacLeish's infamous dictum, "A poem should not mean, but be," echoes in our ears.

In 1938 Christopher Caudwell warned us against what he called "the bourgeois intellectual heresy," that is, "thought without action," or "pure contemplation." In describing the error of the bourgeoise intellectual, Caudwell was predicting, better than he knew, the reigning illusion of literary scholars. What he said of G. B. Shaw can be said of every English department in the country:

This is a familiar spectacle: the intellectual attempting to dominate hostile reality by "pure" thought. It is a human weakness to believe that by retiring into his imagination man can elicit categories or magical spells which will enable him to subjugate reality contemplatively. It is the error of the "theoretical" man, of the prophet, of the mystic, of the metaphysician, in its pathological form the error of the neurotic. It is the trace of the primitive believer in magic that remains in us all. (p. 148)

Arthur Efron's article "Criticism and Literature in the One-Dimensional Age,"[2] written thirty years later, was one of the few cracks in the aesthetic ice to appear during that entire academic generation. (While it is true an occasional critic like Arnold Kettle managed to write and publish, even he could not keep a position in academia. He is generally ignored by established critics, is unknown by professors and students alike and even had to go to Tanzania in 1968 in order to teach in a university!) Mr. Efron identifies the reason for modern criticism's refusal to deal with values and actions in life. Behind all the mazes of quotes and scholarly prose with which he feels constrained to camouflage his courageous contention (understandable when you know the super-cerebral department he comes from), lies his main thesis: Present criticism prevents literature from "telling it" by concentrating on the technological (formal) aspects instead of literature's "oppositional" (contextual) nature. By ignoring all opposition to the status quo, criticism helps to preserve it. Modern critics have a "widely-shared need for critical defenses against any possible connecting of literature with the rest of life." (p. 156) In severing themselves from other disciplines, they have "mistakenly divorced themselves from the huge act of criticism performed by the modern literary imagination," which projects "a need for sustained and multifaceted personal resistance to the one-dimensional world," "and hence from the chief critical matter that it attempts to examine."

The answer to his own question, "Why do none of the major developments in criticism since the New Criticism (rhetorical, myth and archetypal, McLuhan media analysis, phenomenological, perspectivism, linguistic, etc.) evince a recognition of essential alienation?" (p. 52) is not completely satisfactory. He finds that "these approaches . . . are merely in the style of the world at large, and as the New Criticism anticipated it: the age of technological supremacy." (p. 55) The article establishes that critics are

fiddling while Rome burns, but it never really comes out
and identifies them with "the functional sociologists most
present-day laboratory psychologists, or any other intel-
lectuals who have wedded themselves to an ideology within
the status quo. . . ." (p. 55) In fact, Efron assures us,
"we have nothing vital" in common "with these men who
have sold out to the powers that be." (p. 55) How can
Efron separate literary critics from the rest of the intellectual peddlers when he has said that they practice the sin
of omission, "a speciously neutral criticism." And that
they practice the sin of commission perpetuating the status
quo both by defusing the anti-social implications of art,
and by participating in an education of the young that is,
in his own words, "the inculcation of a very limited range
of categories for thinking and feeling." Even as he seeks to
protect his colleagues from the logical conclusions of his
argument he anticipates their hostile reaction.

Now, three years later, we are seeing a true revival in
sociological criticism. And foremost among those makers
of "a genuinely critical approach to literature," are those
whom Mr. Efrom was least likely to consider, the women.
No statistics are needed to demonstrate the chauvinism
that accompanies formalism. Mary Ellmann's book, *Thinking About Women*, should have laid the ghost of "pure"
art considered by "pure" criticism once and for all.
"Books by women are treated as though they themselves
were women, and criticism embarks, at its happiest, upon
an intellectual measuring of busts and hips."[3] "The working rule is simple, basic: there must always be two litera-
tures like two public toilets, one for Men and one for Wom-
en." (p. 32-33) The situation of women as students of
literature or professors is as bad.

Almost every major graduate school in the country gives strong
preference to men in admission, arguing that statistics prove that
women are a poor bet to go through and to become teachers of literature in colleges and universities. That is supposed to end the argument, because the preparation we give for this career is beyond ques-

tion. Yet most of the literature we teach has to do with the relationships between men and women, and much of it concerns itself with the experience of women. Because women drop out of graduate school to bear our children, they disqualify themselves from teaching that literature.

There is no question of female critics getting lost in the merely formal aspects of literature once they become aware of the contradiction it would prove to their own reality. This awareness of the quality of their own lives is increasingly leading women to produce books like Millet's *Sexual Politics* and Figes' *Patriarchal Attitudes*. They have, as Mr. Efron put it, "been through the experience of active disloyalty to the mores of society at large," and these books are, among other things, attempts to reintegrate literary studies into the rest of human inquiry from which it has been so adamantly absent. Ms. Millet states her conviction in the preface of *Sexual Politics* that literary criticism "is capable of seizing upon the larger insights which literature affords into the life it describes, or interprets, or even distorts." She feels that "there is room for a criticism which takes into account the larger cultural context in which literature is conceived and produced. Criticism which originates from literary history is too limited in scope to do this; criticism which originates in aesthetic considerations, New Criticism, never wished to do so."[5]

These women naturally assume that literature self-evidently belongs to the larger scheme of things human. It is necessary to go to an established male critic to get an argument in favor of rejoining literary criticism to other intellectual disciplines.

While Mr. Crews's purpose in "Anesthetic Criticism" is limited to an advocacy of psychoanalytic criticism, his argument is remarkably similar to Caudwell's condemnation of pure thought, for as he deals with "some of the more common academic resistances to Freudian discourse," he comes face to face with academic resistances to anything outside pure, i.e., formal, criticism.[6]

The most important point that Crews's essay makes,

however, is political.

> The history of literary study is transparently a history of intellectual and political fashion, never more so than in recent formalism and neo-religious moralism. . . . Unless one had decided in advance to find criticism "coherent and progressive," he would be hard pressed to justify calling it an intellectual discipline at all. (p. 6)

Although he brings up the connection between criticism and its "educational impact" he never says what that impact is. Exactly how does the use of New Critical method as a teaching device affect the students who are subjected to it and the professors who use it? Does the critical approach to a work alter, as Mr. Efron would have it, the meaning of that work? All Mr. Crews is willing to comment upon is the psychological effect of such teaching. The despair resulting from "suppression of effect" (why not just suppression?), the "genteel" atmosphere which rewards politeness rather than creativity, "the dull, safe, provincial work," is not confined to students. It is "the occupational disease of English . . . a debilitating fear that literary scholarship as we have been practicing it is a useless and elitist pastime." (pp. 9, 10, 11)

Perhaps it is a matter of political orientation and more than a touch of vested interest (or is Mr. Crews "repressing" threatening political knowledge?) that prevents him from identifying the problem as political and sociological. What Mr. Crews can't quite see or say is that criticism *is* the teaching of literature and, it is said the people who teach the young control the society. It is the method by which we teach the young to believe that what the artist says either has something to do with their lives (not only the "life of the imagination" as Mr. Crews has it) or we turn art into a meaningless, aesthetic exercise. The illusion of the pure being of literature has lost a whole generation of students to it, indeed it has lost them to reading anything. The small percentage who gritted their teeth all through college and graduate school and who suppressed their frustration and boredom were either hopelessly dull people to begin with or found their stimulation in intense activity, often political, outside the department. Needless to say they gave very little of themselves to "the required literature" and most of them still haven't finished their dissertations. The very fact that most graduate students in literature refuse to finish their degrees even though it means a waste of usually ten years in preparation for the Ph.D. should tell the professors something. Mainly, that the fear that "literary scholarship as we have been practicing it is a useless and elitist pastime" accurately reflects reality.

Actually, while literary criticism is an "elitist pastime" it performs a useful function. But we must look outside aesthetics to find out what that function is.

The history of criticism in the United States is intimately bound up in the history of politics. Not only did New Criticism rise with and support the reactionism of the past twenty-five years, it reflects the thoroughness with which anti-communism and anti-Sovietism have penetrated even literary studies. It has become standard literary procedure to decry the tyranny of social realism in socialist countries but no one seems to notice the mirror effect in this country. At the time when formalism became the major artistic heresy in the Soviet sphere, a non-formalist critic (even worse if he were a Marxist) became a dead person in American academic circles. Some, like Edmund Wilson, recanted and some, like Margaret Schlauch, left the country. Certainly the political atmosphere here as well as there influenced so-called purely aesthetic opinion.

Professor Bruce Franklin, recently fired at Stanford, sees a direct relationship between fascism and formalism in the United States. He says that the majority of literary critics and professors in the United States desperately believe that there is no relationship between art and life which allows them to study literature as a privately created world completely independent of its social and political context.[7] But this stance was not always accepted in academic circles. It arose in a suspiciously short period and at a time when American and English businessmen were arming Hitler as "a bulwark against communism." The latter 1930's saw both the birth and rise of New Criticism and the death of an extraordinarily vigorous sociological approach which, now conveniently forgotten, dominated the middle 30's. Along with the leftist poetry of Auden, C. Day Lewis, Stephen Spender and Archibald MacLeish came the journals. *Modern Quarterly, New Masses* and *Left Review* were dedicated to Marxist criticism. One of the first books of the time to take the sociological approach was V. K. Parrington's *Main Currents in American Thought*, 1927-30. Then came V. F. Calverton's *The Liberation of American Literature*, 1931, John Strachey's *The Coming Struggle for Power*, 1933, Granville Hicks' *The Great Tradition*, 1933, and Ralph Fox's *The Novel and the People*, 1937. Hicks also edited *Proletarian Literature in the United States*, 1935, C. Day Lewis put together *The Mind in Chains*, 1937, and Bernard Smith did *Forces in American Criticism*, 1937. We should be aware of where and when the most influential new critics arose. Brooks, Warren, Ransom and Tate all came from ultra-conservative Vanderbilt University via elite Oxford. Their first works just preceded the outbreak of World War II. Brooks and Warren's *An Approach to Literature* came out in 1936, the same year as Allen Tate's *Reactionary Essays*. In 1938 came John Crowe Ransome's *The World's Body* and Brooks and Warren's *Understanding Poetry*.

By the 1950's New Criticism had reached its zenith with the rise of Senator McCarthy. Although McCarthy's anti-communist witch-hunt was not primarily directed against left-wing professors, the brainwashing was so successful that the faculties themselves took over the purge. The Assembly of the Academic Senate of the University of California passed a resolution in 1950 barring any member of the Communist Party 'proved. . ., by reason of commitments to that party, are not acceptable as members of the faculty.' The loyalty oaths still required at many state colleges and universities are mementoes of the same politics. As Professor Franklin comments: "Ideology, after all, is more influential than laws."

The effect of formalism in the classroom is indeed political. Students are taught to be formal snobs despising the technical inferiority of proletarian literature. Even when a work is formally superior any undesirable content can be obscured by directing students' attention away from the undesirable subversive message. Eric Hoffer is right when he says that no intellectual believes the common people can rule themselves. After all, they can't even speak "good English." Aesthetics can even be twisted, as Walter Pater has, to prove the superiority of "manliness in art" over what is "feminine." The male aesthetic is "a full consciousness of what one does, of art itself in the work of art, tenacity of intuition and of consequent purpose, the spirit of construction as opposed to what is literally incoherent or ready to fall to pieces, and in opposition to what is hysteric or works at random, the maintenance of a standard."[8] This particular injection of sexism into an aesthetic value system is only an explicit example of what is a Western cultural rule.

According to an historian of the Women's Rights Movement, the feminist revolution ended in reform and reaction in the early 1930's. The puny reforms with which the male establishment obliterated the feminist vision did little but erode patriarchal ideology: the social order remained virtually intact. The causes for the failure of the revolution have been identified as the persistence of the patriarchal family; the collapse of organized feminism in 1920; the Depression and the death of radicalism in the thirties; post-war reaction after 1945—and the labor situation which accompanied it; and, finally, the general conservatism of the fifties.[9] The connection between the feminist cause and the need for sociological literary criticism begins to take shape when it is clearly understood why both movements were crushed at the same time, and by the same forces. Both were seen as radical political movements which attempted to undermine and expose the ideology of established power relationships. Both preached that freedom was not an inherent quality of the soul, but an objective material condition that all people had a right to.

The main attempt of Kate Millett's *Sexual Politics* is to show the correlation between literature (and by the way, criticism) and reactionary political attitudes of which sexism is one expression. Her main fault is in not seeing those reactionary political attitudes in any way but the sexual when they are also linked to racial, capitalist and colonial attitudes. In fact woman may consider herself a member of the first oppressed class. Millett correctly maintains that it is the cultural agents who are ultimately more responsible than the law for the perpetuation of the established order. She indicts three major novelists, Mailer, Miller and Lawrence, as counterrevolutionary politicians. These three are only part of present century's Virility School. We must add Roth, Hemingway, Jones, Algren, O'Hara and many others to the list. One feminist writer has observed that this movement in twentieth-century literature "is a direct response, indeed a male cultural backlash, to the growing threat to male supremacy. . . ."[10]

What has been said of the writers applies no less to the critics. (So Norman Mailer is doubly guilty). They not only emphasize male works, they determine the reasons why the male authors' works are invariably better. This biased criticism is usually conducted under the auspices of formalism (the writing is sentimental, sloppy; the tone is hysterical), but it always results in a nasty attack on women. Criticism is, in Mary Ellmann's words, "phallic criticism." Aesthetics, despite the philosophical overtones Kant lent to it, merely deals with relative cultural norms of taste. What the male cultural establishment decides is beautiful is often more a function of the dominant cultural values than any inherent artistic merit.

Kate Millett has demonstrated that at least one of the dominant male cultural values discriminates against women. Sexism in art propagates the mystique of women's natural inferiority in order to sustain their social and political inferiority. She discerns that men are conditioned into a ruling class from which women are excluded by birth. The artistic violence done to women by writers like Miller and Mailer logically progresses to the physical violence of a Charles Manson.[11] Mailer himself graphically demonstrated, when he assaulted and wounded his own wife, how easily his misogynous hatred moves from the pages of *The American Dream* into the real world.

It is not surprising, then, to see the phallic critics, Mailer at the fore, rise to avenge Millett's 'sexual' transgressions. Sex and violence and literary criticism go together. Irving Howe, ever a political reactionary, takes eight long pages of insulting *ad feminam* prose to call Millett's mind "middle class." Feeling that "squalid," "feckless" and "morally shameful" are merely neuter abuse, Howe resorts to the sexual taunt and calls her a female impersonator.[12] Soon after came Norman Mailer's long confessional cum diatribe on Millett. Aside from his outrage that Millett would dare to disturb the hitherto impenetrable sanctuary of Art, Mailer is incensed that she thinks "the sexual force of the man was the luck of his birth, rather than his finest moral product. . . ."[13] Neither man even attempts to answer the basic feminist argument that men have oppressed women economically, politically, mentally and physically. The very fact that Millett has aroused such enmity and provoked such attention must mean her views contain much painful truth.

Why are male critics so eagerly, if not cleverly, denouncing feminist criticism? Obviously these ideas threaten their own position. The artistic elevation from which they dispensed their own brand of male prejudice has been turned into a live volcano. The feminist critic is finally seeing that criticism was never judicially dispassionate but only used its self-proclaimed autonomy to discourage questioning of its (male) value system. The dangers of a value system, which is only relative, being elevated to the status of a divine absolute are again being exposed. To borrow a term from sociology we might say that with formalism, literary criticism became "functional," that it studied the operation of literature only within the given value system, thus promoting the status quo. When feminist criticism questions the values of the culture, it weakens the supports which have kept men on top.

Feminist criticism can never be merely formal because women recognize, out of the experience of their own oppression, what a powerful weapon art, especially literature, is. Literature is a major component of the educational process, and that process, not biological determinism, shapes our destiny. In seeking to destroy patriarchal ideology in order to better the position of women in society, feminist criticism is a political act.

Feminist criticism is a materialist approach to literature which attempts to do away with the formalist illusion that literature is somehow divorced from the rest of reality. Formalism insists that critics must exclude any material such as personal or social conditions behind the work because they are "extrinsic" or tangential to an understanding of the work. In opposition, feminist criticism reasserts the essential fact that books: "are not spun in mid-air by incorporeal creatures, but are the work of suffering human beings and are attached to grossly material things like health and money and the houses we live in."[14] Reality, above all, is the concern of feminist criticism. Unlike the masculine critics, feminists have nothing to lose by revealing the truth about our sexist society and a literature that commends its values and conceals its limitations. The actual grotesqueness of a reality distorted by prejudice cannot be corrected until it is perceived.

NOTES

[1]Christopher Caudwell, "George Bernard Shaw: A Study of the Bourgeoise Superman," *Studies in a Dying Culture, in Five Approaches of Literary Criticism*, ed. Wilbur Scott (N. Y. 1962), p. 147.

[2]Arthur Efron, "Criticism and Literature in the One-Dimensional Age," *Minnesota Review*, VIII, No. 1 (1968), pp. 48-62.

[3]Mary Ellmann, *Thinking about Women* (N. Y. 1968), p. 29.

[4]Bruce Franklin, "The Teaching of Literature in the Highest Academies of the Empire," *100 Flowers*, No. 1 (1971), pp. 48-49.

[5]Kate Millett, *Sexual Politics* (N. Y. 1970), p. xii.

[6]Frederick Crews, "Anesthetic Criticism," *Psychoanalysis and Literary Process* (Cambridge, Mass. 1970).

[7]Northrup Frye: Four Essays (Princeton 1957), pp. 6-7.

[8]Walter Pater, "Plato's Esthetics," *Plato and Platonism* (N. Y., 1899, pp. 253-254.

[9]Aileen Kraditor, *Up From the Pedestal, Selected Writings in the History of American Feminism* (Chicago 1968), p. 13.

[10]Shulamith Firestone, *The Dialectic of Sex* (N. Y. 1970).

[11]Gore Vidal, "In Another Country," *N. Y. Review of Books*, (July 22, 1971), p. 11.

[12]Irving Howe, "The Middle Class Mind of Kate Millett," *Harper's* (December 1971).

[13]Norman Mailer, "The Prisoner of Sex," *Harper's* (March 1971).

[14]Virginia Woolf, "A Room of One's Own," *A Virginia Woolf Anthology* (N. Y. 1969).

MARCIA R. LIEBERMAN

SEXISM AND THE DOUBLE STANDARD
IN LITERATURE

Feminist criticism is needed to effect a re-examination of sexism as it is found in literature and as it is imposed on literature by critics. The feminist critic will seek to expose the tangle of misconceptions, distortions, and malicious as well as benevolent prejudices which frequently govern the depiction of women in literature, and the response of male critics to female characters and to works by female authors.

Sexism affects literature at three levels, of which the easiest to detect is criticism. The bias of a critic may be clearly seen when he makes judgments based upon sexist preconceptions. It is also apparent that some male writers impose sexist views of female psychology upon the characters they create, but to perceive this second level of sexism may require the reader to challenge the implicit assumptions within a work of art. The most subtle, pervasive level at which sexism affects literature, however, is that of literary convention. The treatment and fate of the heroine, for example, may be controlled by conventions that inherently impose a sexist view on the author and the reader, male or female: they may affect the way an author treats his heroine, and constitute the reason why readers will find her acts credible and her fate acceptable. These conventions, in effect, reflect the values of the culture, and still need to be defined and analyzed.

The problem of sexism at each of these three levels, authorial, critical, and conventional, can be explored through a work like *Anna Karenina.* Anna is generally regarded as one of the great, unforgettable women in literature, a sort of fictional Garbo: beautiful, passionate, and tragic. Tragic, of course, she must be: who would have her be otherwise; who would consider her tragedy to be anything but fitting to the story—so, at least, many readers feel. Anna belongs to a class of great tragic (or pathetic) heroines that includes such women as Mme. de Renal, Nastasya Filipovna, Hawthorne's Zenobia and Hester Prynne, Tess Durbeyville, Eustacia Vye, and their sisters before them, Desdemona, Ophelia, Lady Macbeth, and Cordelia. Some of these women are virtuous, others are not, but all are tormented, and nearly all are either murdered or commit suicide. In the main, they are used to provide a story with pathos. Apart from the class of stories in which two lovers die together and for each other, as in the Tristan and Iseult stories or in *Romeo and Juliet*, the death or suicide of female characters is often more pathetic but less noble than the death of male characters within the same story. Female tragic heroines, unlike male tragic heroes, frequently die without having attained illumination. Lady Macbeth is at first bolder than her husband, but by the end of the play she is a pitiful figure, wandering deliriously through the castle, rubbing her hands. Ophelia and Desdemona are also depicted as members of the frail sex; Ophelia's mind snaps, like Lady Macbeth's, and Desdemona literally sits on the edge of her bed, waiting to be murdered. It appears that a literary convention exists in which a link is established between pathos and femininity; this convention may govern the outcome of *Anna Karenina*.

Anna Karenina is admired by many readers who consider her to be warm-hearted and "womanly," rather like Stendhal's Mme. de Renal. Attractive, lively Anna, married to a cold, pedantic bureaucrat, is clearly a *mal mariée*, a figure descended from the conventions of troubadour poetry. Readers sympathize with her moral struggle when Vronsky begins to court her, admire her when she breaks convention in going off to live with Vronsky, and are moved by her suicide, which occurs nearly at the end of

the novel; of course, it is not the end, but merely the low
point, for Levin's story continues after Anna's death, allowing the book to conclude serenely and hopefully. It is
clear that Anna is punished for her transgressions, but by
whom? Society closes its ranks against her, but in showing
this Tolstoy is only being realistic, for society would indeed have rejected such a woman. Yet is Tolstoy merely
showing the world as it is? Or does he intervene on the
world's side against Anna? Moreover, the novel's haunting
epigraph suggests that she has angered God as well; at the
beginning of both Books I and II, Tolstoy quotes the
Bible: " 'Vengeance is mine; I will repay.' " Against
whom is the force of this threatening prophecy directed?

The question is whether Anna's suicide is authentic
in terms of her character and situation. If a convention of
the pathetic heroine exists, it would suggest or require that
Anna die, whether or not the logic of events and of character necessitates her death. Indeed, we are accustomed
to the suicide or death of such heroines, especially of
adulterous ones: in nineteenth-century fiction these include Mme. Bovary, Mme. de Renal, Lady Dedlock, and
Therese Raquin. In 1870 Tolstoy told his wife that he had
an idea for a novel about " 'a certain type of woman, married, of high society, who had gone astray. He said his
object was to make this woman merely pitiable, not
guilty. . . .' " He did not, however, work on the novel
at once, and before he began to write he heard of the
suicide of his neighbor's mistress, Anna Pirogova,

who, on learning of her lover's attachment to another woman, sent
him a note which he did not receive in time and threw herself under
a train. Tolstoy saw her mangled body at the post-mortem. . . .
The following year Tolstoy began to write his book with the suicide
of an adulteress as its *terminus a quo*. This fact should be remembered when he is accused of 'killing off' Anna, or driving his heroine
to destruction. Had there been no suicide, there would have been no
novel.[1]

In the first railway scene in the novel, in which Anna first appears, and is introduced to Vronsky, a watchman is accidentally run over by a train. Anna is disturbed, and Vronsky sends money for the widow, in order to impress Anna. Anna, close to tears, calls it " 'a bad omen.' " Thus Anna's own fate is foreshadowed.

Anna is a strong woman, more intellectual than Kitty, less conventional than Dolly. She is attractive to Vronsky not only because of her vitality and a certain firmness and sense of decision about her. When Vronsky first sees her at the railway station he notices her firm but graceful step and movements. When at last he is introduced to her, he shakes her "little hand, and the firm grip with which she shook his gave him unusual pleasure."[2] Tolstoy remarks that Anna's "quick, firm yet light step" distinguished her from other Society women. (Unfortunately, Tolstoy tells us more about Anna's beauty, posture, and step than about her thoughts and motives in the first part of the novel. He does not really show us her inner life until just before her death.) She breaks convention by smoking, she plays lawn-tennis (a game too strenuous for Dolly), she is a serious reader. She is forthright and honest, but this leads to her undoing.

It has been pointed out that society would not have condemned Anna for having an affair if she had been discreet and observed certain conventions:

Vronsky's mother thought it entirely *comme il faut* that her son should have a liaison with a charming woman such as Anna; it added a degree of social polish to a rising young careerist. . . . Anna, however, is no casual adulteress. . . . She places herself beyond the pale of her social class, but only because of the manner in which she transgresses its hypocritical moral code.[3]

This is a telling point. If a woman is frivolous or has no soul, like Anna's friend, Princess Betsy, she can survive, but if she has a conscience or cannot live in hypocrisy she is destroyed. This only applies to women; Vronsky, who is serious about Anna, is not destroyed.

Karenin was willing to give Anna a divorce when she

left him, but she refused to accept it at the time. Later, when she wants the divorce so that she can marry Vronsky and feel secure with him, Karenin has changed his mind about it. Her inability to obtain the divorce contributes to Anna's anxiety in the second part of the novel. But. Tolstoy provided her with no clear or convincing motive when she first rejected the proferred divorce. It seems that he has her reject it because of the demands of his plot. Since Anna's suicide was the novel's *"terminus a quo,"* Tolstoy had to find means to drive Anna to despair. Indeed, Anna is deeply troubled on many counts after she goes to live with Vronsky: her separation from her son, her expulsion from society, the question of a divorce, and her anxiety about keeping Vronsky's love. All her actions, however, like her step and her gestures, show the decisiveness of her character. But although Anna suffers from guilt and worry, she is not compelled to commit suicide by a particular chain of occurrences nor by an internal weakness. When she goes to her death she has not heard of Karenin's final, categorical refusal to give her a divorce; Vronsky has not left her. In the last weeks before her suicide, Anna is harrowed by a jealousy which, we realize, is unfounded. Having been barred from society, she can go nowhere, no one will receive her, and so she must literally live for Vronsky. Vronsky is not courting another woman, yet he could do so; he is still accepted in society, he goes out into the world where he can meet other women. The problem is complex: Anna has broken social conventions and religious law, but she was unhappily married, and she loves Vronsky; Vronsky, we know, loves her, and moreover is faithful to her. Despite her suspicions, even Anna know this at a deep level. Emma Bovary's suicide is both credible and logical; she is indeed at the point of ruin when she takes her life. The same cannot be said of Anna. Her suicide is thus not a necessary ending, yet it is made to seem dramatically inevitable, perhaps because Tolstoy is not only depicting the double standard but also, consciously or unconsciously, applying it. It also operates in the comparative treatment of Anna and Levin, who is the other major protagonist of the novel. In one important respect their mental lives are alike. The questions about the meaning of life and death that haunt Anna towards the end of the novel are precisely the same ones that haunt Levin. Both try to understand human suffering, and both question the meaning and the use of reason; yet again we have the contrast: Anna can find no light, and in her despair destroys herself; Levin is vouchsafed the illumination that both had sought. He has found understanding, and he will live.

The sexual double standard is indeed a structural element of the novel. The theme of adultery is first treated in the story of the Oblonskys, foreshadowing Anna's adultery. The connection is close because Stiva Oblonsky is Anna's brother. He is a healthy, handsome, charming man, weak-willed and warm-hearted, optimistic, extravagant, a *bon vivant*. He deceives his thirty-three year old wife because after seven pregnancies she has lost her looks. Oblonsky, incapable of self-deception, does not pretend that he regrets his conduct:

He repented only of not having managed to conceal his conduct from her. . . . He even thought that she, who was nothing but an excellent mother of a family, worn-out, already growing elderly, no longer pretty, and in no way remarkable—in fact, quite an ordinary woman—ought to be lenient to him, if only from a sense of justice.[4]

Oblonsky must have a pretty mistress, just as he must have oysters and champagne. To be sure, Tolstoy portrays him as a frivolous man, but not in a derogatory way. Everyone likes him for his kind, joyous, and honest nature. His bright, handsome face had

a physical effect on those he met, making them feel friendly and cheerful. 'Ah! Stiva Oblonsky! Here he is!' said almost every one he met, smilingly. Even if conversation with him sometimes caused no special delight, still the next day, or the next, every one was as pleased as ever to meet him.[5]

And at the end of the novel he is going on in the same way, weak-willed, extravagant, alive and well. His sister Anna, guilty, like himself, of adultery, has thrown herself under a train.

The story of the Oblonskys' marital troubles is a minor element in the novel, but not because they are minor characters. The possibility of tragedy is not inherent in their story. Dolly Oblonsky must swallow her pride and be reconciled with her husband: she has five children, faded looks, no money, nowhere to go. And Stiva has no reason to commit suicide because his wife is angry upon discovering his infidelity; it simply is not necessary. Stiva suffers a brief period of inconvenience during Dolly's anger, but all is put right, ironically by Anna, when she comes to restore peace to the Oblonsky household. Underlying the entire novel is the daily unhappiness of Dolly Oblonsky:

'Altogether,' she thought, looking back at the whole of her life during those fifteen years of wedlock, pregnancy, sickness, dullness of mind, indifference to everything, and above all disfigurement. . . . And I when I am pregnant become hideous, I know. Travail, suffering, monstrous suffering, and that final moment . . . then nursing, sleepless nights, and that awful pain!'[6]

That the Oblonskys' story, however, is seen as being inherently less than that of the Karenins is shown by the remarks of several male critics. Logan Speirs describes the beginning of the novel: "We are shown a family quarrel. A husband has wrecked the happiness of his wife, but the presentation is gay, even charming. Stepan Oblonsky is a delightful hero of farce. When we see his wife our opinions change, but the situation apparently cannot be helped and Stepan remains delightful."[7] George Steiner says that, "as classical poets would have it, we plunge *in medias res*—the trivial and yet harrowing infidelity of Stepan Arkadyevich Oblonsky (Stiva). In recounting Oblonsky's miniature adultery, Tolstoy sets forth in a minor key the dominant themes of the novel. . . ."[8] Steiner enjoys the "comic brilliance" of the interview between Stiva and Dolly, "his outraged wife," and he refers to "the warm, comical whirl of Dolly's indignation." Dolly's humanity is reduced by this kind of criticism. Her sorrow at the loss of her figure and looks after seven pregnancies, her shame, her awareness that she is an uninteresting object to her husband, her real lack of options, all this is defused of its poignance and made into comic relief; Dolly is squeezed into the stereotype of the Humorless Deceived Wife.

Whereas Tolstoy's attitude towards Anna and his treatment of her raise certain questions concerning the effect of the double standard and social conventions on the novelist, *Moll Flanders* presents a different aspect of the problem. Defoe's heroine is a remarkably energetic woman who struggles to make the best of her difficult and highly eventful life: as recorded in the novel's subtitle, Moll, born in prison, was "Twelve Year a Whore, five times a Wife . . . Twelve Year a Thief, Eight Year a Transported Felon in Virginia, at last grew Rich" and returned to England to enjoy her fortune. Moll is disembarrassed of her romantic illusions at an early age. As a pretty young orphan, she is taken in by a rich family to be a companion to their own daughters. The handsome eldest son, promising marriage, seduces Moll. But when the youngest son announces to the family that he wants to marry Moll, the older son is delighted and urges Moll to marry his brother. Moll is horrified to see her lover receive "the thanks of a faithful friend for shifting off his whore into his brother's arms for a wife."[9] This episode alters Moll: she says, when next she must look for a husband, "I had been tricked once by that cheat called love, but the game was over," and she is resolved to look out for herself.

After this, Moll practices self-interest vigorously, first in finding husbands and later, when she is too old to be marriageable, in her career as a thief. She has been roundly criticized for this: Dorothy Van Ghent, for instance, comments on the "meagerness and abstractness of a sensibility which frantically converts all sense experience into cash value . . . a morality suited to the human species in its peculiar aspect as cash-calculator, and a morality, therefore, most particularly suitable to the prostitute."[10] Van Ghent appears to forget that Moll lived in an age when the poor were free to starve to death without exciting any particular attention. Moll, who is sexually exploited at various times in her life, becomes an essentially solitary person who takes a functional view of her fellow creatures. She is a disguise artist; in order to protect herself, she conceals her thoughts, her past, and even her name from everyone she deals with, including her readers ("Moll Flanders" is not her real name, but rather the name conferred on her by thieves who have heard of her but never met her. The reader never knows her original name in full). Moll conceals everything from everyone: her name, how much money she has, her address, how many times she has been married, how many children she has had. When she becomes a thief she wears innumerable disguises: "generally I took up new figures, and contrived to appear in new shapes every time I went abroad."[11] Moll is thus a paradigmatic woman. In order to secure herself in an economically and socially brutal world, Moll must often conceal her identity from others. In her own words, an unprotected woman "is just like a bag of money or a jewel dropped on the highway, which is a prey to the next comer. . . ."[12] Given the terms of the game, many women still play it the same way today, concealing their natural physical attributes through cosmetics and clothes in order to conform to arbitrary standards of beauty and to attract men. Moreover, women are advised by women's magazines and by "traditional female wisdom" to conceal their inner natures and thoughts from the men they need to attract: they are urged not to show off their intelligence, to agree with their man's ideas and tastes, to admire his opinions and conceal their own. If this is an essential principle of female behavior, not innate to women but practised by them as a security mechanism, then Moll is a quintessential female. She consciously adopts the strategy of disguise but is not destroyed by it; her personality remains intact and she retains a sense of self-worth.

Defoe chose to have his heroine narrate her own story, and since he is thoroughly concealed behind Moll's narration, it is difficult to perceive his attitude towards her. This has led those critics who, like Van Ghent, are uncomfortable with Moll's robust materialism and her single-minded will to get rich, to speculate upon whether Defoe's intentions may have been ironic. One critic, in considering the problem of Defoe's relation to Moll, reveals an implicitly sexist view of human nature. Ian Watt would disagree that Moll is a quintessential female. He finds that Defoe's tough, hardy, practical heroine is

suspiciously like her author, even in matters where we would expect striking and obvious differences. The facts show that she is a woman and a criminal, for example, but neither of these roles determines her personality as Defoe has drawn it. Moll Flanders, of course, has many feminine traits; she has a keen eye for fine clothes and clean linen, and shows a wifely concern for the creature comforts of her males. . . . But . . . the essence of her character and actions is, to one reader at least, essentially masculine.

Although Moll loves fine clothes and clean linen, it is her toughness and strength of character that Watt cannot see as feminine, moving him to assert that her character "is not noticeably affected" by her sex. Her most "positive qualities," he says,

are the same as Crusoe's, a restless, amoral and strenuous individualism. It is, no doubt, possible to argue that these qualities might be found in a character of her sex, station and personal vicissitudes; but it is not likely. . . . Defoe's identification with Moll Flanders was so complete that, despite a few feminine traits, he created a personality that was in essence his own.[13]

Watt's confident pronouncements are based on an essential ignorance of the difference between sex and sex role. It is evident that Watt believes he knows which traits are feminine, and which are not. He does not question his own assumptions about this, but takes it for granted that Moll, as a tough individualist, must be a reflection of her author, hence masculine herself. Watt confuses sex, a biological attribute, with sex role, which is culturally determined. In so doing, he applies not only a sexual but also an intellectual double standard to his material. Irving Howe betrays the same carelessness when, in his review of *Sexual Politics*, he first says that "there are times when one feels the book was written by a female impersonator," but shortly afterwards calls Kate Millett "a little girl who knows nothing about life."[14]

Many disturbing aspects of the treatment of women in literature have been ignored, or accepted, or have even been seen as factors contributing to the beauty or charm of the works in which they appear. The feminist critic has to struggle with her dual consciousness of the inaccuracy or distortion of the depiction of women in novels, poems and plays which she considers to be great works of art. This does not necessarily mean, as men often hastily assume, that she is going to throw out the baby with the bath water; she can continue to love Milton's poetry without also admiring his representation of Eve. She might not give up *Anna Karenina*. But the same unease which is permitted to the Black critic or teacher, and even respected in him (when he deals with Faulkner, for example) is treated as a joke when expressed by women. The feminist critic must also struggle with the laughter and scorn of male colleagues who reject the application of the rigorous critical approach which men apply to literary form, language, and characterization, to the double standard in literature. Some men reject feminist criticism out of hand as being silly, trivial, non-scholarly, or, most often, by denying that it is literary criticism at all. It was in this spirit that Irvin Howe called Kate Millett "brilliant in an unserious way."

The same man who avers that Norman Mailer really has a touch of genius, and who gently tolerates Mailer's lack of discipline (which may even be appropriate, allowing him to be placed in the class of Lovable, Unruly Geniuses), will excoriate Kate Millett, declare that she is a rotten scholar and a lousy writer, and even deny that what she has written about Lawrence, Meredith, Charlotte Bronte, Hardy, Mailer, Miller, and Genet *is* literary criticism. Irving Howe wrote of her book, "that such a farrago of blunders, distortions, vulgarities, and plain nonsense could be passed by the English Department of Columbia University for the doctoral degree is an interesting fact."[15]

Feminist criticism can expose and overturn the double standard that is manifested in literature and in criticism. Sexism is not only revealed in the overt bias of male critics and authors, but also in the social conventions that shape both the creation of literature and our response to it. We must establish and at the same time defend feminist criticism, not only to correct literary distortions but also to expose the sources of covert bias, and to free women from the unchallenged assumptions that limit their lives.

NOTES

[1]R. F. Christian, *Tolstoy, A Critical Introduction* (Cambridge University Press, 1969), pp. 166-167.

[2]Leo Tolstoy, *Anna Karenina* (New York, W. W. Norton, 1970), pp. 57-58.

[3]Ernest J. Simmons, *Introduction to Tolstoy's Writings* (University of Chicago Press, 1968), pp. 86-87.

[4]*Anna Karenina*, p. 3.   [5]*Ibid.*, p. 13.

[6]*Ibid.*, p. 550.

[7]Logan Speirs, *Tolstoy and Chekhov* (Cambridge University Press, 1971), p. 85.

[8]George Steiner, *Tolstoy or Dostoevsky* (New York, Vintage, 1961), pp. 59-60, 64.

[9]Daniel Defoe, *Moll Flanders* (New York, Modern Library, 1950), pp. 50, 52.

[10]Dorothy Van Ghent, *The English Novel* (New York, Rinehart, 1953), pp. 36, 42.

[11]*Moll Flanders*, p. 250.   [12]*Ibid.*, p. 119.

13Ian Watt, *The Rise of the Novel* (Berkeley, University of California Press, 1964), pp. 113-115.

14Irving Howe, "Books: The Middle-Class Mind of Kate Millett," *Harper's*, 241 (Dec. 1970), pp. 124, 129.

15*Ibid.*, p. 128.

JOSEPHINE DONOVAN

FEMINIST STYLE CRITICISM

In *A Room of One's Own* Virginia Woolf argues that
the great women novelists of the 19th century suffered
from a lack of a feminine tradition in style. The sentence
which was given to the Brontë sisters, Jane Austen and
George Eliot was a sentence forged by male sensitivities.
The women writers had, in short, to deal with a stylistic
tradition that was fundamentally alien to their own way of
thinking. It was almost as if they had to write in a foreign
language.

To illustrate her thesis Woolf gives an example of
"the sentence that was current at the beginning of the
nineteenth century." I cite it here:

The grandeur of their works was an argument with them, not to
stop short, but to proceed. They could have no higher excitement
or satisfaction than in the exercise of their art and endless generations of truth and beauty. Success prompts to exertion; and habit
facilitates success.[1]

Woolf says that this "is a man's sentence; behind it one
can see Johnson, Gibbon and the rest." Moreover, she
states it is a sentence that is "unsuited for a woman's use."[2]
Charlotte Brontë and George Eliot tried to use it and
failed; only Jane Austen managed to ignore it, devising instead her own authentic sentence style.

The fundamental assumption Woolf is making in this
analysis is two-fold: one, that there is a female "mind,"
and, two, that there is or ought to be a feminine style tradition appropriate to that "mind." In this paper I would like
to explore some of the ramifications of Woolf's thesis. My
suggestions will be highly tentative; indeed, my primary

purpose is to elicit discussion of the topic rather than to come to any definitive conclusions.

I might begin by looking at the hypothetical "male sentence" which Virginia Woolf has set up, so as to determine exactly what characteristics she is attributing to a male style. The first observation one might make of the sentence is that it is of a certain rhetorical complexity. The first sentence concludes with balanced antithetical phrases: "not to stop short, but to proceed." The third sentence also reveals a sophisticated sense of rhetorical balance. The semicolon provides a delicate causal hinge between the two segments of the sentence. Is it this rhetorical sophistication which Woolf is labeling male? Probably not. The sophistication of the rhetorical art of a Jane Austen or of Virginia Woolf herself precludes such a thesis.

But there is also in the passage another, more subtle, tonal characteristic which may be more to the point of Woolf's thesis. Clearly whoever is speaking in this passage betrays a certain lofty arrogance, a certain sureness, indeed smugness, which may be what Woolf sees as alien to the female author (who after all was something of a newcomer to the experience of writing in the early 19th century, and therefore, unlikely to be making the kind of bold, unchallengeable assertions as are made in this passage).

The tone reveals the author as one who is quite confident of his own authority. One can indeed picture Samuel Johnson making this kind of declaration. Only a member of a ruling class in a ruling nation—in this case a European patriarch at the height of European ascendancy—could write authentically in this way. Its author shows himself to be the heir of generations of secure "insiders." Only such a mind could utter pompous aphorisms of the kind, "Success prompts to exertion; and habit facilitates success."

It is clear that this tone would of necessity have been

foreign to a woman writing in the same period. For women were not, and are not, the dominant class, and their assertions could never have had the lofty air of authority of, say, a Samuel Johnson.

It is interesting to note parenthetically that Mary Ellmann, one of our foremost feminist critics, has isolated "the *sensation* of authority" as a primary characteristic of contemporary male, as opposed to female, prose style.[3] In *Thinking About Women* Ellmann analyzes three prose passages from recent magazine articles written by men. In each she remarks the tone of "confidence, reason, adjustment, efficacy . . . firmness, directness. . . ." The passages are, she suggests, "fair examples of critical prose now in this country, of an established masculine mode of speaking competently on aesthetic issues."[4]

Dorothy Richardson, a late 19th, early 20th century English writer, who pioneered the use of the "stream of consciousness" technique in her lengthy novel *Pilgrimage*, made an observation about male style that is similar to Virginia Woolf's. In criticizing what she called "masculine realism" she pointed to the "self-satisfied, complacent, know-all condescendingness" of the omniscient (male) narrator found in Conrad and James.[5] ". . . Bang, bang, bang, on they go, these men's books, like an L.C.C. tram, yet unable to make you forget them, the authors, for a moment."[6] Richardson proposed to produce in her own writings "a feminine equivalent of the current masculine realism."[7]

Leon Edel in commenting upon Richardson's theories suggests that her primary criticism was that "male realism" was defective because it left out whole areas of "reality."

What [these] novels left out, if we are to judge by what Dorothy Richardson put in, are whole areas of feeling, the self-absorbing reverie, combined with acute perceptual experience.[8]

Virginia Woolf has suggested that Richardson was able to forge a prose style appropriate to this "feminine realism." Indeed, in attempting to describe what would be a "woman's sentence," Woolf pointed to Dorothy Richardson's accomplishment:

She [Richardson] has invented . . . a sentence which we might call the psychological sentence of the feminine gender. It is of a more elastic fibre than the old, capable of stretching to the extreme, of suspending the frailest particles, of enveloping the vaguest shapes. . . . Miss Richardson has fashioned her sentence consciously, in order that it may descend to the depths and investigate the crannies of Miriam Henderson's [the heroine's] consciousness. It is a woman's sentence. . . .[9]

Richardson and Woolf are, of course, part of the larger literary movement against 19th century realism which was to dominate early 20th century literature as "Modernism." However, more to the point of our concerns is the fact that they both suggest in their critical comments as well as in their own prose fiction that there is such a thing as female consciousness and that women writers must evolve a style appropriate to that consciousness.[10]

They further suggest that the female consciousness is primarily aware of—or concerned with—psychological events, rather than with abstract philosophical assertions or with external, dramatic happenings. The style most appropriate to such a consciousness would naturally be some sort of "monolog intérieur."

Another literary theorist who suggests directions complementary to those offered by Woolf and Richardson is Nathalie Sarraute, the contemporary French "anti-novelist," who Ellmann sees as a descendent of Jane Austen.[11] In her essay "Conversation et sous-conversation" in L'Ere du soupçon Sarraute argues that novelists must concern themselves with the "subterranean" reality which underlies everyday surface conversations. These "sub-conversations" are, she says, really "interior dramas made up of attacks, triumphs, recoils, defeats. . . ."[12]

In another context Sarraute illustrates what these psychic happenings are by calling them "Tropismes," the title of her first novel. Tropisms are the involuntary instinctive movements made by animalcules, like the amoeba, to external stimuli. The psyche responds involuntarily to other psyches or to external stimuli in an analogous fashion. It is the artist's job to capture this preverbal reality.

Moreover, Sarraute insists that the novelist must resist the temptation to classify and analyze this reality. Rather he or she must capture the tropisms as if at the moment they occur. The reader and the author must experience them with the character. The continuity of this experience must not be broken.[13]

Now, while Sarraute does not make any claims that an awareness of this subterranean level of reality is the province of the woman writer, it is clear that her theory complements those of Richardson and Woolf in that she is rejecting the authoritative, objective, analytic mode of the male prose writer. Instead, she is arguing for a fictional technique, a prose style, which will effectively eliminate the objective narrator, which will plunge the reader in the midst of the psychic drama that is taking place in the pages of the novel.[14]

Although it is primarily the new French novelists—Sarraute included—who have tried to follow up on these precepts, it is a British woman novelist, Ivy Compton-Burnett, whom Sarraute singles out for having devised the most effective style to the purposes sought. Sarraute points out that Compton-Burnett uses dialogue in such a way as to reveal the "sub-conversations" which are going on underneath. "The interior movements of which the dialogue is only the end result . . . try to insert themselves into the dialogue itself. . . . There is something present which is constantly threatening to break through."[15]

Mary Ellmann corroborates Sarraute's judgment by suggesting that Compton-Burnett's style is a "mode congenial to feminine talent [probably because] . . . women have had ample opportunity to learn the underlife well."[16]

What all of these remarks tend to be saying is that a female prose style is or should be one which enables the writer to deal with the psychic, personal, emotional "inner" details of life in a way that is neither analytic nor authoritarian. What, then, specifically, is such a female style? Can such a theory be "proven" by analyzing existing specimens of female prose style?

To answer this would require a much more extensive study than I can document here. But to illustrate how such a study might proceed, I will analyze somewhat cursorily five specimens of female prose style drawn from the following major novelists: Jane Austen, George Eliot, Kate Chopin, Dorothy Richardson, and Virginia Woolf.

The first passage is from *Pride and Prejudice*:

Till Elizabeth entered the drawing-room at Netherfield, and looked in vain for Mr. Wickham among the cluster of red coats there assembled, a doubt of his being present had never occurred to her. The certainty of meeting him had not been checked by any of those recollections that might not unreasonably have alarmed her. She had dressed with more than usual care, and prepared in the highest spirits for the conquest of all that remained unsubdued of his heart, trusting that it was not more than might be won in the course of the evening. But in an instant arose the dreadful suspicion of his being purposely omitted. . . .[17]

While the author's style here is extraordinarily elegant (which might lead us to conclude an authoritative distance from author to characters), it is clear that the author is depicting the "inner" reality of a moment in Elizabeth's experience. Briefly, it is the moment of embarrassment/disappointment that occurs when she hears that her "conquest" will not be present that evening. A gentle irony is, of course, conveyed in the fact that she had hoped the conquest would take no longer than an evening. This irony relates to the implicit irony involved in the notion of conversations/subconversations. For, Austen here relates a subterranean drama which in effect undercuts the conventional surface ritual of the would-be *femme fatale* entrapping the male.

It is significant also that the narrator, while distanced from the character and thus a "third person," nevertheless "gets inside" her, such that the point of view in this passage is primarily Elizabeth's, undercut only by Austen's delicate irony. There is nothing assertive or heavy-handed about the narrator's description of the event.

The following passage is from *The Mill on the Floss*:

But the constant presence of her mother's regretful bewilderment was less painful to Maggie than that of her father's sullen incommunicative depression. As long as the paralysis was upon him, and it seemed as if he might always be in a childlike condition of dependence—as long as he was still only half-awakened to his trouble, Maggie had felt the strong tide of pitying love almost as an inspiration, a new power, that would make the most difficult life easy for his sake; but now, instead of childlike dependence there had come a taciturn hard concentration of purpose, in strange contrast with his old vehement communicativeness and high spirit; and this lasted from day to day, and from week to week, the dull eye never brightening with any eagerness or any joy. It is something cruelly incomprehensible to youthful natures, this sombre sameness in middle-aged and elderly people, . . .[18]

There is no question but that Eliot is having problems with her sentence in this passage. Note how she rephrases sections of the sentence in passing, as if dissatisfied with the first phrasing and as if wishing by a cumulation of aspects to overpower the reader with the truth of the situation. In the second sentence this occurs three times: first, the opening phrase "As long as the paralysis was upon him" is broken by the parenthetical observation that the illness may be extensive and repeated with a slight variation in "as long as he was only half-awakened to his trouble." The next instance is where "inspiration" is rephrased as "a new power," and the final example is where "from day to day" is extended to "from week to week."

I believe Virginia Woolf is correct in diagnosing Eliot's problem as being that she has tried to use a "man's sentence" to her own purposes. The length and cumbersome structure of the sentence suggest an attempt at rhetorical distance, but it is an attempt which fails because it lacks the emotional disengagement which stylistic distance must entail.

Austen's irony enables her to achieve distance and yet she does not err into the pompously assertive tone of the "man's sentence" Woolf cites. Eliot's tone does not allow for distance; the narration is clearly engaged in the event being narrated, and yet the sentence structure would be appropriate for a pompous, assertive "male" (in Woolf's conception) style. That the passage here cited concludes with a lengthy, ponderous assertion about human nature suggests Eliot is trying to effect the pose of the "know-all" male narrator decried by Woolf and Richardson. Perhaps the above analysis proves some insight into the question of why her prose style is so turgid, uncomfortable, and inappropriately suited to her content.

The following selection is from Kate Chopin's *The Awakening*, an American novel published in 1899, which deals with the vain attempts of a woman to free herself from an unhappy marriage:

That lady was still clad in white, according to her custom of the summer. Her eyes beamed an effusive welcome. Would not Mrs. Pontellier go inside? Would she partake of some refreshment? Why had she not been there before? How was that dear Mr. Pontellier and how were those sweet children? Had Mrs. Pontellier ever known such a warm November?[19]

In this passage the main character Edna Pontellier is being greeted by her friend Mme. Lebrun, referred to as "that lady" in the passage. Edna never responds to these questions in the narration, as the focus changes to other characters in the next paragraph. One may, however, conclude that she did answer them in actuality but that the answers (and indeed the questions themselves) are of no consequence, being simply a part of a surface social ritual.

Here as in the Austen passage one has a sense of a gentle "décollage" between the surface and the "under-conversation." It is clear that the essential or inner Edna is not "there" during the above exchange of surface niceties. Chopin's handling of the narration gives us a strong feeling that the heroine is operating on two levels: on the automatic level of social ritual, and on another many times removed, at a depth far below the surface. This impression recurs through the novel, and helps prepare the reader for Edna's final submergence below the surface in the death-by-drowning scene that concludes the work.

Whether one wishes to characterize Chopin's sentence as "feminine" or not, it is clear that she has fashioned a style that is an appropriate vehicle for the conveyance of the psychological depths of her heroine's inner life.

Virginia Woolf in the passage cited above says Richardson's sentence is "feminine" because she consciously fashioned her sentence

in order that it may descend to the depths and investigate the crannies of Miriam Henderson's consciousness. It is a woman's sentence, but only in the sense that it is used to describe a woman's mind by a writer who is neither proud nor afraid of anything that she may discover in the psychology of her sex.[20]

It would seem that Austen and Chopin fashioned their sentences similarly.

Let us conclude our summary survey by looking at passages from Richardson herself and from Virginia Woolf. The following selection describes a scene where Miriam, the main character in *Pilgrimage* is waking up:

Miriam lay motionless while Emma unfolded and arranged the screens. Then she gazed at the ceiling. . . . She felt strong and languid. She could feel the shape and weight of each limb; sounds came to her with perfect distinctness; the sounds downstairs and a low-voiced conversation across the landing, little faint marks that human beings were making on the great wide stillness, the stillness that brooded along her white ceiling and all round her and right out through the world; the faint scent of her soap-tablet reached her from the distant washstand. She felt that her short sleep must have been perfect, that it carried her down and down into the heart of tranquillity where she still lay awake, and drinking as if at a source. Cool streams seemed to be flowing in her brain, through her heart, through every vein, her breath was like a live cool stream flowing through her.[21]

The following passage is from *To the Lighthouse*:

. . . the whole bay spread before them and Mrs. Ramsay could not help exclaiming, "Oh, how beautiful!" For the great plateful of blue water was before her; the hoary Lighthouse, distant, austere, in the midst; and on the right, as far as the eye could see, fading and falling, in soft low pleats, the green sand dunes with the wild flowing grasses on them, which always seemed to be running away into some moon country, uninhabited of men.[22]

In both these passages it is clear that the primary content has now become the inner, under-the-surface life of the heroines. No longer is it a question of pointing to the ironic distance between the surface and the inner depths of the characters' lives as it was in Austen and in Chopin; rather it is taken for granted that the surface is of little consequence. What matters are the inner lives.

In Richardson, however, the narrator enters into the flow of the characters' thoughts in a way slightly different from Woolf. There is little or no distance between the narrator and the character, even though the thoughts are still being indirectly narrated.[23] The emphasis in Richardson is on the sensual experience of Miriam: her feeling, smelling, hearing, etc.

The effect of her style is one of a hurried accumulation of impressions. Richardson's disregard of conventional punctuation is quite evident in the sentence which begins, "She could feel the shape . . ." One has to ask why the semicolon after "limb" instead of a period. It can only be that Richardson wanted to suggest a close connection between Miriam's feeling the weight of the limbs and the sounds. In other words, the shift is one that takes place in Miriam's consciousnes: she is aware first of the limbs, then of the sounds. The semicolons used in the sentence suggest that all of the "events" described in the sentence are part of one continuing moment of awareness in the mind of the heroine. Periods would have suggested breaks too abrupt to effectively connote the continuing mood of a span of mental awareness as is conveyed in this sentence.

The last sentence also gives a sense of emotional flow:

phrases "through her heart," "through every vein" seem to give the sentence itself a rhythmic fluidity. It is apparent that Richardson has devised a sentence appropriate to her own purposes, which are to express the inner reality, the inner stream, of her character's consciousness.

In the Woolf passage, however (and I do not presume here to do a thorough analysis of Woolf's magnificent style), it is clear that while the eye of the narrator and that of Mrs. Ramsey appear to merge, it is not the narrator who loses ground to Mrs. Ramsey, as the narrator in *Pilgrimage* does to Miriam. The distinction is perhaps subtle but may explain why *To the Lighthouse* remains a masterpiece and *Pilgrimage* does not. Woolf's style remains the controlling voice in the episode here described; whereas Richardson's style "gives into" the pressure, the flow of the experience being related.

However much we may feel that the eye which is observing the scene in the Woolf passage is that of Mrs. Ramsey, we nevertheless never sense ourselves (through the style) lost in her experience. Rather the experience and the view become subsumed to a greater vision, which is that enforced by the style itself. The impeccable design of the sentences, that not a word could be changed, creates an aesthetic control over the "events" narrated that makes this great work more like a poem than the series of dramatic encounters of the traditional novel. One might wish indeed that had anyone attempted Flaubert's great ambition, to write a novel about nothing, it might have been Virginia Woolf.

And yet, the aesthetic control is not the pompous authoritarianism of the male sentence she herself cited as unsuitable for women's uses. Rather—and this I believe is one of the unique attributes of Woolf's genius—she manages to create the effect that the world she is describing is a world of the "inside" where no assertive authoritarian distance could possibly exist. Follow the rhythm of the sentence fragment which begins "and on the right." "As

far as the eye could see" suggests anyone's eye, an un-
identified eye, and yet also Mrs. Ramsey's personal perspective is included in the sweep over the horizon. "Fading and falling, in soft low pleats, the green sand dunes
. . ." is a sentence which creates a rhythmic effect in
sounds which corresponds to the rhythm *both* of the eye
observing the dunes and of the dunes themselves. The
rhythm of the observing mind (inner reality) and that of
the outer reality coalesce in the controlling aesthetic
rhythm of the sentence, the "inner mind" of the novel
itself. In the last phrase the word "seemed" suggests that
we are back in the mind of Mrs. Ramsey and yet the image
of the desolate uninhabited moon country universalizes
the vision beyond her particular mind.

In this inadequate way I have hoped to show how
Woolf manages to retain stylistic control over a passage
while still entering within and universalizing the experience
being narrated. If one accepts that this "tropismic" level
of awareness—that is, the awareness of the underlife or the
inner mind of the world's reality—is one which women
and/or women novelists have to a high degree, then it is
perhaps Virginia Woolf who has fashioned the most effective sentence style to the purposes of transmitting this
reality, while not in the process losing the sense of aesthetic control necessary to great art. She is able to do this
because the psychic rhythms conveyed in her style are her
own.

The final question I would like to leave with the
reader is whether close stylistic analyses such as we have
attempted here on an extensive number of women writers
would lead us to make further conclusions about "feminine style." Would we continue to find recurring traits?
If we did, could we reach conclusions about the female
mind in the way Erich Auerbach, for example, was able to
characterize the Homeric and Hebraic minds through his
close stylistic analyses of *The Odyssey* and *Genesis*?[24]
Surely such an approach is worth further exploration.

NOTES

[1] Virginia Woolf, *A Room of One's Own* (New York: Harcourt, Brace and World, 1929), p. 79.

[2] *Ibid.*, p. 80.

[3] Mary Ellmann, *Thinking About Women* (New York: Harcourt, Brace and World, 1968), p. 150.

[4] *Ibid.*, p. 154.

[5] Dorothy Richardson, *Dawn's Left Hand*, as quoted in Leon Edel, *The Psychological Novel, 1900-1950* (London: Rupert Hart-Davis, 1955), p. 74.

[6] *Ibid.*, p. 74.

[7] Dorothy Richardson, Forward to 1938 Edition of *Pilgrimage*, as quoted in Edel, p. 73.

[8] Edel, p. 74.

[9] Virginia Woolf, *Contemporary Writers*, pp. 124-25, as quoted in Ellmann, p. 172.

[10] The issue of whether there is or is not a female consciousness is not one which can be settled here. For further enlightenment, however, I refer the reader to two articles: David C. McClelland, "Wanted: A New Self Image for Women" in *Dialogue on Women* (Indianapolis: Bobbs-Merrill, 1967), pp. 35-55, and Meredith Tax, "Woman and Her Everyday Life," *Notes from the Second Year: Womens Liberation* (New York: 1970).

[11] "Jane Austen's minutiae are liminal, Nathalie Sarraute's are subliminal, but they are alike in refusing to bypass detail." Ellmann, p. 222.

[12] Nathalie Sarraute, *L'Ere du soupçon* (Paris: Gallimard, 1956), p. 118. Translations of passages from Sarraute are mine.

[13] See Sarraute, *L'Ere du soupçon*, p. 124.

[14] Sarraute, p. 140.   [15] *Ibid.*, p. 144.

[16] Ellmann, p. 227. It is only fair to note, however, that Ellmann generally tends to resist the thesis that there is such a thing as a female "mind" and/or a feminine literary style.

[17] Jane Austen, *Pride and Prejudice/Sense and Sensibility* (New York: Random House, 1950), p. 75.

[18] George Eliot, *The Mill on the Floss* (New York: Pocket Books, 1956), p. 294.

[19] Kate Chopin, *The Awakening and Other Stories* (New York: Holt, Rinehart and Winston, Inc., 1970), p. 273.

[20] In Ellmann, p. 172.

[21] Dorothy Richardson, *Pilgrimage, Vol. I* (New York: Alfred A. Knopf, 1967), p. 149.

[22] Virginia Woolf, *To the Lighthouse* (New York: Harcourt,

Brace and World, 1927), p. 23.

23For the latest discussion of the issue of what to label "stream of consciousness" see Paul Hernadi, "Dual Perspective: Free Indirect Discourse and Related Techniques," *Comparative Literature*, 24, No. 1 (Winter, 1972), pp. 32-43.

24See Erich Auerbach, *Mimesis* (New York: Doubleday, 1957), pp. 1-20.

GILL GANE
ANN KAUTZMAN
KATHLEEN KELLEY

NANCY JAINCHILL
SUSAN MULLINS
SUSAN TENENBAUM

BIBLIOGRAPHY*

In fall 1971 six of us started a seminar on Women and Literature at the Cambridge-Goddard Graduate School. At the beginning
we didn't know much about where to look for books that could be
usefully studied from a feminist perspective; now, at the end of the
year, we have learned something about literature by and about
women, and we thought it might be helpful to others if we drew up
a bibliography presenting the fruits of our experience. We hope that
this bibliography will be of some use to women wanting to study the
female experience as it has been portrayed in literature, to individual
women simply looking for good reading, and to women teaching literature (we make occasional comments on books we consider especially suited to raising the consciousness of various groups of
readers).

This is a selective bibliography based on our personal prefer-
ences and the resources available to us. Most of the original works
we read were prose fiction—novels and short stories; poetry we considered only in the twentieth century, and drama we hardly looked
at at all. We also restricted ourselves to women writers, with so few
exceptions that we haven't bothered to include the handful of male
authors we read. (Of course, this doesn't mean that male writers
should be ignored; the best of them have given some excellent portraits of women, the worst can raise consciousness by their evident
misogyny.) In the case of secondary sources, we looked at a much
wider range of material; our list *Works About Literature* includes
many surveys and critical works by authors of both sexes and offering a variety of perspectives on relationships between literature and
the lives of women.

All the annotated entries are books that we have read, or, more
precisely, that at least one of us has read. In most cases it probably
is just one of us that has read the work, and so the comments generally represent individual judgments.

Lists I and II are of original prose works by women writers,
published before and after 1900 respectively. In these lists we include biographies and critical works dealing with a particular writer

immediately after the entries for the work of that writer. List III is works about literature. These are followed by two summary checklists of books by black women and books which deal with lesbianism; for quick reference purposes these simply give author and title of works dealt with more fully in the other lists. We welcome comments and suggestions for inclusion in the revised bibliography which will be available for 75 cents after April 1973 from:

Gill Gane/Ann Kautzman/Kathleen Kelley/Nancy Jainchill/Susan Mullins/Susan Tenenbaum
> Women and Literature Seminar
> Cambridge-Goddard Graduate School
> 1878 Massachusetts Avenue
> Cambridge, Mass. 02140
> June 1972

First, two anthologies which do not fit into the boundaries of our categories:

Greenwald, Harold, and Krich, Aron, eds. *The Prostitute in Literature.* N. Y., Ballantine, 1960. A paperback original: selections from literature, starting with the Bible and ending with Joyce. Commentary by the editors, but no documentation or references. The term "prostitution" is stretched to include excerpts on mistresses, "ruined" women, and a dialogue by Lucian on lesbianism. With the exception of a moral piece by the tenth-century abbess Hrotswitha, all the selections are written by men: the fascination of male writers and scholars with prostitution is surely an extension or displacement of the client's interest.

Showalter, Elaine, ed. *Women's Liberation and Literature.* N. Y., Harcourt Brace Jovanovich paperback, 1971, $3.50. This is an anthology of writings with commentary and questions, evidently designed for use in a college course. Literature is defined broadly to include "Major Texts of Feminism" (excerpts from J. S. Mill and Mary Wollstonecraft) and writings on psychology. Only one section, "Literature By and About Women," containing seven pieces, consists of literature in its more narrow definition; another section is on literary criticism. The goal of the collection seems to be consciousness-raising at a fairly basic level. Impressionistically, it might be useful in a class including male students. Women hoping for real insights into liberation and literature will be disappointed.

I. WOMEN WRITERS BEFORE THE TWENTIETH CENTURY

Austen, Jane (1775-1817). The never-married daughter of a country clergyman, Jane Austen led the narrowest of lives. Her novels do not move beyond the limits of her life; with her light, ironic touch she paints the day-to-day lives of the country gentry of her time, her largest dramas having generally to do with marriage. Her literary excellence is now widely recognized by all but a few tough-guy male critics. What makes her work particularly interesting to us is its healthy realism: her heroines are plausible young women without unnaturally perfect attributes, and the relations between women and men are presented with unvarnished honesty—there are misunderstandings and conflicts of personality, and, underlying it all, the money and class bases of the marriage market. If the idealization of an unreal vision of love is one of the ways in which the novel has oppressed women, Jane Austen was a courageous rebel against this literary tradition.

————. *Love and Freindship.* In *Love and Freindship and Other Early Works*, N. Y., Frederick A. Stokes, 1922. Reprinted as *Volume the Second*, Oxford, Clarendon Press, 1963. Written when Austen was only in her teens (though not published until 1922), this is a hilariously funny parody of the sentimental novel and its absurd conventions. It had us in fits of laughter.

————. *Pride and Prejudice.* 1813. N. Y., Signet, 1964, 60 cents. A classic worth re-reading to find out something about the politics of marriage in early nineteenth-century middle-class England.

————. *Emma.* 1816. N. Y., Signet, 1964, 60 cents. An intimate and detailed look into the lives of middle-class women and men, showing the importance and economic necessity of marriage for women.

————. *Northanger Abbey.* 1818. N. Y., Signet, 50 cents. Satirical put-down of gothic novels and their unreal conventions; a healthy and realistic antidote to the popular cult of romantic sensibility. Catherine Morland, whom no one would have supposed born to be a heroine, is a gullible innocent much nourished on novels. She yearns for high romance and drama, and instead comes up against the harsher realities of life, and, in particular, of the marriage market. Even the conventional happy ending is described with tongue in cheek.

Brontë, Charlotte (1816-1855) and Emily (1818-1848). The Brontës are now established muses on the literary scene, and most of us have read at least *Jane Eyre*. All of the Brontës' works, and their lives as well, however, deserve reconsideration from a feminist vantage-point.

————, **Charlotte.** *Jane Eyre.* 1847. Many cheap editions. A deservedly well-loved classic. Criticisms can be made of it—Jane Eyre is masochistic, and the book has been identified by some as the precursor of popular best-sellers which achieve their effects through manipulating the reader's emotions.

————. *Shirley.* 1849. Everyman, $2.95. Set against the background of Luddite riots in Yorkshire country, this is the story of two young women, Caroline Helstone and Shirley Keeldar. Of particular interest is the character of Shirley, who is a portrait of Emily Brontë; she is active, confident, out-going, and occasionally seen as almost androgynous.

————. *Villette.* 1853. Boston, Houghton Mifflin, 1970, $1.95. This novel centers around Lucy Snowe's experience teaching in Brussels. Much of the material for it comes from Charlotte's own experience at a girls' school in Brussels, and it casts into fictional form the unhappy love she felt for M. Heger there. Kate Millett's *Sexual Politics* has some good analysis of *Villette.*

————, **Emily.** *Wuthering Heights.* 1847. Many cheap editions. A great and powerful story by the most mysterious of the Brontë sisters.

Hardwick, Elizabeth. "Working Girls: The Brontës": review in the *New York Review of Books*, Vol. XVIII, No. 8 (May 4, 1972), 11-18. From among the masses of critical and biographical works on the Brontes, this short and recent article can be particularly recommended. One of its excellent points is that the romantic and extraordinary side of the Brontës' achievement has been overemphasized; Hardwick instead points out their precarious position as unmarried women without prospects, and stresses that, "Necessity, dependence, discipline drove them hard; being a writer was a way of surviving, literally keeping alive." The central question in Charlotte's work she identifies as "How to live without love, without security?"

Burney, Fanny. *Evelina.* 1778. N.Y., Norton, 1965. Burney was twenty-six when she wrote *Evelina*, her best work. It was a re-working of a story which she had written when she was about thirteen, but which she had destroyed when her stepmother disapproved of her writing. The novel is a remarkable and enlightening account of the daily reality of British eighteenth-century women of Evelina's class.

Chopin, Kate. *The Awakening.* 1899. N.Y., Capricorn Books, 1964, $1.65. This is the story of a young woman, wife and mother, thoroughly dissatisfied with her life. She knows what she must do but feels it is impossible. The book is simply written; its point is crucial, unavoidable. It has been successfully used for consciousness-raising in undergraduate courses, and would be excellent for highschool use as well.

Eliot, George (Mary Ann Evans). *The Mill on the Floss.* 1860. Several cheap editions. This novel has many autobiographical elements in it. Particularly fine are the childhood scenes showing the intelligent and rebellious Maggie Tulliver growing up in the country as the mill-owner's daughter. The adult Maggie, more sub-dued, is independent enough to insist on earning her own living, but the story at this point becomes essentially a love story. It's difficult to avoid feeling some resentment of George Eliot for making her heroines so much less venturesome than she was in her own life; she is, however, an excellent novelist.

————. *Middlemarch.* 1872. N.Y., Signet, $1.50. A portrait of early nineteenth-century British society. The book gives a complex description of the social stratification of a small town, though it deals most intimately with the lives of middle-class women and men. Besides giving her readers a careful portrait of the daily reality of her subjects, Eliot also gets across a good sample of her personal philosophy of life, which is some variety of scientific positivism. Her philosophy did not seek to change the limited opportunities open to women, but rather to "understand" women's reality in Middlemarch society. She fits this into a sociological explanation in which women and men are complementary and are to learn from each other—women's unique contribution being her "moral superi-ority." Reading Eliot is very helpful in reconstructing the history of western women.

Freeman, Mary E. Wilkins. "A New England Nun." Short story in *A New England Nun And Other Stories.* N.Y., Harper Brothers, 1891. When circumstances force a woman to live alone, she dis-covers that she does not wish to marry because a man in the house would mean the end of her lifestyle (caring for flowers, sewing pretty things, etc.) and the domination of his. Freeman's other works include *A Humble Romance* (1887) and *Pembroke* (1894).

Fuller, Margaret (1810-1850) edited the trancendental journal *The Dial* from 1840 to 1842. Her book *Summer on the Lakes* was an account of her travels in the mid-west and western states in 1843; it attracted the attention of Horace Greeley, who gave her a job as literary critic for the *New York Daily Tribune.* In 1845 she pub-lished her most important work, *Woman in the Nineteenth Century.* As a critic of patriarchy and its plunder and waste of human re-sources, she lists abolition of slavery and a feminist reorganization of society as keys to liberation of the human spirit. In another volume, *At Home and Abroad,* can be found many of Fuller's later essays and letters from Europe. In 1847 she married the Italian

Marchise Ossoli; the two of them supported the Roman Republic in the Italian revolution of 1849. They and their son were killed in a shipwreck.

Gaskell, Elizabeth (1810-1865). An extremely interesting English author of the mid nineteenth century. She is particularly revealing of how women's lives changed with the changing economic situation of the early nineteenth century, and is a good writer with lively characters and good dramatic situations besides.

————. *Mary Barton.* 1848. N.Y., Norton, $1.95. Gaskell's first novel, which brought her instant and tremendous popularity. It is set among the working people of early industrial Manchester during a depression and deals with the lives of the poor, especially the women. Good for background, but not so much for the story, which is melodramatic and overdone.

————. *Cranford.* 1853. N.Y., Dutton, $2.95. A sympathetic portrait of a community of spinsters, with insights into their attitudes towards men, marriage, sexuality, and, most of all, each other.

————. *Sylvia's Lovers.* 1863. Everyman. A well-done if somewhat depressing tale of a young woman in early industrial England and what happens to her and her relationships with men and her family as she moves off the peasant farm and into the bourgeois village. Don't be put off by the title; Sylvia is not a frivolous young thing stringing men along, but a real person with a changing life and real problems.

Radcliff, Ann. *The Mysteries of Udolfo.* 1790. Everyman, 2 vols. Earliest of the English gothic novels. Very popular in its time, and mentioned in many later novels as well, and with reason: it is a wonderfully-paced adventure story with a not-completely-passive heroine.

Sand, George (Aurore Dupin). *The Devil's Pool, or Germain's Marriage.* France 1846. Unlike George Eliot, George Sand believed that "the mission of Art is a mission of sentiment and love . . . the artist's end ought to be to cause the objects of her solicitude to be loved." She went on to say that "art is not a study of positive reality, it is the seeking for ideal truth." Though *The Devil's Pool* was written in a time of great social upheavel in Europe, not a word of this is mentioned; it is "a simple tale of rustic life, both fertile and happy." The hero seeks a wife, is appalled by a scheming widow, and finally made blissfully happy by a virtuous and hard-working woman.

————. *Consuelo.* France 1842. A talented singer traipses around European haunts of gothic horror, remaining as pure and infantile, and showing as little initiative or change, as ever was possible on paper—it certainly wouldn't be in real life.

Schreiner, Olive (1855-1920) was a South African; her novel *Story of an African Farm* and her serious treatise *Woman and Labor* (1911) were influential feminist works. Her own life, too, is a fascinating story, though there is no really good biography of her.

————. *The Story of an African Farm.* 1883. Penguin, 1971, $1.45. Schreiner's heroine is an overt feminist who refuses to marry a man she does not love. The book had a strong feminist impact in its time, and still makes good reading. There are also some excellent portrayals of childhood in it.

Meintjes, Johannes. *Olive Schreiner: A Portrait of a South African Woman.* Johannesburg, South Africa, Hugh Keartland, 1965. As Schreiner's most recent biographer, Meintjes (an Afrikaner) has had access to most information about her, and he provides interesting details on, among other things, her sex-life—unfortunately without documenting his sources.

Shelley, Mary (daughter of Mary Wollstonecraft, wife of Percy Bysshe). *Frankenstein.* 1818. N.Y., Dell, 45¢. A horror story with a profound symbolic theme.

————. *Journal of Mary Shelley.* Norman, Oklahoma, University of Oklahoma Press, 1947. Not a useful journal; the usual entries are just a date and a place along with some book she or Percy Shelley may have read.

Some other women writers before the twentieth century who sound interesting (we didn't read them) are:

Edgeworth, Maria. An important early novelist whose works include *Castle Rackrent* (1800), *The Absentee* (1812), and *Patronage* (1813).

Haywood, Eliza. Her novels include *Lasselia* (1724), written before the publication of *Pamela* in the romance or chapbook genre, *The Unequal Conflict* (1725), and *The History of Miss Betsy Thoughtless*, a four-volume novel which may have been an important early influence on Fanny Burney.

Hobbes, John Oliver (Pearl Craigie). Her novels, written in the late nineteenth century, include *Some Emotions and a Moral* and *Robert Orange*.

Jewett, Sarah Orne. She published *A Country Doctor* (1884), *A White Heron* (1886), *A Native of Winby and Other Tales* (1893), and *The Country of the Pointed Firs*.

Martineau, Harriet. A well-known reformer who wrote, among other things, her own *Autobiography* (1877).

Leads to other early women writers may be found in several of the books listed under *Works About Literature* in this bibliography; particularly useful on obscure women novelists is Utter and Needham's

Pamela's Daughters.

II. TWENTIETH CENTURY WOMEN WRITERS OF FICTION

Anderson, Barbara. *Southbound.* N.Y., Farrar, Straus & Co., 1949.
Laura Crane, a powerful, independent black woman, is left with the
task of raising her granddaughter, Amanda, in racist Alabama. Determined that Amanda will have the same opportunities as the
"best" (wealthiest) southern whites, Laura moves the child and her
old mother Persy to Ohio, where a rich white woman wishes to
"adopt" Amanda and raise her as her own. Amanda, who is very
light-skinned, experiences the pain and sometimes the joy of both
worlds. During the Ohio period, Laura is forced to act as the child's
nurse, a position which forces her to restrain her real feelings for
Amanda, creating a gap which can never really be overcome. Laura
wants so much for Amanda to "make it" that she literally works herself to death. Persy, the great-grandmother, is probably the most
loving and real portrayal of an old woman that I have ever read; she
is constant in her black pride. While the story of Amanda seems a
little contrived at times, the three main characters come across as
individuals.
Angelou, Maya. *I Know Why the Caged Bird Sings.* N.Y., Bantam,
1970, $1.25. An autobiography of the author's Arkansas childhood
and her adolescence (mostly in San Francisco). It is written with a
wonderful tone of irony and seriousness combined; a fine combination of black consciousness and of the special experience of being a
black woman. There are many brilliant descriptions, from the farce
of hypocritical pompous white speakers at a highschool graduation
to adventures with a group of drop-out teenagers on the road in
California and a job as the first streetcar conductorette in San Francisco.
Arnold, June. *Applesauce.* N.Y., McGraw-Hill, 1966. A novel
"about the impossibility of being a woman." A female tries on and
kills of three 'feminine' roles—sexmate, intellectual, and earth
mother and ends up finally as a man-self. Book ends with affirmation of woman-self and promise of growth. (SKC)
Austin, Mary. *A Woman of Genius.* N.Y., Doubleday, Page & Co.,
1912. What is the place in the world of the woman of genius? Shall
it be sacrificed that one man may be fed and made comfortable?
Must she sacrifice personal happiness if she is to exercise her gift?
(SKC)
Baker, Dorothy. *Cassandra at the Wedding.* 1962. N.Y., Signet,
1966, 60¢. Cassandra and Judith are twins and deeply attached to
each other. Cassandra, who is gay, tries to prevent Judith's marriage.

A highly readable novel.

Banning, Margaret Culkin. *The Vine and the Olive*. N.Y., Harper and Row, 1964. Stylistically weak, this is the story of a Catholic woman who is "successfully" married to a prominent corporation man but who becomes involved in the birth control movement. This involvement becomes a major conflict between Clare and her husband, who feels that her speech-making about this topic is going to ruin his career. The end is a total cop-out: Ann (the narrator) marries one of the Planned Parenthood crusaders, though Clare and Ann have both grown and dared to commit themselves for their beliefs.

Barnes, Djuna. *Nightwood*. 1937. N.Y., New Directions, $1.50. This is the story of a woman who cannot be contained by society or by the women and men who love her. Stylistically complex and difficult to get into, it has a high literary reputation.

Bawden, Nina. *A Woman of My Age*. N.Y., Harper and Row, 1967. The story of a woman making what she can of a mediocre marriage, told with honesty and humor. Bawden is an unusually fine contemporary English writer and deserves more recognition than she now has.

————. *Tortoise by Candlelight*. N.Y., Harper & Row, 1963. Excellent portrayal of a fourteen-year-old girl's interal life and relationship with others. (SKC)

Beauvior, Simone de. *She Came to Stay*. France 1943. Cleveland, World Publishing Co., 1954. Closely based on an episode in her own life (recounted in *The Prime of Life*), de Beauvoir's first novel is the story of a *ménage à trois* where the young Xavière comes to threaten the relationship between Françoise and Pierre, arousing profound emotions and jealousy.

————. *Memoirs of a Dutiful Daughter*. France 1958. Cleveland, World Publishing Co., 1959. This first volume of Simone de Beauvoir's autobiography describes her Catholic girlhood and how she frees herself from it. It ends in 1929, when, at the age of twenty-one, she has become a brilliant student and has met Jean-Paul Sartre.

————. *The Prime of Life*. France 1960. N.Y., Lancer, $1.25. This second volume of Simone de Beauvoir's memoirs covers the years from 1929 to the liberation of Paris in the second world war. It chronicles with remarkable honesty her continuing intellectual and emotional development and gives a fascinating picture of the intellectual and political climate of the time.

————. *Force of Circumstances*. France 1963. N.Y., Putnam, 1965. This third autobiographical volume runs from the war to the date of its publication, Simone de Beauvoir's fifty-fifth year. In these years, she writes, "the point was no longer to educate but to fulfil myself." As always, absorbing reading, and an impressive portrait of an independent woman.

Bedford, Sybille. *A Favourite of the Gods*. N.Y., Simon & Schuster, 1963. The history of three generations of upper-class women: Anna, the New England heiress who marries an Italian prince in the late nineteenth century, Constanza, their daughter (the favorite of the gods), who, briefly, marries an Englishman; and their daughter, Flavia, who, now in her late teens (the time is the late '20's), tells much of their story. A mystery centers around Anna's reasons for leaving the prince after twenty years of marriage; was it really that she only then discovered that he had had a mistress the whole time? Anna's past reaches into the future in the influence she has over the young Flavia.

————. *A Compass Error*. 1968. N.Y., Ballantine, 1970, 95¢. A sequel to *A Favourite of the Gods*, starting where the first left off and carrying through to their conclusion earlier hints about the shaping of Flavia's life; much of the background material from the earlier book is recapitulated. The young Flavia is alone in Provence while her mother is off on a secret trip with a lover. It is she who initiates an affair with an older woman, Thérése; then she falls in love with the beautiful Andrée. There follow drama and intrigue which we won't disclose, leading to an unhappy dénouement.

Bowen, Elizabeth. *The Death of the Heart*. 1939. N.Y., Vintage, 1958. This is the story of Portia Quayne, a refugee of the upper-middle class. After the death of her mother, Portia is taken into the leisurely London existence of her step-brother Thomas. He and his wife Anna do not care about Portia, though at times they find her a diversion from their boring routine. The inability of these two to express their feelings, or really to have feelings, is presented in the context of their privileged, socially atrophied lives. Portia keeps a diary, and it is from her own careful self-evaluation, her relationship with the housemaid Matchett, and a girlish romantic fling with one of her step-sister's admirers that most of Portia's self-development is presented.

Boyle, Kay (1903-   ) began her career doing freelance reviewing for *The Dial*. She was consistently involved with the political struggles of the people and places which made up her life, and she reflected this in her work. Her book *Primer for Combat*, for example, relates through the diary of an American woman in the France of 1942 the horrible effect of Nazism on that society. She took her writing career very seriously.

————. *Plagued by the Nightingale*. 1931. Carbondale, Ill., Southern Illinois University Press, 1966. A novel dealing with the pressures a couple must deal with when they decide to remain childless (because of hereditary bone disease); interesting insights into exclusively female experience. Style a bit difficult.

Brookes, Gwendolyn. *Maud Martha.* N.Y., Harper, 1953. A novel of Chicago through the eyes of a girl growing up, experiencing marriage and motherhood.

Brophy, Brigid. *In Transit: An heroi-cyclic Novel.* London, Macdonald & Co., Ltd. 1926. Through the fantastic vehicle of a protagonist unable to identify her/his sex, sex-roles, conventions, language and culture are investigated. (SKC)

Cade, Toni, ed. *The Black Woman.* N.Y., Signet, 1970, 95¢. An exciting collection of essays, short stories, and poems written by black women concerning the lives of black women in America.

Canfield, Dorothy. *Four Square and Other Stories.* N.Y., Harcourt Brace, 1949. A good writer, but limited by the moral message of her writing, and especially by her unstinting praise of the good Vermont country life.

————. *The Home Maker.* N.Y., Harcourt Brace, 1924. An accident allows Evangeline, who is unhappy as a homemaker, and her husband, a poet and dreamer, unhappy in the business world, to reverse roles. Interesting insights into the pressures to fulfull social expectations, what those pressures can do to personal relationships and child-rearing. (SKC)

————. *Her Son's Wife.* N.Y., Harcourt Brace, 1926. Interesting study of relationships between a strong, competant woman, her "inappropriate" daughter-in-law and her granddaughter. (SKC)

Cather, Willa. *My Antonia.* 1918. Boston, Houghton Mifflin, 1971, $2.00. A story of the early settlers in Nebraska, narrated through the eyes of a man, but telling about the women of that period. It brings out interesting points not mentioned elsewhere, e.g. that the immigrant families had women working side by side with men in the fields, and that they progressed more rapidly. Antonia ends up a breeder of children.

Colette. *The Innocent Wife.* N.Y., Farrar & Rinehart, 1934. Annie, the wife, functions as a dependent child and slave in relation to her husband until she meets the sophisticated, exciting, intelligent Claudine, who makes her aware of the possibilities of a more independent lifestyle. Finally, Annie leaves her husband's home.

————. *The Pure and the Impure.* France 1932. N.Y., Farrar Straus & Giroux, 1967. An exceptionally interesting collection of pieces on love and sexual relationships which Colette herself thought her best book. There is a woman who simulates ecstatic

orgasm for the sake of her sick young lover; there are male Don
Juans with their violent hostility towards women; there are gay
men and a good many gay women. All are viewed from Colette's
special perspective, which is at the same time peculiarly feminine
and peculiarly French.

———. *Earthly Paradise: Colette's Autobiography Drawn From
the Writings of her Lifetime.* N.Y., Farrar Straus & Giroux, 1966,
$2.65. Childhood scenes in the country, three marriages, a lesbian
interlude, episodes on the stage and in Paris literary society—well-
written vignettes of a fascinating life.

Davis, Angela, and many other political prisoners, including Bettina
Aptheker, Ericka Huggins, Margaret Burnham, Fania Davis Jordan,
and Kendra Alexander. *If They Come in the Morning.* N.Y., Signet,
1971, $1.25. Good analysis of the nature of prisons in America.
Includes some good material on women in prisons (Angela and
Ericka). The poems by Ericka Huggins show her incredible spirit.

Didion, Joan. *Run River.* N.Y., Bantam, 1963, $1.25. A novel
about an upper class Southern family, somewhat in the Faulkner
tradition. It is the story of Lily, a woman always associated with
wealthy men. She herself had few, if any, alternatives in her life.
It shows that the actual quality of a woman's life does not vary
that dramatically from class to class.

———. *Play it as it Lays.* N.Y., Bantam, 1970, $1.25. The story
of Maria, who is incredibly masochistic and alienated. Men control
her every move. She experiences nothingness, and, of course, winds
up in a mental institution.

Dinesen, Isak [Karen Dinesen Blixen] (1884-1962). Isak Dinesen
married a titled cousin in the early 1900's and went to East Africa
(now Kenya) to manage a coffee plantation. After their divorce,
she kept up the plantation, writing to bring in money to keep it
going. Finally she was forced to sell and return to Denmark. She
wrote in Danish and English.

———. *Out of Africa.* 1926. N.Y., Vintage, 1972, $2.45. Written
like poetry or music, these short stories recount Dinesen's life in
Africa and are also interesting for the information they give about
life and customs among the women of Africa. They present an unusual portrait of an upper-class woman running a coffee plantation
by herself in Kenya.

———. *Winter's Tales.* 1942. N.Y., Random House, 1969, $1.95.
Beautifully written gothic stories.

DiPrima, Diane. *Memoirs of a Beatnik.* N.Y., Olympia Press, 1969.

A short autobiographical novel; very accurate depiction of a young girl grabbing for womanhood. Good pornography from a female perspective. (See DiPrima under *Poetry*.)

Disney, Doris Miles. An excellent and prolific mystery novelist with a penchant for brilliant portrayals of children, middle-aged married women, and elderly women. Her mysteries are vehicles for the exploration of character. (SKC)

Drabble, Margaret. *Thank You All Very Much.* 1965 as *The Millstone.* N.Y., Signet, 1969, 60 ¢. Rosamund is guilty of "a brand-new twentieth-century crime"—virginity. She remedies this and falls pregnant; the book tells how, as a graduate student, she goes through with the pregnancy and keeps the child. Fairly light and entertaining reading.

Drexler, Rosalyn. *One or Another.* 1970. N.Y., Dell, 1971, 95¢. Drexler is bright, innovative and very modern, exploring the zany and freaky areas of life in the '70's. This book is about a desperate woman, married to a right-wing sadist and having an affair with one of the high school students he teaches. The border between fantasy and reality blurs as she flips out.

Ferber, Edna. *So Big.* 1923. N.Y., Avon. The story of the successful son and the sacrificing mother. Selina Peake DeJong defies her neighbors and the little farm community and takes on the "work of a man" when her husband dies.

Figes, Eva. *Equinox.* 1966. London, Panther, 1969. An extremely well-written account of the slow break-up of a marriage by an English feminist (Figes is the author of a serious analysis called *Patriarchal Attitudes*).

Fitzgerald, Zelda. *Save Me the Waltz.* 1932. N.Y., Signet, 1968, 95¢. This short novel is an autobiographical account of a woman's struggle to realize herself and her potential as an artist. The book recounts Zelda's Southern upbringing, her marriage to a famous artist (a self-centered egotist who ignored his wife's personal dilemma), her great love for her child which conflicted with any possibility of fulfilling herself as an artist. Probably the most impressive section of the book is the one in which Zelda struggles against the stacked deck of upbringing, marriage, her age and health, to become a dancer.

Glasgow, Ellen (1873-1945). Was born and spent most of her life in Richmond, Virginia. She was burdened as a child with a sickly constitution which plagued her throughout her life, as well as a nervous disability and encroaching deafness. She faced other struggles: surviving the deaths of loved ones one after another, a lack of money in her early writing career, her audience's preference of sentimentality to an author's own vision of truth, and the dominance of wealthy old men in literary circles. She remained faithful to her artistic vision, which ebbed and flowed and changed directions, as did her life. She was determined until she died not to marry. Her works indicate sensitivity to some oppressive conditions, though she relates to the individual rather than the societal causes.

————. *The Battle-ground.* 1902. N.Y., Doubleday. The Civil War through a woman's eyes. It could be used as a contrast to Crane's *Red Badge of Courage.*

————. *Barren Ground.* 1925. N.Y., Hill & Wang, 1959, $2.25. The story of Dorinda Oakley's fight to obliterate romantic love as a force in her life. Set in pre-WW I times.

————. *They Stooped to Folly: A Comedy of Morals.* 1929. A late and interesting Glasgow, told first by a husband and then by his wife, revealing the distance between them and gently questioning the nature of the marriage tie.

————. *The Woman Within.* 1934. N.Y., Harcourt Brace, 1954. Autobiography; the story of the personal and social struggles Glasgow had to write; revealing of the relationship between her life and her art.

————. *Vein of Iron.* 1935. N.Y., Harcourt Brace, 1971, 95¢. A strong woman supports her man in West Virginia in the late 1800's. Not as interesting as some other works by Glasgow.

Rouse, Blair. *Ellen Glasgow.* New Haven, Twayne, 1962, $1.95. A good treatment of Glasgow's major works; biographical material is presented only when relevant to her writings.

Glaspell, Susan. *Plays.* Boston, Small Maynard & Co., 1920. In the play *Woman's Honor*, a man is being tried for a murder of which he is supposedly innocent; however, he will not say where he was at the time of the murder, because, as he says, he is "protecting a woman's honor." In answer to this, one of the female characters says, "Did it ever strike you as funny that woman's honor is only about one thing, and that man's honor is about everything but that thing?" Glaspell is delightful reading, portrays a woman's consciousness, and has been hidden from us for too long.

Harvin, Emily. *The Stubborn Wood.* Chicago, Ziff Davis, 1948. Stylistically weak and hard to read, but about a subject that concerns us very much, this novel is an autobiographical work about a woman whose husband railroads her into a private insane asylum. The woman is middle-class and obviously a victim of the "feminine mystique"; she exhibits all the symptoms of masochism and super-dependency which sap her strength and keep her husband in control of her fate. The book may not be good literature, but it is interesting and useful as non-fiction.

Holiday, Billie. *Lady Sings the Blues*. 1956. N.Y., Lancer, 1969, 95¢. The autobiographical story of the struggles of this black singer as a child when she was raped and consequently imprisoned; and later as a prostitute, an addict, and a fine artist.

Hull, Helen R. *The Quest*. N.Y., Macmillan, 1922. A young woman from an unhappy home struggles for freedom from her environment, for light upon the road she must travel and against the weaknesses that assail her. (SKC)

————. *Labyrinth*. N.Y., Macmillan, 1923. Interesting style. The problem of an intellectual woman who seeks to fulfill herself through work and is betrayed and confused by the demands of a career-oriented husband and young children. (SKC)

————. *Islanders*. N.Y., Macmillan, 1927. A brave, self-reliant woman bears the burdens of a large family and becomes convinced that most women are prisoners, immured in humdrum domestic islands while men sail blithely forth on the exciting seas of adventure. (SKC)

Hurst, Fanny. *Lummox*. N.Y., Harper, 1923. The story of Bertha, an immigrant girl and an orphan who supports herself as a domestic servant. Her only education was working for her board in the sailor's lodging house where her mother had died giving birth to her. At one point she spent six years working for a Mrs. Farley who did "charitable" work for the "Human Welfare League" and who paid Bertha twenty dollars a month. She hated her work but the alternative was waiting in endless employment agencies which she described as "a shambles of stock awaiting inspection." Slowly Bertha made a life for herself. Though she did not rebel against her limited fate she came to know herself. Bertha is a conscious and interesting person. The novel is written in a readable, very flowing style.

Hurston, Zora Neale. *Their Eyes Were Watching God*. N.Y., Negro University Press, 1937. Her style is rather poetic; that is, she experiments and innovates with words and phrases. She does not warp her portraits to make them fit into English Department English; instead she forms the language and her characters; they both come alive. The heroine is Janie, and the book is the story of her life as she tells it to her best woman friend on returning to her small village community in Florida after the death of her husband and love, Tea Cake. Hurston is very high in woman's consciousness, and the book is a joy to read. Other works include *Jonah's Gourd Vine*, which pictures country life and the role of religion in the far South, and *Mules and Men*, which records folk tales of store porches.

Jhabvala, R. Prawer. *Amrita.* N.Y., Norton, 1955. This is the story of a young Indian woman of marriageable age weighing romance against practicality in deciding whom she will marry. The virtues and drawbacks of the extended family come in for some examination.

———. *A Stronger Climate.* N.Y., Norton, 1968. This is a short story collection of Westerners meeting the East. One story is a fine tale of the niece of a famous politician trapped at home by the conventions of both the East and the West. Another story deals with a grandmother who has just fallen in love with an elderly Dutchman, much to the dismay of her children and grandchildren.

Karp, Lila. *The Queen is in the Garbage.* N.Y., Belmont, 1971, 95¢. In labor, the heroine thinks back angrily, unhappily over her life.

Kellogg, Marjorie. *Tell Me That You Love Me, Junie Moon.* N.Y., Popular Library, 1968, 75¢. This is the story of three ugly, physically handicapped, psychically damaged human beings who decide to try and make it together in a hostile world. Junie Moon, the female of the trio and physically repulsive due to serious burns and scarring, is developed by Kellogg as a unique and beautiful individual. The two men, Warren and Arthur, are suitable complements for this portrayal. Probably one of the most interesting aspects of this book is the idea that persons rejected by social norms are in fact unique and complex people. They are portrayed with great dignity and sensitivity.

Kerr, Sophie. *Golden Block.* N.Y., Doubleday, 1918. "There's no sex in brains." A woman's successful career in Big Business. (SKC)

Larson, Nella. This author is considered to be part of the Harlem Renaissance school of writers. Her novel *Passing* was praised by W. E. DeBois upon its publication in 1929. He called it a "studied, singular, and consummate work of art." In 1930 Larson was awarded the Guggenheim Fellowship to enable her to write a novel about the "different effects of Europe and the U. S. on the intellectual and physical freedom of the Negro," but for unknown reasons she never published another work after *Passing.* She died in obscurity in New York City in 1963.

———. *Quicksand.* 1928. N.Y., African/American Series, Collier, 1971, $1.50. Adelaide C. Hill states in her introduction that this novel "helps us to see how one Black woman viewed the problem of the Black community, its relation to white society, the survival of the individual Black person in a totally White society abroad, and the basic problem of sex as it expresses itself for Black women." The novel is probably largely autobiographical. She experiments with exaggeration and fantasy at the end to get her point across. Probably the most basic problem confronted in the book is that of

Sexual Politics—woman's control of her own body.

————. *Passing.* N.Y., African/American Series, Collier, 1971, $1.50. This novel seems more limited in scope than her earlier novel, *Quicksand.* She deals with only one theme—that of a light Negro passing into white society—and she does this in terms of only one small clique (bourgeois black society in Chicago and N. Y.). This theme has many implications and is complex, but Larson does not develop her characters enough. The two main characters are women—Irene Redfield, the narrator, and an acquaintance, Clare Kendry, the woman who has chosen the material advantages of white society but longs for her own people and former friends.

Leduc, Violette. *La Batarde.* France, 1964. N.Y., Farrar, Straus & Giroux, 1965. "A woman is descending into the most secret part of herself and telling us about all she finds there with an unflinching sincerity, as though there were no one listening," writes Simone de Beauvoir in her foreword to this book. It is an absolutely fascinating autobiography of an extraordinary woman, covering the years from her birth in 1908 to the end of World War II. Born illegitimate, convinced all her life of her own ugliness, Violette Leduc's first loves were for women. Later there was an unhappy marriage and finally an unfulfilled passion for the homosexual author Maurice Sachs. Meanwhile, she worked in menial clerical jobs in the world of publishing and film production, moving on the fringe of Paris literary and intellectual society. By the end of the book she has started her first novel. A sequel to this, *Mad In Pursuit,* covering the years 1945 to 1949, is now available.

————. *Therese and Isabelle.* France, 1966. N.Y., Dell, 1967, 95¢. The ninety-five short pages of this book describe one day in the lives of two French schoolgirls in love with each other. A substantial part of the book consists of explicit descriptions of sex, but it is a good deal more than gay pornography: for one thing, the sex is embedded in a context of deeply felt emotion; for another, real life problems and frustrations impinge even on the sex scenes, thus removing the book from the arena of unreal, idealized, mechanical gratification which Steven Marcus calls "pornotopia"; and, finally, it is too well written.

Lehmann, Rosamund. *Dusty Answer.* London, 1927. Young Judith grows up, moving from the big house by the river with the intriguing neighbors to a women's college at Cambridge, England. She becomes romantically involved in turn with three of the men in the family next door, and has an intense relationship with Jennifer, a fellow student.

Lessing, Doris May (1919-   ). Doris Lessing grew up in Rhodesia, moving to England in 1949. She is a first-class novelist who gives a superbly honest and penetrating account of the female experience. Neither she nor her women characters are strictly feminist, but they are very conscious of their femaleness and struggle to be "free" according to their own definitions; their intellectual and political interests may, however, be alienating to some women.

————. *The Grass Is Singing.* 1950. N. Y., Ballantine, 1964, 60¢. Lessing's first novel presents the story of the relationship between a young English-woman, Mary Turner, and an African worker on her farm. The book starts off with the announcement of Mary Turner's murder by the African Moses, then the events which preceded the murder are unfolded: simultaneously attracted and repelled by the black worker, guilty, mystified, feeling isolated and helpless, Mary Turner ended up sexually involved with him—the ultimate horror and degradation in the context of that society.

————. *Children of Violence.* This is the cover title of the following series of five novels: *Martha Quest.* 1952. N. Y., New American Library, 1970, $2.95. This book starts with Martha as a rebellious adolescent growing up on a farm in Rhodesia in the late '30's, reading voraciously, worrying about clothes. After finishing highschool she moves into the town to take an office job, gets swept into a feverish social life, is sexually initiated, and finally gets married on the spur of the moment. The dating scene, the parent problems, the first disillusioning experiences of sex will strike responsive chords in many women. *A Proper Marriage.* 1954. N. Y., New American Library, 1970, $3.50. This is the story of Martha's marriage, which ends in her leaving her husband and child; it raises important questions on nearly all the issues the woman of today who seeks liberation faces. Both these first two volumes are straightforwardly written and deal with experiences common to a wide range of women. *A Ripple From the Storm.* 1958. N. Y., New American Library, 1970, $3.50. Martha is involved in the intense political activity of a communist group in Rhodesia during the war. She marries a German communist exile, Anton Hesse, and ends up somewhat disillusioned both with him and with politics. *Landlocked.* 1965. N. Y., New American Library, 1970, $2.95. Martha's political activities continue as the war draws to a close. Her father dies, and she falls deeply in love with Thomas Stern, who eventually dies. There is an African strike. Martha plans to go to England. *The Four-Gated City.* 1969. N. Y., Bantam, 1969, $1.25. This book is rather dramatically discontinuous with the others in the series: Martha's life in London is much more complex than her life in Rhodesia, and Lessing's own greater intellectual and technical sophistication are evident here, as is her concern with ever-widening areas of experience. Martha in London eventually moves beyond politics to venture over the very edges of reality—first in a trip into the area commonly called insanity (R. D. Laing has clearly influenced Lessing), and second in a futuristic projection of a nuclear cataclysm. The book is extremely thought-provoking; we differ over the healthiness of Lessing's final response.

————. *In Pursuit of the English*. N. Y., Simon and Schuster, 1961. This book recounts Lessing's search after her arrival in London for real English people, and in particular for the English working class. What she finds is a household full of people who are undoubtedly working-class, but striking in their individuality—"sub-Dickensian," one of the reviews said. The book is light reading, very funny and touching.

————. *The Golden Notebook*. 1962. N. Y., Ballantine, 1968, $1.25. This is the story of Anna Wulff's struggle to unite the personal, political, and artistic fragments of her life. The struggle is represented by her attempt to combine the red, blue, black, and yellow notebooks into a single unifying golden one. Lessing's style here is highly sophisticated and complex. The value of Anna's struggle and the degree of success she achieves must be left to the reader to decide, but it is clear that in a very serious way Lessing is attempting to deal with many of the difficulties the modern woman faces in seeking to be whole.

————. *A Man and Two Women*. N. Y., Ballantine, 1963, 75¢. A collection of fantastic short stories portraying the objectification of women today. "A Woman on a Roof" explores the reactions of three men of different ages when they see a woman sunbathing on a roof. "Notes for a Case History" tells the story of a young woman whose only possibility for social advancement is to use her beauty and acquire a successful husband. Any one of these eighteen short stories would be very useful in a course where there is little time for whole books.

————. *African Stories*. N. Y., Ballantine, 1969, $1.25. A collection of Lessing's stories with a Southern African background.

McCarthy, Mary. *The Group*. N. Y., Signet, 1963, 95¢. This is the story of eight women who grew up in the age of the sexual revolution; it contains insights into marriage, sexuality, lesbianism, and the life of the single woman, and raises serious questions about the fruits of that "revolution."

————. *Memories of a Catholic Girlhood*. N. Y., Medallion, 75¢. Eight connected episodes in McCarthy's early life, which was heavily influenced by cruel Catholic guardians and Catholic schools. The final chapter deals with her Jewish grandmother and gives a fine commentary on the aging woman.

McCullers, Carson. *Reflections in a Golden Eye.* 1941. N. Y., Bantam, 1967, 75¢. Life in the military for the men and their wives. The book is concisely written, but each person is well-developed and the book is worth reading.

———. *The Member of the Wedding.* 1949. N. Y., New Directions, $1.50. This is the story of Frankie, an adolescent girl growing up in the South during World War II and her attempt to become the third party in her brother's wedding.

———. *Clock Without Hands.* N. Y., Bantam, 1961, 95¢. This novel, while not giving us any female characters of interest, is perhaps a very important book from a feminist viewpoint. It is essentially the portrait of a Southern patriarch, Judge Clane. There is also a very fine and sensitive love story in the book between two men. Old Clane's grandson Jester feels very close to (and in a really new sense in love with) a black man, Sherman Pew. The old judge's bigotry is based on racism and male supremacy; he sees women and blacks as people who exist to service his needs.

Mansfield, Katherine. *Stories.* New York, Vintage, 1956, $1.65. These stories were written between 1908 when Mansfield was twenty and her early death in 1923. Many of them, besides being excellent by literary standards, present perceptive analyses of the conditions of women's lives and of relations between the sexes. To mention only a few from this collection of twenty-six stories: "The Tiredness of Rosabel" shows a shopgirl fantasizing herself leading the life of a rich woman customer; "The Little Governess" encounters a dirty old man on her first terrifying journey to German; "Prelude" and "At the Bay" deal with the same case of characters, a boisterous, insensitive male and a gamut of finely-drawn women covering virtually all stages of the female life cycle.

Meriwether, Louise. *Daddy Was a Number Runner.* New York, Pyramid, 1970. This is an autobiographical novel about the heroine's experiences as a young black female growing up in Harlem.

Miller, Isabel. *Patience and Sara.* 1969 under the title *A Place For Us.* New York, McGraw-Hill, 1972. A simple and moving story of the love between two nineteenth-century women who finally overcome all obstacles in their way and move into new country to start their own farm. The book is of major interest for its open and honest treatment of a lesbian relationship.

Moody, Ann. *Coming of Age in Mississippi.* New York, Dell, Laurel Edition, 1965, 95¢. This is the autobiographical story of a black girl growing up in the deep South. It is particularly interesting to note the change of consciousness of the girl—that is, when she realizes that "black" is all right in and of itself, not something to be whitened.

Mortimer, Penelope. *The Pumpkin Eater.* New York, McGraw-Hill, 1962. This is the story of an anonymous woman's emotional breakdown and her attempt to regain her touch with reality. It contains fine insights into the psychology of women, abortion, sexuality, love, motherhood, and marriage.

————. *My Friend Says It's Bullet-Proof.* 1967, London, (English) Penguin, 1969. Muriel has just had a breast removed: "convinced that no one could ever feel anything for her, sexually, but pity and disgust," she breaks with her lover. The English women's magazine she writes for sends her on a journalist's tour of America, and in the course of the trip and of her different relationships with two men she comes to accept herself. The book is well-written and perceptive.

Nin, Anais. *Ladders To Fire.* Denver, Swallow Press, 1959, $1.45. A novel that describes the relationship between two women with fantastic depth and understanding in Nin's controlled, evocative use of language.

————. *The Diary of Anais Nin*: three volumes. New York, Harcourt-Brace, Harvest Book, 1966, 1968, 1969, $2.85 each. The journals are most revealing about the author's struggles as a woman, lover, writer, individual, spanning the years 1931 to 1944.

Nwapa, Flora. *Efuru.* London, Heinemann Educational Books, 1966. Efuru is the name of the heroine in this novel by Flora Nuapa of Eastern Nigeria. The novel may be a little hard to read, but it is interesting and gives us a model of a woman in another culture. Efuru ends up as a kind of priestess, pledging her life to a river goddess.

Oates, Joyce Carol. *Expensive People.* Greenwich, Connecticut, 1968, Fawcett, 95¢. Billed as "a tale of gothic horror," this is the story of the child hero's murder of his mother. The book is an indictment of the upper class nuclear family and a fine statement of the integrity of childhood.

————. *Them.* Greenwich, Connecticut, 1969, Fawcett, $1.25. *Them* is primarily about the life of Loretta Wendall, a working class woman, and her children, Maureen, Jules, and Betty. The characters are all believable and the limitations of education and class against which they struggle are neither exaggerated nor glossed over. Loretta is both courageous and continually optimistic, though she lives through episodes of male violence and is, of course, unable to escape poverty—having many children and usually no man. She always manages to find one or two close female friends to share her troubles and joys with. Jules and Maureen represent the struggle to rise above such a debilitating beginning, from the female and the male point of view and position in reality. An excellent book, it examines in a sympathetic way the complexities of violence, sexism, and racism that are perpetuated by a system in which some people are hopelessly trapped in poverty and ignorance.

O'Brien, Edna. *Girl With the Green Eyes.* Published in London under the title *The Lonely Girl*, 1962. The novel is the story of Caithleen, her desperate love for Eugene and his consequent abandonment of her. It raises important questions about the nature of romantic love, and deals with questions about sexuality, the class status of women, the church, and the family.

O'Connor, Flannery. *A Good Man is Hard to Find.* 1955. Harden City, New York, Image, 1970, $1.25. This is a short story collection about life in the South where O'Connor grew up and spent most of her life. She is a powerful writer and many of her characters and descriptions have a haunting quality about them that stays with you long after you've put the book down.

Olsen, Tillie. *Tell Me A Riddle.* New York, Dell, 1971, $2.25. Short stories. The title story, about an aged, dying woman, is a sensitive portrayal of the aging woman and the problems she faces in our society. The story contains vital insights into the nature of marriage, the role of woman as wife and mother, and the husband-wife relationship.

Parker, Dorothy. *Collected Works.* 1936, New York, Viking, 1944. Never taken seriously enough as an author, Dorothy Parker's short stories contain great and appalling truths covered by a little laughter. She is an artist of the short form, saying all that she wants in that short space.

Petry, Ann. *The Street.* Boston, Houghton Mifflin, 1946. This novel is about a young woman in Harlem, Lutie Johnson, who is raising her one child Bub and just trying to survive. Not only is Lutie a well-drawn character, but so are the minor characters who live jammed into the rundown, overcrowded apartments of Harlem. The novel gives us insights into their personal motivations and needs. Petry does not paint a rosy picture. By the end of the book, Lutie has not escaped. Reading the novel is painful at times—but certainly worth it.

Piercy, Marge. *Dance the Eagle to Sleep.* Greenwich, Conn., Fawcett, 95¢. This is a satire describing an aborted revolution. In the

novel the failure is due largely to the ego-tripping of the male leadership and the fact that there is never allowed to females a chance for
equal participation. The book is set in a garish future that reminds
one a lot of the past few years (Chicago, Kent State . . .). Piercy
keeps her woman's consciousness well hidden, choosing to lead the
reader clearly through the oppressiveness of male domination rather
than directly building for us a new model or vision of a movement
which could actually achieve human liberation.

Plath, Sylvia. *The Bell Jar.* 1970. N. Y., Bantam, 1972, $1.50. An
autobiographical novel of a young woman going insane because of
her environment. The book shows dramatically the limited alternatives even for supposedly brilliant women.

Rau, Santha Rama. *Remember the House.* N. Y., Harper, 1956. A
well-written Indian tale of a young woman confronting some choice
in whom she will marry and discovering her different motives and the
different possible outcomes. The book is valuable for its excellent
and unusual view of the extended family.

Richardson, Dorothy. 1873-1957) was a pioneer in the use of the
stream-of-consciousness technique in the novel. An excellent writer
with a strong feminist consciousness, she deserves to be rescued from
the obscurity into which she has fallen. Her greatest drawback is her
length; she wrote a single autobiographical novel, *Pilgrimage*, in thirteen volumes. We indicate briefly its content below, but to sum-
marize it does not do it justice, since its essence is not in the narrative, but in the exploration of a developing consciousness. Reading
Pilgrimage can be an exciting experience; Richardson's prose has the
density and intricacy of poetry, and she gives one the feeling of being
inside her heroine, Miriam.

————. *Pilgrimage.* Collected edition, Richardson, Knopf (4 vols.),
1967. Twelve volumes of this work originally appeared between
1915 and 1938 and a final, incomplete volume was included for the
first time in the 1967 edition. Voluem I of the collected edition contains *Pointed Roofs* (the seventeen-year-old Miriam is a governess at a
German girls' school), *Backwater* (after an interlude with her family,
Miriam goes on to teach at a school in London), and *Honeycomb*
(she works as a governess in a wealthy family). Volume II contains
The Tunnel and *Interim*: Miriam finds more independence working
in a dentist's office and living in a boarding-house; *The Tunnel* can
be particularly recommended. In Volume III are *Deadlock, Revolv-
ing Lights,* and *The Trap*: Miriam has a romantic involvement with
Michael Shatov and goes to meetings of the Lycurgan Society (the
Fabians). Volume IV contains *Oberland, Dawn's Left Hand, Clear
Horizon, Dimple Hill,* and *March Moonlight*: Miriam has several un-

happy loves, and moves towards becoming a Quaker. *Dawn's Left Hand* is a particularly interesting volume, which covers both Miriam's affair with Hypo Wilson (H. G. Wells in real life) and the intense relationship she has with the young woman Amabel.

Richardson, Henry Handel [Henrietta]. *The End of a Childhood.* N. Y., W. W. Norton, 1934. An Australian writer. Very highly recommended are the eight stories in this collection grouped together under the title *Growing Pains: Sketches of Girlhood.* Although there are no recurrent characters, the stories can be seen as a sequence, building up gradually an atmosphere of girlhood friendships, interwoven with the fear and distrust of growing up, of men, and of sex; this culminates in a pretty clearly lesbian episode in the final story. All the stories, however, will be evocative of many women's experiences; any one individually could serve as a good discussion-starter to touch off memories of girlhood in any group of women. Another good story in the collection is "The Professor's Experiment," where the professor's spinster sister is presented as a totally unsympathetic character, until at the last minute she revolts against the way she has sacrificed her life.

Rule, Jane. *This Is Not For You.* N. Y., McCall, 1970. A very finely written and sophisticated novel. Kate, the narrator, who has been gay since high school, falls in love with Esther at college. The story of this love, which Kate chooses never to fulfil, is interwoven with the lives and loves, gay and otherwise, of several other characters.

Sackville-West, Victoria. Her novels cover the period from the early to mid 1900's. She was the best friend of Virginia Woolf and the model for the book *Orlando* as well as a fine writer in her own right who has undeservedly fallen into obscurity.

———. *All Passion Spent.* 1931. Possibly her best novel. A beautifully constructed review of one woman's life: the main character's husband dies when she is eighty-eight, leaving her the leisure to reflect on her life, on the changes that occurred at her marriage, on her desire to be an artist, on her new-found chance to be herself at eighty-eight.

———. *The Edwardians.* 1934. Set between 1906 and 1910, the novel asks the question whether persons can escape the class into which they have been born. The central character is an upper-class male, and women are used as representatives of other classes rather than described as people in their own right.

———. *The Easter Party.* 1950. The story of an upper-class woman sacrificing herself to a troubled man and an outmoded ideal.

Sarton, May. *Plant Dreaming Deep.* N. Y., W. W. Norton, 1968. Brilliant essays about a woman's internal adventures with solitude, self, work, and life styles. Profoundly moving. (SKC)

————. *Joanna and Ulysses, The Small Room, Mrs. Stevens Hears the Mermaids Singing.*—See essay in this book for discussion of these novels. (SKC)

Sayers, Dorothy (1893-1957). Best known for her Lord Peter Wimsey detective stories, Sayers is a fine story-teller and writer. She is one of the few mystery novelists to care enough about her characters to have them change and grow in the course of their sleuthing.

————. *Strong Poison.* 1930. N. Y., Avon, 1970, 95¢. This is the first Wimsey in which the highly likable Harriet appears—accused of murder.

————. *Gaudy Night.* 1936. N. Y., Avon, 1970, 95¢. Here it is Harriet who is the detective. The scene of the crime is her old college at Oxford, a citadel of female scholarship. When obscenities start appearing on the walls and various other horrible events take place, everyone suspects these "frustrated" female academics—but read on.

————. *Busman's Honeymoon.* N. Y., Harper & Row, 1937. The last of the Peter Wimsey-Harriet Vane collaborations on crime, this one on their honeymoon. Not only a good detective story, but remarkable in the growth shown by the main character.

Sheehy, Gail. *Lovesounds.* N. Y., Berkely Medallion, 1966, 95¢. Part of this book is full of cheap, stock literary devices, part of it is rather intersting—the story of a young wife obsessively trying to save her own life. The marriage ends positively in divorce.

Shulman, Alix Kates. *Memoirs of an Ex-Prom Queen.* N. Y., Alfred A. Knopf, 1972. "A novelistic rendering of neo-feminist ideology, cultural analysis and consciousness." (Ellen Morgan) Well-written story of a woman's education and struggle for self-affirmation.

Sinclair, Jo (pseudonym of Ruth Seid). *Wasteland.* N. Y., Harper, 1946. Unfortunately Freudian orientation, but sympathetic, sensitive portrayal of adult sibling relationships. Major secondary character and model-focus of protagonist-brother is a lesbian-sister author. (SKC)

————. *Sing at My Wake.* N. Y., McGraw, 1951. Brilliant study of young woman growing through insecurity, lack of self-esteem, sexual ignorance and disappointment to self-knowledge, successful career, sexual confidence. Wonderful portrayal of mother-son relationship from birth through early adolescence. (SKC)

————. *The Changelings.* N. Y., McGraw, 1955. A pre-teen woman struggles with conflicts between family and ethnic loyalty and moral knowledge and decisiveness. A female bildungsroman. (SKC)

Slade, Caroline. *Mrs. Party's House*. N. Y., Vanguard, 1948. Though this novel is written in an uneven, at times slightly didactic style, it deals with a question that reflects the function and status of women in a male-dominated culture. The central character, Mrs. Party, is used as a vehicle for describing the life of several groups of prostitutes in an average middle-sized city; she is portrayed as a kind of big-hearted, bewildered woman who gets into "the life" after her husband is killed in an accident, leaving her with an invalid mother and no means of support. She becomes a madam, in which position she treats "the girls" in her house with great humanity. Among the best parts of the book are the descriptions of the courts and the cops—insights into how the system works.

Smedley, Agnes. *Daughter of Earth*. N. Y., Coward-McCann, 1929. Mental journey of a poor girl to an understanding and awareness of the forces of oppression (SKC)

Stannard, Una. *The New Pamela: Or Virtue Unrewarded*. N. Y., Ballantine, 1969, 95¢. Pamela in the age of the sexual revolution and her struggle against the double standard. A novel in letters by a feminist academic.

Stein, Gertrude. *Three Lives*. N. Y., Vintage. Important studies of three poor working women's lives, internal consciousnesses, rhythms. (SKC)

————. *Q. E. D.* Three young women on an Atlantic crossing discover the depths of their feelings for each other. (SKC)

Tey, Josephine. *Miss Pym Disposes*. 1956. N. Y., Berkeley, 1971, 95¢. Unusually fine characterizations of the students at a British women's college, who all become suspects in the murder of the least popular of their number.

————. *Brat Farrar*. 1949. N. Y., Berkeley, 1971, 95¢. Perhaps the finest and certainly the best-known of all Tey's works. This is less a mystery than a hair-raising adventure story with appropriately wicked malefactors.

————. *To Love and Be Wise*. 1950. N. Y., Berkeley, 1971, 95¢. The disappearance of a talented young photographer, with a denouement unique in mystery writing. Highly recommended for feminists.

————. *A Shilling for Candles*. 1952. N.Y., Berkeley, 1971, 95¢ The personality of an exceptionally human actress emerges slowly during the investigation of her murder.

Walker, Alice. "Her Sweet Jerome." Short story in *Red Clay Reader* 7. Charlotte, North Carolina, Southern Review, 1970. A story about a black woman's descent into madness after she gets her man, a young, intellectual leftist who beats her, uses her for her money, takes another woman, and completely leaves her out of his life.

Walker, Margaret. *Jubilee.* Boston, Houghton Mifflin, 1968. The novel has three sections: 1) "Sis Hetta's Child—the Ante-Bellum Years"; 2) "Mine Eyes Have Seen the Glory—the Civil War Years"; 3) "Forty Years in the Wilderness—Reconstruction and Reaction." It is the story of Margaret Walker's great-grandmother, as told to her by two grandmothers.

Wasserman, Barbara Alson, ed. *The Bold New Women.* 1966. Greenwich, Conn., Fawcett, 1970, 95¢. A good collection of writings by contemporary women authors. Some excerpts drawn from larger works give an impression of incompleteness, but there is a lot of fine material.

Watts, Mary S. *The Rise of Jennie Cushing.* N.Y., The Macmillan Co., 1914. Midwestern slum girl grows through, up and out of a pressurized environment to become decisive and self-determining. (SKC)

Weirauch, Anna Elisabet. *The Scorpion.* Germany, 1930. N.Y., Greenberg, 1932. In her late teens Metta Rudloff falls passionately in love with Olga Rado; persecution and tragedy follow. The presentation, though clearly sympathetic to lesbianism, is detached and straightforward, without sensationalism, moralizing, or emotionalism. There is a sequel called *The Outcast.*

West, Rebecca. *The Birds Fall Down.* N.Y., Popular Library, 1966, 95¢. A rather splendidly described tale of an English-reared girl confronting her aristocratic Russian heritage, and knowing fear and deception at the same time. Limited in interest perhaps by its single-minded concentration on the upper class.

Wharton, Edith (1862-1937). Born into New York upper-class society, Wharton married into her class, became disillusioned with her marriage, and was separated for many years before her divorce in 1932. She wrote as a girl and was advised by the family doctor to take it up again to relieve the nervous strains of marriage. Her novels are marked by a sense of the futility of struggle against social circumstances.

———. *The House of Mirth.* 1905. Boston, Houghton Mifflin, 1964, $1.45. The story of yet another victim trapped by circumstances. This time a wealthy product of New York society, no less vicious than the New England winter for holding its members in line or destroying them. Wharton has said that she attempted to show "how both wealth and poverty annihilate every impulse to excellence."

———. *Ethan Frome.* 1911. N.Y., Scribner, 1970, $1.45. The

story of a man trapped by poverty, ignorance, the Christian ethic, and the New England winter. It could be a book about anyone of either sex.

―――. *Summer.* 1917. N.Y., Scribner, 1964, $1.45. The central character, a young woman trapped by poverty and ignorance, is one of the few Wharton creations ever to yield to the inevitable, supposedly through her own choice. An interesting parallel to *Ethan Frome,* with the same setting, sensitivity, and hopeless desires.

―――. *The Custom of the Country.* 1913. N.Y., Scribner, 1971. Portrays a woman of zero sensitivity who gets exactly what she wants.

―――. *The Age of Innocence.* 1920. N.Y., New American Library, 1962, 95¢. This is perhaps the most complex of Wharton's good novels; it is about a man and a woman both trapped by the inflexibility of their upper crust New York society. Wonderful characterizations, fine timing and story line.

―――. *Old New York.* 1924. N.Y., Scribners, 1964, $1.65. A collection of short novels; these stand among her most memorable works.

―――. *The Children.* 1928. N.Y., Scribners, 1971. One finishes with a vague pity for, but no sympathy with, the ineffective male main character, searching for the charms of a lost youth among children and a woman far younger than he. Much less effective than her other books.

Widdemer, Margaret. *More Than Wife.* N.Y., Harcourt Brace & Co., 1927. The story of what happens to a woman architect who tries to combine marriage and a career.

Wittig, Monique. *Les Guérillères.* France, 1970. N.Y., Viking, 1971. Though Wittig calls her book a novel, it is obviously an attempt to break into a new form. On several pages we find only a black circle, the symbol of female wholeness and affirmation. There is a flow and rhythm in the book which makes the short, seemingly unconnected paragraphs as delightful as a good poem. One problem is that many of the references to female mythology, symbolism, and culture flow by unrecognized unless you do a bit of research while you read. Wittig's fine positive female sexual imagery is enough in itself to make the book worthwhile.

Woolf, Virginia. *Orlando.* 1928. N.Y., Signet, 1960. Elizabeth Bowen called *Orlando* not a novel but a "fantasy." It was an experiment, an attempt to break into a vivid new way of combining fiction and historical reality, and a vision of what this reality was for real men and women. Woolf wanted to escape from the oppressive method of presenting a few cold dates and facts as history.

Orlando, the central person of the book, begins as a sixteen-year-old male in the Elizabethan period. As the fantasy continues time spins by while Orlando's time moves very slowly. Toward the end of the seventeenth century Orlando's sex is changed from male to female, and she/he experiences the eighteenth, nineteenth, and twentieth centuries as a woman. What we have is a brilliant portrait of British history, so much so that we can almost taste the unique flavor of each period; even more importantly, we have a vivid picture of how gender molded the existence of the individual in the various periods. Many critics have ignored *Orlando*, as they have tried to ignore equally innovative pieces by Gertrude Stein or other women who dared to experiment with fictional forms to give us women's historical reality.

————. *The Years.* N.Y., Harcourt Brace, 1937. This novel covers a span of fifty-seven years, from 1880 to 1937. Instead of building a single character Woolf sketches some of the various real and psychological events of the Pargiter family through the evolution of three generations. The Pargiters are solid middle class. The novel portrays the role divisions that class and sex impose upon human beings in our culture. It is the women in the book who are moving and memorable as characters.

Bennett, Joan. *Virginia Woolf.* N.Y., Harcourt Brace, 1945. Bennett says in her prefatory notes that her intention is to write about Woolf's vision of human life, her sense of values, and to attempt to analyze the form of the novels. Unlike many critics who attempt to sterilize and objectify the artist and her work, Bennett talks about the works as reflections of Woolf's intentions.

III. WORKS ABOUT LITERATURE

Auchincloss, Louis. *Pioneers and Caretakers: A Study of Nine American Women Novelists.* Minneapolis, Minneapolis Press, 1965. Ellen Glasgow, Katherine Anne Porter, Carson McCullers are among the writers he discusses. He seems to find the little details of their lives more important than any of the ideas they present in their works. Except in rare instances he seems to be very caught up with trivia.

Beauvoir, Simone de. *The Second Sex.* France, 1949. N.Y., Bantam, 1970, $1.25. Among the vast store of information in this book is a section on "The Myth of Woman in Five Authors"—Montherlant, D. H. Lawrence ("or Phallic Pride"), Claudel, Breton, and Stendhal. The work as a whole is sprinkled with literary allusions.

Bradford, Gamaliel. *Elizabethan Women*. Freeport, N.Y., Harold A. White Books for Libraries, 1937. Not recommended, except as an example of this typically chauvinist critic. For example, he indicates that many women wrote plays at this time but he reviews none of them. He cautions us not to judge the quality of education afforded Elizabethan women by modern standards. He admits that many Elizabethan dramatists totally ignored or hated women in their plays, but he review none of their works.

Cade, Toni. *The Black Woman*. N.Y., Signet, 1970, 95 ¢. A solid and well put together collection of political, historical, and critical essays by black women. The collection also includes several short fictional and biographical pieces, and poems by Nikki Giovanni, Kay Lindsey, and Aude Lorde. In her introduction Cade says, "there have been women who have been able to think better than they've been trained and have produced the canon of literature fondly referred to as 'feminist literature'; Anais Nin, Simone de Beauvoir, Doris Lessing, Betty Friedan, etc. And the question for us arises how relevant are the truth, the experiences, the findings of white women to Black women?"

Cantarow, Ellen. "The Radicalizing of a Teacher of Literature," *Change, the Magazine of Higher Learning*. Vol. 4, No. 4, May, 1972. Cantarow says "our particular responsibility as teachers of literature is to act on the humanizing knowledge art can give us to construct with our students new, revolutionary ideas of culture, and to construct with them outside the classroom both an active socialist movement and culture." Cantarow graduated from Wellesley and Harvard, and it was from her experience in these mills that she began to realize the contradictions involved in being a female in a male-dominated culture. "In graduate school I began vaguely to realize that the gender of the critical mind (of literature, art, etc.) was masculine and that to be a 'critic' I would have to neuter my understanding."

Ellmann, Mary. *Thinking About Women*. N.Y., Harcourt Brace, Javanovich, 1968, $2.65. Essentially a critique of the sexism that pervades literary culture, though Ellmann would probably not use the term "sexism." There are chapters on "Sexual Analogy," "Phallic Criticism," "Feminine Stereotypes," "Differences in Tone" (between male and female writers), and "Responses" (of women writers to experience). A wide range of writers from the nineteenth century to the 1960's get critical jabs from Ellmann's acid pen, and women are by no means exempt. Ellmann is difficult to read: her style and arguements are often convoluted and her witticisms occasionally irritating. If you can get through this, she makes some provocative points.

Fiedler, Leslie A. *Love and Death in the American Novel.* N. Y., Dell, 1960, $1.25. Important criticism of American male novelists. The book deals with their immaturity—that is, their inability to deal with their sexuality, their relationships with women, and their obsession with death.

Firestone, Shulamith. *The Dialectic of Sex.* N.Y., Bantam, 1970, $1.25. This book presents a brilliant general feminist analysis. The chapter on culture is unfortunately one of the weakest.

Foster, Jeannette H. *Sex Variant Women in Literature.* N.Y., Vantage, 1956. A scholarly and comprehensive study of women portrayed in literature who might be considered lesbians, from Sappho to the twentieth century. Some speculation on women writers is made. The book is a good source of references. Foster's sympathy shows through the scholarly apparatus.

Gagen, Jean Elizabeth. *The New Woman: Her Emergence in English Drama 1600-1730.* N.Y., Twayne, 1954. This is a study of female characters in English plays and their relationship to real women over the period specified. Particular attention is paid to education and the figure of the learned lady as she emerged following Renaissance theories on the education of women.

Gloster, Hugh M. *Negro Voices in American Fiction.* Chapel Hill, North Carolina, University of North Carolina, 1948. An excellent study of black writers since their first work in the Antebellum era to about the end of the Depression. Discusses the work of Pauline E. Hopkins, Frances E. Watkins Harper, Sarah Lee Fleming, Jessie Fauset, Nella Larsen, and Zora Neale Hurston. These writers' works are described within a framework of the black political and social position and movements of each era.

Gornick, Vivian. "Woman as Outsider" in *Woman in Sexist Society,* ed. Gornick and Moran, N.Y., Basic Books, 1971. Gornick discusses the idea that women, blacks, Jews, some overly sensitive males, etc., are closed outside the norms culturally defined as meaningful or powerful. As "outsiders" these people become careful observers of what is happening in the inner circle from which they are excluded— but they are typically denied access to forms of action which would make them part of it. This phenomena is perpetuated in western (male) literature. Examples are cited.

Hinkley, Laura L. *Ladies of Literature.* N.Y., Hastings House, 1946. The book is not as bad as the title sounds. It contains information about Fanny Burney, Jane Austen, Charlotte and Emily Brontë, Elizabeth Barrett Browning, and George Eliot.

Jessup, Josephine Lurie. *Faith of Our Feminists.* Biblo., 1950. The book contains criticism and review of the works of Ellen Glasgow,

Edith Wharton, Willa Catha. It is uninspired. The author's standard
seems to be simply to find women characters who exceed men characters in strength. She rejects the finest and most realistic of these
authors' novels in favor of those where the women can be seen as
triumphing easily over all situations.

Klein, Viola. *The Feminine Character: History of an Ideology*.
N.Y., International University, 1948. "The hypothesis of this study
has been the view that the social and cultural situation at any given
time is expressed in ideologies and reflected in all products of the
human mind: in art, in science, in literature." She analyzes a long
novel by a Dutch author that covered three generations: 1) pre-
Industrial Revolution with the female characters completely subjected, 2) late nineteenth century and the beginnings of emancipation, and 3) pre-World War I. Klein's study is extremely interesting.

Lane, Margaret. *Purely For Pleasure. A Collection of Literary-
Biographical Essays*. N.Y., Knopf, 1967. Lane is not an obvious
feminist, but she clearly has a special interest in women. Apart from
a number of essays on women writers (three on the Brontës, three on
Elizabeth Gaskell, two on Beatrix Potter, one on Jane Austen, and
one on the little-known Flora Thompson, who wrote the story of
her childhood in poor, rural England in the late nineteenth century),
this volume includes several essays which deal with other little-
explored areas of life and literature. Her three essays on Dr. Johnson
deal respectively with his home-life, his eating habits, and his relations with women. An entertaining and perceptive book about
topics men would not think important enough to write about.

MacCarthy, Briget G. *Women Writers: Their Contribution to the
English Novel*. Cork, Ireland, Cork University Press, 1948, two
volumes. A very valuable and comprehensive piece of work.
Volume 1 covers the work of women from 1671-1744, while
Volume 2 deals with later women writers from 1744-1818. Highly
recommended for both its factual and interpretive material.

McCarthy, Mary. *On the Contrary: Articles of Belief*. N.Y., Noon-
day, 1962. A collection of critical essays written between 1946 and
1961. Twelve are under the heading "Politics and the Social Scene";
three are under the heading "Woman" (the brilliant "Tyranny of the
Orgasm," a discussion of women's magazines called "Up the ladder
from *Charm* to *Vogue*," and one on "The Vassar Girl"); six are under
the heading "Literature and the Arts." Among these last, "The Fact
in Fiction" and "Characters in Fiction" can be recommended as
excellent general discussions of the novel.

Marcus, Steven. *The Other Victorians: A Study of Sexuality and
Pornography in Mid-Nineteenth-Century England*. 1964. N.Y.,

Bantam, 1967, $1.25. An extremely interesting study of the under-side of Victorian life that the novelists ignored—the sizable sub-culture that wrote, sold and/or read pornography. There is a percep-tive analysis of *My Secret Lift,* the sexual memoirs of a Victorian gentleman. A concluding chapter discusses "pornotopia," the utopian fantasies pornography creates. Marcus contrasts pornography with literature.

Martin, Wendy. "Seduced and Abandoned in the New World: the Image of Woman in American Fiction," in *Woman in Sexist Society,* ed. Gornick and Moran, N.Y., Basic Books, 1971. The eighteenth-century Puritan origins of the American novel perpetuated the myth of the "fallen," carnal woman from Hester Prynn to Hemingway's Catherine Barkley—heroines who cannot (and must not) make it on their own. The Puritans based their rigidity on the Biblical story of Eve: thus divine mythical support was given to the evolving economic and social system of industrialism. The reality of bourgeois women in the eighteenth century was that they were totally dependent on marriage for economic survival. Martin's thesis is that "fiction not only reflects and expresses social values but transmits them to future generations."

Maurois, Andre. *Seven Faces of Love.* N.Y., Didier, 1944. Maurois discusses the differences between concepts of love embodied in seven French works of fiction—the seventeeth century *Princess of Cleves,* eighteenth century *Nouvelle Heloise* and *Liaisons Dangereuses;* Stendhal, Balzac, and Flaubert's *Madame Bovary* in the nineteenth century; and the work of Proust in the twentieth. He says, "feeling inspires literature, and literature in turn transforms and at time creates feeling."

Millett, Kate. *Sexual Politics.* 1969. N.Y., Equinox, 1971, $2.95. Millett first explains her theory of sexual politics, by which she means all male-female power-structured relationships, then gives examples from literature to illustrate her theory. There is a solid chapter on the historical background of sexual politics, drawing on several writers; the twentieth-century writers D. H. Lawrence, Henry Miller, Norman Mailer, and Jean Genet are examined at length.

Olsen, Tillie. "Silences—When Women Don't Write." *Harper's,* October, 1965. A very interesting article, discussing the many things that prevent women from writing and from developing into serious writers.

Ozick, Cynthia. "Women and Creativity: the Demise of the Dancing Dog." In Gornick and Moran, eds., *Woman in Sexist Society.* 1971. N.Y., Signet, 1972, $1.95. "Art must belong to all human beings, not alone to a traditionally privileged segment. Every endeavor, every passion must be available to the susceptible adult, without the intervention of myth or canard. Woman will cease solely to be man's Muse—and It (as she is, curiously, for writers as disparate as Graves and Mailer, as she was for Freud)—when she ceases to be bemused with romances and lies about her own nature."

Papishvily, Helen Waite. *All the Happy Endings*. Port Washington, N.Y., Kinnikat Press, 1956. A study of the popular novels ordinary women wrote in the nineteenth century and how these books helped women at home develop "survival techniques" that are still considered part of female culture even now. Much helpful information.

Rideout, Walter. *The Radical Novel in the United States 1900-1954*. N.Y., Hill & Wang, 1956. A critical history of the radical and socialist in American literature, drawing interrelations between literature and society. Reference is made to several women who wrote in the early socialist or realist tradition, such as Caroline H. Pemberton who wrote *The Charity Girl* (1901) and Rebecca Harding Davis who wrote a story "Life in the Iron Mills," which was published in the *Atlantic Monthly* in 1861.

Rogers, Katherine. *The Troublesome Helpmate*. Seattle, University of Washington Press, 1966, $2.95. A historical survey of both direct and indirect manifestations in literature of hatred, fear, or contempt for women from Biblical and classical times to the twentieth century.

Rougemont, Denis de. *Love in the Western World*. France, 1939. N. Y., Fawcett, 1966, 95 ¢. De Rougement, a Catholic theologian, develops the thesis that passionate unhappy love was first set up as an ideal in the twelfth century in Provence in the form of courtly love. His argument is highly complex. He gives a detailed analysis of the Tristan and Iseult myth and traces the development of the "myth of passion" through various other works of literature.

Showalter, Elaine. "Women Writers and the Female Experience." In *Notes From the Third Year: Women's Liberation*. Available from Box AA, Old Chelsea Station, N.Y., N.Y. 10011, 1971, $1.50. ". . . feminine experiences have not been fully explored, or honestly expressed by women writers. . . . Women have, in fact, been kept from their own experience by a double critical standard, by a double social standard, by external censorship, and, most dangerous, by self-censorship—which is sometimes exercised in self-defense, more frequently in self-hatred."

————. "Women Writers and the Double Standard." In Gornick and Moran, eds., *Woman in Sexist Society*. 1971. N.Y., Signet, 1972, $1.95. This article discusses the pressures and prejudices experienced by female writers in the nineteenth century, when "virtually all experience that was uniquely feminine was considered unprintable matter."

Snitow, Ann. "Women's Private Writings: Anais Nin." In *Notes From the Third Year: Women's Liberation*. 1971. Available from Box AA, Old Chelsea Station, N.Y., N.Y., 10011, $1.50. A short but interesting article about the struggles of Anais Nin to express her experience and reflect upon her creativity. She, like many other women, has done her most personal and perceptive work in diary or journal form. Snitow examines this as a possible form of expression for women.

Strainchamps, Ethel. "Our Sexist Language." In *Woman in Sexist Society*, ed. Gornick and Moran. 1971. N.Y., Signet, 1972, $1.95. Some useful information about the derivations of so-called taboo words in English, a language which, she points out, "retains more vestiges of the archaic sexual attitudes [of male supremacy] than any other 'civilized' tongue." An excellent article about the relationship between language and cultural attitudes.

Violette, Augusta Genevieve. *Economic Feminism in American Literature Prior to 1848*. Orono, Maine, University Press, 1925. Violette examines the feminism in the writings of Thomas Paine, Sarah Grimke, Margaret Fuller, Emerson and others, in short, "any American writers who evinced any positive interest in the extension of legal and political privileges to women." She ends the study in 1848 as she feels that this year marks the beginning of the organized suffrage movement in the United States.

Utter, Robert Palfrey and Gwendolyn Bridges Needham. *Pamela's Daughters*. N.Y., Macmillan, 1936. A study of changing fashions in heroines of novels since *Pamela*. Much of the book is concerned with trivia, and Utter takes pleasure in putting down women novelists, but there is a great deal of very useful information.

Wallace, Ada. *Before the Bluestockings*. London, Allen, 1929. A study of the lives of educated Englishwomen from the Restoration to the end of the first third of the eighteenth century.

Watt, Ian. *The Rise of the Novel: Studies in Defoe, Richardson and Fielding*. Berkeley, University of California Press, 1957, $2.50. Excellent background on the economic and social setting of the eighteenth century, linking the rise of the novel to social conditions. A good chapter on love and the novel with insightful information on the changing position of women.

Woolf, Virginia. *A Room of One's Own*. 1929. N.Y., Harcourt Brace and World, $1.95. A fine essay dealing with socio-economic factors preventing women from writing. There is historical data, literary criticism on Jane Austen and the Brontës, and thoughts on the stylistic differences between male and female writers.

IV. SUMMARY REFERENCE LISTS

Unless otherwise stated, all books listed here are annotated in Section II. TWENTIETH CENTURY WOMEN WRITERS OF FICTION.

A. BOOKS BY BLACK WOMEN

Anderson, Barbara. *Southbound*
Angelou, Maya. *I Know Why the Caged Bird Sings*
Brooks, Gwendolyn. *Maud Martha. Riot*
Cade, Toni. *The Black Woman*
Davis, Angela, and others. *If They Come in the Morning*
Fields, Julia. *A Poet.* See entry in Section III.
Hurston, Zora Neale. *Their Eyes Were Watching God*
Larsen, Nella. *Quicksand. Passing*
Merriwether, Louise. *Daddy Was a Number Runner*
Moody, Anne. *Coming of Age in Mississippi*
Petry, Ann. *The Street*
Walker, Alice. *Once* (Poetry). "Her Sweet Jerome" (Short story)
Walker, Margaret. *Jubilee*

Some further books by black women (not listed elsewhere here) are:

Fauset, Jessie R. *There is Confusion. Plum Bun. The Chinaberry Tree. Comedy, American Style*
Giovanni, Nikki. *Gemini*
Harper, Frances. *Iola Leroy: or, The Shadows Lifted*
Hopkins, Pauline. *Contending Forces*
Hurston, Zora Neale. *Jonah's Gourd Vine. Mules and Men*
Leake, Grace. *House of Refuge*
Marshall, Paule. *Brown Girl. Brownstones. Soul Clap Hands and Sing. The Chosen Place. The Timeless People*
Spenser, Mary Ella. *Resentment*
Swados, Felice. *House of Fury*
West, Dorothy. *The Living is Easy*

B. BOOKS PRESENTING LESBIAN RELATIONSHIPS

Baker, Dorothy. *Cassandra at the Wedding*
Barnes, Djuna. *Nightwood*
Bedford, Sybille. *A Compass Error*

Colette. *The Innocent Wife. The Pure and the Impure. Earthly
    Paradise*
Di Prima, Diane. *Memoirs of a Beatnik*
Foster, Jeanette. *Sex Variant Women in Literature* (under *Works
    About Literature*)
Leduc, Violette. *Therese and Isabelle. La Batarde.*
Lehmann, Rosamund. *Dusty Answer*
McCarthy, Mary. *The Group*
Miller, Isabel. *Patience and Sarah*
Richardson, Dorothy. *Dawn's Left Hand*
Richardson, Henry Handel. *The End of a Childhood*
Rule, Jane. *This is Not for You*
Sarton, May. *Mrs. Stevens Hears the Mermaids Singing. The Small
    Room*
Sinclair, Jo. *Wasteland*
Stein, Gertrude. *Q. E. D.*
Tey, Josephine. *To Love and Be Wise*
Weirauch, Anna Elisabet. *The Scorpion*

For further sources we refer the reader to:

Damon, Gene and Lee Stuart. *The Lesbian in Literature: A
    Bibliography.* 1967. Available for $2.00 from
    The Ladder, Box 5025, Washington Station,
    Reno, Nevada.

*Supplementary entries by the editor are marked (SKC).

INDEX

A hat can't tell if it's on a boy or a girl or a hamburger.

by Nathan Cornillon - 3½